T0100683

IFIP Advances in Information and Communication Technology

IFIP – The International Federation for Information Processing

IFIP was founded in 1960 under the auspices of UNESCO, following the First World Computer Congress held in Paris the previous year. An umbrella organization for societies working in information processing, IFIP's aim is two-fold: to support information processing within its member countries and to encourage technology transfer to developing nations. As its mission statement clearly states,

> *IFIP's mission is to be the leading, truly international, apolitical organization which encourages and assists in the development, exploitation and application of information technology for the bene t of all people.*

IFIP is a non-profitmaking organization, run almost solely by 2500 volunteers. It operates through a number of technical committees, which organize events and publications. IFIP's events range from an international congress to local seminars, but the most important are:

- The IFIP World Computer Congress, held every second year;
- Open conferences;
- Working conferences.

The flagship event is the IFIP World Computer Congress, at which both invited and contributed papers are presented. Contributed papers are rigorously refereed and the rejection rate is high.

As with the Congress, participation in the open conferences is open to all and papers may be invited or submitted. Again, submitted papers are stringently refereed.

The working conferences are structured differently. They are usually run by a working group and attendance is small and by invitation only. Their purpose is to create an atmosphere conducive to innovation and development. Refereeing is less rigorous and papers are subjected to extensive group discussion.

Publications arising from IFIP events vary. The papers presented at the IFIP World Computer Congress and at open conferences are published as conference proceedings, while the results of the working conferences are often published as collections of selected and edited papers.

Any national society whose primary activity is in information may apply to become a full member of IFIP, although full membership is restricted to one society per country. Full members are entitled to vote at the annual General Assembly, National societies preferring a less committed involvement may apply for associate or corresponding membership. Associate members enjoy the same benefits as full members, but without voting rights. Corresponding members are not represented in IFIP bodies. Affiliated membership is open to non-national societies, and individual and honorary membership schemes are also offered.

Ana Pont   Guy Pujolle   S.V. Raghavan (Eds.)

Communications: Wireless in Developing Countries and Networks of the Future

Third IFIP TC 6 International Conference, WCITD 2010
and IFIP TC 6 International Conference, NF 2010
Held as Part of WCC 2010
Brisbane, Australia, September 20-23, 2010
Proceedings

Volume Editors

Ana Pont
Polytechnic University of Valencia
Department of Computer Engineering
46022 Valencia, Spain
E-mail: apont@disca.upv.es

Guy Pujolle
Pierre et Marie Curie University (Paris 6), LIP6
75016 Paris, France
E-mail: guy.pujolle@lip6.fr

S.V. Raghavan
Indian Institute of Technology Madras
Department of Computer Science and Engineering
Chennai 600 036, India
E-mail: svr@cs.iitm.ernet.in

Library of Congress Control Number: 2010933096

CR Subject Classification (1998): C.2, H.4, H.3, D.2, J.1, K.4.4

ISSN	1868-4238
ISBN-10	3-642-15475-1 Springer Berlin Heidelberg New York
ISBN-13	978-3-642-15475-1 Springer Berlin Heidelberg New York

springer.com

© IFIP International Federation for Information Processing 2010
Printed in Germany

Typesetting: Camera-ready by author, data conversion by Scientific Publishing Services, Chennai, India
Printed on acid-free paper   06/3180

IFIP World Computer Congress 2010 (WCC 2010)

Message from the Chairs

Every two years, the International Federation for Information Processing (IFIP) hosts a major event which showcases the scientific endeavors of its over one hundred technical committees and working groups. On the occasion of IFIP's 50th anniversary, 2010 saw the 21st IFIP World Computer Congress (WCC 2010) take place in Australia for the third time, at the Brisbane Convention and Exhibition Centre, Brisbane, Queensland, September 20–23, 2010.

The congress was hosted by the Australian Computer Society, ACS. It was run as a federation of co-located conferences offered by the different IFIP technical committees, working groups and special interest groups, under the coordination of the International Program Committee.

The event was larger than ever before, consisting of 17 parallel conferences, focusing on topics ranging from artificial intelligence to entertainment computing, human choice and computers, security, networks of the future and theoretical computer science. The conference History of Computing was a valuable contribution to IFIPs 50th anniversary, as it specifically addressed IT developments during those years. The conference e-Health was organized jointly with the International Medical Informatics Association (IMIA), which evolved from IFIP Technical Committee TC-4 "Medical Informatics".

Some of these were established conferences that run at regular intervals, e.g., annually, and some represented new, groundbreaking areas of computing. Each conference had a call for papers, an International Program Committee of experts and a thorough peer reviewing process of full papers. The congress received 642 papers for the 17 conferences, and selected 319 from those, representing an acceptance rate of 49.69% (averaged over all conferences). To support interoperation between events, conferences were grouped into 8 areas: Deliver IT, Govern IT, Learn IT, Play IT, Sustain IT, Treat IT, Trust IT, and Value IT.

This volume is one of 13 volumes associated with the 17 scientific conferences. Each volume covers a specific topic and separately or together they form a valuable record of the state of computing research in the world in 2010. Each volume was prepared for publication in the Springer IFIP Advances in Information and Communication Technology series by the conference's volume editors. The overall Publications Chair for all volumes published for this congress is Mike Hinchey.

For full details of the World Computer Congress, please refer to the webpage at http://www.ifip.org.

June 2010   Augusto Casaca, Portugal, Chair, International Program Committee
Phillip Nyssen, Australia, Co-chair, International Program Committee
Nick Tate, Australia, Chair, Organizing Committee
Mike Hinchey, Ireland, Publications Chair
Klaus Brunnstein, Germany, General Congress Chair

Preface

Communications: Wireless in Developing Countries and Networks of the Future

The present book contains the proceedings of two conferences held at the World Computer Congress 2010 in Brisbane, Australia (September 20–23) organized by the International Federation for Information Processing (IFIP): the Third IFIP TC 6 International Conference on Wireless Communications and Information Technology for Developing Countries (WCITD 2010) and the IFIP TC 6 International Network of the Future Conference (NF 2010). The main objective of these two IFIP conferences on communications is to provide a platform for the exchange of recent and original contributions in wireless networks in developing countries and networks of the future.

There are many exiting trends and developments in the communications industry, several of which are related to advances in wireless networks, and next-generation Internet. It is commonly believed in the communications industry that a new generation should appear in the next ten years. Yet there are a number of issues that are being worked on in various industry research and development labs and universities towards enabling wireless high-speed networks, virtualization techniques, smart networks, high-level security schemes, etc.

We would like to thank the members of the Program Committees and the external reviewers and we hope these proceedings will be very useful to all researchers interested in the fields of wireless networks and future network technologies.

July 2010

Ana Pont
Guy Pujolle
S.V. Raghavan

WCITD 2010

International Advisory Board

Edward Knightly	Rice University, USA
Ramon Puigjaner	Universitat de les Illes Balears, Spain
Tharam S. Dillon	Curtin University of Technology, Australia
Leonard Barolli	Fukuoka Institute of Technology, Japan
Augusto Casaca	Instituto Superior Técnico, Portugal

General Chairs

Mieso Denko	University of Guelph, Canada
Albert Y. Zomaya	The University of Sydney, Australia

Program Committee Chair

Ana Pont	Universidad Politécnica de Valencia, Spain

Program Committee Members

Pedro Cuenca	University of Castilla La Mancha, Spain
Benjamín Baran	National University of Asunción, Paraguay
José A. Gil Salinas	Universidad Politécnica de Valencia, Spain
Jason B. Ernst	University of Guelph, Canada
Joel Rodrigues	University of Beira Interior, Portugal
Rajkumar Buyya	The University of Melbourne, Australia
Krithi Ramamritham	IIT Bombay, India
Jose Neumann de Souza	Universidade Federal do Ceará, Brazil
Yacine Ghamri-Doudane	ENSIIE, France
Ramon Puigjaner	Universitat de les Illes Balears, Spain
Antoine Bagula	University of Cape Town, South Africa
Rodrigo Santos	Universidad Nacional del Sur, Argentina
Siraj Shaikh	Cranfield University, UK
Benoid Vaidya	Tribhuvan University, Portugal
Dimitris Varoutas	University of Athens, Greece
Tadeusz A. Wysocki	University of Nebraska – Lincoln, USA
Aruna Jayasuriya	University of South Australia, Australia
Noureddine Boudriga	University of Carthage, Tunisia
Adnan Al-Anbuky	Auckland University of Technology, New Zealand
Augusto Casaca	Instituto Superior Técnico, Portugal

NF 2010

Program Committee Chairs

Guy Pujolle   UPMC, France
S.V. Raghavan   IITM, India

Program Committee Members

Ozgur B. Akan   Middle East Technical University, Turkey
Pedro A. Aranda Gutierrez   Telefonica, Spain
Luis Orozco Barbosa   UCM, Spain
Alessandro Bassi   Hitachi, France
Chris Blondia   University of Antwerp, Belgium
Raouf Boutaba   Waterloo University, Canada
Dariusz Bursztynowski   TPSA, Poland
Lee Bu Sung, Francis   NTU, Singapore
Georg Carle   TUM, Germany
Matteo Cesana   Milan, Italy
Chih-Yung Chang   Tamkang University, Taiwan
Omar Cherkaoui   UQAM, Canada
Arek Dadej   University of South Australia, Australia
Simon Dobson   University College Dublin, Ireland
Mischa Dolher   CTTC, Spain
William Donnelly   WIT, Ireland
Emmanuel Dotaro   Alcatel, France
Otto Duarte   UFRJ, Brazil
Wissam Fawaz   Lebanese American University, Lebanon
Luigi Fratta   Milano, Italy
Dominique Gaïti   UTT, France
Alex Galis   UCL, UK
Mario Gerla   UCLA, USA
Annie Gravey   Telecom Bretagne, France
Gunther Harring   University of Vienna, Austria
Bijan Jabbari   Mason University, USA
Shengming Jiang   South China University of Technology, China
Daniel Kofman   Telecom ParisTech, France
Matti Latva-aho   University of Oulu, Finland
Herman de Meer   Passau, Germany
Edmundo Monteiro   DEI, Portugal
José-Marcos Nogueira   FUMG, Brazil
Mai Trang Nguyen   UPMC, France

Table of Contents

Preface

It is a great pleasure to present the proceedings of the Third IFIP International Conference on Wireless Communications and Information Technology for Developing Countries (WCITD 2010) held in Brisbane, Australia, September 20–23, 2010 jointly with the IFIP World Computer Conference.

The conference attracted papers on various topics in wireless and mobile communications, wireless and mobile networks, information technologies and systems. After a rigorous review process we selected 7 best papers, from 17 submissions, for the presentation and publication in the conference proceedings. This results in a 41% acceptation rate. The Program Committee members generously contributed their time so that the submissions were evaluated by at least two and often by three different reviewers, ensuring the highest standards for the selection process, which resulted in a small but high-quality program.

The technical program included two technical sessions and a keynote speech given by Aruna Seneviratne entitled "Technological Challenges for New Service Models in Developing Countries."

I would like to thank all those people who directly or indirectly contributed to the success of this conference. In particular, I would like to thank IFIP Technical Committee 6 for providing travel grants for some authors, and Augusto Casaca who devoted a lot of time to ensure the success of the IFIP WCC.

My special gratitude to the General Chairs, Albert Zomaya and Mieso Denko, for their support and guidance.

During the selection process of the best technical program and speakers for this conference last April, Mieso Denko passed away at age of 42. This unexpected and sad news shocked all those who were working with him. Dr. Denko was the driving force of WCITD since he proposed the organization of this conference in 2006 with the joint aims of presenting innovative technical research in communication systems and information technology, and delivering practical technical solutions in often harsh environments.

Last but not least, I would also like to thank all authors of WCITD 2010, for supporting the conference by choosing it as a forum to report their quality research results, and the industry experts for sharing their experience with researchers in academia.

In memory of Mieso Denko.

July 2010   Ana Pont

Semantic Clustering in Wireless Sensor Networks

Atslands Rego da Rocha[1], Igor Leão dos Santos[2], Luci Pirmez[2], Flávia C. Delicato[3],
Danielo G. Gomes[1], and José Neuman de Souza[1]

[1] Federal University of Ceará – Brazil
[2] Federal University of Rio de Janeiro - Brazil
[3] Federal University of Rio Grande do Norte - Brazil
{atslands,danielo,neuman}@ufc.br, igorlsantos@poli.ufrj.br,
luci@nce.ufrj.br, flavia.delicato@dimap.ufrn.br

Abstract. Wireless Sensor Networks have critical resource constraints and minimizing resources usage is crucial to extend the network lifetime. Energy saving in WSNs can be achieved through several techniques, such as topology control and clustering, to provide a longer lifetime and scalability to the network. In this paper we propose a semantic clustering model based on a fuzzy inference system to find out the semantic neighborhood relationships in the network. As a case study we describe the structural health monitoring domain application which has been used to illustrate and verify the proposed model.

Keywords: Wireless sensor networks, semantic clustering, fuzzy logic system.

1 Introduction

A typical wireless sensor network (WSN) consists of spatially distributed nodes with sensing, processing, storing and communicating capabilities that cooperatively monitor environmental conditions. Due to critical resource constraints of the sensor networks it is important to design techniques which minimize their resources usage and consequently extend their lifetime.

Clustering has been used in ad-hoc networks and WSNs as an effective technique for achieving extended network lifetime and scalability [1]. The general idea is to perform the cluster formation based on the received signal strength, and to use local cluster heads (CHs) as routers of data gathered by the sensors in their clusters towards the sink node. Several works on WSNs have been developed in the context of clustering [2]. However, although there is often some correlation between sensor nodes grouped in a same cluster, a semantic correlation is not frequently exploited.

In this paper we propose a semantic clustering for heterogeneous WSNs in order to minimize the communication resource usage and energy cost. Our proposal is based on the computation of semantic neighborhoods relationships by finding correlations between information from sensor nodes. Sometimes neighbor nodes sense areas that are not related at all, or neighbor nodes provide measurements that are not correlated. For example, in the airport security applications [3], sensor nodes both do video and audio processing and communicate with their neighbors nodes in order to share a global view of the sensing environment. However, nodes fixed on different sides of

A. Pont, G. Pujolle, and S.V. Raghavan (Eds.): WCITD/NF 2010, IFIP AICT 327, pp. 3–14, 2010.

the same wall observe different areas of environment that are not related at all. Therefore, since closely located sensors generated data that are not semantically correlated, they should not exchange information, since this would be a waste of network resources.

In our work, the set of sensor nodes which are semantically correlated among each other is grouped into *semantic clusters*. The semantic clustering is a service provided by a semantic middleware for WSNs described in our previous work [4]. A fuzzy system is responsible to establish the relationships of the semantic neighborhoods. Fuzzy inference systems match two of the most challenging requirements [5] of WSNs: (i) they are simple and can be executed on limited hardware and (ii) they accommodate imprecise data. The ability of handling imprecise data is desirable since individual data from sensor nodes often are inaccurate due to calibration problems, environmental noise, wireless transmission loss, faulty sensors among other itens.

In this work, our proposal is applied in the Structural Health Monitoring (SHM) domain. Extending the network lifetime is crucial to enable SHM systems to perform a high density sensing of the monitored environment, so that sampled data can be reliably analyzed.

2 Related Works

There exist some approaches in WSN that address semantic clustering techniques or structural monitoring issues, but not both in conjunction. Bouhafs et al. [6] propose a semantic clustering algorithm for energy-efficient routing in WSNs that allows data aggregation. Our work differs from it since the neighborhood relationships are inferred by using fuzzy logic in the CHs.

Ulieru and Madani [7] present a bridge monitoring application of WSNs using both agent technology and ubiquitous computing. The authors use an optimization strategy inspired in ant colonies to control the network topology based on context information. In contrast, we use semantic clustering in order to extend the lifetime of network. Moreover, our method allows reclustering when environmental changes.

Bruckner et al. [3] show how a network of smart sensor nodes can be established by using high-level semantic knowledge that is gathered by loopy belief propagation between sensors with overlapping sensing areas. The semantic neighborhood relationships are inferred by smart nodes using statistical analysis of the shared environment. The authors do not use clusterization at all.

Perianu et al. [1] present a method for spontaneous clustering of mobile wireless sensor nodes based on a common context, namely Tandem, which allows reclustering in case of topological or contextual changes. Our method allows saving communication and energy resources by (i) turning on/off sensor nodes which are not involved in monitored variables and (ii) controlling messages are sent between semantic neighbors and sink nodes.

3 Methodology

In our work, there are two phases of clustering: a physical clustering and a semantic clustering. At the network start up process, a physical clustering of sensor nodes is done. The physical organization is hierarchical and consists of two levels. The upper level is composed of CHs that do not perform any sensing tasks, but perform both processing on data received by the sensors and inter-cluster communication. The lower level is composed of sensors that are responsible for collecting the data and are subordinated to one of the CHs. For the physical clustering phase, algorithms such as LEACH [8], among other protocols [2], can be used.

The semantic organization[1] is also hierarchical and consists of two levels. The upper level is composed of semantic collectors. We define a semantic collector as a node that is in charge of making a report containing all data received by the sensors that are semantically correlated and sending this report to the sink node. The lower level is composed of sensor nodes that are semantically correlated to each others and are subordinated to one of the semantic collectors.

We designed a methodology (Fig. 1) to perform the semantic clustering phase that is performed after the physical clustering previously explained. Our proposed methodology is applied in three steps: (i)creating Low Level Symbols (LLSs) for each sensor input; (ii) performing fuzzy system to calculate the semantic neighborhood relationships of the network; (iii) (re)grouping in semantic clusters the set of sensor nodes which are semantically correlated to each others. Step 1 is processed locally in each sensor node, while Steps 2 to 3 are processed locally in each CH.

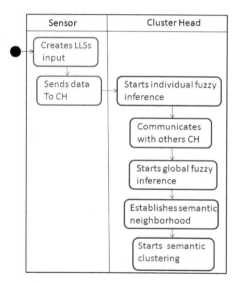

Fig. 1. Methodology (UML Diagram)

In the first step, each sensor node creates LLS to represent mono-modal symbols, as in [3]. A sensor input variable, such as acceleration, temperature, humidity is considered a mono-modal symbol. The several achieved LLSs are represented in XML format. Thus, the LLSs specify the variables which can be analyzed in the

---

[1] The concept *cluster head* do not exist in the semantic organization. Thus, whenever we refer to the concept *cluster head* in this document, we are referring to the physical clustering.

environment in order to support a decision making process. For example, in a SHM domain, a semantic correlation can be performed between LLSs such as acceleration, temperature and stress in order to detect possible damages in the civil structure. In the next step, a fuzzy system is responsible to establish semantic neighborhoods relationships by finding correlations between information from sensor nodes. The fuzzy inference system is divided in two phases: (i) an individual fuzzy inference process is performed in each CH considering only the sensor nodes correlation that belong to its cluster and (ii) a global fuzzy inference process is performed in each CH considering the neighbors CHs "opinion" about their sensor nodes correlation. The information correlation is gathered when the CHs communicate each other. In the last step, the set of sensor nodes which are semantically correlated to each others is (re)grouped in semantic clusters.

4 Semantic Neighborhood Process

We use a rule-based distributed fuzzy inference system for WSN similar to the work described in [5] to establish the semantic neighborhood relationships. Briefly, a fuzzy logic system is composed of four basic components: fuzzifier interface, knowledge base, inference process and defuzzifier interface. The fuzzifier maps crisp inputs into fuzzy sets by using the membership functions. A membership function gives the degree of similarity of a crisp input to the fuzzy set. Next, the fuzzified values activate the rules of knowledge base that are provided by experts or extracted from numerical data. Next, the fuzzy inference process combines the rules to obtain an aggregated fuzzy output. Finally, the defuzzifier interface maps the fuzzy output back to a crisp number that can be used for making decisions. The fuzzy inference system uses two types of inputs: individual observations of the sensor nodes (individual fuzzy inference) and neighborhood observations (global fuzzy inference).

The individual fuzzy inference process is explained as following. The fuzzy logic system starts whenever a CH notices that one or more sensors inside its cluster are "candidates" to become semantic neighbors. The sensors are considered "candidates" to become semantic neighbors when their data satisfy a domain rule related to the event monitored by the WSN. For example, in the SHM domain, if there is any relevant change in the modal frequency values of a sensor node, the sensor node will be considered a "candidate" to become a semantic neighbor. In this example, the domain rule is "acceleration is higher than a specified threshold". The fuzzifier utilizes as input data the aggregated data (crisp input) of the sensors that satisfy a domain rule. The fuzzifier can also utilize as input data some sensor's data that were processed by the CH. The fuzzifier maps crisp inputs into fuzzy sets by using the trapezoidal membership functions. The most common membership functions are trapezoidal and triangular. Triangular membership functions are used whenever there is a single element that has the pertinency value equal to 1 (one). The trapezoidal membership functions are used if there are several (> 1) elements that have the pertinency value equal to 1. We use the max-min inference since it proves to be computationally fast in the system implementation [5]. Each CH stores their fuzzy inference results. The CHs communicate to each others (one-hop) by sending and receiving messages containing their individual fuzzified results about semantic neighborhood relationships inside their respective clusters. Every CH which receives these messages from neighbor CHs performs the fuzzy inference using the neighbors fuzzified observations (global fuzzy inference). It is used a sigma-count factor [9], a measure of fuzzy cardinality that allows to generalize counting techniques, in the quantification of neighborhood observations:

$$\sum Count(F) = \sum_i \mu F(xi).$$ (1)

where a fuzzy set F is characterized by a membership function $\mu F(x_i)$ which gives the degree of similarity of x to F. F is a property of interest related to the sensor nodes observations, e.g. "acceleration value is high" or "humidity level is low". Finally, X = {x1, ..., xn} is the set of neighbors.

A fuzzy majority quantifier is used to get a fuzzified indication of the consensual neighborhood opinion. A fuzzy majority is defined as a fuzzy linguistic quantifier. In our case, we use the *most* [10] quantifier to characterize the fuzzy majority, i.e., the consensual neighborhood opinion in order to take a more accurate decision:

$$\mu_{most}\left(\frac{\sum Count(F)}{|X|}\right) = \mu_{most}\left(\frac{\sum_i \mu F(xi)}{n}\right).$$ (2)

$$\mu_{most}(x) = \begin{cases} 0 & \text{if } x \leq 0.3 ; \\ 2x - 0.6 & \text{if } 0.3 < x < 0.8 ; \\ 1 & \text{if } x \geq 0.8 . \end{cases}$$

Next, the fuzzified values activate the inference rules. The fuzzy inference system incorporates both the fuzzified individual observations and the quantified neighborhood observations in the rules. For example, concerning a SHM domain:

IF acceleration is High AND stress/strain is High AND
most(accelerationtNeigh) is High AND most(stress/strainNeigh) is High
THEN SemanticNeighborDecision is High

The fuzzy inference system combines the rules to obtain an aggregated fuzzy output. Finally, the defuzzifier maps the fuzzy output back to a crisp number which it is used for making decisions related to the semantic neighborhood. To reduce the computational complexity, we use a simple defuzzification method denoted as *maximum* method in order to produce a crisp output.

5 Semantic Clustering

The following steps illustrate an overview of the proposed method:

1) A new semantic cluster may be composed of the semantically correlated sensor nodes which are identified in the messages sent by CHs, although those sensor nodes may be either in the same physical cluster or not.

2) In a given neighborhood, the CH that has the highest number of semantic neighbors in its cluster is elected as a semantic collector.

3) The semantic collector is responsible for sending the reports to the sink nodes. The reports may contain both the agregated values of the semantic neighbors, the semantic collectors IDs associated to the detected damage and the semantic neighbors IDs.

6 Case Study: Structural Damage Detection, Location and Extent Estimation

The main goal of a SHM application is to assess the integrity of the monitored structures performing damage detection, localization and extent estimation tasks. Our proposed method is based on the Sensor-SHM algorithm [11]. Sensor-SHM is a distributed algorithm for WSNs which performs damage detection, localization and extent determination in civil structures, making use of the shifts in the structure's modal frequencies. Sensor-SHM is described as following.

6.1 Sensor-SHM

There is a cluster formation[2] at Sensor-SHM algorithm start up process. The CHs are determined and each CH is aware of its CH neighbors. CHs do not perform sensing tasks, and are at a higher level in the network. The lower level is composed of sensors responsible for collecting the signatures of the structure and are subordinated to one of the CHs. Sensor nodes are identified by the index i, in the lower level of the network, while CHs are identified by the index j, from the higher level of the network.

The presence of damage in a structure may cause shifts in all of its modal frequencies, at a given sensor node location. Then, the perceived change depends on the position of the sensor node, if it is close to the damage site or not. Briefly, the Sensor-SHM algorithm is explained as following:

1) Each sensor node individually collects acceleration values from its position on the civil structure in the time domain. A Fast Fourier Transform (FFT) is then performed on the collected acceleration measurements and a simple method is used in order to extract the modal frequencies shown in the frequency spectrum generated by the FFT algorithm. A vector $\overrightarrow{\omega}_{i,t}$ (3) of M extracted modal frequencies represents the signature of the structure, considering a sensor i in the data collection stage t. Thus, each sensor node i obtains a $\overrightarrow{\omega}_{i,t}$ vector in each data collection stage t. Every sensor node sends to its CH the $\overrightarrow{\omega}_{i,t}$ vector at each sensing stage t.

$$\overrightarrow{\omega}_{i,t} = \begin{bmatrix} \omega_{i,t}^{1} \\ \vdots \\ \omega_{i,t}^{M} \end{bmatrix}. \tag{3}$$

---

[2] Semantic clustering is not used in the original Sensor-SHM algorithm.

2) Each CH analyzes incoming signature vectors from each sensor node contained in its cluster, in order to notice any modal frequency change. Each CH compares the modal frequency vectors $\varpi_{i,t}$ sent at the current data collection stage by the sensor nodes with a modal frequency vector $\varpi_{i,0}$ sent by each sensor i in the first data collection stage, containing the initial signature of the structure for each location. Each $\varpi_{i,0}$ means a signature from a healthy state of the civil structure, which means it has no damage or undesired perturbations. The comparison is made through the absolute value of the vector $\Delta\varpi_{i,t}$, which stores the subtraction of the actual values with the ones from the undamaged state, for each mode of vibration. The initial signature of the structure of each sensor node is sent to the CH by the sensor nodes. If there is a relevant change in the modal frequency values in $\varpi_{i,t}$ related to those of $\varpi_{i,0}$, considering a certain amount of tolerance threshold specified at the network start up process, the algorithm assumes the possibility of damage presence in the monitored structure. The tolerance threshold vector $\vec{T_i}$ is defined for each sensor node. The threshold values depend on the sensor node position on the civil structure and are defined by a structure specialist.

3) A $D_{i,t}$ coefficient is calculated for each sensor node i. For the first five modal frequencies, see the $D_{i,t}$ formal definition:

$$D_{i,t} = \vec{A_i}\ \overrightarrow{\Delta\varpi_{i,t}} = \begin{bmatrix} A_i^1 & A_i^2 & A_i^3 & A_i^4 & A_i^5 \end{bmatrix} \begin{bmatrix} \Delta\varpi_{i,t}^1 \\ \Delta\varpi_{i,t}^2 \\ \Delta\varpi_{i,t}^3 \\ \Delta\varpi_{i,t}^4 \\ \Delta\varpi_{i,t}^5 \end{bmatrix}. \tag{4}$$

The $D_{i,t}$ coefficient value means how close a sensor node i is to the detected damage site. The $\vec{A_i}$ vector is composed by weights associated to each modal frequency shift. The sink node informs the A_i values to the CHs at the network start up. However, the A_i values can be modified during the operation of the network. Since changes in the higher modal frequencies mean there are changes in the local modes of vibration, the $\vec{A_i}$ vector is responsible for identifying the sensor nodes which are closest to the damage position, once higher weight values should be set to the higher modes of vibration. Therefore, in the network startup process, the highest weight values are associated with the highest modes of vibration and are stored in the CH of each sensor node i. Thus, the sensor nodes contained in a cluster formation which is closest to the damage position have the highest $D_{i,t}$ coefficients of the whole network.

4) A $C_{j,t}$ coefficient is performed through the sum of all $D_{i,t}$ coefficients for all k sensor nodes contained in a cluster j of the network:

$$C_{j,t} = \sum_{i=1}^{k} D_{i,t}. \tag{5}$$

The $C_{j,t}$ coefficient means how close to the detected damage site the cluster is, as a whole.

5) In the network startup process, a L_j threshold value is set in the CHs, which depends on the structure local attributes where each cluster formation is installed. Whenever $C_{j,t} \geq L_j$, the CH sends to its neighbor CHs (one-hop) a message including its $C_{j,t}$ coefficient value. This action avoids a large number of false damage detection notifications, because in a real damage detection situation it is expected that some neighbor CHs also detect the same event and also send their $C_{j,t}$ coefficients to the neighbor CHs.

6) Every CH which receives the $C_{j,t}$ coefficients from neighbor CHs compares those values to its $C_{j,t}$ coefficient. In a given neighborhood area, the CH which has the highest $C_{j,t}$ coefficient value is considered a collector CH. The collector CH is responsible for making a report containing all $\varpi_{i,t}$ values of the neighbor CHs and send it to the sink node, emitting an alert notification to the engineers.

Therefore, the damage localization and extent determination are determined by the sensor positions which its CH has $C_{j,t} \geq L_j$. In multiple damage detection case, or in case of a large area of damage situation, the occurrence of multiple collector CHs is expected. These collectors may send multiple reports from different positions in the structure to the sink node.

6.2 Semantic Clustering in SHM

Sensor-SHM algorithm uses the cluster position in the structure in order to localize and estimate the extension of detected damage. However, depending on the sensors position in a cluster j, some sensors can be closer to the detected damage site than other sensors in the same cluster. Such fact can impact the $C_{j,t}$ coefficient used by the Sensor-SHM algorithm since this coefficient is composed of the $D_{i,t}$ values of the sensor nodes contained in a cluster j. And as we previously mentioned, the $D_{i,t}$ coefficient denotes how close a sensor node i is of the detected damage site. So, that fact consequently can affect the Sensor-SHM method results related to this aspect.

We applied our proposed clustering in the SHM domain, using the Sensor-SHM algorithm as a base and our proposal as an enhancement to this algorithm aiming at achieving best performances regarding the energy consumption thus extending the WSN lifetime. Whenever a damage is detected, the network organization is modified based on semantic correlation between the sensors. The sensors which are closest to the damage site are denoted semantic neighbors. Such sensors are easily identified since they have the highest $D_{i,t}$ coefficient values of the network. However those sensor nodes may be in the same physical cluster or not (considering the physical clustering).

A damage detection in a civil structure is illustrated in Figure 2. Using the Sensor-SHM algorithm, possibly the clusters C, D, E and F have the highest $C_{j,t} \geq L_j$ coefficients values in the network, since they are close to the detected damage. Sensor-SHM determines the damage area (represented by blue dashed lines) by the clusters positions which $C_{j,t} \geq L_j$. However, we can observe that in the clusters C, D, E and F, some sensors are closer to the damage site than other sensor nodes. In this same example, using our clustering method, the semantic neighborhood is composed of sensors node with ID 13, 14, 17, 18 ,21, 25 and 30 that are grouped in a semantic cluster. The damage area is only determined by the semantic cluster position in the structure (represented by yellow dashed lines). Thus, considering the crosslayer nature of the WSNs systems, using both Sensor-SHM and our proposed semantic clustering method we can improve the precision of the damage localization and extent estimation tasks. Briefly, our method works as following:

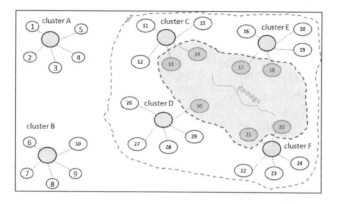

Fig. 2. Semantic Clustering

1) At the network start up process, a physical clustering scheme (explained in section III) is performed. Using the Sensor-SHM algorithm for damage detection, each sensor node i obtains vectors $\varpi_{i,t}$ (3) in each data collection stage t and sends them to its CH. If the CH notices a relevant modification in the frequency vectors $\varpi_{i,t}$, it assumes the possibility of a damage presence in the observed structure. A $D_{i,t}$ coefficient (4) is also calculated for each sensor node i contained in a physical cluster j which presents a relevant modification in the frequency vectors.

2) Next, our fuzzy system starts whenever a CH notices that one or more sensors inside its cluster are "candidates" to become semantic neighbors because they satisfy the domain rule:

$$\overrightarrow{\Delta\omega_{i,t}} \geq \overrightarrow{T_i} = \begin{bmatrix} \Delta\omega_{i,t}^1 \\ \Delta\omega_{i,t}^2 \\ \Delta\omega_{i,t}^3 \\ \Delta\omega_{i,t}^4 \\ \Delta\omega_{i,t}^5 \end{bmatrix} \geq \begin{bmatrix} T_i^1 \\ T_i^2 \\ T_i^3 \\ T_i^4 \\ T_i^5 \end{bmatrix}. \tag{6}$$

3) In the individual fuzzy inference process, a partial set of semantic neighbors is selected in each physical cluster. The bases for the fuzzy logic system are built from data generated in extensive simulations. One linguistic variable was labeled as *coefficient* (Fig. 3), representing the $D_{i,t}$ coefficient of sensor nodes. For this linguistic variable, two labels are defined as Low (L) and High (H) in order to

represent the two simulated coefficients. For the coefficient variable, the universe of discourse was defined considering the closed interval of real numbers between zero and the largest simulated value for this variable. Regarding the membership function, that determines the shapes that represent each fuzzy set, the trapezoidal shape was chosen for this variable. Similar to [12], the boundaries of the shape are defined using a adopted confidence interval (95%). The value that represents the adopted confidence interval is used for each fuzzy set on the left side (lower boundary) and the smallest simulated value whose membership degree in the next fuzzy set is equal to 1, on the right side (upper boundary). In the start up process of the network, a Ld_j threshold value (Fig. 3) is informed to the CHs, which depends on the structure local attributes where each sensor node is installed. The Ld_j threshold is specified to determine if a *sensor node* is close to the damage site or not.

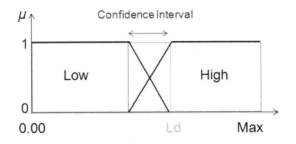

Fig. 3. Membership Functions for the Coefficient Variable

4) The CH sends to its neighbor CHs a message including both the semantic neighbors IDs into a physical cluster *j* and the aggregated data related to the $D_{i,t}$ coefficients of each sematic neighbor. Every CH which receives these messages from neighbor CHs updates the fuzzy inference using the neighbors observations (global fuzzy inference). A fuzzy rule is also defined:

   IF coefficient is High AND nmessages is High AND most(coefficientNeigh) is High AND most(nmessagesNeigh) is High THEN SemanticNeighborDecision is High

   where *nmessages* is a linguistic variable that represents the number of received messages by the CHs. This variable avoids a large number of false damage detection notifications, because it is expected that some neighbor CHs also detect the same event.

5) The semantically uncorrelated sensor nodes should not exchange information since that would waste resources of the network. So, uncorrelated nodes can be temporarily turned off.

6) A new semantic cluster is composed of all detected semantic neighbors and the semantic collector election is performed. The semantic collector might calculate the $CS_{j,t}$ coefficient value:

$$CS_{j,\,t} = \sum_{i=1}^{k} D_{i,\,t}\,. \tag{7}$$

$CS_{j,t}$ is based on $D_{i,t}$ coefficient values of the detected semantic neighbors and it denotes how close the semantic cluster is to the detected damage site. The semantic collector may also send the reports to the sink node including the $\varpi_{i,t}$ values of the semantic neighbors.

Whenever a new damage is detected, both a new election of the semantic neighbors and a new semantic clustering are perfomerd. In cases of multiple damages or large damages, it is possible the occurrence of multiple semantic collectors which can send to the sink node multiple reports from the different positions in the structure. The sink node has a time history of the $\varpi_{i,t}$ values of all semantic neighbors.

7   Conclusion

We propose a semantic clustering for WSNs. One important benefit of our proposal is to allow the network self-organize according to semantic correlation between sensor nodes. Another important benefit is to reduce the number of sensors which are monitoring the environment and consequently save resources such as processing, communication and energy in order to extend the lifetime of the network.

We applied the proposed semantic clustering algorithm in a SHM study case. As future work, it will be interesting to evaluate the semantic clustering algorithm for all detected semantic neighbors of the network and to investigate parameters such as the node degree, transmission power, battery level, processor load, i.e. metrics for choosing the optimal clustering structure as described in [1]. Moreover, we intend in a subsequent work to further explore the process of clustering formation in order to improve the WSN efficiency and performance. If the cluster is large, there is a large overhead due to control messages and more energy consumption. On the other hand, small cluster formations increase the spatial granularization due to the growth in the number of CH nodes. Accordingly, small clusters reduce the amount of collecting points because the CHs do not gather data from the environment. It will be interesting to consider trade-off between CH size, overhead, and energy saving.

Acknowledgments. This work is partly supported by the CNPq through processes 477226/2007-8 for Luci Pirmez and Flávia C. Delicato; 477229/2009-3 and 306938/2008-1 for Flávia C. Delicato; 481638/2007 for Neuman Souza, Danielo G. Gomes, Luci Pirmez and Flávia C. Delicato. This work is also partly supported by the FINEP through process 1979/09 for Luci Pirmez.

References

1. Marin-Perianu, R.S., Lombriser, C., Havinga, P.J.M., Scholten, J., Troster, G.: Tandem: A context-aware method for spontaneous clustering of dynamic wireless sensor nodes. In: International Conference for Industry and Academia. Springer, Heidelberg (2008)
2. Abbasi, A.A., Younis, M.: A survey on clustering algorithms for wireless sensor networks. Computer Communications 30, 2826–2841 (2007)
3. Bruckner, D., Zucker, G., Simo, J., Herzner, W., Mahlknecht, S.: Semantic neighborhood sensor network for smart surveillance applications. In: 3rd International Conference from Scientific Computing to Computational Engineering (2008)

4. Rocha, A., Delicato, F., Souza, N., Gomes, D., Pirmez, L.: A semantic middleware for autonomic wireless sensor networks. In: Workshop on Middleware for Ubiquitous and Pervasive Systems, vol. 389. ACM, New York (2009)

5. Marin-Perianu, M., Havinga, P.: D-fler: A distributed fuzzy logic engine for rule-based wireless sensor networks. In: Ichikawa, H., Cho, W.-D., Satoh, I., Youn, H.Y. (eds.) UCS 2007. LNCS, vol. 4836, pp. 86–101. Springer, Heidelberg (2007)

6. Bouhafs, F., Merabti, M., Mokhtar, H.: A semantic clustering routing protocol for wireless sensor networks. In: Consumer Communications and Networking Conference, pp. 351–355. IEEE Computer Society, Los Alamitos (2006)

7. Ulieru, M., Madani, S.A.: An application of industrial agents to concrete bridge monitoring. In: ICINCO-ICSO (2006)

8. Heinzelman, W., Chandrakasan, A., Balakrishnan, H.: An application-specific protocol architecture for wireless microsensor networks. IEEE Transactions on Wireless Communications, 660–670 (2002)

9. Zadeh, L.A.: A computational approach to fuzzy quantifiers in natural languages. Computers and Mathematics 9, 149–184 (1983)

10. Kacprzyk, J.: Group decision making with a fuzzy linguistic majority. Fuzzy Sets and Systems 18, 105–118 (1986)

11. Santos, I., Pirmez, L., Lemos, E., Vaz, L., Delicato, F.C., Souza, J.N.: Resource Consumption Analysis for a Structural Health Monitoring Algorithm Using Wireless Sensor Networks. In: 28º Simpósio Brasileiro de Redes de Computadores e de Sistemas Distribuídos (2010)

12. Pirmez, L., Delicato, F., Pires, P., Mostardinha, F., Rezende, N.: Applying fuzzy logic for decision-making on wireless sensor networks. In: Fuzzy Systems Conference (2007)

C³TO: A Scalable Architecture for Mobile Tutoring over Cell Phones

Laurie Butgereit[1,2] and Reinhardt A. Botha[2]

[1] Meraka Institute, Pretoria, South Africa
[2] Nelson Mandela Metropolitan University, Port Elizabeth, South Africa
lbutgereit@meraka.org.za, ReinhardtA.Botha@nmmu.ac.za

Abstract. Quality tutoring can be one of the building blocks in the bridges over many of the various "divides" - digital, economic, social and educational. Appalling recent statistics have shown that only 7% of South Africa's first year university students have sufficient mathematics knowledge and background to cope with university work. C³TO (Chatter Call Centre/Tutoring Online) is an architecture which facilitates mobile tutoring by linking primary and secondary school pupils to volunteer tutors from local South African universities to assist with mathematics homework. Pupils use chat software on their cell phones (with the majority using the Mxit instant messaging system) to discuss their mathematics homework with the volunteer tutors. The first implementation of such tutoring system yielded a much higher demand than was expected. This paper specifically reports on the scalability issues that were considered when designing the C³TO architecture. It argues for design interventions at three different levels and presents the current design accordingly.

Keywords: math, mxit, cell phones, tutoring, scalability.

1 Introduction

Quality education is important to the advancement of a person and a country. In the modern digital age, quality education in mathematics, science, and digital skills (such as Information Technology and programming) are even more important. Alas, South African mathematics and science education has been the subject of many critical reports and reviews. A recent report by Higher Education South Africa shows that only 7% of South African first year university students can cope with university level mathematics [1]. Previous international research placed South African Grade 8s last among 50 nations which participated in the study [2].

Amid these dismal statistics about mathematics education, however, is an interesting statistics on cell phone usage. Although there are no definitive statistics on cell phone usage by children and teenagers, recent research by Kreutzer [3] in low income township schools in Cape Town shows that 97% of respondents had used a cell phone the previous day for seeking information, communication, playing games, or multi-media. In a larger study, Kreutzer [4] found that 77% of the respondents owned a cell phone and 66% of the respondents' phones were internet enabled.

A. Pont, G. Pujolle, and S.V. Raghavan (Eds.): WCITD/NF 2010, IFIP AICT 327, pp. 15–25, 2010.

The "Dr Math" project was started in January, 2007, and was an attempt to see if school pupils would use their own personal cell phones at their own personal cost to get assistance with mathematics homework. The basic interactions involved with "Dr Math" are depicted in Figure 1. Pupils used the popular Mxit instant messaging system on their cell phones to chat with "Dr Math". In effect they would reach tutors who were connected to "Dr Math" using normal desktop workstations. This project grew from an initial expectation of approximately 50 participants to more than 4000 pupils using the system. The project has been well documented [5, 6].

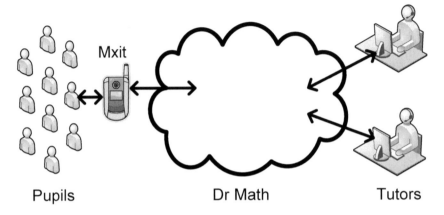

Fig. 1. Interactions with Dr Math

However, any software platform or project which is designed to originally cater for 50 users and then unexpectedly grows to more than 4000 users can have one expected outcome. Butcher found that delays were occurring with the "Dr Math" platform and that some pupils were waiting an unacceptable amount of time for responses from tutors [7]. Later in this paper we discuss these problems in more detail.

The problems led to a complete redesign of the "Dr Math" architecture, dubbed C³TO or Chatter Call Centre/Tutoring Online. C³TO is specifically designed to address the scalability issues for mobile online tutoring system. In particular, this paper discusses how scalability is achieved within the C³TO architecture. However, first consider what scalability really means.

2   What Is Scalability?

The "scalability" of a solution can be defined as how well the solution works when the size of the problem increases [8]. The concept of scalability is not limited to software. Consider aviation. An airplane design which is for an aircraft intended to carry 4 people cannot just be made proportionally larger in order to carry 200 people. The design of a 4 person aircraft does not scale to an aircraft to carry 200 people. In some industries scalability is less important than in other industries. Consider civil engineering. A bridge which was built in 1900 over a river will not have to scale in length. However, the traffic which goes over the bridge may become heavier and denser.

In the case of software, especially networked based software and social networking software, the number of total users will continually increase. This increase, however, may not be linear. It may have daily, weekly, monthly or annual cycles. Scalability in terms of software solutions is the ability of reducing or increasing the scope of methods, processes and management according to the problem size [9].

Scalability as part of an architecture essentially strengthens the capability to manage capacity. Capacity management is required to balance demand (the need for tutoring) and supply (the availability of a "Dr Math" service) in a cost-effective and timely manner. Scalability concerns itself with the ability to adjust the supply when demand changes.

For software services, Laitinen, Fayad, and Ward [9] argue that one way of assessing scalability (and therefore capacity) is the notion of "scalable adequacy." Scalable adequacy is the effectiveness of a software engineering solution when used on differently sized problems. Inherent to this idea of scalable adequacy is that the software should provide good mechanisms for partitioning, composition, and visibility control. The software should be configurable to cater for particular problem needs, contractual requirements, and even budgetary goals. Software which can omit unneeded facilities without destroying overall functionality possess scalable adequacy.

In the next section, we will consider how C³TO was developed framed against the scalability requirements.

3 C³TO and Scalability

The process to develop the new C³TO architecture started with a careful analysis of the scalability concerns in the original "Dr Math". This section commences by describing these scalability concerns in more detail in the first sub-section. Thereafter the second sub-section reflects on the development of the new "Dr Math". Finally the third subsection presents a typology of scalability design decisions, which the rest of the paper mimics to discuss the design choices in detail.

3.1 Scalability Concerns in the Original "Dr Math"

The initial implementation of Dr Math raised several scalability concerns including:

1. Hardware scalability: During the first few months of existence, "Dr Math" ran simply on the author's office laptop using Open Source chat software such as Gaim and Pidgin. As the number of participants increased, merely moving Gamin and Pidgin to faster hardware did not solve the underlying problem because of the addressing mechanisms used in the chat protocols. In order to take advantage of the faster hardware, a different software solution would be necessary.

2. The number of connections: As the number of participants grew during the first year of operation, various limitations were hit using Mxit chat protocols. For example, at one point in time, Mxit limited a chat account to only having 500 contacts. As "Dr Math" attempted to grow beyond 500 pupils, the original software needed to be modified to monitor more than one Mxit account. This limit on the number of contacts dramatically affected the scalability of the initial implementation of "Dr Math".

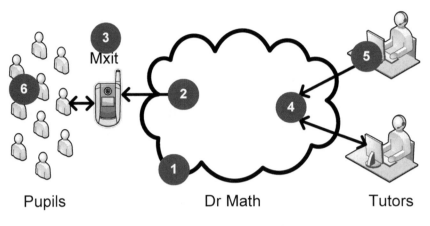

Fig. 2. The major scalability concerns in Dr. Math

3. The type of connection: During the first year of "Dr Math's" existence, it migrated from Jabber chat protocols, the Google chat protocols, and finally to Mxit proprietary protocols. During this time, only one chat protocol could be supported at any one time. This limitation meant that only users on a particular chat system could access Dr Math.

4. Managing the workload of tutors: The initial implementation of "Dr Math" assumed that all tutors had the same tutoring ability. Pupils were merely evenly split up across all tutors who were logged in regardless of the individual tutors' abilities. This often resulted in some tutors being given more questions than they could handle while, at the same time, other tutors were idling because they could type faster or had better mathematical knowledge.

5. The physical accommodation of tutors: During the initial implementation of "Dr Math", tutors needed to physically come into our offices in order to act as tutor. This was due to a number of software limitations implemented at that time. For example, the tutoring software was implemented originally as a Java application and needed to be physically installed on the computers where the tutors worked. In addition, the log files of the conversations were primarily protected by the corporate firewall and computer username and password. There was no internet access.

6. Tutors were being (mis)used: Once the pupils became familiar with the "Dr Math" project, they often misused (or even abused) the services of the tutors by asking them to lookup textual information on the internet (such as historical facts about Isaac Newton) or to test them on their times tables. Although the tutors were happy to do this, this limited the number of other pupils who also needed access to tutors.

3.2 Re-development of "Dr Math"

The "Dr Math" software had to be completely re-developed according to the new architectural decisions. Since the "Dr Math" project deals primarily with minor children, ethics clearance requirements originally received from the Tshwane University of Technology had to be re-implemented in C³TO. These include:

1. Code of conduct signed by human tutors
2. Various disclaimers sent to participants at critical times
3. Recording of all conversations
4. Securing all cell phone numbers so that they are not visible to others
5. Password protection and role based security on web interfaces
6. Various algorithms in place to attempt to intercept the passing of telephone numbers between pupils and tutors.

Some other changes, like additional security mechanisms, were also made, but since these do not directly impact the scalability concern discussed in this paper they are omitted here. "Dr Math" running under the new C³TO architecture was made available to pupils in November, 2009. In South Africa, November is "exam season" with most pupils writing extensive end of year exams. The platform was available over the Christmas holiday season (primarily for games, lookups, and competitions but not actual tutoring) and is being used extensively (including tutoring) during the new 2010 academic year. At the time of writing this paper, tutors are currently being recruited from a number of tertiary institutions in South Africa. One tutor is actually from the UK. More information on the actual results of this scalability exercise will be available at the presentation of this paper.

While considering the problems to be addressed the authors realized that the design choices are characterized by different principles. The next sub-section describes a typology that will be used in the rest of the paper to discuss the actual design decisions in more detail.

3.3 Typology for Scalability Decisions

Critical reflection on the problems experienced and the design choices made yielded the realization that the design choices in C³TO can be described at three different levels:

1. At the *technical* level certain design choices had to be made. These design choices are specific and concern mostly "what" is being chosen and/or implemented in C³TO to address certain issues.
2. At the *tactical* level, design decisions were more concerned with "how" things are done. As such it is concerned with the governing "behavior" of the system.
3. At the *strategic* level, higher order design decisions had to be made. Here one is concerned with the basic principles followed and adapting the essential nature of the system to address demand concerns.

The rest of this paper discusses the decisions in more detail according to each of the three levels.

4 Technical Scalability Choices

Certain technical choices had to be made with respect to the implementation of C^3TO. These technical choices are mostly concerned with which products, standards and protocols were chosen and supported. Essentially these choices were attempting to re-use generally known solutions to scalability. In the next three subsections we discuss the three main technical choices that were made with a view to enhance scalability.

4.1 J2EE, Jboss and Mobicents

The Java 2 Platform, Enterprise Edition (J2EE), is a model for developing distributed applications with particular emphasis on standards, reliability and scalability [10]. JBoss is an open source implementation of the J2EE standard which has found commercial success [11].

In order to provide developers with standardised Java APIs for network applications, the Java APIs for Integrated Networks (JAIN) initiative was started. JAIN SLEE (Service Logic Execution Environment) defines an application server similar to J2EE but designed for telecommunications related applications [12]. JBoss implements JAIN SLEE through its Mobicents Communication Platform [13]. Mobicents was the first (and currently the only) open source platform certified for JAIN SLEE compliance [14].

Mobicents provides for two types of artifacts. Resource adaptors are low level communication artifacts. The standard Mobicents release comes with a handful of resource adaptors, including HTTP, XMPP, and timer facilities. Service Building Blocks are higher level artifacts which use multiple resource adaptors to provide a service.

The actual communication portion of C^3TO is implemented as a Mobicents service building block. The XMPP resource adaptor provided by Mobicents receives messages from the pupils. These messages are forward to the C^3TO service building block which processes them. These choices are depicted graphically in Figure 3.

Jboss and Mobicents, especially when hosted on a Linux operating system, provide a scalable architecture which is able to run on a wide range of hardware configurations including small "netbooks" , high end servers, and virtual hosted environments. This aspect of the scalability of C^3TO primarily addresses the ease of migrating to faster and more powerful hardware as the need arises.

4.2 Multiple Connections

C^3TO provides for easy configuration of multiple XMPP connections through the XMPP resource adaptor supplied with the default Mobicents distribution. Mobicents implements an event driven model where a service building block can be interrupted by a "call back" from a resource adaptor. By allowing easy configuration of multiple XMPP connections, C^3TO implements the partitioning and visibility control indicated by Laitinen, Fayad, and Ward [9] to be important in scalability.

In the specific case of "Dr Math" running under C^3TO, the initial implementation provides for one national chat address for "Dr Math." If, however, the numbers

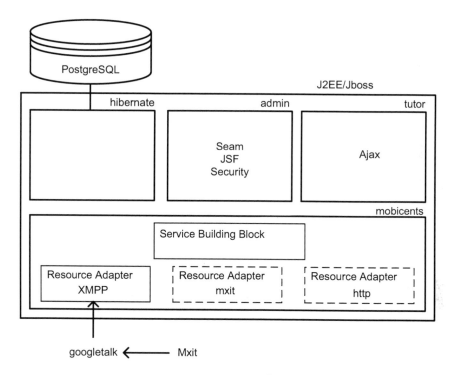

Fig. 3. Conceptual overview of C³TO architecture

increase to such a size where one national address is unmanageable, then it would be easy to implement provincial or regional addresses for "Dr Math" by configuring addition XMPP connections. This aspect of the scalability of C³TO primarily addresses the implementation of similar systems on the same server as the need arises.

The choice of Mobicents as communication platform also enables the future development of resource adapters that support other protocols than XMPP. This possibility is depicted in Figure 3 by the resources adaptors drawn in broken lines. It may, for example be possible to develop a resource adaptor that supports the native mxit protocol, rather than relying on the mxit-googletalk interface. Since all of these resource adaptors communicate with the Service Building Block supporting additional connections and protocols would be seamless to the tutors.

4.3 Web-Based Tutoring

The initial implementation of "Dr Math" required tutors to be physically present at a specific venue. This clearly has implications in terms of the availability of tutors as they may need to travel. This made for fairly inefficient use of the tutors time. It was thus necessary to completely redesign the tutoring module to allow volunteers to tutor over the Internet. The tutoring interface was implemented as a typical web application.

This web-based tutoring is crucial to the scalability of C³TO as it allows volunteers to tutor for short periods of time whenever it was convenient for them.

Because of the ease of configuring resource adaptors under Mobicents, in the near future we hope to implement a system whereby "off duty" tutors could be sent an SMS (or text message) whenever the "on duty" tutors are overwhelmed with questions and need additional tutors to assist with the pupil load.

This aspect of scalability of C³TO primarily addresses the effective management of scarce resources (the human tutors) as the need arises or the "scalable adequacy" as defined by Laitinen, Fayad, and Ward [9]

5   Tactical Scalability Choices

Once decisions regarding the "what" will be used is made, one needs to consider specific ways "how" these technologies will be used. These choices allow us to design features that may change the behavior of the system. Next we discuss two choices that allow the behavior of the system to be adapted seamlessly.

5.1   Web Configurable

While the components as technical choices allow for many different uses it is also important that those changes can be incorporated into the system as seamlessly as possible. Re-compiling a system because of "growth" is clearly counter-productive – many users will be unable to use the system. For this reason C³TO has been designed to be completely configurable and maintainable over the Internet.

The administration is a typical three tiered web application, with configuration details contained in the database in a fairly elementary meta-model. Consider some of the configuration options:

- Additional XMPP connections can be created and maintained by various web based administration pages.
- New volunteer tutors can register their interest in tutoring over the web. Authorised administrators can then give these volunteers access rights for tutoring over the internet.
- Volunteer tutors can set preferences in terms of certain subjects or at certain levels.
- Additional components such as mathematics competitions, web scrapes, lookups, etc. can be configured over the web. These components came about from some strategic design decisions that will be discussed later.

This web based configurability assists in the scalability of C³TO by making it easy to add additional features remotely when necessary, without interrupting the service.

5.2   "Busy-Ness" Model

Volunteer tutors have different backgrounds, knowledge, and skills. C³TO addresses this fact through a rudimentary "busy-ness" model. The "busy-ness" model is based on the following aspects:

- Only questions which fit the tutors qualifications and preferences are forwarded to him or her. This do require the pupils to communicate to an appropriate "Dr Math" account say dr.math.junior rather than the general account.

- Whereas typical web applications are "pull" information from websites, the tutoring portion of C³TO simulates a "push" of information from the server to the tutors by using AJAX. The polling rate of the AJAX components is configurable per tutor to allow for the difference in capacity between tutors.
- The number of conversations a tutor is involved with does provide help. However not all chats are very interactive, there might be "salvos" of messages, or chats may not be ended when done.
- The total number of chats and tutors available defines the basic scale of the overall busy-ness of the system.

This aspect of scalability of C³TO primarily addresses the effective use of human resources. To a certain extent the "busy-ness" model is the key to managing current supply and demand in as an efficient way as possible. The refinement and extension of the current model is seen as a definite future challenge.

6 Strategic Scalability Decisions

Some capacity problems appeared because the systems weren't used according to expectation. For example pupils used the tutors as calculators, asking answers to questions such as "what is sin 60?". Clearly this is not an effective use of tutor's time and may even make the tutors somewhat negative. It was then decided to adopt a different strategy, that of automated responses.

6.1 Automated Responses

The function of the automated responses is to give pupils the information they need without requiring intervention by a tutor. Even, if an intervention by a tutor is initially required, the tutor could then refer the pupil to one of the automated responses or "bots" to get the information required. Examples of these automated responses include, for example, a scientific calculator, a scrape of Wikipedia, and a list of definitions and formulae.

From an architectural perspective any communication with C³TO which is not intended for a human tutor is handled by the service building block which implements these "bots".

This aspect of C³TO addresses scalability in that it frees up tutors' time, i.e. increase supply, for more pressing demands. The initial success of "Dr Math" also led to reconsidering the types of mathematics interventions one can provide through this platform. The introduction of games followed.

6.2 Games

Computer games have enticed and addicted players for many years. From the initial "pong" game which debuted in the 1970s, on through "zork", "space invaders" and "pacman" in the early 1980s, and advancing to realistic graphical first-person-shooters of the current era, young people have played computer games. The current generation of high school pupils have lived their entire life in the presence of computer games (do the math, the current group of 18 year olds were born in 1992). Although researching the history of games is not the focus of this paper, annecdotal evidence clearly shows that young people will play computer games for hours if the topic is fun.

Although games does not address a specific scalability problem that was occurring it can still be seen as a strategic intervention that aids with scalability. The uptake of the "Dr Math" service shows that a demand for help exist. Providing additional "services" other than pupil-tutor chats do address the general demand for help, specifically during times human tutors may not be available.

7 Conclusion

C³TO leverages children and teenagers natural use of cell phones and chat protocols in order to provide quality educational content using a medium that they adore. The development of C³TO provided many lessons.

"Chat-based call centers" is a relatively new concept. The development of C³TO contributed knowledge towards developing these type of systems. Choices of specific technology with scalability in mind were investigated and carefully considered choices made. The code base for the project was done using open source software and will also be distributed as such, aiding in future work in this direction.

Re-thinking scalability in this specific context also contributes to a more holistic view of scalability. The scalability choices typology presented allows future researchers to think systematically about the problems associated with scalability and could aid in identifying often overlooked strategic and tactical interventions.

Finally the development of C³TO and the specific emphasis on scalability allows for the continuation of providing mathematics (and possibly other educational) assistance to pupils in a country desperate of a higher level of mathematical literacy.

The "Dr Math" service has been running on the C³TO architecture since January 2010. The performance issues often experienced in the old "Dr Math" service has largely disappeared. In addition other tutoring services have also been added to the same instance of the C³TO architecture; this caused no noticeable performance degradation. As of 13 May 2010 the platform facilitated interaction with 10074 registered users, of which around 2000 can be considered "active" users. Five different services are hosted on the platform implementing the C³TO architecture: two of those run on a continuous basis, while one only run periodically, with the other two being of a once-off short period nature. At most three of these services were active at one time, with no noticeable degradation of performance.

Formal performance testing is unfortunately difficult as the real bottleneck at this point in time seem to be the availability rather than the technical infrastructure. Specifically "Dr Math" and "Dr Lols" (a life skills tutoring service) has had 1557 and 378 active users during 2010 utilizing 24 chat connections. During April 2010 a total of 190512 messages (both in- and outbound) were handled with the system.

C³TO has without a doubt positively contributed to the performance-related issues experienced in the previous incarnation of the chat-based tutoring service.

Acknowledgements

C³TO makes use of many open source projects including Jboss, Mobicents, Seam, Postgresql, HtmlParser, and Linux. Although at the time of writing this document, it has not yet been released as open source, it will be released in the near future as open source under a Creative Commons, attribution, no commercial value, share alike South Africa 2.5 license.

References

[1] Yeld, N., Bohlmann, C., Cliff, A.: National Benchmark Tests Project as a National Service to Higher Education (Draft Copy). Higher Education South Africa (2009)

[2] Mullis, I.V.S., Martin, M.O., Gonzalez, E.J.: TIMSS 2003, International Mathematics Report: Findings from IEA. TIMSS & PIRLS International Study Center, 465 (2003)

[3] Kreutzer, T.: Assessing Cell Phone Usage in a South African Township School. In: E/Merge 2008 Proceedings (2008)

[4] Kreutzer, T.: Generation Mobile: Online and Digital Media Usage on Mobile Phones among Low-Income Urban Youth in South Africa, vol. 30 (retrieved on March 2009)

[5] Butgereit, L.: Math on MXit: using MXit as a medium for mathematics education. In: Meraka INNOVATE Conference for Educators (2007)

[6] Butgereit, L.: Using instant messaging over GPRS to help with school work. In: 2nd IFIP International Symposium on Wireless Communications and Information Technology in Developing Countries, Pretoria, South Africa, pp. 6–7 (2008)

[7] Butcher, N.: Evaluation of the Imfundo yami/yethu Project: Executive Summary. Neil Butcher and Associates (2009)

[8] Macri, D.: The scalability problem. Queue 1(10) (2004)

[9] Laitinen, M., Fayad, M.E., Ward, R.P.: The problem with scalability. Communications of the ACM 43(9), 115–118 (2000)

[10] Singh, I., Johnson, M., Stearns, B.: Designing enterprise applications with the J2EE platform. Sun MicroSystems, Inc., Palo Alto (2002)

[11] Richards, N., Griffith, S.: JBoss A Developer's Notebook. O'Reilly, Sebastopol (2005)

[12] Van Den Bossche, B., De Turck, F., Dhoedt, B.: Evaluation of current java technologies for telecom backend platform design. In: Proceedings of the 2005 International Symposium on Performance Evaluation of Computer and Telecommunication Systems, pp. 699–709 (2005)

[13] Deruelle, J.: JSLEE and SIP-Servlets Interoperability with Mobicents Communication Platform. In: The Second International Conference on Next Generation Mobile Applications, Services and Technologies, NGMAST'08, pp. 634–639 (2008)

[14] Kumlin, V.: Open Source SIP Application Servers For IMS Applications: A Survey (2007)

Wireless Mesh Networks for Infrastructure Deficient Areas

Roman Seibel, Nils-Hendrik Klann, Tim Waage, and Dieter Hogrefe

Georg August University of Göttingen
Computer Science Institute & Faculty of Economics
37077, Germany
seibel@cs.uni-goettingen.de, hhk@uni-goettingen.de,
tim.waage@stud.uni-goettingen.de, hogrefe@cs.uni-goettingen.de

Abstract. Provision of internet access in infrastructure deficient areas is expected to bring profound economic and humanitarian benefit to developing countries. Notwithstanding, achieving this goal poses an economic and technical challenge. Due to technological and economical reasons cellular networks are regarded to be unable to deliver affordable distribution in the short term. Instead 802.11s wireless mesh networking standard is identified to be a more viable and affordable partial solution to deliver broadband internet in the periphery of developing countries. A general focus is the individual incentive to participate in a mesh network rather than reliance on organisational bodies. This paper designs an architecture and business model for a low cost, low range distribution of internet access. The technical architecture is evaluated using simulation and is found to be viable, but demands optimisation.

Keywords: developing; ICT; cellular; 802.11s; mesh; business model; revenue sharing; simulation; capacity.

1 Introduction

This contribution takes a holistic approach to understand the peculiar situation of developing countries with regards to Internet access distribution and finds and evaluates a technical solution. We find that the barriers to internet provision in developing countries are of both economic as well as technical nature. Consequently we conceptualize on a new approach to distributing Internet access which combines theories from the fields of economics and computer science to tackle the above mentioned challenges. Holistic also refers to the fact that prior to finding yet another technical solution, an economic and technical perspective is applied to determine the solutions requirements. Following this the technical solutions and economic rules, in terms of a business model, are designed. Eventually the solution is being technically evaluated.

1.1 Economic Perspective

Affordable access to reliable Information and Communication Technologies (ICT) poses a key element to economic growth, human development and social progress of

A. Pont, G. Pujolle, and S.V. Raghavan (Eds.): WCITD/NF 2010, IFIP AICT 327, pp. 26–38, 2010.
© IFIP International Federation for Information Processing 2010

societies. Following the argument of [1] the broader availability of computers as well as information and communication technology has been recognized as a major contributor to the growth experience of industrialized countries during the 20th century. In quantitative terms the growth-enhancing effect attributable to the increased availability of ICT in industrialized countries is estimated to amount to as much as one additional percentage point of annual growth for countries such as the United States, Great Britain or Germany. [2] An additional percentage in growth has a non negligible impact over time, for it is exponential by nature.

Unfortunately access to this technology and thus its inherent advantages is distributed very unevenly around the world – a fact often described as the "digital divide" [3], [4]. As access to ICT infrastructure remains asymmetrically distributed on a global scale, so are the advancements. Societies and individuals are potentially able to reap from technologies such as broadband internet and mobile communications.

Much like in the case of the industrialized countries the availability of ICT is expected to act as a stimulant to economic growth in developing countries. As noted in [4] an average increase of 10 percent in mobile phone penetration in a developing country is expected to boost economic growth by around 0.81 percent annually. A similar increase in broadband penetration is expected to have an even higher growth effect of 1.4 percent annually. In addition to the issue of economic growth alone, the importance of ICT technology like "road, rail or electricity." infrastructure, is to an increasing extent recognized as an equally important pre-condition for human development [5]. In a similar vein broad provision of ICT infrastructure is identified as an important target within the Millennium Development goals, where an increase in the access to telephones, cellular networks and broadband internet is seen as a crucial development target.

The gravity created by a lack of access is most visible when contrasted with examples where individuals in these countries were able to make use of ICT. One important aspect is the provision of easy access to market information. [6] and [7] provide illustrative examples for the cases of India and Niger where the new availability of market information through mobile phones created major increases in the wellbeing of society. Other benefits include the improved operation of health services, schools and government services [5], [8], [9] The positive linkage between access to information and human development is further elaborated in [10].Although the positive impact of a reliable and affordable access to ICT services is by now beyond doubt, less clarity exists in concepts aiming at the actual delivery of such services to individuals in poor countries. Efforts have clearly been undertaken in connecting countries – for example on the African continent via undersea cables with the Internet. [11] This represents a crucial step towards achieving indiscriminate access to ICT services for as many individuals as possible, yet falls short of a complete solution. Obviously the sole establishment of a network connection through an undersea fiber represents a useful but also potentially insufficient measure if not combined with a solution to disseminate access to this connection throughout the entire country. As an isolated measure alone achieving an undersea wire without having a dissemination strategy only serves for replicating the *between-country* digital divide within the borders of the same country thus creating a *within-country* gap in ICT access. Instead a framework is required which provides solutions helping to overcome both the technical as well as economical obstacles, policy makers and enterprises face when extending access to ICT from the shorelines of countries to doorsteps of the actual users.

If we accept the fact that network connection is becoming viable on the country level the focus of attention has to be concentrated on solving downstream part of the provision challenge which describes the establishment of ICT services on a more local village or household level. We identify the following requirements for a distribution concept.

- Low regulatory effort for spectrum licensing.
- Low reliance on large organizational bodies.
- Simple entrepreneurial business model, with individual incentives.
- Low cost, mass market equipment availability.

In the discussion around this topic it is generally assumed that persisting structures on developing countries provide no practicable environment for wired-based approaches as usually seen in industrialized countries. Last have the luxury of a dense telephony cable network, installed in the previous century, suitable for broadband access distribution. Further, as [12] points out, even if installed, earth wire solutions are extremely prone to cable theft as the copper material used in the process represents a significant revenue source for delinquents. Since cellular networks become more ubiquitous globally, a typical suggestion to bridge the so-called "last mile" between an internet provider and the actual household relies on cellular networks. Basically the argument is that already existing mobile phone technology simply needs to be upgraded to data service capability to provide mobile internet access throughout society. We provide some discussion in the upcoming chapter and argue against cellular networks and pro 802.11 mesh, which is fulfilling the above mentioned requirements for a provision of ICT services at the provincial, village and even urban level.

1.2 Cellular Unfitness

Historically GSM (2G) based networks have expanded rapidly in developing areas, offering low cost voice services and slow high cost data services based on GPRS or EDGE. These networks can be upgraded to WCDMA networks to facilitate broadband data services, that can offer up to 7,2[1] Mbps with HSDPA, a path that has been taken in developed countries during the last decade. Further 3G hardware production has gained a large momentum on world markets and economies of scale allow manufacturers to produce low cost equipment, suitable for low income countries.

As we have discussed in the previous section, developing areas lack of infrastructure that could support access distribution on household level. Facilities such as telephone-, television- or even sufficient electric grid cable work is a scarce good. It is natural to assume that cellular networks can also be used for the last mile in developing countries, to offer Internet access to consumers and small businesses. However we argue that 3G cellular networks have certain limitations, that will render them an expensive solution, which can only serve a small percentage of the population, mainly high income households and larger enterprises.

---

[1] HSDPA category 8, using QPSK and 16-QAM modulation with up to 10 codes.

With cellular architecture Base Station Transceivers (BTS) are set up in a certain location with a certain radio coverage radius of a few hundred meters to a few kilometers (depending on parameters like transmit power, antenna design, frequency and environmental obstacles). This area, the cell is used to provide clients such as handsets and cellular modems with 2G/3G voice and data services. It makes sense to cover greater developing areas with so called macro cells, to reach as many customers as possible, while investing in as few cell sites as feasible.

The problem with WCDMA as multiple access technology is that its effective cell capacity, i.e. the maximum number of clients it can serve, is interference limited [13]. This is due to inter symbol interference (ISI) which implies that actual broadband cellular data services are only available to clients if a) they are located near the cells core with a reasonable signal quality and b) the number of simultaneous clients using the cell is small, which results in minimal interference. Nevertheless this fact is contradicting with the macro cell architecture mentioned above and leads to a low effective data rate and reduced effective coverage radius. A low effective radius results in the necessity for a higher cell site density which drives cost and therefore higher price, a property unwanted in low income countries. Currently developed countries counter measure this effect with the introduction of femto cells. Femto cells are small, low power cells, installed on customer premises with IP based backhaul connection to a cellular network operators core network. The IP based backhaul is usually realized via a separate cable, DSL or fiber broadband access of the customer. As a result macro cell load decreases, since the majority of data intensive services are used indoors, mostly at home. This effectively reduces the number of users per macro cell, decreasing interference and augmenting the macro cells effective radius. It can be argued that this solution extends WCDMA to a universal technology, that serves both, high performance data service needs indoors and seamless broadband data services while mobile. Notice, that developing areas generally do not have any kind of infrastructure that could support femto cell backhaul.

As a result, 3G networks, based on WCDMA cannot serve as the technology of choice to provide access to low and middle income households. Among other a key disadvantage of 3G cellular networks are the associated regulatory issues as well as the high costs associated with the service. As [14] points out 3G cellular networks are based on a vertical and centralized business framework with which users solely act as clients without much possibilities of actually participating in the provision process. Furthermore internet provision through 3G infrastructure faces considerable technical and legislative challenges in developing countries. As 3G services rely on a fixed spectrum the technology becomes vulnerable to issues such as spectrum scarcity on the one hand as well as insufficient spectrum management by government agencies and potentially ICT providers [15]. As [16] points out licenses to use bandwidth associated with a 3G cellular network structure can imply considerable costs for companies wishing to enter the market.

Long Term Evolution (LTE), successor of WCDMA networks uses Orthogonal Frequency Division Multiple Access (OFDMA) for downlink. It reduces the interference problem that occurs with WCDMA networks, by assigning individual, quasi non overlapping sub channels to clients. It needs to be analyzed how well LTE could be used in developing countries for the last mile, regarding performance and capacity. Although LTE is an interesting alternative, but it underlies the same economic and regulatory constraints as 3G networks and it might take a decade or more until LTE reaches economies of scale in order to be able to be rolled out in the majority of developing countries.

At large cellular networks do not fit the above mentioned requirements. Spectrum is licensed and tends to be expensive, especially if auctioned amongst multinational telecommunication companies. A large organization is necessary to operate a cellular network and equipment such as base stations, controllers and end user modems are not as low cost as alternatives. As opposed to this 802.11 networks provide more room for innovative concepts given their "decentralized, bottom-up" structure. Low regulatory effort through usage of Industrial Medical Scientific (ISM) and Unlicensed National Information Infrastructure (UNII) spectrum is possible. The fact that individuals can easily buy and install standard equipment secures low reliance on organizational bodies such as mobile network operators. It is further possible to implement simple entrepreneurial business models as will be discussed shortly. Finally low cost mass market equipment makes it affordable even for lower income households. Further low cost mesh routers offered by [17] are suitable for the supplier side of the market, whereas low cost computers such as netbooks and tablet PCs equipped with 802.11 Wireless LAN interfaces are a fit for clients, i.e. demand side of the market.

We have now discussed the ICT situation of developing countries and how access to Internet services can have a significant positive economic and humanitarian impact. We have established key properties for a technical and economic solution and introduced and criticized cellular networks as an obvious but problematic approach. We will now introduce the concept of wireless mesh networks, based on afore mentioned IEEE 802.11 standard, its architecture, a business model and capacity simulations, in order to consider it as a further alternative for infrastructure deficient areas for household level access distribution.

2   Wireless Mesh

This section describes the architecture of a 802.11 based wireless mesh network for the last mile of infrastructure deficient areas, followed by a business model and simulation results of the architectures capacity in worst case/peak period scenarios.

2.1   Architecture

Fig. 1 depicts 9 elements which are being introduced from left to right.

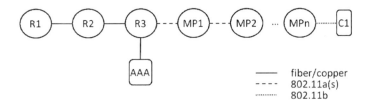

Fig. 1.

The left most element shows a router R1, belonging to a Tier 1 Internet Service Provider (ISP). Tier 1 ISPs voluntarily or commercially peer with each other and thus establish the backbone of the global Internetwork. Tier 1 uses broad band fiber- and copper cables to interconnect routers. Tier 2 router R2 is connected to Tier 1 via broad band infrastructure. Tier 2 ISP is customer of Tier 1, it resells Internet access to individual customers termed Tier 3, which can be end customer or a further reseller i.e. ISP. R3 is connected to R2 via last mile copper cable or radio channel (DSL, 802.16, WCDMA, Satellite).

Tier 3 maintains an Authentication, Authorization and Accounting (AAA) entity, interconnected with R3. Mesh Points (MPs) are routers with a wireless 802.11a (5 Ghz) interface, that uses mesh mode (802.11s) to interconnect with each other and establish a mesh backhaul. MPs carry a second interface based on 802.11b/g/n (2,4 Ghz) to connect to client devices, here C1. We separate the client radio access from the mesh backbone to reduce interference. We choose ISM 2,4 Ghz band for the client domain, because it is the most ubiquitous interface in end devices und more robust and far reaching, since it uses a lower frequency compared to 802.11a. We identify the 5 Ghz band as less crowded by other technologies (Bluetooth, cordless phones, microwave ovens, etc.). Also its lower spatial coverage, due to the higher frequency, is less relevant, because in multi hop architectures, distance between nodes can be relatively low, compared to single hop architectures. Notice: In case 802.11n is used for the client spectrum domain, only single band (2,4Ghz) mode should be used, to prevent interferences with 802.11a (5Ghz).

2.2 Business Model

The broad aim of every technological innovation is to realize some sort of benefit or value to participating parties. For end users the benefit is Internet access and for providers it is economic benefit of financial transactions made for that service by end users. In order to describe how the logic of value creation and capturing is conducted with this particular technology, we use a simplistic business model, described by a value chain and accounting relationship model. This business model focuses on two afore mentioned requirements of low organizational dependence and simple entrepreneurial incentives.

Fig. 2 introduces following entities of the value chain from left to right. Tier 2 ISP purchases access form Tier 1 and resells it to Tier 3. Tier 3 purchases Internet access from Tier 2 and resells it to Clients. Tier 3 can be a subsidiary of Tier 2 or an independent individual. The revenue earned by Tier 3 is shared with MP maintainers that evidently participate in routing of traffic to and from an associated client.
MP maintainers are individuals in contractual relationship with Tier 3.

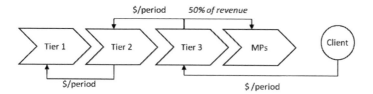

Fig. 2.

The accounting relationship is the following. Client 1 purchases credit with Tier 3 via micro payment for a certain amount of US$, per certain period, e.g. days. Notice this example uses (mobile) micro payment[2] rather than cash exchange. This allows simple automated and secure transactions. The situation in developing countries shows a widespread adoption of GSM based micro payment systems, due to lack of banking services for various economic reasons. The client uses the credit and generates traffic via a first hop to an access point and several following hops via wireless mesh backhaul. After the period has passed, MP1, .. MPn report to AAA entity their routing/forwarding effort for Client 1. AAA verifies reports, calculates respective share for each MP and transfers a certain amount of currency to MP maintainer via micro payment.

The architecture described is standard mass market equipment. The used protocols on 802.11 networks such as hybrid wireless mesh protocol (HWMP) studied and suitable, if still not optimal for this scenario as will be shown in the next section. The innovation of this approach is not the technical refinement, but the combination of affordable mass market equipment and a business model, that applies micro economic incentives to individuals, in order to motivate the participation in a wireless mesh network in vicinity to a broad band gateway. Thus meeting above requirements, the solution capitalizes not only on low organizational participation and entrepreneurial incentives but also on low cost mass market products and low regulatory effort.

2.3 Example Scenario

The following describes an example ISP Tier 3 sets up a router, connected to Tier 2 and a AAA element in a urban or rural area. This individual is most likely someone already reselling internet access in his internet café/shop. Neighboring individuals (MP maintainer) of Tier 3 premises obtain mesh points and install and associate them with router and AAA element of Tier 3 via 802.11a (mesh mode). Micro payment details are shared between Tier 3 and MP maintainer. The service is setup and ready to use by clients. A user (Client1) detects a wireless network, based on 802.11b in the vicinity of a MP associated to Tier 3. Client 1 associates to MP and is greeted with a captive portal of Tier3. Payment instructions are presented for a pass for a certain period, e.g. 24 hours for 1US$. Client 1 uses micro payment to transfer 1 US$ to Tier3's mobile payment account. The client no uses the Internet connection realized by Tier 3 and cooperating MP maintainers for 24 hours and generates traffic along certain mesh path(s). At the end of 24 hours, MP maintainer receive a share of for example 50% of the revenue, i.e. 50 US. Each MP maintainer receives a portion of this share according to performed forwarding effort on his mobile payment account. For example if three MP were involved MP1, MP2 and MP3 and all MPs have contributed the same amount of data forwarded to and from Client 1, the share will be distributed equally, 16.66US¢ per MP. Notice: This will be the case in a mesh scenario, with static routing topology throughout the alleged period, but will vary if routing topology changes.

One consequence of this revenue sharing model needs to be mentioned. If the topology is, as shown in Fig.3, with R3 as the root node and a hierarchical arrangement

---

[2] See M-PESA www.safaricom.co.ke, www.roshan.af, www.vodacom.co.tz

of MPs around it, there will be sets or rings of MPs closer to R3 and more distant. We classify those nodes with hierarchy number tuples such as MP1.2, which means Mesh Point ring 1, number 2. MP1.2 which is closer to R3 will play a greater role in traffic forwarding for clients than MP2.1, since also MP2.2 and MP2.3 are associated to it with its clients. Clients are denominated C1, C2 … Cn. Hence MP1.2 is crucial to the functioning of a significant part of the network. Since its indispensability it makes sense that MP1.2 will receive greater revenue shares for forwarding effort. The greater the number of clients in outer rings, the greater the income for MPs in inner rings will be relative to the income of MPs in more distant rings. This creates an incentive for MP maintainers in crucial positions to keep MPs active and reachable by other nodes. This may include the necessity to provide a stable power source such as grid, batteries, wind or solar power. Notice: Also MPs in inner rings have associated clients, these are left out of the diagram for simplicity.

2.4 Capacity Simulation

The following section describes the simulation setup produced with Qualnet simulator[18], a commercial derivate of GloMoSim[19]. We used Qualnet 5.0, Wireless Library, with an implementation of IEEE P802.11s/D1.00 draft standard. 802.11s uses a hybrid path selection protocol on medium access (MAC) layer, which means that either on demand or tree based modes are supported. In order to analyze the capacity of the architecture and evaluate the viability of the set up and business model, the following two scenarios are being created. One small area scenario to test general short distance two hop access to a nearby Internet gateway and one large area scenario to test for upper boundaries of the topology.

Fig.3 shows 36 Mesh Points (MPs) that are placed around a Mesh Portal Point (MPP), that has a 10 Mbps backhaul to a Tier 2 ISP. The distance between two neighbor MPs is 100m. Thus the mesh backhaul radius is 300m. This covers an area of $282.600m^2$ (area of circle) with equal MP density. MPs are interconnected with 802.11a on UNII 5Ghz band. The figure shows only MP1.1-1.6 denominated and all "leaves" of MP1.2s connection tree, in order to simplify the figure. All MPs are attached to MPP in the same manner. Each MP provides access to a certain number of clients via 802.11b ISM 2,4 Ghz band. All dataflow is directed to and from the central MPP. Tier 2 Router. Tables below show the actual average throughput per client in case every client produces a constant bit rate (CBR) of 64 kbps between itself and Tier 2 Router. Although in practice website traffic is more arbitrary and generates high bit rate bursts, we use CBR to create a steady and controlled load, to provoke the topology and used protocols to reveal its limitations. We use 64 kbps rather than a more realistic 1 Mbps per client, to prove if it is possible to establish a data service that allows basic applications such as email and web browsing. These scenarios are supposed to simulate peak time traffic with all clients active at the same time. It can be assumed that a single clients connection will perform better most of the time.

The first simulation uses MP1.1-1.6" the number of clients per MP varies from 4 to up to 32. We aim to investigate the maximal number of clients that can obtain a reasonable quality of service, near to an Internet gateway. The data flows over two hops, one from client to MP and second from MP to MPP. Table 1 shows results with

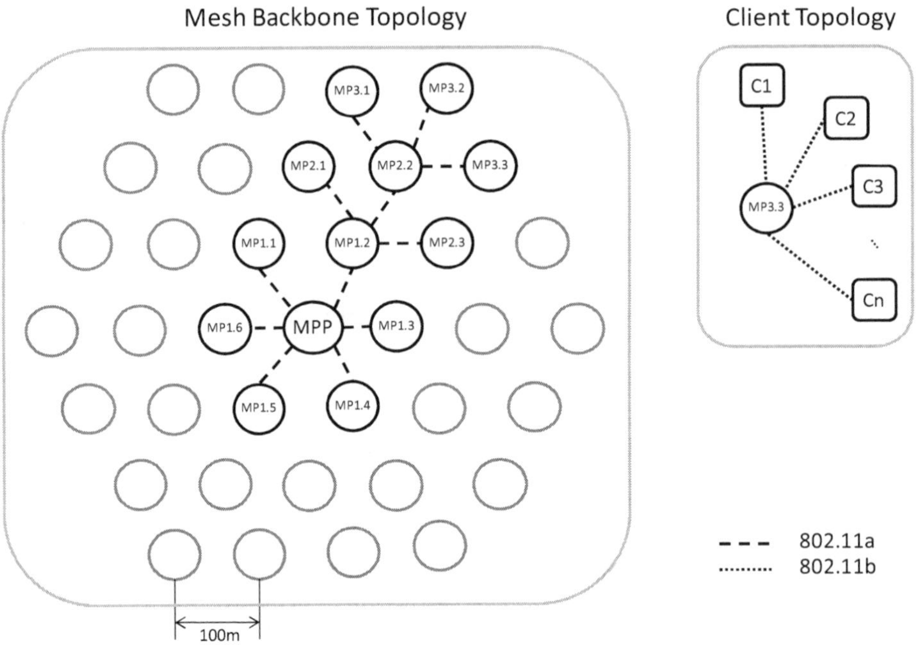

Mesh Backbone Topology

Client Topology

100m

--- 802.11a
.... 802.11b

Fig. 3.

average throughput per client in kbps. Because performance per client varied, variation is captured as the standard deviation and presented in parentheses. The lower the value is in relation to throughput, the more equal or fair network bandwidth is shared.

Table 1.

clients per MP	Total number of clients	Avg. Throughput (standard deviation) [kbps]			
		TCP traffic		UDP Traffic	
4	24	64.40	(00.08 $\triangleq$ 0%)	64.24	(00.00 $\triangleq$ 0%)
8	48	59.36	(04.80 $\triangleq$ 8%)	64.24	(00.00 $\triangleq$ 0%)
16	96	33.44	(21.44 $\triangleq$ 64%)	40.56	(30.96 $\triangleq$ 76%)
32	192	23.44	(25.60 $\triangleq$ 109%)	20.08	(29.44 $\triangleq$ 146%)

It is possible to provide fair and reliable Internet access at a rate of ca. 60kbps for 48 clients in a dense area around the MPP. It is further possible to deliver 30-40 kbps with high deviation of 60-70% to 96 clients. More clients will augment the deviation up to 100% of the average throughput and render the service useless for some clients. From this initial simulation experiment we speculate that a single broadband connection can provide reasonable low bandwidth Internet access to clients in the vicinity of two hops for 50-100 clients. We assume that establishing a six MP topology, with up to 100 clients combined with traffic shaping of 128kbps or 256 kbps per client and a more realistic arbitrary traffic behavior could deliver viable low cost quality of data service on household level.

Under the simple assumption that one household covers about 500m² (small house), the area in the first scenario could accommodate about 60 households (31.400m² with 100m radius), one access per household is therefore feasible. If such Internet gateways, owned by Internet shops, private higher income individuals or others were densely available, the six MP, two hop topology would solve a significant part of the last mile connection problem. But in reality density of broadband infrastructure is low and therefore more hops are required to serve more clients not close to the infrastructure. In our second experiment we investigate how well the technology scales in terms of increased hop counts.

The second simulation uses all 36 MPs covering the complete area. Clients use two to four wireless hops to and from the MPP. As Table 2 displays the bandwidth equality amongst clients is less, compared to the previous scenario. Standard deviation for only 36 simultaneous clients amounts 50% of the average throughput for TCP and about 70% for 72 clients. We observe that in larger networks the inner nodes often achieve much higher throughput than outer nodes. Therefore fairness mechanisms could be established in order to provide equal service all over the network. The comparison of UDP to TCP reveals that fairness is a greater issue for TCP.

Table 2.

clients per MP	Total number of clients	Avg. Throughput (standard deviation) [kbps]			
		TCP traffic		UDP Traffic	
1	36	48.48	(24.88 ≙ 51%)	46.96	(03.44 ≙ 7%)
2	72	29.04	(20.26 ≙ 69%)	30.80	(14.32 ≙ 62%)
3	108	24.80	(24.32 ≙ 98%)	15.20	(08.00 ≙ 52%)
4	144	17.68	(25.04 ≙ 141%)	12.48	(08.08 ≙ 64%)

Considering our household example above, this topology could fit 500 households ($282.600m^2$, 300m radius), but less than 100 clients (one out of five) can be served a reasonable Internet access. Hence the D1.00 802.11s mesh networks scalability as implemented in the simulator is low.

This scenario shows that for large multi hop networks, the wireless mesh topology and protocols will be a significant bottleneck in peak periods and can only serve a low overall number of clients. Here further investigations of protocols and measures of fairness need to be conducted.

3   Related Work

A framework of a multitude of wireless technologies for infrastructure deficient areas is provided by [20]. There exist several projects implementing urban and rural WMNs for city and communal population [21-22], but none of which implements incentive systems for individual participants. These networks are either for free use or for commercial use, financed and maintained by a third party.

A micropayment scheme for a captive portal for wireless internet access is designed and implemented by [23]. The concept is based on premium Short Message System (SMS) messages, it is not useable with current mobile payment schemes such as MPESA[24].

The capacity or scaling capability with increased hop count is identified as the main challenge of 802.11s as a possible last mile technology. The following related work gives an insight into possible solutions and further challenges.

As [25] point out, the medium access scheme of 802.11s is based on traditional 802.11 MAC protocol Enhanced Distributed Channel Access (EDCA), which is designed for 1 hop scenarios and therefore is not a mesh aware access scheme. [26] analyses the general capacity problem of wireless mesh topologies. They apply a concept called bottle neck collision domain to identify a link, that creates a bottleneck for the whole topology, considering load of all involved links affected by the medium access scheme. Usually one of the links between MPP an MP1.1-1.6 constitutes a bottleneck.

Several alternative [27] schemes exist, such as Mesh Deterministic Access (MDA) an optional 802.11s scheme or Mesh Network Alliance (MNA) scheme. The latter applies the concept of segregating mesh backhaul traffic from client access traffic in contention and non contention periods and spatial frequency reuse, by considering signal strength of neighbor nodes. The former uses a distributed time division access scheme. Both schemes try to reduce the unnecessary delay of multihop mesh packets, which leads to low scalability as we have encountered. A further method of increasing scalability is the employment of multiple channels for mesh backhaul traffic, thus reducing the bottleneck collision domain significantly as proposed in [28].

4 Summary and Future Work

In this paper we have analyzed developing markets from the economic point of view and pointed out the immense economic and humanitarian benefits of a broader distribution of Internet access in infrastructure deficient areas. We have identified requirements for a solution that approaches low cost, low regulation and entrepreneurial properties. Further we have designed a solution that based on 802.11s can bridge the "last mile" to low income households on a short range. The solution implements low cost equipment paired with a revenue sharing business model that promises rapid decentralized deployment. We have finally evaluated the capacity of the architecture and found it to be viable for certain scenarios, with demand for further optimization. Future works on this concept may cover open architectural questions and optimization investigations, such as collected below.

- Exact AAA architecture: designed, implementation and evaluation regarding performance and security.
- Security analysis for mesh backbone and client association with regard to authentication and encryption is necessary.
- The possibility of roaming between different Tier 3 networks or administrative domains: investigation and incorporation into business model and architecture design.

- The possibility of Tier 3 administrative domain merger and split: investigation regarding AAA and general architecture design.
- Financial transfer architecture and integration to AAA: implementation and evaluation.
- Further performance tests: evaluation of mobility inside the network with regard to basic service set handover, possibly based on IEEE 802.11r.

Nevertheless as we have identified the main weak point to be scalability and related work research point to unsuitable medium access schemes, the main challenge remains unsolved. We assume that the reduction of bottlenecks in the medium around the Internet gateway (MPP) is most likely to be possible with a combination of time divided access, spatial frequency reuse and application of multiple channels.

References

1. Jorgenson, D.: Information technology and the US economy. American Economic Review, 1–32 (2001)
2. Colecchia, A., Schreyer, P.: ICT investment and economic growth in the 1990s: is the United States a unique case? A comparative study of nine OECD countries. Review of Economic Dynamics 5(2), 408–442 (2002)
3. Bhavnani, A., et al.: The Role of Mobile Phones in Sustainable Rural Poverty Reduction, p. 22 (retrieved November 2008)
4. Muente Kunigami, A., Navas Sabater, J.: Options to Increase Access to Telecommunications Services in Rural and Low Income Areas. World 1(2), 3–4 (2010)
5. Qiang, C., Rossotto, C., Kimura, K.: Economic impacts of broadband. Information and Communications for Development 2009: Extending Reach and Increasing Impact, 35–50 (2009)
6. Aker, J.: Does Digital Divide or Provide? The Impact of Cell Phones on Grain Markets in Niger (2008)
7. Jensen, R.: The Digital Provide: Information (Technology), Market Performance, and Welfare in the South Indian Fisheries Sector*. The Quarterly Journal of Economics 122(3), 879–924 (2007)
8. Marasinghe, V., Abeykoon, P., Wootton, R.: Strategies to promote ehealth and telemedicine activities in developing countries. Telehealth in the Developing World, 79 (2009)
9. Lucas, H.: Information and communications technology for future health systems in developing countries. Social Science & Medicine 66(10), 2122–2132 (2008)
10. UNCTAD, Information Economy Report 2006: The Development Perspective. United Nations Publications (2006)
11. Williams, M.: Advancing the Development of Backbone Networks in Sub- Saharan Africa. Extending Reach and Increasing Impact, 51
12. Mbarika, V.: Re-thinking Information and Communications Technology Policy Focus on Internet versus Teledensity Diffusion for Africa's Least Developed Countries. EJISDC 9, 1–13 (2002)
13. Knisely, D., et al.: Standardization of Femtocells in 3GPP. IEEE Communications Magazine, 69 (2009)
14. Lehr, W., McKnight, L.: Wireless internet access: 3G vs. WiFi? Telecommunications Policy 27(5-6), 351–370 (2003)

15. Wellenius, B., Neto, I.: The radio spectrum: opportunities and challenges for the developing world. Info-Cambridge-Camford Publishing Limited 8(2), 18 (2006)
16. Garber, L.: Will 3G really be the next big wireless technology? Computer, 26–32 (2002)
17. Open-Mesh. Open-Mesh Webpage (2010), https://www.open-mesh.com/
18. Technologies, S.N.: Qualnet Product Webpage (2010), http://www.scalablenetworks.com/products/qualnet/ (cited 2010 05/11/2010)
19. UCLA, P.C.D., Global Mobile Information Systems Simulation Library (2010)
20. Gunasekaran, V., Harmantzis, F.: Emerging wireless technologies for developing countries. Technology in Society 29(1), 23–42 (2007)
21. Ishmael, J., et al.: Deploying rural community wireless mesh networks. IEEE Internet Computing, 22–29 (2008)
22. meraka.org. testbed networks (2010), http://wirelessafrica.meraka.org.za (cited 20.01.2010)
23. Barcelo, J., Oliver, M., Infante, J.: Adapting a Captive Portal to Enable SMS-Based Micropayment for Wireless Internet Access. In: Stiller, B., Reichl, P., Tuffin, B. (eds.) ICQT 2006. LNCS, vol. 4033, pp. 78–89. Springer, Heidelberg (2006)
24. Njenga, A.: Mobile phone banking: Usage experiences in Kenya
25. Hiertz, G., et al.: Principles of IEEE 802.11 s (2007)
26. Jun, J., Sichitiu, M.: The nominal capacity of wireless mesh networks. IEEE Wireless Communications magazine 10(5), 8–14 (2003)
27. Hiertz, G., et al.: IEEE 802.11 s: WLAN mesh standardization and high performance extensions. Language 890, 8044
28. Kyasanur, P., et al.: Multichannel mesh networks: challenges and protocols. IEEE Wireless Communications 13(2), 30–36 (2006)

Establishing Low Cost Aquatic Monitoring Networks for Developing Countries

Jarrod Trevathan[1], Ian Atkinson[1], Wayne Read[1], Ron Johnstone[2],
Nigel Bajema[1], and James McGeachin[1]

[1] eResearch Centre, James Cook University, Australia
eResearch@jcu.edu.au
[2] School of Geography, Planning & Environmental Management/Centre for Marine Studies,
University of Queensland, Australia
rnje@uq.edu.au

Abstract. Effective monitoring of natural resources in developing countries is vital to ensuring the sustainability of the environment and major industries such as aquaculture. Sensor networks are a promising technology that can be employed to remotely gather real-time data on important environmental parameters. This data can be exploited by operators/policy makers to better manage environments and maximize the production from aquaculture ventures. However, developing countries face numerous problems in deploying and using sensor network technology. The main issues include cost, limited technological infrastructure, and inexperience with collecting, storing and analyzing data. This paper examines these issues and defines the level of quality that would be sufficient for providing developing countries with usable environmental data. We describe how a country's existing infrastructure can be combined with scalable middleware (SAL) to integrate disparate technologies. We also present results from a test sensor network featuring heterogeneous technologies that is being used for environmental monitoring.

Keywords: Sensor networks, aquaculture, enabling technologies, middleware integration platform, communications infrastructure.

1 Introduction

The commodity of the natural environment is a precious reserve and means of income for many *developing countries* (DCs). Conserving the natural environment is vital to ensure the sustainability and economic progress of such countries. However, it is all too common that environmental degradation is the first thing to occur when these economies move along a path towards industrialization. For many South-East Asian countries, the harnessing of the natural environment to support aquaculture is an important economic resource and provides much needed protein for their populations. As such, these ventures are extremely sensitive to pollution and human activity.

The main reason for environmental damage in DCs is the lack of government policies, limited means to monitor resource usage, and the inability to act on such information if it was available. *First world countries* (FWC) are now starting to

A. Pont, G. Pujolle, and S.V. Raghavan (Eds.): WCITD/NF 2010, IFIP AICT 327, pp. 39–50, 2010.

employ sophisticated *sensor network* (SN) systems to augment traditional environmental monitoring programs used to monitor and analyze environmental phenomena. However, there are many issues facing DCs which presently has made these potentially more effective approaches unviable. Significant obstacles are associated with the costs related with setting up a monitoring system, and also the availability of IT and engineering expertise. Many examples of systems in FWCs have been overly expensive, and for the most part ineffective. Furthermore, generally DCs have very limited ICT infrastructure. Such infrastructure is required to collect, collate and communicate the information to, and perform analysis on the behalf of policy makers/end-users. Furthermore, whatever infrastructure policy makers have access to can be disparate and tends not to be designed to smoothly integrate.

In recent years, middleware software solutions have emerged that can be used to integrate heterogeneous IT [1, 2, 3, 4, 5]. The effect of this middleware approach is that the existing IT infrastructure in a DC, no matter how basic or incompatible can be used to establish basic SNs for environmental monitoring. Despite only possibly having access to older and/or obsolete hardware/software platforms, SN middleware technology can bridge the gaps between hardware systems and allow DCs to use low cost and pervasive sensors. When combined with emerging standards such as Sensor Web Enablement [6, 7], data collected from SNs can be archived so that external monitoring agencies can view and analyze the data. Such end-to-end monitoring systems will be of great value for remotely monitoring aquatic environments and assist, for example, in managing the sustainability of the aquaculture industry.

This paper examines the issues facing DCs in deploying SNs for remote aquatic monitoring, and contrasts the approaches taken in more developed countries. This analysis allows us to define the level of quality that would be sufficient for providing DCs with valuable data for the purposes of environmental monitoring and management. We describe how software mechanisms can be used to integrate disparate hardware and communications technologies existing in DCs. The software middleware we have developed (referred to as *SAL* [1, 2]) is scalable and can support a SN of almost any complexity. Finally, we present real world examples of how the proposed software is being used for environmental monitoring, and how it is being tailored specifically for aquatic settings.

This paper is organized as follows: Section 2 discusses the issues facing DCs and draws comparisons with FWCs in terms of establishing viable and sustainable SN systems. Section 3 presents the software technologies we are developing in order to address some of these issues. Section 4 gives a series of test deployments to illustrate its scalability and resourcefulness to handle SNs containing dissimilar technologies. Section 5 examines the SEMAT project and our contribution to the development of its technologies. Section 6 provides some concluding remarks.

2   Issues Facing Developing Countries

This section describes the issues facing DCs for the deployment and management of SN systems. We contrast these issues with the ICT requirements for SNs and the lessons learned from projects in FWCs. This allows us to define the quality of service and the minimal technological infrastructure needed to deploy a network that will at the very least provide valuable data for end-users.

The underlying core issues for deploying environmental monitoring systems in DCs are basically the same problems as in FWCs. However, there are several features that make key differences. Firstly, FWCs generally have access to some pervasive broadband infrastructure. That is, communications technology is usually high speed, reliable and has wide coverage. Secondly, FWCs have access to an abundant amount of current generation computing hardware and software platforms for collecting, archiving and analyzing data. Finally, most FWCs have established policy making/endorsing bodies that use the collected data to ensure that phenomena under study conforms to the established policies and legal practices.

In contrast, DCs often only have access to basic ICTs. However, there is a very large range – between the ultimate extreme of having absolutely nothing, or being relatively in league with FWCs. In any case, we have to allow for the fact that there will be heterogeneous technologies which might be as basic as ordinary radio communication, or it might be equivalent to FWC broadband and cellular network standards. Computing and software platforms within DCs are often older, or in many cases obsolete compared to the latest technology in use by FWCs. Furthermore, there may be no established policy making mechanism, or this may be primitive with only a mediocre level of effectiveness. The resounding question this raises is, *"what is the minimum technological infrastructure required to establish an environmental monitoring SN system in a DC"?* To answer this question it is prudent to examine similar systems for FWCs.

An example of a system is not particularly suited for use in a DC is being established by the *Australian Institute of Marine Science* (AIMS)[1] as part of the *Australian Integrated Marine Observing System* (IMOS). This project involves the deployment of remote sensing buoys at strategic locations around the Great Barrier Reef[2] [8]. Their purpose is to detect oceanographic features such as salinity, temperature, light, etc. However, the solution falls short for use in by a DC in multiple ways. The first major shortcoming is cost. Each buoy costs an estimated $50,000 AUD, with deployment and maintenance also requiring significant technical infrastructure and expertise. Furthermore, it is not pervasive and gives only localized answers. That is, there are only four sampling points across a reef that spans 344,400 square kilometers. Therefore, the effectiveness of the data for any sort of modeling is limited. As such, this sort of approach is unsuitable for a DC.

With this example in mind, let us examine the features of cheaper alternatives. Regardless of the cost, the system must be able to deploy "enough" sensors to measure with "sufficient" accuracy to present useful information. (Note that less precise assumes sufficient accuracy.) Four million cheap sensors with limited precision are arguably of much greater value than four expensive sensors of extremely high precision. Furthermore, four million sensors will cover a larger geographical area thereby maximizing the coverage for the network and environments sensed. In terms of an aquatic setting, the geographic dimensions are important. Sensor readings are not just required horizontally between locations, but also need to be at multiple points vertically between the surface and the bottom of the water body. This makes the cost of the sensors extremely important in order to take the most measurements.

---

[1] www.aims.gov.au
[2] http://imos.org.au/faimms.html

Cheap   Expensive

pervasive/broad WSN   few/localized
less power   high power
small size   large size
short life   long lasting/enduring
capable   highly proficient

Fig. 1. The cost spectrum for SN systems

Figure 1 illustrates the cost spectrum for SN systems. As the design choice moves between the extremes, the features of either extreme will become more pronounced. A cheap system will allow for a pervasive network of low-cost sensors and gateways to be deployed on a potentially massive scale. Whereas expensive systems (as in the AIMS example [8]) can only result in a few sensor nodes thereby giving localized readings. Low-cost systems potentially have lower power requirements and the components are physically smaller than in an expensive infrastructure. However, cheap systems typically do not have the same endurance and life span as more expensive setups. Although the pace of improvement in technology means that sensors can be outdated within two/three years in any case. In general, cheap sensor nodes can be easily replaced which means their lifespan may not be a significant limiting factor. Furthermore, expensive systems that are damaged, lost or stolen are quite difficult to replace making less expensive systems more attractive. While expensive systems are highly proficient (and precise) due to their sophistication, cheap systems are usually capable albeit with less precision.

In light of the cost structure and requirements, we define the parameters for a suitable/feasible solution for remote SNs in DCs as follows:

- The system must be cost effective, to provide the most coverage and is affordable for a DC. (Sensors embedded in packaging can be as cheap as $10-$15 each.)
- It must use existing hardware and communication infrastructure. Even though solutions may interconnect to high technology front ends when they are available, there must be basic, low cost solutions that do not depend on any advanced technology. For example, a SN deployment using second hand/obsolete computers with very low cost sensors communicating via early technology mobile networks. There is also scope to capitalize on initiatives that telecommunications companies are offering DCs. For example, Ericsson in collaboration with the *Swedish Program of ICTs in Developing Regions* (SPIDER) has initiated investigation of wireless SNs in developing regions, including the allowance for bandwidth on GSM mobile phone networks to be used for environmental monitoring.[3]
- The data collected must be valuable to the end users and accessible to all interested parties. External bodies such as a government or a United Nations agency can in theory access the collected data. This would aid in the establishment of sound, or in the very least accountable environmental management policies.

---

[3] http://www.spidercenter.org/project/national-research-and-development-center-wireless-ad-hoc-and-sensor-networks-wasn

It is interesting to note that low technology solutions may also be viable in some locations and not others. For example, deploying and manually cleaning sensors on a daily basis (as would be required with some very low-cost infrastructure) would be cost prohibitive for most FWCs. However, this solution may in fact fit very well with the structure of a DC where labor can be both effective and relatively inexpensive. This may be a consideration that affects any SN deployment in a DC.

Much of the hardware that is present in a DC typically will come at least in part *via* aide from FWCs. It might be in the form of money to purchase the equipment, but it is more likely to come in the form of donated second hand equipment. Whatever, the method for acquiring the hardware, the underlying point is that there will be a menagerie of heterogeneous and incompatible technologies to work with.

To achieve a system that satisfies the aforementioned constraints requires the use of a software stack to handle the range of communication and hardware technologies. That is, a middleware solution to bring together disparate technologies which range in computational power and cost.

3 Scalable Software Solutions for Abstracting Hardware and Communications Technologies

Lack of standards makes it difficult to integrate heterogeneous sensors in a single SN. Therefore it is important to have middleware which is able to manage all types of sensors. This middleware is often implemented specifically for one SN, which makes it very hardware dependent. Changes in the network, such as adding a new sensor, lead to the need for manipulating the code of the middleware. This section describes the *Sensor Abstraction Layer (SAL)* which is designed to address these issues.

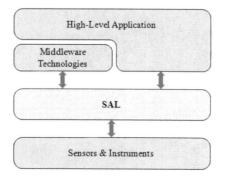

Fig. 2. Architectural overview of a system stack using SAL

SAL is a middleware which provides a plug-in-based model where support for new types of sensors can be loaded to the running system via plug-in. The system automatically detects and configures new sensors, if permitted by the hardware and underlying OS. Furthermore, it provides a unified interface to all sensors by abstracting the sensor specific features. With this it aims at simplifying the access to a SN as well as the management and control of its sensors [1, 2].

SAL can be seen as a low-level software layer as it bridges a network of sensors with high-level applications or further middleware technologies, e.g., a ring buffer. Figure 2 presents an architectural overview of a system stack using SAL.

SAL is implemented as a client-server application and thus consists of two components, the *SAL client* and the *SAL agent*. The *SAL client* represents an interface for SAL to either the user via a user interface or to other applications. It implements the SAL agent *Application Programming Interface* (API) in order to provide the functionality of the SAL agent. The API is grouped into the following categories:

Sensor Management – Methods to manage the pool of sensors and including operations for enumerating, adding and removing sensors.
Sensor Control - Methods to report on a sensor's capabilities and control the streaming of the data.
Platform Configuration - Methods to adjust the platform, e.g., add support for a new sensor type.

Each category uses a different markup language. The *Sensor Management* methods use *SensorML* [6], which describes a sensor's configuration. The methods in the category *Sensor Control* use *CommandML*. The CommandML documents contain a list of commands which are supported by a sensor. The last category, *Platform Configuration,* uses *Platform Capabilities and Configuration Markup Language (PCML)*. Documents of the type PCML contain information on how the platform is to be configured in order to support a certain type of sensor technology.

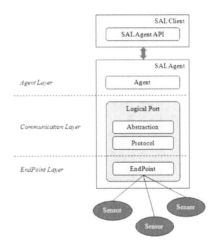

Fig. 3. SAL components and software layers

The *SAL agent* implements the various features of SAL. It runs on a platform which is connected to the sensors and therefore is regarded as a *sensor gateway*. The connection between the platform and the sensors can be either direct using platform specific I/O ports like USB or indirect by using wireless technology. The *SAL agent* manages the sensors which are directly connected and are found by the agent and the indirectly connected sensors it has been told of. The *SAL agent* consists of three layers: *Agent Layer, Communication Layer,* and *EndPoint Layer* (see Figure 3).

The *Agent Layer* is responsible for the communication with the *SAL client*. It receives messages, parses and forwards them to the underlying *Communication Layer* and sends the response back to the client.

The *Communication Layer* provides methods for managing and controlling sensors. The managing methods are used to configure and set up hardware while the controlling methods translate a generic command into a sensor native command, which then can be transmitted to the sensor. The generic commands are provided in the SAL API. For translating the generic commands the two sub-layers *Abstraction Layer* and *Protocol Layer* are used. The *Abstraction Layer* is an adapter layer where the generic commands are implemented. From here the sensor-specific methods are called, which are implemented in the *Protocol Layer*.

The *EndPoint Layer* is tightly coupled to the I/O ports available on the sensor gateway. It is responsible for transmitting native sensor commands produced by the sub-layer *Protocol* to the sensor. In the other direction, data from the sensor is transmitted to the SAL agent. The software code for this layer is normally included in the operating system. SAL ensures it is available and configured correctly.

The two sub-layers *Abstraction* and *Protocol* and the *EndPoint Layer* together form a *Logical Port*. Each sensor is connected to a Logical Port. SAL allows a specific client to control multiple agents (*horizontal scalability*). Furthermore, the logical port allows SAL to scale vertically (*vertical scalability*) in that an agent can control other agents in a hierarchical manner. This is due to the logical port treating the attached device as a data source, independent of whether it is a sensor or another agent. The ability to scale allows SNs of almost any topology or configuration.

SAL is also integrated with the RBNB Data Turbine developed by the San Diego Super Computing Group [9]. The Data Turbine allows for near real-time streaming of data from multiple sources (as is common in a SN). All incoming data is temporarily stored in a time-stamped buffer prior to being consumed by the end-user. The end-user can essentially fast-forward and rewind the buffered data which is extremely useful for time series analysis and presentation.

SAL has been trialed on the Davies Reef SN project [10] whereby it controls a sensor array via a low cost/power computer in a remote reef. Of greater importance to this paper's objectives is SAL's role in the SEMAT project [11] which aims to develop low cost pervasive aquatic SN systems (see Section 5).

4 A Test Implementation

To show SAL's feasibility for deployment in a low cost heterogeneous environment, we created a series of sample SNs of varying scales. This section describes the test setup and SAL's performance at increasing levels of complexity.

One Client, One Agent – The first test involved using one agent that had multiple heterogeneous sensors attached. There was a single client controlling the agent. The aim for this test was to illustrate SAL's ability to connect, manage and collect data from numerous heterogeneous sensor types simultaneously from different vendors.

The sensors included a one wire dongle sensing temperature and humidity, a Web camera streaming live data, fifteen Java sun SPOTs[4] (which contains a package of multiple sensor types), and a one wire bus containing ten independent thermistors.

For this test the SAL agent and client were run on separate single board computers (WAFER-945GSE SBC from ICP Electronics[5]) which communicated wirelessly. Each computer had a processor speed of 1.6 Ghz and 2 GB of RAM. The price for each computer was $427 AUD. Once registered, each sensor type could be plugged and unplugged without affecting other devices. The number of devices we could attach and the amount of data transferred essentially was only limited by number of USB connections and the network bandwidth respectively.

The tests were then repeated with a Gumstix[6] device. These are miniature computers (approximately the size of a stick of chewing gum) designed to run in purpose built applications. These devices are indicative of what would be deployed in the field for a wireless SN. The processor speed is 400 MHz with 128 MB RAM. Our tests used the Vertex series package which retails for approximately $300 AUD. These tests were designed to examine how SAL performs on lower powered devices as what might occur in a DC.

There was no notable deviation in performance from the tests run on the single board computers. The entire price for the test SN was approximately $3,000 AUD depending on the computers used and the number of desired sensors.

Multiple Agents at the Same Level (Horizontal Scalability) – The second test involved testing SAL's ability to scale horizontally. There was one client controlling multiple agents. Each agent was independent to and peer with each of the other agents. Each agent had a varying array of sensors attached.

This test involved the single board computers and also some relatively old desktop computers (which ranged in processing power and memory capacity). This test was used to examine SALs performance by combining some equipment that might be representative of what is available to DCs.

As per the previous tests, the system performed well. We theorized that SAL can be used on any computer that has the processing power equivalent of the early Pentium range (i.e., 1.6 MHz). The memory requirements are only constrained by the ability to support the Linux operating system and the Java run-time environment.

Multiple Agents at Differing Levels (Vertical Scalability) – The final test determined how well SAL scales vertically where one client that controls one agent. This agent then controlled two agents directly below it, each of which had differing arrays of sensors (refer to the discussion of a logical port in Section 3). The results showed that this worked seamlessly in line with how SAL handles data sources.

In conclusion, regardless of the technology employed, SAL was able to seamlessly integrate the entire SN. Almost any computer from the mid 90s onwards can run SAL. The price for an entire SN can be as little as $500 - which only increases with the number of agents/clients used and the number of and costs of the sensors desired.

---

[4] http://www.sunspotworld.com/
[5] http://www.icp-australia.com.au/
[6] http://www.gumstix.com/

5   Pervasive, Low Cost and Intelligent Aquatic SNs

This section describes the *Smart Environment Monitoring and Analysis Technologies* (SEMAT) project as an example of an end system that could be used in the context of a DC [11]. SEMAT is largely driven by the need to create a low cost intelligent SN system for monitoring aquatic and coastal environments, and importantly the analysis of that data into information which can be used for management and planning. The specific goals for SEMAT are as follows:

1) Underwater wireless communications – As aquatic environments are remote and vast, it is not economically viable or practical to have sensors wired together. Often in such an environment the positioning of the cables represents a significant practical problem. The cable itself is also vulnerable to breakage or degradation over time.

2) Short-range wireless and power transmission – Interconnecting cables for data communications and/or power *in-situ* is complex in a marine environment. SEMAT aims to develop technologies whereby neighboring cables can be connected underwater and inductive methods used transfer power and data between nodes.

3) Plug and Play – A major problem facing the deployment of wireless SNs is the disparate technologies used as equipment must be combined from different manufacturers. Even the simple case of adding a new type of sensor usually involves reconfiguring the entire system so that the end user can view the sensor's output. SEMAT will use SAL to allow new equipment to be added to the network such that it is instantly recognized and configured for use. This is analogous to plugging in a new peripheral device for a computer such as a printer or mouse, which the operating system automatically detects and allows instant use. Making a wireless SN plug and play removes much of the technical overhead for managing the network by novices.

4) Minimal deployment expertise – SEMAT will offer end users a complete package. The end user will only need to choose what sensors they require and SEMAT will auto-configure the necessary parameters. Essentially once deployed, the user could take a laptop down to the beach (for example) and can begin to view the sensed data.

5) Near real time analysis tools – SEMAT will provide software tools that allow data to be streamed in near real-time from sensors. Users will have the ability to buffer large amounts of data and sift through the data at hand using the RBNB Data Turbine [11]. Data collected is put into a format that is recognized by standards bodies (i.e., Sensor Web Enablement [7]) and therefore can be imported into sophisticated data modeling and visualization tools.

6) Intelligent sensors – Sensor nodes in SEMAT will have a level of intelligence in that they have two way communications with each other. This will allow sensors to have a degree of autonomy from the end user such that if there is a sudden change in a condition which affects the phenomena under study, then sensor nodes can communicate with each other to change their parameters to better study the changes in the environment. For example, if one set of sensors detects that significant rainfall is occurring, it might communicate with the salinity sensor to increase its sensing rate from daily to hourly. There are almost limitless uses for such intelligence.

SEMAT is an ambitious and large project which draws on expertise from multiple disciplines including marine biology, engineering, mathematics, and computer science. There are several parties involved with the development of SEMAT including: DHI Group[7] (Denmark); University of Queensland (UQ)[8] (Australia); James Cook University (JCU)[9] (Australia); and the Torino Foundation (Italy).

DHI and UQ are responsible for the marine science and high level modeling of marine phenomena. For the purposes of SEMAT, this study is related to the prevalence of *Lymbia algae* blooms at Deception Bay in Queensland Australia.

DHI have developed hydrodynamic modeling software that is being used for the initial studies SEMAT will be conducting. The Torino Foundation specializes in developing and commercializing sensor technology. They are tasked with designing purpose built intelligent sensors for the SEMAT system. The initial sensors under development will be geared towards the studies being undertaken by DHI and UQ.

The Information Technology and Electrical Engineering school at UQ is designing the wireless power transfer and communications systems. They are working in conjunction with the Torino Foundation to decide on the electrical standards for the power transfer. UQ is also working in conjunction with JCU on the communications protocols that will be used between sensor nodes and how the information will be relayed back to the gateway devices.

The eResearch Centre at JCU is responsible for providing the middleware (i.e., SAL) and end user interface for the data acquisition, storage and presentation from the SEMAT system. This is perhaps one of the most challenging components of the SEMAT project. JCU is essentially tasked with making the system plug and play and allowing for near real time analysis of the collected data.

Lymbia Algae Study at Deception Bay

Lymbia Algae is a particularly virulent form of algae that attaches itself to sea grass. As the algae grows, it absorbs nutrients from the sea floor and surrounding areas and physically covers sea grasses preventing light reaching the sea grass – essentially killing it off. Once the algal has finished growing (blooming), it breaks off and typically washes up on the beach/shore line. It leaves scaring along the sea bed where it was present and it usually prevents future sea grass from growing.

While it is uncertain what causes the algae to bloom, it is suspected that it forms mainly in warm conditions, shallow and calm water, and human activity (possibly in the form of nutrient run off) may affect its life cycle. The initial case study for SEMAT will be to study the influences that contribute to the spread of Lymbia algae. Ideally the result will be to suggest a plan for environmental management to control its spread in aquatic environments.

In recent years Deception Bay in Queensland Australia has experienced significant Lymbia algae blooms. The bay is largely protected from the greater ocean and doesn't

---

[7] www.dhigroup.com.au
[8] www.uq.edu.au
[9] www.jcu.edu.au

contain any significant wave action. It is shallow with high tide only raising the water depth to approximately three meters at its peak. Deception Bay is situated between the mainland and the southern region of Bribie Island therefore it is heavily influenced by human activity.

As the initial application for SEMAT is for monitoring aquatic environments for marine science studies, UQ and DHI selected Deception Bay as the premiere site for testing the initial SEMAT system. There were several factors influencing this decision including: proximity to Brisbane; prevalence of algal blooms; subtropical environment; shallow water; and calm conditions

Ultimately, the SEMAT development environment will use six different sensors to examine different potential influences and their interaction on Lymbia algae blooms. The types of sensors include: *temperature, total light, photo synthetically active radiation* (PAR), *salinity/conductivity, turbidity, pH,* and *dissolved oxygen.* Several data sinks will be deployed at strategic locations around Deception Bay. Each sink will host the aforementioned sensors.

6   Conclusions

DCs are heavily reliant on their aquaculture resources for food and exports. Effective management of this vital resource is critical to ensuring the future sustainability and economic progress of a DC. SN technology can be used to actively monitor resource use to provide end-users, policy makers and external third parties with the information they need in order make more informed decisions. However, excessive cost, lack of infrastructure, and limited expertise/experience, hinders the adoption of SN technology in DCs.

This paper examined these issues and provided a framework for how a DC can use low cost sensors in combination with a country's existing infrastructure to deploy a capable SN for aquatic monitoring. We propose that SAL can be used as a viable middleware solution to establish a SN in a DC regardless of conflicting technologies. Preliminary test results and real world deployments indicate that SAL is both scalable and capable of suiting any network configuration and sensor types. The cost is only constrained by the computers used (which can be as old as a Pentium), and the number and expense of the desired sensors. The proposed solution is being integrated into the SEMAT project as the nexus for a fully plug and play system capable of being easily deployed in any aquatic environment.

Future work involves increasing the magnitude and scale of the tests conducted with SAL. That is, we are aiming to test SAL on a large-scale horizontal and vertical level incorporating sensors from numerous vendors. We are also going to perform a series of 'wet tests' whereby SAL is used with submersible sensors and low cost computing devices as a proof of concept. Finally, SAL's versatility will be further developed and tested in conjunction with the aims of the SEMAT project.

Acknowledgments. This work was supported in part by the Queensland Government National and International Research Alliances Program.

References

1. Gigan, G., Atkinson, I.: Towards a uniform software interface to heterogeneous hardware. In: Proceedings of the International Conference on Intelligent Sensors, Sensor Networks and Information Processing (ISSNIP), pp. 429–434 (2008)
2. Gigan, G., Atkinson, I.: Sensor Abstraction Layer: a unique software interface to effectively manage SNs. In: Proceedings of the International Conference on Intelligent Sensors, Sensor Networks and Information Processing (ISSNIP), pp. 479–484 (2007)
3. Handziski, V., Polastre, J., Hauer, J., Sharp, C., Wolisz, A., Culler, D.: Flexible Hardware Abstraction for Wireless Sensor Networks. In: Proceedings of the 2nd European Workshop on Wireless Sensor Networks (2005)
4. Heinzelman, W., Murphy, A., Carvalho, H., Perillo, M.: Middleware to support Sensor Network applications. IEEE Network Magazine Special Issue, 6–14 (2004)
5. Rmer, K., Kasten, O., Mattern, F.: Middleware challenges for wireless sensor networks. ACM SIGMOBILE Mobile, Communication and Communications Review 6(2) (2002)
6. Aloisio, G., Conte, D., Elefante, C., Marra, G.P., Mastrantonio, G., Quarta, G.: Globus Monitoring and Discovery Service and SensorML for Grid Sensor Networks. In: Proceedings of the 15th IEEE International Workshops on Enabling Technologies: Infrastructure for Collaborative Enterprises (WETICE), pp. 201–206 (2006)
7. Botts, M., Percivall, G., Reed, C., Davidson, J.: OGC Sensor Web Enablement: Overview and High Level Architecture. In: Nittel, S., Labrinidis, A., Stefanidis, A. (eds.) GSN 2006. LNCS, vol. 4540, pp. 175–190. Springer, Heidelberg (2008)
8. Bainbridge, S., Rehbein, M. A., Feather, G., Eggeling, D.: Sensor Networks on the Great Barrier Reef - managing marine sensor data. In: Proceedings of the Environmental Information Management Conference, pp. 19–25. University of New Mexico (2008)
9. Tilak, S., Hubbard, P., Miller, M., Fountain, T.: The Ring Buffer Network Bus (RBNB) Data Turbine Streaming Data Middleware for Environmental Observing Systems. In: Proceedings of the Third IEEE International Conference on eScience and Grid Computing (2007)
10. Huddleston-Homes, C., Gigan, G., Woods, G., Ruxton, A.: Infrastructure for a Sensor Network on Davies Reef, Great Barrier Reef. In: Proceedings of the International Conference on Intelligent Sensors, Sensor Networks and Information Processing (2007)
11. Johnstone, R., Caputo, D., Cella, U., Gandelli, A., Alippi, C., Grimaccia, F., Haritos, N., Zich, R.E.: Smart Environmental Measurement & Analysis Technologies (SEMAT): Wireless Sensor Networks in the marine environment. In: Proceedings of Wireless Sensor and Actuator Network Research on Opposite Sides of the Globe, SENSEI (2008)

Infrastructure and Business Model for Universal Broadband Access in Developing Regions: The Ceara State Digital Belt

Cid F. Gomes[1], Fernando C. Gomes[1,2], and Marcial P. Fernandez[3]

[1] Ceara State Government,
Centro Administrativo Barbara de Alencar, 60811 Fortaleza, Brazil
cidgomes@gabgov.ce.gov.br
[2] Computer Science Department, Universidade Federal do Ceara,
Campus do Pici, Bloco 910, 60455 Fortaleza, Brazil
carvalho@lia.ufc.br
[3] Computer Network and Information Security Lab,
Universidade Estadual do Ceara,
Campus do Itaperi, Av. Paranjana 1700, 60740 Fortaleza, Brazil
marcial@larces.uece.br

Abstract. With regard to digital services access, many rural and remote urban area in developing countries are underserved, if served at all. In a monopolized environment, telecommunications are of low quality and costly. Broadband Internet and other digital services are restricted to small percentage of people. In some cases the operator prefers to pay fines instead of providing services to remote areas. In this paper we present an infrastructure together with its business model that is being installed in the Brazilian Ceara state. This infrastructure was entirely constructed by the state government, but the operational costs (OPEX) will be paid by investors willing to share data transportation. Different groups will be chosen among interested investors by public auction, in order to enforce competition. Moreover, a new state company will be created that will offer low cost data transportation services, assuring that high bandwidth will be available to more than 80% of the state population.

Keywords: Optical Networks, Wireless Communications, Telecommunication Policy-Developing Countries.

1 Introduction

Broadband is a vital driver of economic growth, not only in the demand it generates directly, but also in gains in economic efficiency and the creation of new applications. Waverman, Meschi and Fuss [9] confirm that the GDP growth impact of mobiles is large in both developed and developing countries, but around twice as important in the latter group. The policy implication of their results for developing countries is clear: it will be worth investing in telecommunications to get close to universal service. Governments around the world are seeking to

A. Pont, G. Pujolle, and S.V. Raghavan (Eds.): WCITD/NF 2010, IFIP AICT 327, pp. 51–59, 2010.
© IFIP International Federation for Information Processing 2010

improve digital inclusion and maximize the economic benefits of Internet access, Distance Learning, Telemedicine, Electronic Entertainment, Security Systems, etc. These examples illustrate only a few of the ways in which broadband technology is changing our lives.

The United States President Obama recently signed into law the $ 787 billion stimulus package, which includes $ 7.2 billion for broadband grant and loan programs. France has determined that apartments and offices in new buildings must be connected by optical fiber. Other governments around the world are seeking to improve digital inclusion as they strive to create modern information societies.

As noted in ITUs Trends in Telecommunication Reform 2008, the first approach that operators can adopt to roll out advanced connectivity is the deployment of fibre as rapidly as possible [1].

In this paper we present the infrastructure (fiber backbone and wireless last mile) deployed by the state government in Ceara, Brazil. Moreover, we propose a sustainable business model that will be applied in order to bring competition to remote areas and, as a consequence, increase the offer of affordable digital services to the population.

2   Environment

Most of the country lack telecommunications infrastructure.

2.1   Brazilian States Are Underserved

Much of the data communication for the final leg of delivering connectivity from a communications provider to a customer (also known as last mile) in Brazil relies on ADSL (Asynchronous Digital Subscriber Line) technology, which uses the fixed telephony network infrastructure. This refers to the main obstacle to the development of telecommunications in the country: the monopoly on fixed telephony. In every region of the country, only one company holds the ADSL infrastructure. On the top of that, since the monopoly does not invest on deploying fiber, many Brazilian states lack a wired optical fiber backbone and updated ADSL. As a consequence, most of the country suffers with low speed narrow bandwidth and high telecom costs [2,4,6].

In the monopoly environment, the sole company that holds the infrastructure does not see broadband connection as an essential service that must be spread out, even to low income population. They see it as a highly profitable business, for which its infrastructure should be kept available to those, and only to those, who can afford to pay very high connectivity prices. Competition among broadband providers would be the best way to lower costs and to have the state-of-the-art communication technology available.

Ceara is a Brazilian state located in the northeastern developing region that counts 8 million inhabitants spread out in a 148,825 km area. Estimates show that in 2008 only 3% of the state population has broadband access (equal or greater than 1 Mbps), most of them live at the capital, Fortaleza. These facts reveal that a huge rural area is underserved, if served at all.

2.2   Brazilian Broadband among World's Worst

Oxford and Oviedo universities recently presented a broadband quality joint study showing that Brazils Broadband Quality Score (BQS) ranks 40th among 42 countries [2]. If one considers the Northeast of Brazil only, he or she would obtain even worst results. As a matter of fact, according to the Brazilian Internet Steering Committee 2009 survey [3], Internet access (low speed bandwidth) in Northeast is available only to 7% of the population. These facts reveal that people in the region have no ability to benefit from todays and next-generation web applications and services.

The Ceara state contributes only to 2% of the Brazilian GDP. Its population is about 8,7 million people, including 89,7% of urban population. The state telecommunication company has been privatized in 1998. Like other Brazilian states, although there is the last mile monopoly, four cellular telephony operators provide cell phone lines throughout the state. They use long distance radio backhaul for communication between cities. However, since the radio infrastructure available does not allow higher speed communication, they offer 3G service effective only to Fortaleza, the state capital.

Facilitating the widespread deployment of next-generation broadband Internet with download speeds of at least 20 Megabits per second (Mbps), and ideally 50 Mbps or upwards will enable the emergence of a whole host of online applications and services, many of which we can barely imagine today [5,7,8].

2.3   Costs Are High

The Ceara state government communications needs are comprehensive. Schools, police stations, hospitals, fiscal agents, and so on, have to be connected through a 3.000 nodes data network, in order to access e-gov applications and Internet. Since there is no competition, communication service is not only expensive, but also low quality. For example, most of the schools have only 64 Kbps. Government pays for each school link R$700.00 monthly (approximately US$ 300.00, as of February 2010). The annual data link bill amounts to R$ 20 million (approximately US$ 9 million per annum) altogether. Besides, one will find low speed broadband (1 to 2 Mbps) only in five out of 185 state counties.

3   The Digital Belt: An Infrastructure for Governance and Development

The government has started to launch a digital belt around the state, composed of a 3,000 kilometers optical fiber redundant ring and ramifications. The states digital belt will initially cover 82% of the population. It has two main roles:

I. To fulfill the government needs in the 50 most populated cities;
II. To give telecom carriers and service providers incentive to use and share the infrastructure, in order to foster the digital inclusion across the state, and create an environment in which broadband innovation and competition could flourish.

The states Digital Belt will cost R$ 65 million (approximately US$ 36 million), and will be finished by June 2010.

By making it possible to access, use, and share information, news, and entertainment with ever increasing speed, broadband knits geographically-distant individuals and businesses more closely together, increases productivity, and enriches quality of life. In so doing, it fuels economic growth and job creation that, in turn, provide unparalleled new opportunities for citizens.

Besides, states economy must benefit from broadband connection. Population has to access ubiquitous, lower price digital services. Business, societies, low-income communities

Connectivity with sustainability is the central idea behind the Digital Belt. As a matter of fact, government agencies will not operate the infrastructure. It should be sustained and operated by private companies, interested in providing digital IT services. Nevertheless, it is not evident how to transfer the infrastructure to the companies, so one could assure competition among them. Besides, it is important to give broadband Internet access the low-income population.

3.1   Technological Challenges

To specify the technology used in the Ceara State Digital Belt it was needed to consider several factors. Many of these factors are not exclusive to the particular situation of the state of Ceara, but are also present in other developing countries.

The first point was to choose the appropriate technology for the network topology. As we stated, the state of Ceara has a very large geographic area and different population densities. Forty percent of the population lives in the Metropolitan Region of Fortaleza, which represents less than 4% of the land area of the state. So the technologies chosen should encompass both situations: a densely populated area and a huge sparse population area.

The second point was to choose a technology that could support the connectivity demands for, at least, 10 years. At this point we must mention that an important fact is the government network, contracted from operators. Therefore, there are no legacy technologies to be considered, giving freedom to choose the best technology.

Finally, the third important point is to choose technologies with low cost of installation and operation. As the major goal of the government is the population coverage, as much cheaper is the technology chosen, the increase of coverage is achieved with the same budget. Low cost operation allows a longer use of the network, with less chance to being restricted during an economic crisis, for instance.

Optical Backbone. The backbone technology adopted is the fiber optic, both in metropolitan and rural areas. We agree that optical technology is suitable to permit long hauls transmission and almost infinite increase of transmission capacity. Building a network with fiber optics is not the cheapest alternative, but considering the transmission quality and capacity scalability achieved, is a valuable investment.

As Data Link technology Giga-Ethernet was adopted. As the main objective is the connectivity and Internet access, Ethernet technology is quite appropriate. The Ethernet evolution in recent years allowed the extension of the distance achieved with this technology, that is also called Metro-Ethernet and Carrier-Ethernet.

To ensure recovery in case of failure, the entire network uses the ring architecture, moreover, Ethernet Automatic Protection Switching (EAPS) protocol was adopted to ensure failover in less than 50 ms, which is in compliance with to recovery requirements of telecommunications network based on Synchronous Digital Hierarchy (SDH). Another architectural approach was the implementation of a double ring as shown in Figure 1.

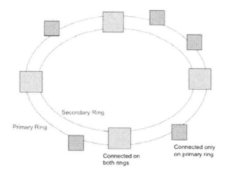

Fig. 1. Redundant double ring, implemented by frequency multiplex

The most considerable problem in a ring Metro-Ethernet network is the dependence of all nodes that should be active to ensure redundancy, because if two nodes turn off, one sector of the ring comes down. Thus, we chose some points with better infrastructure and big traffic demand, to connect a second ring. As they are larger sites, we offered a data rate twice than the others, and, in these places, there are also better infrastructure 24 hour a day. If two intermediate nodes are disconnected, there will be another way through the second ring, improving network reliability. As the second fiber is on the same cable, when the cable break both primary and secondary ring will be interrupted, but the experience shows that most problems on the network were due the shutdown of switches in nodes with less infrastructure, like short time of UPS and lack of qualified personnel.

The optical solutions adopted were different in the metropolitan and rural area. In the metropolitan area Ethernet switches with optical interfaces for long distance were used. As each node is 2 Km to 5 Km far from each other, 1 GBPS LX interfaces was used (up to 10 Km).

Within the rural area of state, the distances are significantly higher, despite an average of 40 km between nodes, many spans have more than 80 km, beyond the reach of ZX optical interfaces in switches (typically up to 80 Km). In the rural area we used the Dense Wavelength Division Multiplexing (DWDM) technology.

Due to support the increase of bandwidth demand and the reduction of optical interfaces costs, we adopted a 10 GBPS basic rate. As all the DWDM equipment is modulated on the ITU-T hierarchy (2.5 GBPS, 10 GBPS, 40 GBPS), the use of 2.5 GBPS becomes inefficient because the maximum Ethernet speedy below 2.5 GBPS is only 1 GBPS and 1.5 GBPS is wasted. A 10 GBPS WDM interface cost only slightly higher than the 2.5 GBPS but allows the transmission of full 10 Gigabit Ethernet.

Like the situation on metro network, in long distance we also adopted the doublering architecture, putting a second ring in some nodes with higher demand and better infrastructure. But unlike metro network, that a second fiber was used, in this situation we used a second lambda to receive the second connection. In the intermediate nodes we adopted Optical Add-Drop Multiplexer (OADM) that does not interrupt the connection of adjacent points even in case of shutdown.

Wireless Last mile. To define the access technology for the last mile we needed to consider different characteristics of population density found in the State. Likewise, it is also necessary to standardize the technology to facilitate the network operation and management and take advantages to get lower cost due to quantity purchased. Considering all technologies available, Pre-Wimax was chose because it fulfils most of the requirements needed.

Another issue is the situation of the frequency licenses for use in Brazil according to the Telecommunication Regulatory Authority (Anatel). The 3.5 GHz frequency auction is in legal dispute since 2006. Therefore, the only frequency available are the license exempt frequencies, such as 5.4 and 5.8 GHz. Several Internet providers also use these frequencies, leaving the radiofrequency spectrum congested in various locations. The 5.4 GHz radio offers more channels and is less congested in major cities, but the transmission power is limited, reducing the range. The 5.8 GHz radio has fewer channels, but the higher power increases the range, but it has a very congested spectrum, that brings interference in many places.

However, in 2008, Anatel authorized the use of 4.9 Ghz licensed frequency for use in public safety. As the Digital Belt aims to connect public places in the state, including, hospitals, police and fire stations, these organizations could use this frequency, freeing license-exempt frequencies for other applications, not categorized in this use.

Thus, the Digital Belt Pre-WiMAX network uses 4.9 GHz frequency for public safety. In urban areas, with more users or congested spectrum, the 5.4 GHz frequency was used. As the users density increases, the limited range due to lower power does not cause problems. For point-to-point connection in rural areas with lower density and larger distances, up to 60Km, the 5.8 GHz frequency was used. Usually in these places the spectrum is free and the interference was much smaller.

Figure 2 below shows the optical fiber infrastructure. Its topology takes into account that the number of citizens to be connected to the network must be maximized. As a matter of fact, the infrastructure passes across the biggest cities of the state.

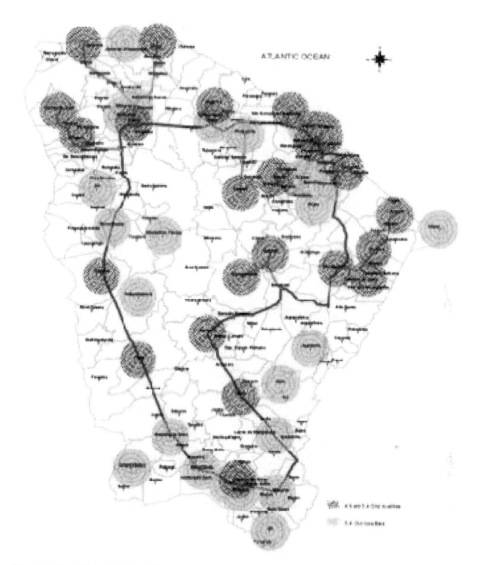

Fig. 2. The Digital Belt. The main redundant ring (red) the ramifications (green) and wireless base stations locations (blue).

3.2   Partnership with Electricity Utility Company

All the optical cables are supported by electrical high tension electricity poles. An agreement with the local electricity utility company Coelce has been signed, where the government provides four optical fibers to Coelce, and the company provides power transmission poles, towers, and electrical stations to host network equipment. Coelce intends to deploy a last mile network, using Power Line Connection (PLC) technology.

The fibre infrastructure comes up in order to fulfill important part of the government communication needs. Initially, the effort will cover 82% of urban population with Next Generation Network. Public schools, police, fire departments, hospitals, bureaucratic offices all around Ceara will take advantage of this infrastructure.

4   The Business Model

Considering the two main foregoing roles of the infrastructure, and the fact that optical fibers will already be illuminated at with ultrahigh speed broadband, many questions arise, for example:

- How to assure competition among service providers?
- Who are the main players?
- What if new service providers want to offer new technology, such as, IPTV, VoD, VoIP?
- How to assure sustainability of the model?
- Will service providers pay for maintain the network?
- Should major service providers hold the infrastructure?
- The players will pay for network expansion?
- How to deal with regulatory obstacles?

Clearly, the government will launch the Digital Belt and then hand it over to service providers. The latter will have to invest in order to provide last mile infrastructure.

The proposed business model depends on four steps to be accomplished by the government:

1. Creation of a joint venture company. This company will be composed of three different investors with equal shares. One of them may be the government itself. The digital belt company has two main purposes: i. to supply high-speed data transportation throughout the state; ii. to manage the network;
2. Promote a bid in order to choose the investors that will participate in the venture. The total amount obtained in the bid will be applied to the new company;
3. Immediately provide 2 GBPS for each private investor in every county of the state.

The government held a workshop on November 2009 with telecoms, Internet services providers and municipalities, in order to gather and discuss propositions to the business model. Many telecom companies, such as, Telemar Norte Leste (largest operator in Brazil), Telecom Italia Mobile, Brazil Telecom, Telefnica, Telmex (Embratel) were present. They appear to be interested in participating in the joint venture.

The Digital Belt is an original enterprise. In order to fulfill governments goals, its business model must be carefully studied and followed up by an experienced team, specialized professionals on feasibility study, telecom billing, and telecommunications technologies.

5   Discussion and Conclusion

The Ceara state government perceived that broadband access is a key value to the population. Large telecom companies would not invest in bringing fiber optics backbone to poor, remote areas. Then the government decided to invest in infrastructure and hand it to the operators in order to achieve almost universal broadband access in a sustainable environment.

In this work we presented the necessary infrastructure (cabled and wireless) and a business plan designed to bring competition to offer affordable digital services to the population.

The infrastructure chosen is based on optical cables and wireless last mile. The business plan calls telecom companies for participation in a new joint venture that offers high-speed data transportation. The government covered all the capital expenditures (CAPEX) in order to build the infrastructures, however, the private sector will cover the operational costs (OPEX).

Since beginning 2008, high-speed broadband demanding services have been funded by the government. Forbidden applications due to low quality dialup connection will become possible. Telemedicine, video-conferencing, videosurveillance, distance learning, remote data access to police cars and firemen are among the applications that will be available to the citizens in a short period of time.

The Digital Belt is an original enterprise. In order to fulfill governments goals, its business model must be carefully studied and followed up by an experienced team, specialized professionals on consultancy in telecommunication market, telecom billing, and state-of-the-art technologies.

References

1. Biggs, P.: Confronting the Crisis: Its Impact on the ICT Industry. International Telecommunication Union Report (2009)
2. Angani, P., Kim, T., Guleri, U., Misawa, Y., Vicente, M.R.: High-Quality Broadband Essential to Growth of the Worlds Knowledge Economies. University of Oxford and University of Oviedo Joint Report (2008)
3. Brazilian Internet Steering Committee: Survey on the Use of Information and Communication Technologies in Brazil, http://www.cetic.br/tic/2008/index.htm
4. Crandall, R.W., Jackson, C.L.: The $500 Billion Opportunity: The Potential Economic Benefit of Widespread Diffusion of Broadband Internet Access. Criterion Economics (2001)
5. Parikh, T.S.: Engineering Rural Development. CACM 52(01) (2009)
6. Fornefeld, M., Delaunay, G., Elixmann, D.: The Impact of Broadband on Growth and Productivity. Micus Management Consulting GmbH (2008)
7. Sein, K.S., Ahmad, I., Harindranath, G.: Sustaining ICT for Development Projects: The Case of Grameenphone CIC. Emerging Markets in Telecommunications. Telektronikk 104(02) (2008)
8. Ezell, S., Atkinson, R., Castro, D., Ou, G.: The Need for Speed: The Importance of Next-Generation Broadband Networks. The Information Technology & Innovation Foundation Report (2009)
9. Waverman, L., Meschi, M., Fuss, M.: The Impact of Telecoms on Economic Growth in Developing Countries. In: Moving the debate forwards. Vodafone Policy Paper Series, vol. 3 (2005)

ICT Driven Knowledge Management in Developing Countries: A Case Study in a Chinese Organisation

Jin Tong and Siraj A. Shaikh

Department of Computing and the Digital Environment,
Faculty of Engineering and Computing, Coventry University, Coventry, CV1 5FB,
United Kingdom
jintongcn@gmail.com, s.shaikh@coventry.ac.uk

Abstract. Current research of knowledge management (KM) is mostly based on experience in developed countries that are already becoming knowledge economies [16]. In general, ICT (information and communication technologies) is playing an important part of KM in these countries. Applications of their KM models and frameworks might not yield expected results in developing countries. It is necessary to help organisations in developing countries to understand the issues of KM in their local context. Towards this goal, this paper explores current KM practice in China through a case study of a recently created Chinese mobile phone company (referred to as Lotus). The researchers present a model demonstrating how ICT can promote effective KM based on the Lotus case findings. However, this model is more applicable in the wider developing countries context than just China.

Keywords: Knowledge Management, ICT adoption, Chinese organizations.

1 Introduction

Increasingly organisations are keen to adopt knowledge management (KM) strategies to achieve organizational objectives, including competitive advantages, shared intelligence, improved business performance and higher levels of innovation. This trend started in developed countries (such as Japan, US and EU) decades ago. KM applications within these countries have reached a mature level. KM implementations within developing countries, however, are still at an early stage. In the case of China, for example, KM is a relatively new concept and its importance has not yet been fully explored [2].

The role of information and communication technologies (ICT) as technical support for KM is widely acknowledged and emphasised in current literature. ICT tools, for example, have been proposed to develop knowledge databases or to support effective communications for knowledge sharing purposes. Current work on the application of ICT to promote effective KM mostly aims to help organisations in developed countries. There is not much work on effective KM for organizations in developing countries, such as China, especially how ICT acts as a facility to promote positive social change in supporting KM.

A. Pont, G. Pujolle, and S.V. Raghavan (Eds.): WCITD/NF 2010, IFIP AICT 327, pp. 60–71, 2010.
© IFIP International Federation for Information Processing 2010

To address this gap, this paper reports on a case study conducted in a Chinese organisation called *Lotus*. *Lotus* is a recently created mobile phone manufacturing company. Established by a group of 15 active professionals from the mobile phone industry, who decided to come together in 2005 to form *Lotus*, it designs and manufactures tailor-made mobile phones and other wireless terminal products for markets in China, South America and Europe. Their clients are brand manufactures, mobile phone distributors and small-medium sized wireless product operators. *Lotus* is representative of a typical small organisation in China and KM practices observed in the organisation reflect on the wider sector in the country. It has also been studied in authors' another paper [1], which explored cultural influences on KM in Chinese organisations. This paper, in contrast to the previous one, aims to focus on the role of ICT as the driver underlying KM and attempts to analyse it from a non-cultural perspective.

The rest of this paper is organised as follows. Section 2 reviews background and literature relevant to the ideas presented in this paper. Section 3 describes the research methodology used to study the *Lotus* case. Section 4 conducts an analysis of the findings of this case study. Section 5 presents a model explaining the role of ICT in KM specifically in the context of developing countries. Section 6 finally concludes the paper with observations and remarks.

2 Background

This section sets the context and discusses why ICT is important for developing countries, such as China, and how it has been applied for effective KM up until now. Given *Lotus* as a choice of case study, Section 2.3 pays particular attention to China in this regard.

2.1 The Importance of ICT for Developing Countries

There is ample evidence from developed world to acknowledge that ICT is a major driving force for economic development. The invention of the Internet and its widespread applications are even held by some [3], [4] as the twilight of the third industrial revolution, comparable to the role played by the internal combustion engine and the railroad in the second industrial revolution. Hoffman [5] believes that effective ICT adoption will help organisations to substantially enhance their international competitiveness. ICT has become a "critical infrastructure for competing in an information-intensive global economy" [6, p. xi]. Meanwhile, some studies [7], [8], [9] have developed the argument that ICT investments are necessary to stimulate economic development and as a means of enhancing national productivity and competitiveness. This has been called the "information technology-led development" strategy [9]. It is recognised that ICT applications can enable improvements in productivity and quality in a number of sectors relevant to developing countries, such as agriculture, manufacturing, infrastructure, public administration, and services such as finance, trade, distribution, marketing, education, and health [10]. The following statement from a World Bank discussion paper strongly supports this:

"Information technology dramatically increases the amount and timeliness of information available to economics agents – and the productivity of processes to organize, process, communicate, store, and retrieve information... [and this] has major implications for developing countries, as producers and users of this technology." [6, p. 1]

2.2 ICT Applications in KM

KM is one of the emerging trends for organisations to sustain competitive advantages. Many firms that embrace KM as a key organisational policy eventually go on to become industry leaders [11]. Their success shows the benefits of effective KM to an organisation. KM is about directing people's view on knowledge, guiding people's behaviors of sharing their knowledge, designing right strategies and using effective approaches to promote knowledge creation, dissemination and leveraging to fulfill organisational objectives.

Nonaka and Takeuchi [12] developed a knowledge creation model that obtained widespread acceptance within the KM community. It identifies four different processes through which knowledge is created – *socialization, externalization, combination* and *internalization.* This SECI model has convinced many practitioners that organisational KM practice can be effectively improved if the knowledge is managed in an explicit / codified format. Since then, many researchers have attempted to apply ICT technologies to maximally capture, codify and store knowledge within organisations [13]. Organisations in the developed world have made considerable progress in implementing effective KM. However, many developing countries, such as China, started this progress relatively much later. With rapid economic development over the past 25 years, most Chinese organisations are at a stage that massive fundamental knowledge – knowledge that can be easily captured, codified and stored – has not been effectively managed. Analysis in subsequent sessions of this paper serve to highlight that such a situation still exists in the case of *Lotus* for example.

2.3 Current ICT Adoption in China

Learning from developed countries' experience, Chinese government has made significant investments in ICT and has come to view it as an important contributor to industrialization and economic development [17]. While reviewing China's ICT adoption and diffusion, Meng and Li [4] insist that compared to relatively high IT expenditures on hardware (88.1%), the consumption of software and IT service in China is very low (7.3%). It indicates that there is lack of ICT usage in Chinese organisation. They also believe that "it is reasonable to assume that as computer usage reaches a point of saturation within the next several years, the percentage of software and IT services will go up significantly" [4, p. 281]. However, there is little literature available on how ICT is adopted in China for management purposes in organisations.

3 Research Methodology

This paper attempts to investigate the current KM practice within *Lotus*, and explores some of the reasons underlying such a state of practice. A qualitative research methodology was adopted in this study. To ensure that adequate care was taken in structuring and analyzing the case, the following four steps were taken.

1. A *learning day* was organised as part of an organisational day trip. Within a relaxed environment, the authors established initial communications with all employees and helped them to have a common understanding of knowledge management, and the purpose of the present case study.
2. *Observation at the work place* was organised, lasting three days, to achieve an overview of knowledge flows within *Lotus*, and identify the key interviewees for in-depth interviews. Through participant observation at the work place, the authors managed to get familiar with the potential interviewees' working language.
3. *In-depth interviews with the management team and selected employees* was organised, which included interviews with 18 *Lotus* staff members, including the Chief Manager, R&D director, Human Resources manager, 5 R&D design team leaders, and 10 selected general employees. Each interview lasted approximately 1.5 hour. The interview contents have been tape-recorded and subsequently transcribed.
4. In order to ascertain the *validity of findings*, meetings with volunteered *Lotus* participants were held regularly. Meanwhile, consultations with the management team on findings created opportunities to introduce necessary KM solutions to business processes. The study process also resulted in consensus and commitment of research participants on formal KM approaches (e.g. applications of knowledge maps, [14]).

4 Field Results and Analysis

Traditional Chinese cultural values pervasively influencing the management mode and organisation is one of the outstanding characteristics of Chinese organisations [15]. From a cultural perspective *Lotus* has been studied earlier [1]. The study explored the practice of keeping knowledge implicit in Chinese enterprises. The study revealed that employees like to keep their knowledge implicit and are willing to informally share their knowledge. A series of factors derived from the Chinese culture including

-   hierarchy consciousness,
-   fear of losing face,
-   a sense of modesty,
-   competitiveness, and
-   a preference for face-to-face communication

Can act as barriers to knowledge initiatives within Chinese organisations. Trust in intra personal relationships among employees can partly mitigate the impact of above cultural characteristics. However, at a macro organisational level there is still a need to share knowledge using explicit and formal KM approaches.

Apart from the above cultural factors, some other management related issues, such as working procedures and business strategies, also affect the current KM practice within *Lotus*. Focusing on these issues, this section attempts to explore the KM gap *and identify* the major reasons contributing to this gap in *Lotus*.

4.1 KM Gap within Lotus

Prior to starting the field work, the authors had expected to find KM practices in *Lotus* relatively more effective compared to other Chinese organisations. There are several reasons to allow such an expectation. First, ICT hardware investment in *Lotus* is at a high level. PC and internet coverage inside the company is 100%. Such conditions make *Lotus* very similar to technology-based organisations in developed countries. Secondly, 3 out of 5 senior managers in the *Lotus* management team have a background of working in leading telecommunication companies in developed countries. Because of their rich international working experience, it was also expected that KM concepts should be familiar to them. Finally, given that *Lotus* is a company in the ICT industry, employees' willingness to adopt ICT related KM approaches into daily work is expected to be higher than other Chinese companies. Current KM practices within *Lotus* were found to be on the contrary however. This KM gap is reflected as follows:

Management team members' perceptions towards KM are not encouraging. KM is still a new concept to *Lotus* staff. Apart from the chief manager, the rest of senior managers are not familiar with the concept of KM. General *Lotus* staff do not have sufficient awareness of the importance and needs of applying KM strategies.

There are no formal KM strategies and approaches within Lotus. Codified and explicit knowledge is comparatively rare in this organisation. Like other Chinese organisations, the majority of workforce in *Lotus* is the staff in the manufacturing department, which routinely creates several product lines. However, the nature of business determined that R&D department plays a decisive role for the company, in order to survive within keen competition with other similar organisations, *Lotus* needs to possess an experienced R&D team capable of leveraging competitive advantages. There are approximately 50 design engineers in R&D department. During the daily work process, their own knowledge gaps forced them to obtain new knowledge from other resources. However, knowledge sharing within this department primarily depends on informal approaches, such as social events (e.g. staff have dinner together), seeking personal assistance from others, etc. Therefore, massive fundamental knowledge has not been captured, codified or stored formally.

Knowledge flows are not flexible enough – only top to bottom through the organisational hierarchy. In most successful organisations that have supportive KM environment, knowledge can be transferred / shared through various paths. Knowledge flows in those organisations can be very complex and flexible. However, current KM practice in *Lotus* shows that knowledge flows only from top to bottom level through the organisational hierarchy.

4.2 Reasons Contributing to the Gap

Further investigation reveals several reasons underlying the KM gap that exists at *Lotus*.

Reason 1 – Insufficient ICT adoption in *Lotus*. The IT support team has set up a website for all employees, which facilitated an online forum, document storage, and messages from the company's leadership. In general, IT support staff attempted to design the organisational website as a formal knowledge sharing facility. But the use of the site is not encouraging. Embedded functions in this website are rarely used. When the authors interviewed anticipated users of this website, most of them even did not know the existence of such functions.

This incident reveals the issue of insufficient ICT adoption in *Lotus*. Unlike most successful organisations in developed countries, the potential of ICT is not fully exploited within *Lotus*. Most staff members use the organisation's intranet to send email, chat online with colleagues, or use web search engines to get information. R&D engineers work on PCs everyday to design products by using relevant software. However, administration staff use their computers to do the very basic paper work. For instance, instead of creating a HR database, HR department is still using paper-based folders to maintain employee records. There are no standard written working procedures within any department, though most employees are familiar with their work process because of their work experience in the field. R&D engineers do not maintain problem solving records or any database to manage their design work processes. The traditional training method – of one master supervising one apprentice is still being used in *Lotus*. When a new employee is hired, a mentor (a senior staff member) is assigned by the HR department to assist the new member with any problem he/she may have during the work process. These examples evidently indicate that in *Lotus*, ICT has been only used as a supplement for daily manual work, but not as an essential work force at the general management level.

While organisations in developed countries are trying to avoid excessively depending on ICT to manage their intellectual capital, *Lotus* does not truly recognize the vital function of ICT in its KM. Due to low effective usage of ICT, massive explicit knowledge has been kept implicit within *Lotus*, although such knowledge is normally explicitly managed (codified) through ICT in organisations in developed countries.

Reason 2 – Strict hierarchy within *Lotus*. There is a clearly defined organisational hierarchy in *Lotus*. Within this organisational structure chart, each employee can be located into specific position according to their responsibilities. Meanwhile, there is another informal hierarchy inside this organization (Figure 1). In this informal hierarchy, company managers are still at the top level. Elderly staff and employees who joined *Lotus* are at higher levels then those just joined this company. New graduates (recently employed *Lotus* staff) who do not have any experience in related working field are at the bottom level.

Employees' traditional hierarchy consciousness results in this informal organisational hierarchy. Due to the fear of breaking rules and policies, formal organisational hierarchy always held predominant importance. So even in this informal hierarchy, people who are at managing positions are still at the top level. The tradition of respecting elders and sense of modesty made new graduates volunteered to stay at the bottom level in this hierarchy. In addition, not just age, but also experience and time of working in the organisations can be the reasons for an employee to be respected and rank at a higher level, even though he or she may be biologically younger than others sometimes.

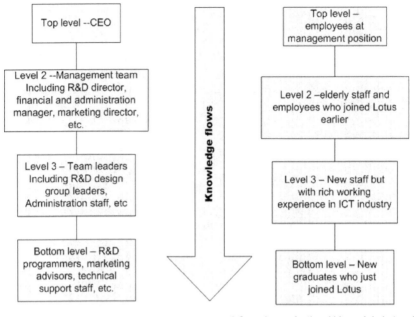

Formal organisational hierarch in Lotus

Informal organisational hierarch in Lotus due to employees' traditional hierarchy consciousness

Fig. 1. Strict organisational hierarchy (formal and informal) in *Lotus*

In both formal and informal hierarchy in *Lotus*, junior employees (staff at lower level, such as lower-position, younger, newer staff) are expected to follow seniors' advice. Seniors are supposed to teach or pass on their knowledge and experience to juniors in organisations. Following seniors' suggestions is the right way to show juniors' respect to them. *Lotus*'s new staff mentoring policy (one master supervising one apprentice) is one example showing that knowledge flows from top to bottom in this company. So obviously, managers and senior staff rarely receive knowledge from their subordinates and juniors. This situation causes an 'unequal' knowledge sharing environment.

Reason 3 – Lack of supportive policies and practitioners. Investigation shows that there are no qualified KM personnel within *Lotus*. KM in China only started in 1990s. Only a few Chinese universities set KM courses and foster KM professionals. There are very few qualified KM professionals available compared to the size of Chinese KM market. Organisations with mature knowledge management facilities in developed countries, senior managers and HR administrative personnel are normally the KM principals. However, such administrative staff at *Lotus* do not have required KM skills and knowledge to be responsible for KM related tasks.

Hoarding knowledge is a natural tendency. Knowledge sharing hence must be encouraged and rewarded. The organisational website mentioned earlier provides a convenient platform to staff to share ideas and exchange knowledge. But hardly anyone visited this website. Obviously, *Lotus* staff did not take this seriously, because they are not encouraged to use it. Without senior managers' support and encouragement, KM activities always do not have high execution priority. As a result, when activities of knowledge sharing conflict with other action plan, the organisation's policies specify that other action plans go first. For example in *Lotus*, R&D department is always developing several products for different clients at the same time. All R&D engineers are allocated to different project groups. So employees from the same team are working on different projects. Meanwhile, the organisation has a bonus policy, which allows employees get more bonuses if their project team develops better product. Such bonus policy obviously can increase the employees' commitment on their project. But at the same time, it also creates a harmful atmosphere, in which employees would not like to share knowledge with the project competitors.

In summary, lack of supportive KM policies and qualified practitioners causes a non-supportive organisational environment for effective KM in *Lotus*.

5 Discussion

By explaining why it is necessary to improve the current KM practice within *Lotus*, the value of effective KM to Chinese organisations is highlighted in this section. A more widespread adoption of ICT is proposed to bridge the *Lotus* gap. The role of ICT as an essential enabler for KM within Chinese organisations is illustrated in a model. This model also shows applicability in the wider developing countries context than just China.

5.1 The Need to Improve Current KM Practice

China has put high-priority efforts in becoming a more knowledge-based economy and society, and this means KM is very important [18]. Being caught in the global economic downturn, increasingly Chinese organisations have to prepare for more severe marketing competitions. Since effective KM could help organisations sustain their competitive advantages (e.g. higher production and economic efficiencies), improving Chinese organisations' KM practices is necessary. The *Lotus* case sets a good example to demonstrate such a need.

With the expansion of mobile phone market, more and more products have to be designed at the same time. Without a standard R&D design procedure, a *Lotus* employee may waste time in redoing the same job (e.g. some reusable driver programs have been written repeatedly in *Lotus*). Therefore, explicating such implicit knowledge is required to improve employees' work efficiency and minimize the production duration. Furthermore, without a written record of solved problems during the work processes, mistakes can be repeated and solution seeking time can be longer than expected. It is also necessary to produce standard staff training material to effectively pass on necessary knowledge as well as reduce new staff training time. Any formatted documents can also become written evidence for future analysis of one project's success or failure.

According to *Lotus*'s recruitment plan, more inexperienced staff (e.g. new graduates and people who have never worked in this field) will be employed in order to increase saving on the HR budget. It will be very difficult for these potential employees to start delivering high quality work without any valuable codified knowledge available in *Lotus*. In this case, managing knowledge using ICT is a logical starting point to facilitate knowledge sharing.

5.2 The Use of ICT to Bridge the KM Gap

KM in developed countries has provided ample evidence to indicate that one main role of ICT in KM is to accelerate the speed of knowledge capture, transfer and storage. This role emphasized the importance of ICT in the dimension of technical supporting. KM progress always comes with positive organisational changes. Effective KM strategies in an organisation should be able to increase employees' motivation of sharing their knowledge, and to help employees to overcome their psychological barriers in seeking / receiving knowledge from others. Therefore in the dimension of promoting organisational change, will ICT still play an important role? Analysis shows that it will. Figure 2 below clearly explain how ICT application can promote such positive organisation changes.

Once organisations set up KM friendly policies and employ qualified KM practitioners, ICT adoption as a basic KM approach can be encouraged. Good organisational policies should also foster a flatter organisation structure. Employees can take different roles in different projects in organisations, so their position in the formal organisational hierarchy can be more adaptive. As the formal hierarchy became flexible, knowledge flows that pass through this structure can be more dynamic.

However, improvement to the informal organisational hierarchy needs the positive impact of widespread adoption of ICT. Once an organisation starts to use ICT to maximally codify fundamental knowledge, explicit knowledge within this organisation will be available in different format, such as website, shared documents, and so on. Employees will not need to seek for required knowledge in person all the time. This can be extremely helpful for employees that are at the higher level in the organisational hierarchy to receive knowledge from the ones at lower level. Their psychological barrier of feeling embarrassed when receiving knowledge from subordinates and youngsters can be overcome in this situation. Similarly, widespread ICT adoption can also increase employees' motivation of sharing their knowledge, especially the ones at the lower level in the hierarchy. For example, while *Lotus* is training one of the new staff members using their 'one master supervising one apprentice' mentoring policy, the apprentice normally would not like to show their expertise and knowledge in front of their masters. However, transferring their knowledge in another format (e.g. documents, webpage) is less possible to make them feel that they are offending the seniors in the company. Their motivation of sharing knowledge hence increases.

Although this model is generalized based on the *Lotus* case study, its value does not restrict in China only. The role of ICT as an essential driver of effective KM can also be applied to the wider developing countries context. According to this model (see Figure 2), ICT can enable effective KM in two dimensions. First, widespread ICT adoption can technically support managing massive fundamental knowledge,

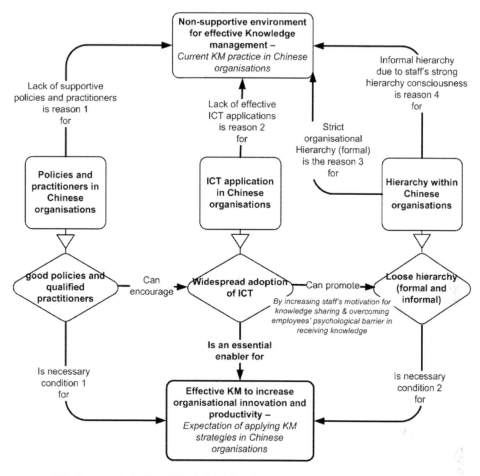

Fig. 2. Extended role of ICT in bridging the KM gap in Chinese organisations

which is the urgent problem in most developing countries [16], [18], [19]. Second, it can also promote a comparatively loose organisation hierarchy by increasing employees' motivation of sharing knowledge and overcoming their psychological barriers in receiving knowledge.

6 Conclusion

Through a case study in a Chinese company, this paper explores current organisational KM practice in China. The study revealed a gap between expectations of applying KM strategies and current experience in Chinese organisations. This gap caused *Lotus* to fail to reach expected business performance levels. Insufficient ICT adoption, strict organisational hierarchy (both formal and informal), and lack of supportive policies and practitioners can be seen as the three major reasons contributing to this gap within *Lotus*. Widespread ICT adoption within Chinese organisations is proposed to bridge gaps in knowledge sharing expectations. The essential role of ICT in effective KM is emphasized in a model (see Section 5.2) that can benefit organisations in both China and other developing countries.

This effort aims to provide an insight into KM practices in the developing world. While *Lotus* serves to be one example from China, it is hoped that such an exanimation is extended to other developing countries to reaffirm general conclusions drawn from this work. The crucial role that ICT plays for effective KM is acknowledged and should serve as a reminder for knowledge managers in China and the developing world at large. Further work aims to focus on a selection of specific ICT tools and technologies in their role to support KM, and the organisational changes necessary for adoption of effective KM processes.

References

1. Tong, J., Mitra, A.: Chinese cultural influences on knowledge management practices: a case study in a Chinese manufacturing enterprise. In: Proceedings of the 3rd Asia-Pacific International Conference on Knowledge Management, KMAP 2006, Hong Kong (2006)
2. Peng, J., Li-Hua, R., Moffett, S.: Trend of knowledge management in China: challenges and opportunities. Journal of Technology Management in China 2(3), 198–211 (2007)
3. Kraemer, K., Dedrick, J.: Information technology and productivity: results and policy implications of cross-country studies. In: Pohjola, M. (ed.) Information Technology, Productivity, and Economic Growth, pp. 257–279. Oxford University Press, Oxford (2001)
4. Meng, Q., Li, M.: New Economy and ICT development in China. Information Economics and Policy 14(2), 275–295 (2002)
5. Hoffman, K.: Microelectronics, international competition and development strategies: the unavoidable issues – editor's introduction. World Development 13(3), 263–272 (1985)
6. Hanna, N.: Exploiting information technology for development: a case study of. World Bank Discussion Paper 264. World Bank, Washington (1994)
7. OECD: OECD Information Technology Outlook 1999. OECD, Paris (2000)
8. Asian Productivity Organisation: Information technology-led development. APO, Tokyo (1990)
9. Mody, A., Dahlman, C.: Performance and potential of information technology: an international perspective. World Development 20(12), 1703–1719 (1992)
10. Sein, M.K., Harindranath, G.: Conceptualizing the ICT artifact: toward understanding the role of ICT in national development. The Information Society 20, 15–24 (2004)
11. Davenport, T.H., Prusak, L.: Working Knowledge: How Organizations Manage What They Know. Harvard Business School Press, Boston (1998)
12. Nonaka, I., Takeuchi, H.: The Knowledge-Creating Company: How Japanese Companies Create the Dynamics of Innovation. Oxford University Press, Oxford (1995)
13. Sparrow, H.: Knowledge in Organisations. Sage, Thousand Oakes (1998)
14. Tong, J., Mitra, A.: Knowledge maps and organizations: an overview and interpretation. International Journal of Business Information Systems 3(6), 587–608 (2009)
15. Pun, K.F., Chin, K.S., Lau, H.: A review of the Chinese cultural influences on Chinese enterprise management. International Journal of Management Reviews 2(4), 325–338 (2000)

16. Okunoye, A.: Towards a framework for sustainable knowledge management in organisations in developing countries. In: Brunnstein, K., Berleur, J. (eds.) Human Choice and Computers: Issues of Choice and quality of life in developing countries, pp. 225–237. Springer, Heidelberg (2002)
17. Press, L., Foster, w., Wolcott, P., Mchnery, W.: The Internet in India and China. Information Technologies and Internet Development 1(1), 41–60 (2003)
18. Burrows, G.R., Drummond, D.L., Martinsons, M.G.: Knowledge Management in China. Communications of the ACM 48(40), 73–76 (2005)
19. Singh, S.K.: Knowledge management practices and organisational learning in Indian Software Company. Int. J. Business Innovation and Research 3(4), 363–381 (2009)

Technical ICTD - A User Centered Lifecycle

Joerg Doerflinger[1] and Tom Gross[2]

[1] SAP Research, CEC Karlsruhe, Vincenz-Priessnitz-Strasse 1,
Karlsruhe, 76131, Germany
joerg.doerflinger@sap.com
[2] Faculty of Media, Bauhaus-University Weimar, Bauhausstrasse 11,
Weimar, 99423, Germany
tom.gross@medien.uni-weimar.de

Abstract. Technical Information and Communication Technology for Development (ICTD) lacks appropriate research methods along the entire development lifecycle spanning design, development, deployment, and evaluation. Many ICTD projects have failed meeting the challenges of technical ICTD because of inappropriate research methods which often left frustrated end users alone with unusable research results. Successful technical ICTD research needs a shared methodology that involves the end user in all research lifecycle phases. With User Centered Design and Action Research the Mobile Human Computer Interaction (HCI) research field offers concepts with a clear end user focus. However, applying Mobile HCI research methods unchanged in technical ICTD will fail due to the specific cultural, infrastructural and governmental context of ICTD research. In this paper we present a set of Mobile HCI research methods adapted for technical ICTD research based on results and lessons learned of a research project in rural South Africa.

Keywords: User Centered Design, Action Research, ICTD, Mobile HCI.

1 Introduction

People in rural areas of emerging economies lack appropriate access to Information and Communication Technology (ICT) which is a key mechanism for socioeconomic development in those regions that need it most. In a globalized world, economical, social, and political life will be more and more digital, and those without access to ICT will be increasingly excluded [1]. Many previous approaches of providing ICT access in developing countries failed because of an often applied "copy&paste" approach of 1st economy concepts in regions with different governmental, cultural and infrastructural contexts [2]. To improve technical ICTD research, the methodologies utilized along the entire development lifecycle need to be adapted from a technology centric top-down approach towards a user centric top-down/bottom-up combination taking into account the specific ICTD context. In this paper we present a set of research methods adapted towards the specific requirements of technical ICTD, which refers to ICTD topics specifically relevant for computer scientists and engineers.

A. Pont, G. Pujolle, and S.V. Raghavan (Eds.): WCITD/NF 2010, IFIP AICT 327, pp. 72–83, 2010.
© IFIP International Federation for Information Processing 2010

Technical ICTD research today is not yet a well established research field because of missing metrics and tools [3]. Metrics clearly define the research goal and make research measurable and comparable. The tools represent agreed-upon research processes and methodologies. Today there is no shared set of research methods supporting researchers in technical ICTD research. With our proposed set of research methods for technical ICTD we contribute exactly to this part. Our proposed research approach combines and adapts existing research methods from the Mobile Human Computer Interaction (HCI) research field along the entire technical ICTD development lifecycle. The adaptation takes place on two levels - the overall research approach and at the individual lifecycle elements.

The overall approach is to move from the technology centric top-down approach of former technical ICTD research, which often led to design versus reality gaps, towards a user centric approach involving end users in all research lifecycle phases. Ignoring end user needs and their potential to contribute valuable insights most probably will lead to inappropriate research results. Technical ICTD could be more effective when involving end users along the entire research lifecycle.

On the second level, the methods used in the individual lifecycle phases need to be adapted to cope with the cultural, infrastructural and governmental challenges of ICTD research like the language barrier, cultural lack of understanding, missing requirements definitions, end user trust creation, low literacy, low computer literacy, spatial separated researchers and end users, and difficult infrastructure and governmental setups.

The following chapter provides information on related work and underlines the need for user centered technical ICTD. In chapter 3 we describe the proposed methodology on an overall and individual lifecycle phase level. Chapter 4 provides lessons learned during our research work, necessary to execute valuable technical ICTD research. With a conclusion and possible future research activities we conclude the paper in chapter 5.

2   Related Work

In this chapter we provide an overview of current ICTD and Mobile HCI research literature, its individual weak points and how they could benefit from each other. We present possible innovation models in theory and with practical examples.

Jonathan Donner's review [4] of roughly 200 studies on mobile phone usage in the developing world reveals the huge variety of different ICTD studies which underlines the broadly interdisciplinary field of ICTD compared to the much more narrowed field of technical ICTD. His review shows that there is still a separation of ICTD and non-ICTD research, which in real life doesn't exist: "people's lives cannot be compartmentalized into separate categories such as economic, social, religious and cultural ... they are all part of the same person's experience and concerns" [5]. Technical ICTD research could be much more effective without this distinction but taking into account the non-technical factors, which are the people and their environment.

In a review of 102 publications on Mobile HCI [6], Kjeldskov and Graham revealed that only very few studies have been done in real settings, using studies of situated use. Most of the studies focused on the technical aspects of prototyping. If at all, prototype evaluations have been executed in artificial environments, often without any information on success, failure or shortcomings of the utilized methods. This clearly depicts a lack of use of end user involvement and real environment methods like action research, case and field studies which are of most value for technical ICTD research. Whereas technical ICTD could benefit from methods for mobile research, Mobile HCI could benefit from a new research field using research methods that are currently not frequently used and thus limit the effectiveness of the research field itself. Due to the huge opportunities of mobile computing in developing countries, Mobile HCI research methods perfectly fit into the technical ICTD research focus.

In the ICT4D Manifesto [2] Richard Heeks addresses the need for new innovation models and identifies three of them. Pro-poor innovation is done outside the target community but on their behalf (e.g. OLPC laptop). This top-down approach contains the risk of design versus reality gaps that could be seen with the initial telecenter model. In the para-poor model, which combines participatory design and action research, the innovation is done with and within the target community, leading to much more appropriate research results. Per-poor innovation is done within and by the community itself. Even if this model might be promising in future and first mobiles, then computers, and now the internet begin reaching the poor communities it will need more time to let the communities themselves innovate on a large scale. Thus, currently the para-poor innovation model seems to be most appropriate for technical ICTD research.

One project that made a successful shift from a failing pro-poor start towards a successful para-poor development is the Warana Unwired [7] research project. It started with the installation of 54 PC kiosks in rural India with goals defined without detailed on-site requirements analysis. In 2005 an ethnographic study on the Warana project revealed that none of the initial goals have been met because the people had completely different demands. With these study results the use case was re-designed towards the real requirements using appropriate technology and content resulting in an appropriate frequently used solution. Another para-poor project is CAM [8], which provides an architecture for developing and deploying mobile services in the rural developing world. To gather the system requirements an extensive field study with all use case stakeholders was conducted. The tight interaction with the end users led to a system appropriate to run in the specific ICTD context. Techniques like ethological studies and field studies to gather the requirements, and evolutionary design or rapid prototyping have been used successfully in a project on HIV/AIDS in South Africa [9]. Due to an extensive stakeholder analysis, requirements gathering and the utilization of a so called "local champion", the project started with a clear definition of the use case scenario. The local champion is a person out of the target community with a high interest in driving the research. He is the local contact and maintains enthusiasm in the target community.

A majority of technical ICTD research today already utilizes user centric methods, but only partially along the entire lifecycle. There is hardly any information on projects covering the complete technical ICTD lifecycle with user centered research methods. This might be a) because of the high costs and time consumption of User Centered Design (UCD) and action research in natural settings b) because of a lack of information on how to efficiently utilize those methods. New combinations of existing methods can make technical ICTD research much more efficient [9]. In the following chapter we describe our proposed set of appropriate research methods to support a user centered approach along the entire technical ICTD research lifecycle.

3 User Centered Technical ICTD Lifecycle

The User Centered Technical ICTD Lifecycle describes a set of research methods with a clear focus on end user interaction and action research. In this chapter we describe our proposed overall approach and the adapted Mobile HCI research methods utilized during the individual technical ICTD research lifecycle phases.

3.1 Overall Approach

The results presented in this paper have been produced during a three year research project in the ICTD context called Collaboration@Rural (C@R) [10]. The focus of C@R was on a procurement use case supporting small shop owners in rural South Africa with only basic mobile phones and erratic network access [11]. The overall framework in which the research took place was the Sekhukhune Rural Living Lab (RLL). The Living Lab concept itself is built upon two main principles: a) involve end users as co-creators and b) experimentation in real world settings [12]. The combination of these two principles makes the Living Lab a suitable playground to investigate the appropriateness of Mobile HCI research methods adapted towards UCD and action research in context of technical ICTD.

The purpose of UCD is to serve the user, not to use a specific technology, or to produce a scientific piece of software. In UCD the user needs dominate the entire design and this is what technical ICTD should be about as well. UCD, or participatory design, has been successfully used in Mobile HCI research [13], and due to the huge opportunities of mobile technology in emerging economies [14] will also be used in technical ICTD research. However, up to now Mobile HCI methodologies haven't been utilized appropriately for technical ICTD research which led to a number of failing projects [1][15]. Many ICTD projects utilized UCD methods unchanged, grounded them on assumptions about end user requirements and failed. The tight interaction with real end users within the Sekhukhune RLL solves this problem and enables UCD based on real facts [9]. Since the Sekhukhune Rural Living Lab approach covered the entire lifecycle from requirements gathering to evaluation, all utilized research methodologies have been used within a UCD and action research setup (see Fig. 1). This ensures to be in natural settings all the time and eliminates the danger of losing focus on real world problems and end users. The combination of top-down knowledge of researchers together with the bottom-up real world knowledge of the end users provides an effective way to conduct appropriate technical ICTD research.

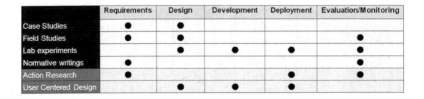

	Requirements	Design	Development	Deployment	Evaluation/Monitoring
Case Studies	●	●			
Field Studies	●	●			●
Lab experiments		●	●	●	●
Normative writings	●				●
Action Research	●			●	●
User Centered Design		●	●	●	

Fig. 1. Research methodologies per technical ICTD lifecycle phase

The UCD approach was used during design, development and deployment realizing an iterative development in collaboration with the end users. Action research was utilized in the requirements, evaluation and monitoring phase. During the utilization of Mobile HCI research methods in our UCD and action research setup we have collected lifecycle phase specific issues necessary to adapt existing Mobile HCI research methods for the use within technical ICTD research.

3.2 Requirements Analysis

To avoid the flaw of previous failing ICTD projects that based their research on assumptions, a detailed requirements analysis needs to build the foundation of valuable technical ICTD research [16]. Current technical ICTD literature concentrates on presenting solutions only and lacks descriptions of research problems, requirements and definitions. Thus there is hardly any data available to ground new technical ICTD research on [3]. This enforces ICTD researchers to do expensive and time consuming on-site requirements analysis. But to avoid doing inappropriate research this is a mandatory requirement, or like Raj Reddy puts it: *"If you want to develop new technologies or innovate old technologies for different contexts, you're crazy if you don't go to those contexts"* [17]. During our research we did extensive on-site requirements analysis using Mobile HCI research methodologies adapted towards the ICTD specific requirements.

Field Studies and Case Studies. *Local contact.* During our research we've had the help of the Infopreneur™[18] - a trusted person within the rural community who offers basic IT services. A local contact is necessary for field and case studies since he often provides much more detailed information about cultural issues, he knows the people, the use case and the scenario. A foreign researcher easily could step over an important requirement just because of a lack of understanding of the local context.

Local language and Trust. During the workshops, interviews, and questionnaires it became clear that using the local language is mandatory. This was done with the help of the Infopreneur™. Since he is a trusted person, the answers he gathered have been much more precise and without distortion due to the fact of people not telling private or "bad" things to foreign researchers. People felt much more comfortable talking to him instead directly to us.

Purpose of individual research methods. Using workshops to gather insights into problems of an existing use case or to get feedback from the users about issues with use case stakeholders might provide misleading answers. People will not talk about governmental or community issues while sitting in a workshop together with other people from the same community. This kind of questions is much better elaborated in person-to-person interviews executed by a trusted person like the Infopreneur[TM]. Workshops work fine to collect general feedback about a use case and especially for prototype testing and feedback rounds because of the community effect. People are much more willing to test a prototype when they are together with known people showing them how to use it instead of a researcher explaining a prototype in a top-down approach. Testing a prototype together with the community members also enables a more natural behavior and might reveal scenario issues that have not been on the researchers list before. Workshops are a well suited for initial design and prototype feedback rounds.

Personas and Scenarios. During the requirements gathering phase not only information on the required functionality of a piece of software is collected but also a lot of information about the end users and use case scenario itself. This information needs to be documented in a comprehensive way to provide basic research input for the technical ICTD community and to give project members that have not been on-site a clear understanding of the end user and use case environment. Personas and Scenarios [13] (pp.160-165) are an effective way to give for example the developer of a prototype, sitting thousands of kilometers away from the end user, a clear view of the end user. It helps researchers to understand that they build something for people within a completely different infrastructural, cultural and governmental environment.

3.3   Design Methodology

The design phase creates the first prototype mock-ups based on the requirements analysis and input from the end users and represents the starting point for the continuous prototype improvement during iterative development cycles.

Participatory design. *End user input.* After an initial design sketch continuous interaction with the end user takes place to create a prototype appropriate to the end users needs. Since it is difficult to keep in contact with end users in the rural areas with limited network access, again the Infopreneur[TM] serves as local contact for participatory design. Since he lives in the end user community and has basic IT knowledge he is a valuable information source during design phase. The Infopreneur[TM] is able to collect information from users during private talks, which often provides much more critical input than guided interviews. He also provides input to the design not possible to gather by a researcher visiting the area for two month and thus bridges the important cultural gap.

Without any assumptions. During design developers often tend to use well known concepts (e.g. semantic, syntax, designs) in their prototypes. However, these concepts might fail in the different context of technical ICTD. For example, today GIS (Geographical Information System) applications are a well known concept in the 1st economy, but there is no evidence to assume people in rural areas of developing countries might ever have been exposed to a geographical map at all. Every detail needs to be questioned and tested in collaboration with the end users.

Mock-ups and Functional prototypes. *Paper based mock-ups.* The first mock-ups will be most probably paper based sketches that can be easily changed during end user interactions. Paper based prototypes are also effective to test basic concepts in rural settings since they are independent of electricity and connectivity and thus can be discussed also with end users in very remote areas without additional equipment.

Functional prototypes. In our research, functional prototypes directly followed paper based mock-ups without any other prototyping technique in between. Due to the lack of computer knowledge end users in developing countries have difficulties to understand concepts like "wizard of oz" where a human acts as a computing device. An example out of our research is that they had problems to understand why to use a specific syntax in a structured SMS (Short Message Service) message (e.g. 2xProductA) instead of clear text (e.g. Two times product A), if even they as a human could understand it - and a computer should be much more clever. Functional prototypes avoid those metaphors and can be tested in real settings. For effective tests, functional prototypes always have been exposed to end users during a workshop, using the community effect, and with the support of the Infopreneur^{TM}. However this approach makes functional prototype testing a very expensive and time consuming task - for both, researchers and end users since they need to travel to the workshop venue.

Rapid Prototyping. *Different context.* Rapid prototyping tests in natural settings are necessary to get end user feedback and to only rely on hardware and infrastructure available in the target scenario. In context of ICTD, the available infrastructure and hardware might be considerable less powerful than available resources in which the developer creates the prototypes. Thus testing on virtual machines reflecting the target environment is a good practice before testing the prototype in the real environment.

Tests are not only about software. Rapid prototyping not only provides feedback about human-prototype interaction but also about the entire system environment the prototype is deployed in. Rapid prototypes reveal all aspects of context specific limitation in the target area like infrastructural, cultural and governmental issues. There are many specific limitation 1st economy developers initially might not be aware of (e.g. some countries don't allow Voice over IP, limitations of telecom providers, different payment models, different usage of symbols, different infrastructure).

3.4   Development Methodology

Technical ICTD research often involves researchers creating solutions for a user community in another environment, even on another continent. To support this setup, additionally to the issues mentioned in the requirements and design phase, the following adaptations need to be made on the development methodologies.

Iterative Development. Especially in the difficult infrastructural and cultural environment of technical ICTD research, iterative development ensures appropriate and end user driven development. Developing something just top-down might be much cheaper and faster in the beginning, but contains the risk of producing just another piece of code no one will or can use. Then, redeveloping things quickly exceeds costs and time efforts for iterative development.

First prototype iteration to build trust. With iterative development and action research, the first development cycle needs to provide a robust prototype, ready to run stable in the target use case. This is necessary to build trust between the end user and the new system introduced by "foreign" researchers. People are skeptical towards innovations brought in by people not known in the community. If now, in this fragile setting, the first deployment of the prototype fails the end users will hardly continue to support the research work. For them the research influences their real life business.

Context simulation. Simulating the context of use during development ensures effective iterative development. It enables early prototype debugging and avoids spending money for a field trip just to find out that something is missing to run the prototype. We've learned this the hard way travelling 400 km to the end user just to recognize that the required flash player was not installed and there was no chance to download a few megabyte over the slow, expensive and erratic GSM (Global System for Mobile Communications) network.

Environment setup as early as possible. Due to the infrastructural and governmental context in which ICTD research takes place simple issues might become much more complicated. This might be governmental processes, infrastructural limitations, or interoperability issues specific to developing country regulations. One example within our research was the setup of a telecom service provider in South Africa. Sorting out the contract details and setting up the mobile phone numbers took much longer than anticipated.

3.5   Deployment Methodology

During our research in the Sekhukhune RLL we came across some important issues that need to be taken care about to ensure a successful deployment of prototypes within the iterative prototyping approach.

Real Use Case - challenging but beneficial. In a Living Lab setup, like the Sekhukhune RLL, prototypes are deployed and tested within a productive real use case. This requires prototypes to be very robust right from the beginning to avoid disappointed end users. Even if it is more challenging to deploy prototypes in a real use case it provides much more valuable results than laboratory tests. A real world deployment immediately provides feedback about appropriateness, acceptance and business value and thus the prototype iteratively becomes a productive system.

Non-technical issues. Before deploying a prototype in the target use case it is necessary to get all use case stakeholders informed and convinced. Since the deployment of an iterative prototype, following our approach, is deployed within a real use case, it is influencing real life business. In the C@R procurement use case we had some issues with one use case stakeholder (delivery truck drivers) because they haven't been seriously trained about the new use case structure and thus felt threatened by the new technology. They are not the end users and have not been the focus of our technical ICTD development but since they belong to the use case they influence the entire research work as well.

Support and Administration. Iterative development with prototypes deployed in a real use case requires support for the end users. In our case the support was mainly done by the Infopreneur^{TM}, helping end users coping with the new system. The Infopreneur^{TM} as local contact is an effective way to continuously provide support to the end user. Beside the end user support, system administration capacities need to be set up to monitor the deployed system and to solve problems immediately. During our research work this was done by the prototype developers themselves using an administration interface to the system. Administrative access to all system components is an important feature when deploying components in rural areas far away from any system administrator. Even if it is just a prototype a broken system always endangers the important trust relationship between end user and system.

3.6   Evaluation and Monitoring Methodology

The evaluation phase is the last step of one iteration within an iterative development approach providing input for the next cycle. The final evaluation phase takes part in the end of the entire development work to evaluate the finel system in productive use. The monitoring phase utilizes the same methods but with focus on cheap long term options like log file analysis or the Infopreneur^{TM} collecting information during regular chats with the end users.

Direct observation. Direct observation is used to get feedback from the end user using several observation technologies - usability expert, human observer and questioner, screen cam, web cam. In 1st economy prototyping it might make sense to utilize this methodology in an early stage already to reveal major design faults. However, in the ICTD context direct observation only makes sense at a late prototype stage since the costs and time efforts to transport the equipment and researchers to the use case scenario and to facilitate the evaluation workshop are high. We've used direct observation to test a very late prototype stage deployed in natural settings and executed it as a scenario based contextual walkthrough. Even in this late prototype stage which was created using iterative development and continuously end user input the direct observation still revealed some valuable usability issues.

Questionnaire and Workshops. Since the prototype evaluation via questionnaires often fails because of low end user literacy we've again used the support of the

Infopreneur^{TM}. When using workshops for evaluation there is often the problem that the participants follow the comments of the person with the strongest voice or try to guess what the researchers want to hear and provide faked answers. When using the Infopreneur^{TM}as workshop host users felt much more comfortable talking to him instead of talking to foreign researchers. Users also feel less "watched" and act much more natural when observed by the Infopreneur^{TM}since he is "just another guy from the community". Workshops provide a good environment for open questions. In an environment with so many differences in infrastructure, government and culture these kind of open minded questions might bring up completely new topics.

Log Files. The most simple but very effective way to evaluate a system is to analyze the system log files providing accurate information on system acceptance and usability issues. We've utilized log files to evaluate the usage of a mobile client within the procurement use case. The log files revealed several usability issues regarding the mobile client user interface and also provided insights in the usage characteristics (e.g. times of order placement). In the ICTD context log files also can be used to find out more about the end user behavior like, how many SIM cards a user has or information on the literacy level.

4   Lessons Learned

During the three year research project in the Sekhukhune RLL we adapted research methods from the Mobile HCI research field towards a UCD and action research approach for technical ICTD. These lessons learned provide practical information for technical ICTD researchers and serve as input for the technical ICTD research body of knowledge. In this chapter we summarize lessons learned necessary to conduct valuable technical ICTD research.

Building trust with the target community is a major requirement. Without the trust of the users in a new use case design, the prototypes and business value the ICTD research falls flat - no user, no research. Action research and UCD significantly impact the daily business of end users and thus ICTD research comes with a huge footprint right from the beginning.

For effective technical ICTD research a local contact person with a good knowledge of the target community and environment, some IT knowledge and English language skills (e.g. Infopreneur^{TM}) is required. This person is important for a valuable execution of workshops, interviews, prototype tests, evaluation and for trust building in general. Using the Infopreneur^{TM}to observe end users provides much more relevant information since they don't feel observed by a foreign researcher but just have a chat with the well known community colleague.

An effective solution for conducting technical ICTD research is user centered iterative development in a real scenario. Beside benefits like the immediate validation by real users it also comes with some requirements like: when deploying a prototype in a real use case it becomes a running productive system and thus needs to be handled as such. Iterative development ensures the appropriateness of the solution regarding infrastructure, culture and governmental regulations.

Beside the technical challenges also human factors play an important role especially in ICTD research. The acceptance of a new technology or the adaptation of an existing use case often requires the "community effect". When introduced by a community member (Infopreneur^{TM}) end users are much more willing to trust in the solution and use it. During the user centered approach continuous contact to the end users is important to let them be part of the entire approach. Ignoring comments from end users might lead to frustrated end users endangering the entire research project.

On a research project level technical ICTD research needs to be consequent in what is promised and what gets delivered. A disappointed end user community will not support research activities anymore. ICTD research, if executed within a real use case, should have the clear goal of being self sustainable. In technical ICTD, this might not be the overall goal since it is only one part of the entire ICTD research. However, when conducting technical ICTD research in a real use case it becomes important to be aware of the risks and consequences of failure.

5   Conclusion and Future Work

In this paper we propose a user centered technical ICTD research approach utilizing adapted Mobile HCI research methods in the individual research lifecycle phases. The proposed methodology set has been successfully used within the C@R research project. The presented methodology set is an initial step towards a clear methodology outline for technical ICTD. We want to encourage other ICTD researchers to evaluate and contribute to this kind of literature to establish a shared information source about technical ICTD research.

Since there was almost no literature available providing guidance on how to execute effective technical ICTD research, most of the research results have been gathered by a "try and error" approach. The missing literature knowledge together with the action research approach in a real use case imposes a huge responsibility on the researchers not to make mistake. The wrong research methods not only could lead to inappropriate research results but also have a real negative impact to the end users.

The presented research results are based on one use case, which is representative for many other developing country research scenarios but however, it is only one example. To prove and improve the concept, the current approach will replicated and evaluated in another ICTD research scenario.

To make technical ICTD research more efficient, a next step will be to improve the currently inaccurate simulation environments in which developing regions contexts are simulated for prototype tests in laboratory settings. This will not replace iterative in-situ prototyping tests within the natural settings but it will decrease cost and time effort for those tests. The aim is to already eliminate most of the prototype bugs in laboratory settings before spending time and money for a field visit. With appropriate heuristics, laboratory simulations might become an effective "low-cost" technical ICTD prototype evaluation technique.

Beside the weak research methodology outline, to which this paper contributes to, missing definitions like "what defines a novice user" or "what is a common device in rural areas" are another weak part of technical ICTD research. Basic definitions like these could help finding a starting point for ICTD researchers. Future work will investigate in the creation of a set of definitions required to execute valuable technical ICTD research.

References

1. Heeks, R.: ICT4D 2.0: the next phase of applying ICT for International Development. IEEE Computer (2008)
2. Heeks, R.: The ICT4D 2.0 Manifesto: Where Next for ICTs and International Development? (2009)
3. Toyama, K., Ali, M.: Computing for global development: is it computer science research? ACM SIGCOMM Computer Communication Review 39(5), 40–43 (2009)
4. Donner, J.: Research Approaches to Mobile Use in the Developing World: A Review of the Literature. The Information Society 24(3), 140–159 (2008)
5. Horst, H., Miller, D.: The Cell Phone: An Anthropology of Communication (2006)
6. Kjeldskov, J., Graham, C.: A review of mobile HCI research methods. LNCS. Springer, Heidelberg (2003)
7. Veeraraghavan, R., Yasodhar, N., Toyama, K.: Warana Unwired: Replacing PCs with Mobile Phones in a Rural Sugarcane Co-operative. In: Proceedings of ICTD (2007)
8. Parikh, T.S., Lazowska, E.D.: Designing an architecture for delivering mobile information services to the rural developing world. In: Proceedings of the 15th International Conference on World Wide Web, Edinburgh, Scotland. ACM Press, New York (2006)
9. Parikh, T.S.: Proceedings of the CCC Workshop on Computer Science and Global Development. In: Proceedings of the CCC Workshop on Computer Science and Global Development, pp. 1-92, Berkeley (2009)
10. Friedland, C., Merz, C., v Rensburg, J.: Stimulating the development of networked enterprises: the added value of Collaborative Procurement in rural South Africa (2008)
11. Doerflinger, J., de Louw, R., Friedland, C., Mengistu, M., Merz, C., Pabst, K.: Mobile Commerce in Rural South Africa Proof of Concept of Mobile Solutions for the Next Billion Mobile Consumers. In: WoWMoM 2009, Kos (2009)
12. Ter Hofte, H., Lovborg Jensen, K., Nurmi, P., Froehlich, J.: Mobile Living Labs 09: Methods and Tools for Evaluation in the Wild. In: Mobile Living Labs 09 at Mobile HCI 2009 Conference, Bonn, p. 48 (2009)
13. Jones, M., Marsden, G.: Mobile Interaction Design. John Wiley & Sons, Ltd., Chichester (2006)
14. Toyama, K., Bernardine Dias, M.: Information and Communication Technologies for Development. IEEE Computer Society 41(6), 22–25 (2008)
15. Heeks, R.: Information systems and developing countries: Failure, success, and local improvisations. The Information Society 18(2), 101–112 (2002)
16. Doerflinger, J., Friedland, C., Merz, C., de Louw, R.: Requirements of a Mobile Procurement Framework for Rural South Africa. In: ACM Mobility 2009, Nice. ACM Mobility, New York (2009)
17. Baker, M.: The Challenges of Emerging Economies. Pervasive Computing 1536-1268, 40–46 (2006)
18. van Rensburg, J., Veldsman, A., Jenkins, M.: From Technologists to Social Enterprise Developers: Our Journey as ICT for development practitioners in Southern Africa (2007)

Preface

Network of the Future Conference deals with important paradigms for the post-IP generation: new architectures, knowledge and piloting planes, network virtualization, green technologies, sensor networks, mobile and wireless networks, and strong security. In these proceedings, these seven paradigms are described in different sections. From the material proposed in this book, it is possible to deduce what could be the future Internet or post-IP generation.

The papers presented in this volume were peer-reviewed by an international Program Committee, resulting in an acceptance rate of approximately 30%.

The first section introduces new architectures either based on ethernet or coming from some theoretical studies. Then, some "green technologies" are presented in detail: green network planning, green communications, and the smart grid. Sensor networks are at the basis of the next session with the Internet sensor grid and efficient transmission schemes. The proceedings also introduced high-security schemes for future fixed or mobile networks. Trusted networks and strong authentication methods are mainly described.

Network virtualization can provide a powerful way to run multiple networks, each customized to a specific purpose, at the same time over a shared substrate. This paradigm permits us to know what the transition will be toward IP or non-IP new architectures.

Performance and wireless networks are also analyzed in this book through different examples.

Thank you to the authors of the papers, the members of the Program Committee, and the reviewers. Without their dedication and active involvement, the conference would not have achieved its current high quality.

July 2010

Guy Pujolle
S.V. Raghavan

An Introduction to the Network of the Future

Guy Pujolle

University Pierre et Marie Curie (UPMC) – Laboratoire d'Informatique de Paris 6 (LIP6),
4 Place Jussieu, 75005 Paris, France
Guy.Pujolle@lip6.fr

Abstract. This paper deals with important paradigms for the future post-IP generation: Knowledge and piloting planes, network virtualization and strong closed authentication. We describe these four paradigms and finally we can deduce what could be the future post-IP generation. We first introduce the architecture and a high security scheme that can be deduced from a strong closed authentication where the customers can get a perfect privacy. Then, we describe network virtualization that can provide a powerful way to run multiple networks, each customized to a specific purpose, at the same time over a shared substrate. Finally, we describe the meta control environment based on Autonomic Networking, associated with a knowledge plane and a piloting plane. This piloting system will be able to control the Quality of Service (QoS) in IP networks and consequently responds to users' requirements.

Keywords: Network architecture, future Internet.

1 Introduction

The main objective of this paper is to present the design of a new Post-IP architecture that merge networks and clouds into a common and cohesive framework. The boundaries between networks and services as well as between future networks and clouds are frontiers that should vanish. Indeed, the two areas should merge. This will result in unprecedented flexibility, extensibility and elasticity in composition of public, private and hybrid infrastructures. Protocol stacks, services, applications and information systems will be deployed and instantiated on a need basis. Acquired or leased hosting platforms and execution environments will be released to reduce investment and operating expenses.

The focus of this paper is what makes this new architecture original and different from proposals and research that address services referred to as Software as a Service (SaaS) or Platform as a Service (PaaS) or Infrastructure as a Service. So, we propose a new architecture that could be at the basis of a post-IP Network and Cloud environment. This post-IP architecture is mainly based on

- a high degree of security,
- virtual networking within the cloud,
- a distributed piloting system.

The paper is divided into four main sections. Section 2 will describe the global architecture and introduces what could be the security in this network and cloud

A. Pont, G. Pujolle, and S.V. Raghavan (Eds.): WCITD/NF 2010, IFIP AICT 327, pp. 87–94, 2010.

architecture. Section 3 will describe the virtualization paradigm. Section 4 is devoted to the piloting system, and finally the last section will describe a very first test bed of the architecture.

2 The Architecture and Its Security

The envisioned network and cloud architecture is depicted in Figure 1. This architecture is composed of :

- A security plane allowing a high-level and mutual authentication of users and servers.
- A cloud plane involving the provisioning of dynamically scalable and virtualized resources as a service over the network.
- A knowledge plane storing information (data and metadata) and high level instructions, detecting when something goes wrong, and automatically feeding the piloting plane for fixing the encountered problem
- A piloting plane acting as intelligent intermediary between control and management entities and the knowledge plane taking into account network and service context.
- A management and control plane containing all algorithms ensuring management and control of virtual and physical resources.
- A virtualisation plane enabling the coexistence of multiple virtual networks on top of the data plane
- A data plane responsible for packet forwarding. This plane contains physical and radio resources to be optimized.

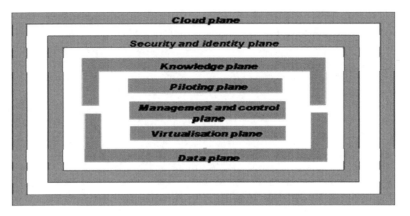

Fig. 1. The Network & Cloud seven-plane architecture

The cloud plane permits to work within the different cloud providers as if they were just one virtual cloud provider. This allows to see the virtual cloud as a service. This vision is described in Figure 2.

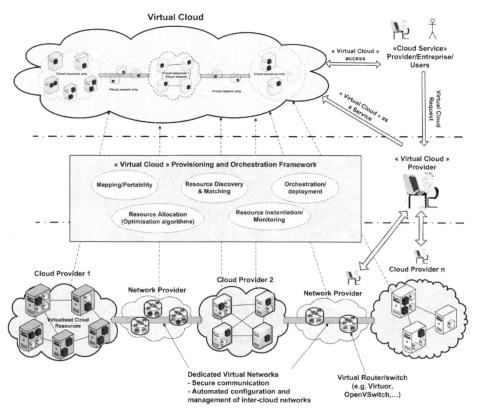

Fig. 2. The cloud environment

The security plane is based on SSL/TLS mutual authentication method and the new paradigm is the execution of SSL/TLS within a smartcard that must be available in all machines connected to the network. Privacy is realized through couples of smartcards so that the connections are anonymous but every connection can be controlled. So a key is necessary to enter the network as shown in figure 3. This solution avoids all logins and passwords and cannot be attacked by viruses and co.

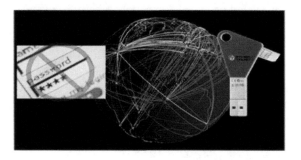

Fig. 3. The Network & Cloud global security

All accesses and mainly web accesses could be realized through an OpenID server or any other identity server with a high security and using the keys of the users. The user will need only his own key protected by his fingerprint (no login, no password, no attack).

3 Virtualization Plane

The virtualisation plane is of a prime importance: all equipments will be virtualized from routers to servers including boxes, firewall, PBX, gateways, etc. Then, the network element hardware is virtualised, enabling different virtual machines on a single device. The virtual networks are isolated from each other and are unaware of their virtualisation, the underlying physical network, or their concurrency to other virtual networks. Virtual machines may be created, destroyed, moved, cloned, started, and stopped on the underlying hardware.

The National Science Foundation (NSF) in the United States announced the Global Environment for Networking Investigations (GENI) [NSF-GENI]. Research that falls under the broad conceptual umbrella of this initiative will focus on designing new network architectures and services that range from new wireless and sensor devices to customized routers and optical switches to control and management software. The GENI project attempts to "de-ossify" the Internet and develop and architecture that will allow an easy migration strategy such that users and applications can migrate effortlessly from the current Internet to a future more robust and secure environment. This ''de-ossification ''is mainly based on the concept of network virtualisation.

Virtual machines provide the illusion of an isolated physical machine for each of the guest operating systems. A Virtual Machine Monitor (VMM) takes complete control of the physical machine's hardware, and controls the virtual machines' access to it.

Most projects on virtualization envisage a clear separation of roles between infrastructure provider and virtual network provider. The latter uses the former like an airline uses airport facilities. A virtual network provider allocates virtual resources provided by a number of different infrastructure providers.

The *OpenFlow* initiative is an alternative approach to providing facilities to test new network architectures. This was initiated by *the Stanford Clean Slate* project and is gaining support from both academia and major vendors. The idea is to exploit the fact that most switches and routers contain flow tables. The structure of these tables differs between vendors but all can support a certain common set of functions. OpenFlow provides the means for experimenters to act on the flow tables to alter the way the router forwards packets of certain flows. This conceptually simple facility can be used to create virtual networks.

Virtual network (VN) embedding or mapping has been addressed with various assumptions and scenarios by [Fan][Zhu][Yu][Ricci][Lu][Chowdhury][Houidi]. The general aim is to allow a maximum number of VNs to co-exist in the same substrate while reducing the cost for users and increasing revenue for providers. Optimal VN embedding satisfying multiple objectives and constraints can be formulated as an NP-hard problem.

To circumvent this difficulty, heuristic algorithms were used to assign VNs to substrate resources including greedy algorithms in [Zhu][Yu][Ri], customized algorithms in [Yu], iterative mapping processes in [Lu] and coordinated node and link mapping in [Chowdhury]. Since the underlying physical network can be highly dynamic, authors in [Hon] propose to decentralize the VN mapping by distributing the algorithm in the substrate nodes. The latter act as autonomous agents making decisions based on partial information built from their local knowledge and cooperation with neighbouring nodes.

The future Post-IP network will also look into the choice of the virtual resources to form virtual networks. The server where the virtual resources are stored could contain several thousand of different virtual objects.

Advanced algorithms must be developed to gather information about virtual networks, the load of virtual resources, the physical network, the remaining capacities of the physical network, and the currently supported and required services. Control schemes are crucial tasks in virtual networks since resources are shared by the different virtual networks. Two kinds of control could be addressed: resources control inside the physical networks and optimization of the performance of each virtual network.

4   The Knowledge and Piloting Environment

The knowledge and piloting plane imply an intelligence-oriented architecture using mechanisms able to control automatically placement of all virtual machines into the physical network. The approach is a particularly attractive solution as it involves the development of an automatic piloting system with intrinsic properties as autonomy, proactivity, adaptability, cooperation, and mobility.

The piloting system is definitely a new paradigm. Indeed, this system includes two sub planes that are aggregated in the piloting system. The two sub-planes are the knowledge plane and the configuration plane. So, within the piloting system some mechanisms have to be integrated to drive control algorithms. Indeed, the partition of the piloting system into two sub-planes has the advantage of simplifying the presentation but indeed these two sub-planes are strongly related: the knowledge and the configuration planes are developed in an integrated way. This piloting system has to drive the network through the control plane. For this purpose, the piloting system has to choose the best algorithms available within the control plane to reach the goal decided by the system. Due to the emergence in network environments of virtual control algorithms the choice of the best control algorithm is crucial. The second action of the piloting system is to decide about values to be given to the parameters of the different algorithms. As a summary, the piloting system has to configure the control plane which itself configures the data plane. Currently, in traditional networks the control algorithms are not chosen and the values of the parameters are selected through information collected directly by the algorithms themselves. The advantage of the piloting system is to react in real time on the behavior of the control algorithms. This piloting process aims to adapt the network to new conditions and to take advantage of the piloting agent to alleviate the global system. We argue that a distributed intelligent agents system could achieve a quasi optimal adaptive control process because of the following two points: (1) each agent holds different processes (behaviour, dynamic planner and situated view) allowing to take the most relevant decisions at every moment; (2) the agents are implicitly cooperative in the sense that they use a situated view taking into account the state of the neighbours.

This architecture has several advantages. First there is a simplification for recovering knowledge necessary for feeding the piloting system. Indeed, in current systems, every control algorithm has to retrieve by itself all the information necessary to execute the algorithm. This behaviour is shown in Figure 4.

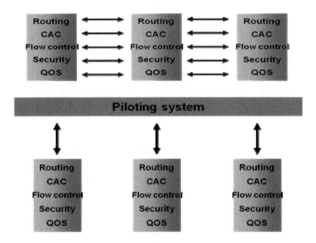

Fig. 4. Advantage of knowledge plane

In this situation, all the control algorithms (routing, CAC, flow control, quality of service, security, availability, mobility management, etc.) have the obligation to look for their own information to decide what is the best routing algorithm, what is the best flow control scheme, what is the best parameters for security control, etc. Indeed, all these algorithms need the same information or knowledge with a strong probability. Thus, in parallel, these algorithms have specific signalling packets to retrieve the same information. Moreover, the different algorithms are not correlated and could decide somewhat contradictory decisions. In the piloting architecture, the decision process is definitely different. This process is outlined in Figure 4. We see in this figure that the control algorithms are fed by the distributed Piloting System encapsulating the Knowledge plane where all the knowledge is. Moreover, this process permits to add new knowledge to pilot the control algorithms. For example, for a routing algorithm in a wireless mesh network, it is possible to add some knowledge on the electromagnetic field if available. This could be crucial in a real time or critical control process.

More precisely, the platform can be built on a multi-agent system to offer some intelligence. The multi-agent system is formed with agents situated in all network equipment (common to all virtual instances). The architecture is shown in Figure 5.

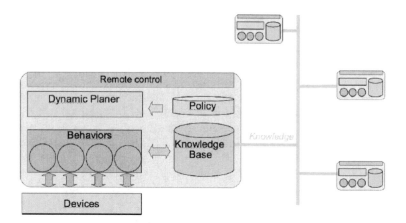

Fig. 5. The agent architecture

The different entities of the agent architecture are as follows. Each agent maintains its own view of the network on the basis of information obtained through the knowledge plane. This agent-centric view of the network is called the situated view, and is focusing on the agent's close network environment. This produces the knowledge basis that forms the knowledge plane.

The behaviours are autonomic software components permanently adapting themselves to the environment changes. Each of these behaviours can be considered as a specialized function with some expert capabilities. Each behaviour is essentially a sense->decide->act loop. Typical categories of behaviours are as follows:

• Producing knowledge for the situated view in cooperation with other agents.
• Reasoning individually or collectively to evaluate the situation and decide to apply an appropriate action, e.g. a behaviour can simply be in charge of computing bandwidth availability on the network equipment (NE). It can also regularly perform a complex diagnostic scenario or it can be dedicated to automatic recognition of specific network conditions.
• Acting onto the NE parameters, e.g. behaviour can tune QoS parameters.

Behaviours have access to the situated view which operates within each agent as a whiteboard shared among the agent's behaviours. Moreover, some behaviours can or cannot be used depending on the memory space and real time constraints. This behaviour exploits the tolerance for imprecision and learning capabilities. At this juncture, the principal constituents are fuzzy logic, neural computing, evolutionary computation machine learning and probabilistic reasoning.

The activation, dynamic parameterization and scheduling of behaviours (the rule engine is seen as a behaviour) within an agent is performed by the dynamic planner. The dynamic planner decides which behaviours have to be active, when they have to be active and with which parameters. The dynamic planner detects changes in the situated view and occurrence of external/internal events; from there, it pilots the reaction of the agent to changes in the network environment.

Finally a policy repository is necessary for defining the rules associated with the physical and the virtual networks.

5   Results and Conclusion

A very first prototype of the environment described above was realized. With this prototype a large number of new algorithms and paradigms have been tested. The platform assembles all the elements described in this paper and mainly the virtualisation process, the autonomic plane, the customized virtual networks and all the control schemes through the piloting system. The platform contains between 20 physical machines (industrial PC with quite a high potential). A physical machine is able of supporting 200 virtual machines. So for a total of 20 machines in the network we have been able to experiment a global network with 4 000 virtual resources. The first tests performed of this testbed show that the global throughput of the network can be doubled keeping the same quality of service.

Moreover, when the situated view is reduced to one hop, the piloting system is able to adapt the network in real time.

As a conclusion, we think that the future Post-IP architecture will contain a virtual plane and a piloting system able to optimize the placement of the virtual resource. A virtualized cloud will also necessary to permit the customer to get information in a quite simple and optimized manner.

References

[Fan]   Fan, J., Ammar, M.: Dynamic topology configuration in service overlay networks: A study of reconfiguration policies. In: Proceedings of the IEEE INFOCOM 2006 (2006)

[Zhu]   Zhu, Y., Ammar, M.: Algorithms for assigning substrate network resources to virtual network components. In: Proceedings of the IEEE INFOCOM 2006 (2006)

[Yu]   Yu, M., Yi, Y., Rexford, J., Chiang, M.: Rethinking virtual network embedding: Substrate support for path splitting and migration. ACM SIGCOMM Computer Communication Review 38(2), 17–29 (2008)

[Ricci]   Ricci, R., et al.: A solver for the network testbed mapping problem. ACM Computer Communication Review 33(2), 65–81 (2003); Lu, J., Turner, L.: Efficient mapping of virtual networks onto a shared substrate, Washington University, Technical Report WUCSE- 2006-35, (2006)

[Chowdhury]   Chowdhury, N.M., et al.: Virtual Network Embedding with Coordinated Node and Link Mapping. In: IEEE INFOCOM 2009 (2009)

[Houidi]   Houidi, I., Louati, W., Zeghlache, D.: A Distributed Virtual Network Mapping Algorithm. In: Proceedings of the 2008 IEEE International Conference on Communications, Beijing, China, May 19-23, pp. 5634–5640 (2008)

Future Internet Is by Ethernet

Marko Luoma, Raimo Kantola, and Jukka Manner

Aalto University, Department of Communications and Networking,
Otakaari 5A, 00076 Aalto, Finland
{firstname.lastname}@tkk.fi
http://www.comnet.tkk.fi

Abstract. This is a position paper describing an approach to the creation of the Future Internet. We argue that the new architecture must respond to two key challenges: (1) increase trust among Internet stakeholders and (2) provide cost efficient scaling of the network to new levels of capacity, number of users and applications. We argue that the solution is to redesign the Internet by gradually replacing IP with a carrier grade transport system. In practice such a packet transport system can be created based on Carrier Grade Ethernet. We call the resulting network Internet by Ethernet. We make some fundamental arguments and outline the research agenda that will open based on the premises that we describe.

Keywords: Future Internet, Packet Switching, Trust-to-Trust, Carrier Grade Transport, Ethernet.

1 Introduction

We argue that (1) the Internet should be redesigned not just from the technological perspective but also from the perspective of business models and contracts that are done based on the business model. It seems pointless to keep scaling network speeds up if the network is filled with traffic that the users do not want to receive and the capacity that is available is hogged by a few percent of the users. We argue that the way forward is to build a federated trust model into business models in order to change the operational principle from "assist the sender" to a more trustworthy "make the selfish and malicious actors pay".

To achieve this goal, from the technological perspective we argue that (2) Internet needs to be redesigned from the bottom-up in terms of the protocol stack. We have seen where the continuous adaptation to the application requirements has led the Internet infrastructure. Our starting point is the concept of Carrier Grade transport which we believe to be packet based and more specifically Ethernet like. Carrier grade transport provides a predictable, reliable and trustworthy service to user's packets. Based on the Carrier Grade transport system, the operators can enhance the level of trust in their business relationship. The goal is that the operators form a federated trust domain where the cost of transport to an operator will depend on the rating of the operator in the community. This federated trust domain is surrounded by a trust boundary towards the customers and users.

A. Pont, G. Pujolle, and S.V. Raghavan (Eds.): WCITD/NF 2010, IFIP AICT 327, pp. 95–107, 2010.
© IFIP International Federation for Information Processing 2010

The consequence of packet based carrier grade transport is profound. With the growing role of the transport system, the role of IP as the network integrator will be gradually decreased. This continues the trend started by MPLS that has become a general purpose network connectivity services platform.

We argue that (3) addressing in the Future Internet is recursive and addresses and customer (device) identifiers are separated. In recursive addressing, a chain of addresses points to a unique end-point. Recursive addressing lets users with a private address in one address space to communicate with users that are in a different private address space. This makes it possible to keep reusing IPv4 addresses. Thus the huge address space defined for IPv6 will not be needed. Address space boundaries co-inside with trust boundaries.

(4) The Future Internet by Ethernet has connection state on address space boundaries. Connection state stores everything that is needed to manipulate address and identity information in the packets. Packets are switched over the address space/trust boundaries and the switching state is managed by implicit signaling that is embedded in the normal traffic patterns that applications use [2], [5].

Inside trust domains forwarding entries can be created by the background routing process like in an IP network. Domains that provide traffic engineered protected connections may use centralized routing while domains providing best effort service may use distributed routing.

Routing is recursive and public network domains are completely isolated from consumer and corporate networks. This means that (5) the public services core does not reveal its addresses or methods of forwarding to its clients. Equally, consumer or corporate networks do not reveal their addressing information to other client networks nor to the core network [2].

Variants of Ethernet such as 802.1ah carry virtual LAN identifiers and service instance identifiers in packets. (6) This can directly be used to virtualize the public network.

(7) A Carrier Grade transport network has full OAM. It follows that connections across links and public network domains are supervised by OAM packet flows. This makes it possible to recover from link or node failures quickly and trace failures to services.

(8) Mobility should be a service on top of the transport network, i.e. mobility should be implemented on Ethernet level. We should also focus first on efficient local mobility, and add the design of global mobility on top.

Based on the arguments, a few initial comments should be made. Connection state and OAM make it possible to protect the users from malicious traffic and the public network from greedy traffic flows. Based on OAM, the traffic entering a public network can be smoothed to a fair share for the flow within network capacity. It will be possible to make use of the information gathered by the OAM system in the host's protocol stack as well as in the boundary elements leading to better end to end transport protocol algorithms and a fairer service. Exactly how far we can take this is a subject for research.

The concept of connection state on trust boundaries leverages the experience of Network Address Translators and stateful Firewalls. Instead of seeing such devices as a nuisance Internet by Ethernet sees them as key elements making Trust-to-Trust advocated by Dave Clark a networking principle rather than an afterthought. Instead of single sided switching usually implemented by a NAT, the new boundary nodes will use implicit signaling to create switching state both for the outbound and the inbound flows. For the customers to brave the creation of switching state for an incoming flow, new protocols leveraging the connection state will be needed. The goal is creating reasonable means for the target customer network to ensure that the incoming flow is legitimate. More details are in [2], [10].

The concepts of carrier grade and connection state will bring more control into the network. The result is that end users will have more freedom of creating end user services because the network is more trustworthy. The end user services must accept the fact that it is no business of the users to see how the public network is implementing its packet transport service edge to edge except in terms of the SLA parameters if such have been put into the contract.

The rest of the paper is organized as follows. Section 2 explains the principles we suggested above. Section 3 discusses migration. Section 4 comments on some obvious objections to the suggested approach. Section 5 outlines research directions that emerge based on the principles. In Section 6 gives a few conclusions and a summary.

2 Principles Explained

In this section we justify and explain the principles (1)(8) suggested. In the last subsection we discuss the scalability of what we propose.

2.1 Federated Trust-to-Trust

The problem of the current Internet is the fact that the technology supports only stakeholder relationships of a low level of trust. First the relationship of customers and network providers need to be addressed. Next the relationships between providers of the different legs on the end to end path need to be supported. We argue that we should see the end to end path as a chain of three trust domains. First is the originating user's trust domain. Next is the federated multi-operator trust domain that provides a public packet delivery service. The third leg is the trust domain of the target user. We show this concept in Fig. 1.

In an ideal world a customer knows that each network provider is tightly bound to provide reliable and secure (trusted) service. We may argue that current Internet aims to do this by the business model where transit and peering agreements are made with interconnecting provider domains. In an ideal world these contracts would form a chain of trust relationships between customers. However, this is not the reality as there are minimal incentives to secure the service - as the service which is agreed in contract is merely a reachability service and there is no control loop for assessing the performance of individual providers in the chain. Current interconnection infrastructure lacks the functionalities allowing the building of more sophisticated services with inbuilt trust.

What shall be changed from the current infrastructure and business model? For one, there needs to be a mechanism to rate providers based on their operational processes and their reputation in the market. As an incentive this rating should be reflected onto the interconnection charges. This operation resembles the way companies are rated by rating institutions for their liquidity. This rating affects the terms and margins which companies pay for their loans.

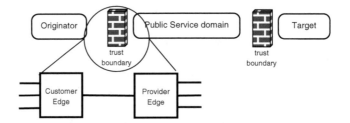

Fig. 1. Communication over Trust Domains

With a proper certification from a rating system, a provider can convince interconnecting providers on its ability to control the influx of traffic so that there is a minimal amount of malicious flows. This certification should be dynamic and based on a continuous rating process. Reputation of the provider should be based on the trouble ticketing of other providers and their customers. These tickets should be escalated onto a reputation system. The tickets are accumulated over a period of time by the reputation system. When the result is over a certain threshold relative to ratings over all providers, the rating of the provider should decrease and automatically increase the interconnection charges of that provider. Ideally, this should be reflected on the access price of individual customers. This will change the current network principle "help the sender" to a more trustworthy principle "help the receiver" by putting variable price for the sending of a packet.

2.2   Bottom-Up

A lot of work is currently being carried out with the idea that IP is the inviolate holy network integrator. Thus, a lot of work concentrates on functions above IP and in practice above TCP/IP. The official truth is that IPv6 will be the successor to IPv4. At the same time, the community is painfully aware of the problems inherent to IP networks. We argue that IPv6 does not meet current networking requirements. Stakeholders have legitimate needs of protecting their networks and their business that is carried over and with the network. A huge address space introduced by IPv6 does not address this need [1].

The users wish to control who can communicate with whom. Let us take two examples. (a) Mobile users are even more adverse to DDOS, SPAM and other unwanted traffic than fixed users. Depending on the pricing model, mobile users may have to pay for such traffic. The mobile operators do not want to see significant amounts of unwanted traffic being sent over the expensive air interface. The idea of a host based Firewall does not fit together with battery powered devices. If unwanted traffic is received for Firewall processing, it depletes the battery. One should note that the batteries in mobile phones last days because most of the time the mobile sleeps. (b) The idea of the Real World Internet tries to put sensors and actuators e.g. in people's homes on the Internet. We do not want other people to meddle with our homes unless we have contracted them to do so. Consequently, a huge address space giving every possible device a globally reachable address as in IPv6 is not a blessing, it is a problem.

Transport for the Internet has changed several times. First IP was carried over TDM lines borrowed from PSTN. The service scaled from modem speeds to 2Mbit/s. Frame relay allowed scaling the service to a few tens of Mbit/s. ATM increased the link speeds to several hundreds of Mbit/s. The current transport method - packets of synchronous digital hierarchy - scales up to 40Gbit/s. Scaling up from this level is done by adopting wavelength division with either 10Gbit/s or 40Gbit/s lambda rates. So, the transport method has changed each time when the maximum link speeds have increased by a factor of 15 to 65. Now the question is: what transport will be used for the next upgrade? We believe that the next electronic transport system will be packet based. In practice the protocol is called Ethernet. We are participating in the work towards 100Gigabit/s Ethernet and see that there is little interest of scaling synchronous transport further than what is currently available.

The reasons for this are the flexibility in division of resources, cost and power saving. Ethernet packets carry addresses and VLAN tags as identifiers for the packet owner. Neither of these is present in SDH frames. The presence of addresses in the basic frame has fundamental implications. One is that transport is asynchronous and the speed can be flexibly adjusted according to need. This is a good starting point for saving energy and network capacity. There is ongoing work towards energy efficient Ethernet in IEEE. Finally, we point to the price difference of POS and Ethernet interface boards in high speed core routers.

In the process of becoming the transport medium for public networks, Ethernet must become carrier grade. Backbone Ethernet connections need to become similar to SDH circuits, recovery from failures should be as fast as or better than in SDH and the service should be accurately managed by each operator. Broadcasting of unknown packets, MAC learning and spanning tree protocols need to be replaced by new solutions in Carrier networks. We have created an example solution in this direction in the ETNA project [3],[9], [10]. ETNA control and data planes support both Carrier Grade intra and inter-carrier native Ethernet networks. Another approach that seems more suitable for corporate networks based on distributed operation and DHTs is being designed and implemented in the Celtic 100GET project [4].

A packet based transport network delivers addressed packets from edge to edge. Most customer and corporate networks are based on Ethernet. So, what we have is a chain of Ethernets end to end. The result is that the role of IP routing is diminished step by step. The remaining role of IP is acting as an identity protocol and for a time, a domain wide routed protocol. In the face of such dramatic changes in the underlying protocol layers, it seems that we must look at the Future Internet starting from the bottom of the protocol stack, not from the applications.

2.3   Addressing, Identification and Routing

Unallocated IPv4 addresses will be exhausted in 2012. IPv6 has long been advocated as the remedy. However, this solution makes existing users pay for the new ones yet to be connected. The dual semantics of IP addresses has led to many difficulties in networking. IPv6 does not change this.

We propose an alternative way forward: let us keep reusing IPv4 addresses as many times it takes and let us re-invent the transport infrastructure as needed. Recursive addressing is possible with protocol stacks such as IP over IP, MAC in MAC, IP over MAC-in-MAC, etc.

We must decide how to identify users, their devices and services at the same time as we choose the addressing system. We argue that we have three options for the identities: (1) identities are random values or (2) we keep using IPv4 addresses as local user identifiers or (3) we reuse identities assured by the mobile network infrastructure in a new way. Introducing a new deterministic global identification scheme for users, hosts and services is costly. Mobile access to Internet is gaining momentum: the number of broadband mobile subscriptions has overtaken the number of fixed broadband subscriptions and grows faster than fixed access. So, leveraging the mobile infrastructure for brokering trust between users is starting to make sense.

In [2], [10] we suggest using random identifiers for users, hosts and services. A quick look at the birthday paradox shows that IP over IP does not scale for random IDs [2]. The ongoing work on Locator/ID Separation Protocol or LISP uses deterministic 32 bit values as End-point Identifiers [6]. Unfortunately, LISP requires that EIDs are globally unique leading to limited scalability. Let us note that it is sufficient to be able to create edge nodes that serve up-to a few million users communicating with several million targets. Only places where the IDs are processed are these edge nodes. Therefore, the random id does not need to be globally unique. It suffices that IDs are unique with high probability in the boundary nodes that will process the IDs. In [2], based on the Birthday paradox, we show that random identities in the order of 60 to 80 bits will be sufficient.

This argument leads to the protocol stack: IP over MAC-in-MAC. In parallel to IP other identity protocols can be used. For stepwise deployment, other stacks are easily accommodated as well.

This addressing structure leads to end to end forwarding over routed or bridged originating customer network (leg 1), followed by (leg 2) a public network that may be a routed Ethernet network like the one we created in ETNA and the terminating customer network (leg 3) that can also be routed or bridged. Leg 2 can be also for example an IP/MPLS network. This is shown in Fig. 1.

2.4 Connection State on Boundaries

The most important trust boundary is between the user (consumer or corporate) network and the public network. On this boundary we move from a private addressing scheme to a core addressing scheme. In our solution outbound packets are encapsulated to backbone frames and inbound packets are de-capsulated. This is similar to what LISP does without specifying any trust architecture.

We can break the boundary to customer edge (CE) and provider edge (PE) functions as shown in Fig. 1. In outbound packets, the customer edge replaces the source address with source id. For a given name of a target host or user or service, the ingress provider edge returns a destination id to a requester in a customer network. An outbound packet leaves the customer edge with source id and destination id information replacing address fields in the payload headers. Using connection state in the PE, the destination id will be appended by the destination address of the egress PE node. Upon reception of a packet to a destination id, the egress PE node finds the locally significant address of the destination and sends the packet to the customer edge. For an incoming packet, the CE will apply any reasonable means, we call packet access control, to find out whether the packet is legitimate or not. We have discussed such methods in [2]. The CE creates its own connection state and executes the policy created by the local network administrator.

The connection state on the boundaries can be leveraged to many uses. For example, multi-homing can be hidden from the core routing system, traffic engineering and packet access control can be stateful and thus more intelligent than simple filtering using rules.

CE processing outlined above renders NAT traversal based on UNilateral Self Address Fixing [7], [8] unnecessary. Any remote target is seen by a host as if residing in the local network. The messy application code related to NAT traversal can be dropped from applications. The downside is that new service description methods will need to be introduced. Instead of using IP addresses and port numbers (like in SDP), service description should use e.g. names and ports. For ease of deployment, the changes in hosts can be postponed by intelligent customer edge processing of packets as we show in [2].

2.5 Network Isolation

Name queries are routed through the CE and PE nodes. Part of the information returned by a name query is stored in connection state in PE and CE nodes. The principle is: *A customer network never publishes any address information. A public network does not show its addressing to customer networks.* As a result, the network structures are hidden.

Because each leg of the end to end connection uses its own forwarding /routing / switching system, network events such as routing configuration errors impacting one leg will not impact the other legs.

2.6   Network Virtualization

ISPs make their money from corporate connectivity while earning money from the consumer services is challenging. Therefore, virtualizing the infrastructure cost efficiently is important to ISPs. Nowadays, MPLS/VPNs and virtual routing are used for the purpose. Often customer Ethernet circuits are run over Pseudo-wires created using IP/MPLS. Depending on the level of traffic isolation, this can lead to a complex and thus a less than cost efficient network structure. Due to IEEE Ethernet lack of support for global networks, MPLS shim is necessary. However, our work in ETNA shows that it is rather straightforward to create a native Ethernet-based control plane that provides carrier grade control and lets the operators cost efficiently create virtual networks that span even several carriers. In another approach we are pursuing in the 100GET project, we can create virtual networks but also turn the Ethernet broadcast traffic into unicast based on Routing Bridges (rbridges) and DHTs, thus enabling the very basic Ethernet technology to scale.

2.7   OAM

In the carrier grade transport network we can run link level OAM, a less frequent OAM flow edge to edge over a domain and even less frequent OAM flow end-to-end. OAM packet frequencies can vary from milliseconds to seconds. Limiting factors are the number of parallel OAM sessions and functionalities that are bound to the sessions. It is rather straightforward to create simple fault notification on link level but to combine more intelligent aspects like resource control and quality reporting in each intermediate point to sessions is not simple.

This problem was touched by the work done with ATM available bit rate (ABR) traffic management. The optimization goal was to maximize network utilization with fair resource division by using OAM messages to convey indications of a fair amount capacity. This was, however, found to be complex to implement and impossible to manage in large networks. Optimizing the use of OAM flows and leveraging them for different needs is an ongoing research challenge.

2.8   Mobility

Most of the next 2 Billion new Internet users will be using a wireless connection. Most of them will do so through a mobile network. According to ITU, the number of mobile broadband subscriptions has overtaken the number of fixed broadband subscriptions. Any networking protocol and architecture that does not support mobile use, will be less than satisfactory and will lead to costly add-on solutions. We should design the Future Internet for mobile use in mind.

It may be argued that mobility is not the function of packet transport, but in large the result of mobility is the change of serving edge node and thus change in the transport connection. It is also true that in order to maintain maximal flexibility the base protocol should be as simple as possible and should therefore not bear the burden of individual functionalities - like mobility management. This leads to a layered structure where the protocol is not the dividing method rather the functionality that is pursued. This means that the base protocol can have extensions for performing value added tasks - like mobility, identity resolution or even charging.

In this respect, the overwhelming use for mobility is in the local access network. Thus, we need to make sure that the base packet transport supports natively the movement of the end-points, and even sub-networks - a concept that is available in IP networks as a complex add-on that barely works. Since Ethernet addresses are not tied to topology, mobility is easier than in IP. In our forthcoming design, mobility is implemented by the network without explicit support from end hosts. We are building such functionality over the rbridges technology. Support for global mobility can be added later, as the add-on when needed.

2.9   Scalability of the Approach

It is a legitimate concern whether the suggested approach with its heavy reliance on connection state on the network edge will scale. For cost efficiency reasons, we must be able to build large CE and PE nodes that can serve up-to several millions of users with their numerous applications. This is a topic for experimentation and research and a good challenge for the vendors.

An alternative is the model that operators give CE devices an address that is globally unique and the CE has a DHCP server that assigns dynamic IP addresses to users, hosts and services. These are used to identify users locally under one CES but never for global routing. The allocation of these identifiers can be e.g. per DNS request. The identifiers are stored in DDNS that can be part of the CE. The protocol stack stays the same as before, the difference is in the source and destination addresses carried in the inner Ethernet header. CE to CE forwarding is based on two NSAP addresses carried in the inner and the backbone Ethernet layers. One NSAP address points to a CES and the backbone has its own NSAP addressing for PE devices. Both NSAP addresses are carried in the DA fields of the respective Ethernet frame. The benefit is that PE processing per packet will be simplified.

In both the alternative model and the suggested one, the CE scalability has similar challenges as NATs do. In the alternative model, an identity for a user or host is allocated by the visited network. In the model using random identifiers, the id is allocated and managed by the home network. This leads to differences in the mobility architecture.

3   Migration

How to move from the present Internet to Internet by Ethernet? The suggested architecture has three tiers on which deployment and migration can progress rather independently of each other. Each of the tiers pursue a common goal of enhancing trust and providing cost efficient scaling of the Internet to higher capacity, cost efficient connection of wireless users and meeting the needs of new applications.

On the transport tier, the first step is that one operator decides to use an Ethernet core network once the technology matures. From the point of view of the carried traffic, Ethernet circuits, E-LANs and E-trees are as good as their IP/MPLS counter parts. These legacy systems can continue to be used in parallel.

On the access tier, the first step is a directory service that provides the information for the Ethernet CE and PE nodes. In another paper, we show how to use DNS for the purpose. Step 2 is that one or several Ethernet core operators start providing customer access at Ethernet layer to CE devices. In step 3, a customer network connected to such an operator can deploy a native Ethernet Customer Edge device and connect it to a PE device owned by an operator. The customer may optionally discontinue its IP connection to the Internet at the same time and access the legacy Internet through NATs hosted by an operator.

Deployment of solutions on the transport and access tiers requires no or minimal changes to hosts. Double-NAT traversal solutions may be reused. It would be clean that the applications that use IP addresses on the application level were revised to use names and other more suitable means of identification. For applications like FTP or SIP that use IP addresses as identifiers and transmit them to remote parties on a control channel, an application specific state machine in the CE function can be used eliminating the need for immediate changes in host software.

The highest in the suggested architecture is the tier of federated trust among the stakeholders. It fits nicely into the overall picture but can progress rather independently of the two lower tiers once cost efficient IP trace back becomes feasible. A way of supporting IP trace back is shown in [10].

Alternative and further strategies are also possible. For example, in the future we could design an end-host stack without IP at all. We could pursue removing IP headers from the packets traversing the core. All communication is done over Ethernet, i.e., transport protocols and their payloads are run directly over Ethernet. When communication with a legacy IP network is needed, we could use remote APIs on CE or PE devices to encapsulate the data into IP packets.

4   Objections and Counter Arguments

Networks with MAC addresses do not scale. Instead of a single MAC address, our approach uses the minimum of two independent Ethernet domains (customer and backbone) each with their own addressing. Scaling to large backbone networks is likely to be based on other than vendor assigned addresses. Nothing stops carrying NSAP like hierarchical addresses in the backbone frames. The address allocation can be managed by the operators. Also, by removing MAC-learning and spanning trees, the basic Ethernet will be scaled up.

Why would Ethernet be any better than IP? The question of forwarding protocol is secondary to control plane structure and allocation of functions in the network. IP has so much legacy that it is better to go for a clean break than try to keep patching IP. The recursive variant of IP over IP does not scale to mobile access [2]. LISP that also uses IP over UDP/IP has scalability limitations. The lack of support for carrier grade concepts in IP is fundamental. We can instead re-invent Ethernet, make it carrier grade and build a cost efficient technology that can be economically upgraded to the future link speeds. We can not communicate without layer 2. Ethernet is becoming ubiquitous. It has addresses in each frame. It is possible to leverage those for global communication. So, why not simplify the stack and get rid of some of the cost?

We have all this functionality in IP - why redesign it all for Ethernet? This is untrue. IP is fundamentally not carrier grade. Further development of IP networking technology has become very challenging because of the erosion of its fundamental principles of end to end and IP over everything. IPv4 addresses will be exhausted soon. Move to IPv6 is not well motivated. IPv6 does not help to hide networks from each other, it does not help to create trustworthy services and it does not help to virtualize the infrastructure. An accepted solution to multi-homing that is essential for mission critical connectivity of businesses to the core Internet is still missing. People want NATs even in IPv6 networks and we may end up with the same or worse routing scalability problems in IPv6 than what we have in IPv4.

It is true that we end up redesigning many functions that are present in current IP networks. Let's not worry about this. We have been doing this always in the history of networking for each new generation of technology. This is not the first and not the last time. Instead of complaining about it let's concentrate on improving the designs.

Why would be need this federated trust system - it can become a target for attack and fail. At the moment we fight unwanted traffic largely only by defense. We use NATs and Firewalls. However, the senders of unwanted traffic are professionals and the sending has become a business. We argue that we "the nice users" are at war and we are being buried in the infoglut. Let us recall that no war has been won by defense only. The Federated trust layer is a proactive response with the goal of making sending unwanted traffic unprofitable.

5   Research Directions

The outlined architecture is a subject for technical research, prototyping and experimentation. Results of the efforts in ETNA [9] and 100GET will be made and partially have been made available for others to build upon.

Fundamental research questions are: how far can we take the suggested trust architecture in term of technology and how can we introduce it in terms of politics and tussle among the stakeholders. The challenge is that probably a new global association of Internet Exchange is needed to govern the federated trust schema. Operation can be given to a private company on a competitive basis every few years.

Instead of starting from global politics, we may also start from better mechanisms for the customer/operator interface. There the challenge lies in finding a deployment path on which each step has an incentive for the critical stakeholders. Our proposal of Customer Edge Switching is easier to deploy than LISP because no "alternative topology" is needed. For CES that connects to an IP core, each access network and each corporate network can make an independent deployment decision [10].

Exact definition of the addressing used in Global Ethernet-like networks needs to be studied and agreed upon. We have made a proposal in ETNA.

Technical methods for protecting customer networks from unwanted incoming traffic are an important area of research although numerous methods known from other contexts can be reused here. New trust related protocols will be needed as well.

A fundamental issue is whether we trust the trust model or we concentrate on protecting the user by all means feasible while the user is engaged in communication with another user who she fundamentally does not trust irrespective of any network supported trust model. Probably, we must assume that no trust model can be absolutely relied upon.

Scalability of nodes that will store connection state will be an important topic.

New means for describing identity in applications need to be studied and defined. These include for example new guidelines of use or a new version of Service Description Protocol. Interactions of the suggested addressing and identification schemas with applications and their impact on the mobility architecture need to be studied.

Mobility management as such in the context of the Ethernet protocol family is an important topic.

Finally, a carrier grade packet transport system that is energy efficient is needed. Probably making full use of the energy efficient Ethernet that introduces variable link speeds for the sake of energy efficiency will require traffic engineering on Ethernet layer.

6   Summary

We have implemented a rather comprehensive prototype of an Ethernet based carrier grade transport architecture that this paper relies upon [1], [3], [9]. We have also implemented a corporate network Ethernet routing solution that seeks to eliminate broadcasting due to ARP and unknown target addresses from bridged networks [4].

In both contexts, we have made our first attempts to integrate mobility management into the Ethernet protocol family. More remains to be done.

This paper seeks to generalize the ideas that lay behind our prototypes.

We propose to make the trust architecture the starting point of designing the Future Internet. We propose a new path of technology development that will seek to satisfy the increasing needs in trusted and scalable communications. Based on the architecture design, we discuss migration challenges and approaches and outline a number of research topics for the networking community.

Acknowledgments. Our thanks go to our partners in ETNA and 100GET projects.

References

1. Kantola, R., Luoma, M., Lamminen, O.-P.: Transport for Carrier Grade Internet. In: 1st IEEE Below IP Networking WS at GlobeCom, Honolulu (2009)
2. Kantola, R.: Implementing Trust-to-Trust with Customer Edge Switching. In: AMCA in Connection with AINA, Perth (April 2010)
3. Lamminen, O.-P., Luoma, M., Nousiainen, J., Taira, T.: Control Plane for Carrier Grade Ethernet Network. In: 1st IEEE Below IP Networking WS at GlobeCom, Honolulu (2009)
4. Varis, N., Manner, J.: Minimizing ARP Broadcasting in Trill. in: 1st IEEE Below IP Networking WS at GlobeCom, Honolulu (2009)
5. Virtanen, L.: Communicating Globally Using Private IP Addresses, M.Sc thesis, Comnet/TKK, Espoo, Finland (2009)
6. Farinacci, D., Fuller, V., et al.: Locator/ID Separation Protocol (LISP) (January 2010) draft-ietf-lisp-06.txt
7. Behaviour Engineering for Hindrance Avoidance (Behave), http://www.ietf.org/dyn/wg/charter/behave-charter.html (referred January 31, 2010)
8. Daigle, L. (ed.): Informational RFC 3424, IAB Considerations for UNilateral Self-Address Fixing Across Network Address Translation (2002)
9. ETNA web site, http://www.ict-etna.eu/index.html
10. Routed End-to-End Ethernet, Protocols, http://www.re2ee.org

On the Way to a Theory for Network Architectures

Thi-Mai-Trang Nguyen

University Pierre et Marie Curie (UPMC) – Laboratoire d'Informatique de Paris 6 (LIP6),
4 Place Jussieu, 75005 Paris, France
Thi-Mai-Trang.Nguyen@lip6.fr

Abstract. The design of the future Internet is facing real challenges on network architecture. Attempts to resolve the issues related to naming/addressing, middle boxes, QoS-Security-Mobility interactions, cross-layer and inter-domain usually lead to endless debates. This is because the structure of the Internet has become too complex and has evolved with new functions added which are not always compatible with the existing functions. In order to analyze the architecture of the Internet in a strict manner, it is necessary to understand in depth the composition of functionalities within a protocol or between protocols. This paper presents a study on the composition of network functionalities and highlights future directions towards a theory for network architectures which includes the principles that network architectures should follow to ensure the normal operation of the member functions, detect all possible conflicts between them as well as figure out impossibilities.

Keywords: Network architecture, future Internet.

1 Introduction

The architecture of the Internet has been much evolved since its creation. In comparison with the beginning of its design, the today's Internet has many new protocols, communication paradigms, device types and applications. Important new protocols include Real-time Transmission Protocol (RTP) [1] for real time multimedia transmission, Mobile IP [2] for mobility at Internet Protocol (IP) level, IPsec [3] and Transport Layer Security (TLS) [4] for security at IP and transport levels respectively, SCTP [5] for multihoming, and IPv6 [6] for a new addressing scheme. New wireless access technologies such as Wi-Fi, Wi-Max, GPRS/3G/4G increase the mobility in the Internet and allow new communication paradigms such as ad-hoc networking and vertical handover. High speed access technologies such as ADSL and optical fiber offer a higher bit rate to end-user enabling service convergence between voice, television and data in the Internet at large scale.

When adding new protocols into the Internet, new architectural elements have been introduced. Mobile IP has defined a Home Agent to make IP address changes transparent to the correspondent node. Network Address Translation (NAT) [7] entity has been added into IP router to translate addresses between private IP addresses and public IP addresses. The complexity of the Internet architecture has been increased with new protocols and elements added. Many conflicts have been raised in the

A. Pont, G. Pujolle, and S.V. Raghavan (Eds.): WCITD/NF 2010, IFIP AICT 327, pp. 108–119, 2010.
© IFIP International Federation for Information Processing 2010

literature. NAT and firewalls conflict with the end-to-end principle of the Internet [8]. Wireless link and mobility make Transmission Control Protocol (TCP) congestion control confuse the reason of packet loss and get poor performances [9]. When incompatible design principles are implemented within the same network without regard to the presence of each other, the protocols cannot operate properly to provide the services expected from the design. The general consensus of the research community is that the methodology of continuously patching the Internet is not sustainable with the continuing growth on size, demands and complexity.

Future Internet design has become a federating theme of European research since 2007 with the activities in the 7th Framework Programme (FP7) [10]. The FP7 4WARD project [11] follows a clean-slate approach to rethink the design of the Internet architecture from scratch taking into account current user needs and technological advents on transmission and devices. Two of main studies carried out within the 4WARD project are the Generic Path (GP) concept [12] and the Architectural framework [13]. The Generic Path concept defines basic entities needed to support a variety of communication paradigms and enable the dynamic setup and control of communication paths which can be rich in functionalities. The Architectural framework defines the concepts of Netlet and Strata as two basic entities encapsulating the functionalities provided by the composed functional blocks. In both studies, the composition of network functionalities plays an important role in the design of protocols for Generic Path, Netlet or Strata. This paper presents a study on network functionality composition which can be used during the design of protocols encapsulated within these entities. This study can be also useful for network protocol design in general and may be combined with existing theory such as graph theory for a theory of network architectures.

The organization of the paper is as follows. Section 2 presents the relationship between network architecture and the composition of functionalities. Section 3 proposes taxonomy of main network functionalities within a network. Section 4 describes the order which can be followed during the protocol design to integrate network functionalities into a protocol. Section 5 presents the design of a multihoming protocol based on functionality composition. Section 6 discusses the possibilities to integrate the functionality composition principles into existing communication theory for a theory of network architecture. Finally, section 7 concludes the paper.

2 Network Architecture

Network architecture specifies the elements defined within a network, their functionalities and the communication between them. Elements can be physical elements or logical elements. Logical elements are defined and associated with different functionalities but may be implemented within the same physical entity in practice. For example, the Session Initiation Protocol (SIP) architecture [14] defines the proxy server and the registration server as two elements with two distinct functionalities, one relaying the SIP requests towards the destination and the other maintaining the binding between SIP address and IP address, but they can be implemented within the same physical machine in practice. The communications between elements are defined as interfaces and protocols. The Global System for Mobile Communications (GSM) architecture [15] has named interfaces between elements and specifies the protocols used over each interface. The Internet architecture only specifies the protocols between the elements without naming the interfaces.

The Internet that we have today relies on the interconnection of many networks following different architectures, one relying on or collaborating with another. The interconnection between networks can follow the layer model, a.k.a. the Open System Interconnection (OSI) model, or in a collaborating model which is not clearly layered. For example, the IP network using the IP protocol relies on the underlying networks which can be Ethernet, Wi-Fi or cellular networks and have completely different network architectures and protocols. This interconnection follows the layer model in which the IP packets are encapsulated within the underlying network protocol's Protocol Data Unit (PDU). However, the collaboration between SIP and RTP is not layered but rather shares the same layer. SIP has its own architecture with User Agent, Proxy Server, etc. and RTP has its own architecture with sender, receiver, translator and mixer. We can consider the nodes supporting the SIP protocol as a sub network and the node supporting the RTP protocol as a sub network. These sub networks co-exist and provide complementary functionalities which are signaling and transport. This concept of sub network corresponds to the concept of Strata [16] or compartment [12] defined in the 4WARD project.

Stratum is modeled as a set of nodes containing functionality for data processing, and a medium which defines how data can be transferred between nodes in the stratum [16]. The nodes within a stratum correspond to the elements defined for a network. The medium corresponds to the communication protocols between them. Compartment is defined as a set of entities with an associated namespace and they can communicate between them using a common (set of) protocol(s) [12]. The entities within a compartment correspond to the elements defined for a network. They can use a protocol or a protocol suite defined for the communication between them. The communication between entities within a compartment is defined as a GP. Both stratum and compartment are expected to be composed not only in a layering manner but also in an arbitrary manner. While stratum concept characterizes the relations between strata by service provider-customer relationship via SSP and peering relationship via SGP, the compartment concept studies the relations between compartments by looking inside the nodes participating in different compartments. It's inside these nodes that the GPs belonging to different compartments are interconnected via hooks or Mediation Point. A hook table can be considered as a simple realization of Mediation Point. More complex Mediation Point can realize complex functionalities such as multiplexing, routing, switching, or scheduling to interconnect different GPs.

While both stratum and compartment can model any network by composing the specified strata or compartments in a flexible manner, there is a need to analyze the interaction between the functionalities encapsulated within these strata or compartments and determine the design trade-offs when composing the functionalities. The study on functionality composition and interaction is also useful to solve the issues within the current Internet. The protocols added to the Internet to provide some new functionality may have bad impact on the functionalities provided by the existing protocols within the network. This study will help network architects for a better design when adding functionalities within a layer or a protocol as well as when adding a layer or a protocol into a protocol stack or a protocol set.

3 Network Functionalities

When having a look at the functionalities that we can have within a network, we can see that network functionalities can be divided into six categories as shown in Fig. 1.

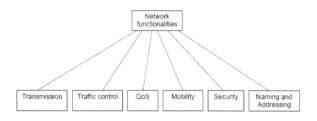

Fig. 1. Network functionality taxonomy

The *transmission* functionality category includes functionalities such as sending, receiving, forwarding, routing, switching, storing, and processing PDUs. Data transmission is the basic functionality in any communication system. The simplest communication system is composed of two nodes, one sending data and the other receiving data without any other additional functionality such as QoS, naming/addressing or traffic control. A more advanced network node could also store data along the path such as in the case of Delay Tolerant Network [17] or even process data in case of network coding [18].

The *traffic control* functionality category includes flow control, error control, congestion control, and reordering control. Flow control is responsible to control the data rate at the sender. Error control deals with errors occurring during the transmission. Congestion control reacts to the congestion experienced in the network. Reordering concerns the out-of-order transmission and puts PDUs back in order. These functionalities can be composed and integrated into a protocol according to the requirement. For instance, if we add error control or flow control functionality to the IP protocol, we will have a network layer protocol with error control or flow control. These functionalities are not dedicated to the transport layer or any other specific layer. A typical example of a protocol using error and flow control is HDLC (High-level Data Link Control) [19], a protocol at layer 2.

Similarly, QoS, Mobility, Security, and Naming/Addressing are main functionality categories in a communication network which are composable. Queuing discipline and admission control are parts of *QoS* functionality group. Handover and location management are examples of *Mobility* functionality group. Authentication, authorization, encryption, data integrity, and key distribution are elementary functionalities of the *Security* functionality group. Naming schemes and name resolution techniques are part of the *Naming/Addressing* functionality group.

4 Composition of Functionalities

We can design new protocols and get a desired network by composing the functionalities, or more concretely composing the functional blocks implementing the functionality needed. Fig. 2 illustrates the idea of functional composition.

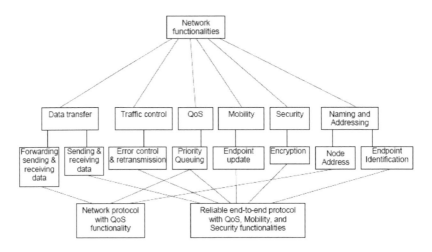

Fig. 2. Examples of functionality composition

As illustrated in Fig. 2, we have in the first composition a network using an addressing scheme, with the ability of sending, receiving and forwarding data, with QoS support (e.g. by selecting the Priority Queuing discipline [20]). In the second composition, it is completely possible to select the functionalities needed to design a new reliable end-to-end protocol with QoS, Mobility, and Security functionalities. This protocol uses an endpoint identification scheme (i.e. node addresses and port numbers). The reliable transmission is provided by the Error control and retransmission functionalities. This protocol can also provide QoS because it uses Priority Queuing in the terminal to serve different connections. To provide security functionality, it integrates an encryption algorithm for user data encryption. To support mobility of endpoint, a functionality detecting endpoint changes and updating endpoint identification can be invented and integrated to the protocol.

Lessons learned from the design of protocols in the Internet [21] show that show that the composition of functionalities should follow the steps illustrated in Fig. 3. In the first step, network architect should consider how to identify uniquely the entities participating in the protocol or in the protocol suite. Depending on the size of the network, flat or hierarchical addressing can be chosen. The size of the address is also chosen based on the size of the network in term of number of participating entities. The architect must decide whether a completely new and independent identifier scheme needs to be defined or an existing identifier scheme can be partially reused. For example, TCP endpoint is identified uniquely within the network by a port number, the TCP protocol number and the IP address. This identifier scheme reuses the IP address which is the identifier scheme of the IP protocol. Mobility has impact on addressing design. If the identity scheme of a protocol reuses the whole or part of the identity scheme of another protocol, the change of address happened within the underlying protocol due to mobility can break the normal operation of the protocol under design. This is the case of mobility issue with the TCP and IPsec protocols. Multi-homing protocol such as LS-SCTP (Stream Control Transmission Protocol for Load Sharing) [22] necessitates two levels of identifier, association level and path level. Virtual circuit based protocol uses two identifier schemes in a collaborative manner, address for signaling and label for data switching. When two protocols use two independent identity schemes, the architect should choose the method for addressing translation such as ARP-based method or address translation server. IP and Ethernet use ARP-based method while ATM (Asynchronous Transfer Mode) [23] and IP use address translation server. Finally, if network architect wants to use a naming scheme in conjunction with an addressing scheme, the naming scheme and the name resolution method have to be defined.

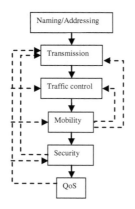

Fig. 3. Order of functionality composition

In the second step, the transfer mode and other details related to data transmission should be defined. In this step, network architect should determine whether the protocol is byte oriented or message oriented, connection oriented or connectionless, and define the minimal PDU format (e.g. PDU length or payload length). Except for end-to-end protocol, the architect should consider the functionalities integrated into intermediate nodes such as routing, multiplexing, switching, duplicating, storing and coding. Depending on the functionality selected, necessary control information will be added into the PDU header and necessary algorithms (e.g. routing algorithm) will be integrated into the protocol as the behavior of intermediate nodes.

In the third step, traffic control mechanisms should be defined. Traffic Control is related to the way to moderate the data rate or to protect data against errors. If there can be errors during the transmission and the application does not tolerate errors, error control such as error detection (e.g. CRC - Cyclic Redundancy Check) or error recovery (e.g. FEC - Forward Error Correction) should be integrated into the protocol. Necessary behaviors of the participating entities, necessary control information carried in the protocol header, and redundant information should be integrated into the protocol. If the application needs in order delivery, sequence number should be added. If the application does not tolerate data loss, retransmission should be defined. If there is a need to avoid overflow that the receiver or there is a need for a fair resource sharing between communications, or there is a need for control the sending rate of a communication, flow control should be integrated. If there is a need to react to network congestion, congestion control should be defined. For each type of control, there are many algorithms available along with the necessary control information to be carried in the header.

In the fourth step, mobility support should be considered. A protocol supporting mobility needs mechanisms reacting to the consequences due to mobility. If the identifier (e.g. IP address) can be changed due to mobility, binding update mechanism should be defined. Binding update can be end-to-end (e.g. SHIM6 [24] or SCTP) or endpoint-to-network (e.g. Mobile IP). If the topology is changed due to mobility, dynamic routing with route updates is necessary (e.g. ad-hoc routing protocol). During this step, it is necessary to check whether the design in steps 2 and 3 need to be adapted. For example, trigger for routing update due to mobility should be integrated into the routing protocol defined in step 2. Handover trigger should be defined. Path condition changes requiring an adaptation of flow control and congestion control parameters after a handover should be taken into account in traffic control mechanisms defined in step 3.

In the fifth step, security should be considered. Basic security services such as authentication, authorization, and data encryption should be integrated into the protocol depending on the application's needs. For each security service, mechanisms, algorithms along with necessary message exchanges should be integrated into the protocol. Many well known authentication methods, authorization mechanisms, and encryption algorithms are available in the literature. Each security service can be integrated in different steps. Authentication and authorization can be integrated into connection establishment defined in step 2. Encryption can be integrated into the transmission mechanism defined in step 2 before sending data at the receiver or intermediate nodes. Mobility should be taken into account during the design of security. Authentication may need to be triggered after a handover. For example, 802.11 terminal needs to be authenticated when changing to a new access point.

In the sixth step, QoS should be considered. As all other categories can impact the QoS of the communication, QoS design is put at the end of the composition procedure to take all these impacts into account. Different dedicated QoS mechanisms such as explicit resource reservation (e.g. Intserv-RSVP [25]) and class-based QoS provisioning (e.g. Diffserv [26]) are available. Each QoS mechanism will need additional message exchanges (e.g. reservation messages) and algorithms (e.g. scheduling algorithms such as priority queuing and weighted fair queuing) to be integrated into the protocol or the protocol suite. The design during all the last steps has impact on the QoS offered to the communication. Virtual circuit facilitates the resource reservation or resource provisioning because we know the nodes belonging to a path and these nodes can keep reservation state for the communication while it's hard to provide QoS in datagram (i.e. routing based) network because every node within the network may involve in the communication. Packet size has impact on the delay. Flow control and congestion control mechanisms have great impact on the throughput or the bandwidth offered to the communication. Retransmission increases the delay. Handover introduces data loss. Interference reduces the bandwidth offered. Security at the same time introduces delay and increases the required bandwidth. Multi-homing can increase packet reordering. These impacts are architectural trade-offs and should be considered in this step regarding QoS requirements of the application. Refinements of the design in the previous steps (e.g. soft handover, pre-authentication, flow control and congestion control adaptation, QoS routing) should be identified and integrated into the protocol.

There exist a large number of network functionalities in both data and control planes within a network. The above discussions show that each functionality can have different implementations. Mobility can be supported by end-to-end or end-to-network binding updates. QoS can be provided by per-flow reservation or class-based priority. Security can be provided by public key or secret key encryption. The choice of specific implementations depends on the degree of the application's requirements on each feature. The interoperability between functionalities should be check during the design following the six steps described in this section especially regarding architectural trade-offs. As the relations between functionalities are complex, the functionality categories and the six steps are organized in the way that these impacts can be all checked. To minimize the protocol refinements, network architect should take important integrations between functionalities into account in advance. If the integration between security and naming/addressing is intended (e.g. Host Identity Protocol [27]), the integration can be done during the first step and only checked and refined during the fifth step. If the integration between QoS and transmission is intended (e.g. QoS routing), the integration should be considered in the second step when designing routing protocol and checked or refined during the last step.

5   Example of Protocol Design

In this section, we will use the procedure of functionality composition presented in section 4 to design a transport protocol supporting multihoming for mobile terminals. Today's mobile terminals are equipped with several interfaces. However, transport protocols widely used by applications do not support multi-homing feature. TCP and UDP do not simultaneously send data over several interfaces. If an application wants to benefit from the bandwidths coming from several interfaces, flow distribution over multiple TCP or UDP connections must be implemented within the application in an ad-hoc manner. The objective of this design is to have a new transport protocol in which the support of multihoming and mobility are in the first priority, with a minimum support of QoS, security and traffic control. It's worth noting that the specification of the requirements of the protocol and hypothesis on network infrastructure should be much more in detail and precise at the beginning. In this paper, the requirement details and hypothesis will be presented during the design to justify the design choices. In practice, network architect should make a list of detail requirements and hypothesis before starting the protocol design. If the requirements and hypothesis change, the designed protocol(s) may have fundamental changes.

In the first step, we consider the Naming/Addressing functionalities. As we are designing a transport protocol for IP networks, we can follow the design of current transport protocol using a port number, protocol number and IP address to identify uniquely a protocol endpoint within the network. The protocol number should be carried within the IP packet while the port number is carried within the transport protocol PDU. Lesson learned from SCTP shows that for multihoming support, each endpoint should be identified by a list of IP addresses instead of a single IP address. The communication between the two endpoints is called an association. Each path within this association is identified by a pair of source IP address and destination IP address. We suppose that each interface is associated with one IP address. No new naming scheme is needed. The organization of the identifier scheme used in this protocol is shown in Fig. 4.

Fig. 4. Identifier scheme used in the multihoming transport protocol

In the second step, we consider the transmission functionalities. We expect to have a multi-homing transport protocol in which data can be sent over different paths associated with different available interfaces. That means we need a flow distribution functional block which distributes data over several paths. Without much consideration about QoS, we can put in this functional block a simple scheduling algorithm which is Round-Robin in which the first PDU is sent over the first path, the next one over the second path and so on. As stream based transmission of TCP is quite complicated in an unnecessary manner in comparison with the requirements of the protocol under design, we decide to use message-based protocol like UDP. Multi-streaming feature like SCTP are judged as unnecessary. Routing or forwarding is not necessary because this is an end-to-end protocol. This is a connection oriented protocol in which a minimum amount of control information is exchanged before sending data between endpoints. The list of IP addresses of each endpoint are exchanged for the maintenance of path list in each endpoint. Message size can also be determined during this exchange if specified in the requirement list. Otherwise, a default value can be defined for the protocol.

In the third step, traffic control is considered. For the sake of simplicity, only sequence number is required for reordering packets and loss detection at the receiver. Flow control and congestion control are not needed. Simple error detection is necessary for PDU header.

In the fourth step, mobility support is considered. End-to-end binding updates learned from SCTP are selected for mobility support in order to reserve the end-to-end communication paradigm of the Internet, which can be considered as a hypothesis or requirement for the protocol design. End-to-end binding update necessitates the definition of control messages for updating with the other endpoint the changes of IP address due to a handover. This binding update helps the other endpoint to avoid sending data to an unreachable address. We can also suppose that there is not mobile IP or SHIM6 used within network. If IP address used as part of endpoint identifier never changes, binding update and mobility support in term of IP address changes are not necessary.

In the fifth step, security is considered. For example, a simple secret key-based authentication with challenge-response and a simple secret key-based encryption are required. Authentication will be integrated within the connection establishment. Data encryption is done for user data before transmission over a path.

In the sixth step, QoS is considered. Suppose that no special QoS constraint in term of delay bound, minimum bandwidth, and jitter are defined. If some QoS requirements are defined, hypothesis about the network infrastructure (e.g. whether the network infrastructure can provide some bound delay should be checked in order to determine whether the QoS requirements of an end-to-end protocol can be met by integrating some QoS mechanism. For example, jitter can be ameliorated by using a buffer at the receiver.

The protocol has been implemented in C++ [12] for the proof-of-concept of functional composition in network protocol design and for further studies on multihoming transport protocol design.

6 Towards a Theory for Network Architectures

Discussions and examples presented in the previous sections show that network functionalities can be classified and flexibly composed during network protocol design. The composition of functionalities within one protocol is quite simple and controllable. Within a protocol suite, the interaction between functionalities provided by different protocols is more complex and will be subject to another paper. Functionality composition principles integrated with existing theories such as graph theory and queuing theory may lead to a theory for network architectures in which both functionalities and performances of a network are evaluated. Tools for both simulation and prototype are needed for functional and performance evaluation. Research on Future Internet Architecture [29,30] shows that a theory for network architecture design and evaluation is needed.

Network architecture encapsulating elements with defined functionalities and communication protocols between them needs to be evaluated for both functional and performance perspectives. Conflicts or design trade-offs between functionalities should be integrated within the design and evaluation tools (e.g. simulator). An end-to-end protocol using IP address as endpoint identifier put over an IP infrastructure with the presence NAT elements should be detected as a conflict on design principle. A multihoming transport protocol wishing may not be able to sent data over a specific interface if the routing protocol at the network level is only based on the destination address.

The composition of functionalities principles integrated with graph theory can also be used to validate the functional design of a network. Two nodes which don't have direct link between them cannot be reachable one by another if there is not forwarding functionality implemented within intermediate nodes.

In a real test-bed, useful information related to network functionality composition should be available to be collected by an architectural validation program which can detect architectural conflicts or trade-offs.

Within the 4WARD project, some initial integration of functional composition principles within the GP concept and the architectural framework is in progress [11]. Within the GP concept, the functionalities are composed within the Mediation Point. In the architectural framework, the functionalities are composed by the composition of functional blocks during the Netlet and Strata design.

7 Conclusions

This paper considered the interaction and composition of network functionality as an important piece towards a theory for network architectures. Taxonomy of network functionalities and a procedure to compose them during network protocol design have been presented. A simple example of multihoming protocol design based on composition of functionality has illustrated the concept. Further directions towards a theory allowing designing and evaluating network architectures have been highlighted. In the next steps, studies on functionality composition and interaction within protocol suite and between networks are needed. Combination between the obtained principles and existing theory in communication networks is an interesting research topic. Tools for both simulation and prototype are also necessary.

Acknowledgments

This work has been partially funded by the FP7 4WARD project and the ANR 3MING project. The author would like to address special thanks to Martin Johnsson, researcher at Ericsson EAB for his useful comments and discussions within the 4WARD project's works.

References

1. Schulzrinne, H., Casner, S., Frederick, R., Jacobson, V.: RTP: A Transport Protocol for Real-Time Applications. RFC 3550 (July 2003)
2. Perkins, C.: IP Mobility Support for IPv4. RFC 3220 (January 2002)
3. Kent, S., Atkinson, R.: Security Architecture for the Internet Protocol. RFC 2401 (November 1998)
4. Dierks, T., Allen, C.: The TLS Protocol Version 1.0. RFC 2246 (January 1999)
5. Stewart, R.: Stream Control Transmission Protocol. RFC 4960 (September 2007)
6. Hinden, R., Deering, S.: Internet Protocol Version 6 (IPv6) Addressing Architecture. RFC 3513 (April 2003)
7. Srisuresh, P., Egevang, K.: Traditional IP Network Address Translator (Traditional NAT). RFC 3022 (January 2001)
8. Carpenter, B.: Architectural Principles of the Internet. RFC 1958 (June 1996)
9. Xylomenos, G., Polyzos, G.C., Mahonen, P., Saaranen, M.: TCP Performance Issues over Wireless Links. IEEE Communications Magazine 39(4), 52–58 (2001)
10. Stuckmann, P., Zimmermann, R.: European Research on Future Internet Design. IEEE Wireless Communications (October 2009)
11. The FP7 4WARD project, http://www.4ward-project.eu/

12. Biermann, T., et al.: Description of Generic Path Mechanism. Deliverable D5.2.0, 4WARD project (May 2009)
13. Callejo, M.Á., Zitterbart, M., et al.: Draft Architectural Framework. Deliverable D2.2 (April 2009)
14. Rosenberg, J., Schulzrinne, H., Camarillo, G., Johnston, A., Peterson, J., Sparks, R., Handley, M., Schooler, E.: SIP: Session Initiation Protocol. RFC 3261 (June 2002)
15. Eberspächer, J., Vögel, H.-J., Bettstetter, C.: GSM Switching, Services and Protocols. John Wiley & Sons, Chichester (2001)
16. Johnsson, M., Huusko, J., Frantti, T., Andersen, F.-U., Nguyen, T.-M.-T., Ponce de Leon, M.: Towards a new architecture framework - The Nth Stratum concept. In: Proceedings of the 4th International Mobile Multimedia Communications Conference (MobiMedia'08), Oulu, Finland (July 2008)
17. Cerf, V., Burleigh, S., Hooke, A., Torgerson, L., Durst, R., Scott, K., Fall, K., Weiss, H.: Delay-Tolerant Networking Architecture. RFC 4838 (April 2007)
18. Ho, T., Lun, D.S.: Network Coding – An Introduction. Cambridge University Press, Cambridge (2008)
19. Halsall, F.: Data Communications, Computer Networks, and Open Systems. Addison esley, Reading (1996)
20. Nichols, K., Blake, S., Baker, F., Black, D.: Definition of the Differentiated Services Field (DS Field) in the IPv4 and IPv6 Headers. RFC 2474 (December 1998)
21. Macedo, D.F., Luiz dos Santos, A., Pujolle, G.: From TCP/IP to Convergent Networks: Challenges and Taxonomy. IEEE Surveys & Tutorials 10(4), 40–55 (2008)
22. Al, A.A.E., Saadawi, T., Lee, M.: Bandwith Aggregation in Stream Control Transmission Protocol. In: Proceedings of the 9th IEEE Symposium on Computers and Communications, ISCC04 (2004)
23. Perros, H.G.: Connection-oriented Networks, SONET/SDH, ATM, MPLS, and Optical Networks. John Wiley & Sons, Chichester (2005)
24. Nordmark, E., Bagnulo, M.: Shim6: Level 3 Multihoming Shim Protocol for IPv6. RFC 5533 (June 2009)
25. Braden, R., Clark, D., Shenker, S.: Integrated Services in the Internet Architecture: an Overview. RFC 1633 (June 1994)
26. Blake, S., Black, D., Carlson, M., Davies, E., Wang, Z., Weiss, W.: An Architecture for Differentiated Services. RFC 2475 (December 1998)
27. Moskowitz, R., Nikander, P.: Host Identity Protocol (HIP) Architecture. RFC 4423 (May 2006)
28. Nguyen, T.M.T., Zhang, X.: Composition of Functionalities Implementation for multihoming transport protocol design, http://www-phare.lip6.fr/~trnguyen
29. European Future Internet Portal, Architecture: Future Internet, http://www.future-internet.eu/home/future-internet-assembly/valencia-april-2010/session-agendas/architectures.html
30. Robert, J.: The clean-slate approach to future Internet design: a survey of research initiatives. Annals of Telecommunications 64(5-6), 271–276 (2009)

Green Network Planning Model for Optical Backbones

Jose Gutierrez, Tahir Riaz, Michael Jensen, Jens M. Pedersen, and Ole B. Madsen

Department of Electronic Systems, Networking and Security Section, Aalborg University
Fredrik Bajers vej 7, 9220 Aalborg Ø, Denmark
{jgl,tahir,mj,jens,obm}@es.aau.dk

Abstract. Communication networks are becoming more essential for our daily lives and critically important for industry and governments. The intense growth in the backbone traffic implies an increment of the power demands of the transmission systems. This power usage might have a significant negative effect on the environment in general. In network planning there are existing planning models focused on QoS provisioning, investment minimization or combinations of both and other parameters. But for designing green optical backbones there is a lack of a model. This paper presents novel ideas to be able to define an analytical model to consider environmental aspects in the planning stage of backbones design.

Keywords: Green network, Network planning, Optical Backbone.

1 Introduction

As FTTH is becoming more widely deployed, bandwidth possibilities for users might increase up to Gbs-order connections. This expansion has a significant effect on the backbone traffic. This increment of traffic implies an increment on the power consumption by the whole network system [1-3].

Network planning tools, usually, are focused on economical or performance aspects, but due to this growth of networks, the consideration of environmental aspects might be necessary in a near future.

Currently, there are tools available to be able to analyze the performance or the economical aspects of a network design before its implementation and deployment, examples are [4] and [5]. Geographical Information System (GIS) data is usually used in order to minimize the digging tasks which are directly related to the deployment investment. In addition, the network topologies are defined in such a way that short path distances between nodes (hops) can be established to improve the performance. Unfortunately, the network planning tools have not followed energy efficiency criteria. There is a relation between how a network is designed and implemented and emissions caused, but there is not a solid base to deal with the problem, however many ideas have been proposed lately [6,7].

This work is intended to define the relations between optical backbone network planning and generic Green House Gases emissions. The goal and main contribution is to define an analytical model to be able to relate important parameters used in network planning such as number of nodes, topology, physical length of the network,

A. Pont, G. Pujolle, and S.V. Raghavan (Eds.): WCITD/NF 2010, IFIP AICT 327, pp. 120–131, 2010.
© IFIP International Federation for Information Processing 2010

number of users , etc, with GHG emissions. This model has been introduced in [7]. It is possible to study how the optical network infrastructure affects the environment and it might be included as design criteria. Furthermore, a case study is presented as an illustration of the potential model use.

This model is partially based on *Life-Cycle Assessment* (LCA) [8], a widely used approach to analyze the environmental effects of products or services from "*cradle-to-grave*" and power usage of the different network task and elements, influenced by publications such as [2,3,8-10].

This model lays the first brick towards a more environmental aware network planning, and hopefully it can be used and adapted to find real solutions for this upcoming environmental issue.

The rest of the document is as follows: Section 2 presents important preliminary concepts. Section 3 introduces the model equations and parameters and Section 4 illustrates the practical use of the model. Finally, Section 5 concludes the work.

2 Preliminary Concepts

Distributed Weighted Average Distance, (*DWAD*):
It is used to calculate the average number of routers and amplifiers the traffic passes through. It is measured in "*hops per bit*" and it is dependent on the traffic distribution, a traffic matrix is required.

For the case study, to create the traffic matrix it is assumed that the aggregated traffic by each node is proportional to its population. This traffic is distributed to the rest of the nodes proportionally to their population. Only the internal backbone traffic is considered. For external traffic other transmission concepts such as "*node to gateway*" should be applied.

The total average distance, $DWAD_T$, should consider failures, Eq. (1). PU_x is the time percentage a network is at a state of x failures.

To determine $DWAD_T$ for the case study, a basic graph analysis script has been implemented. The procedure is to determine the path distance between all the possible pairs of nodes by calculating the corresponding *Spanning Tree* (ideal scenario, no failures). Then, the process is repeated eliminating the corresponding number of links ($[1,f]$) and the average is calculated for each case. The results are deterministic, no simulation involved, in the way that all possible combinations of failure are processed and for all possible pairs of source-destination nodes. This method is more feasible for low f values due to combinational problems.

As a small example, let's consider the possibility of 0 and 1 failures at the same time. The network has no failures 80% of the time, then $DWAD_T=0,8DWAD_0+0,2DWAD_1$. Basic availability concepts are used to calculate the failure probability and *down-time* of any element [4] and [11].

$$DWAD_T = \sum_{x=0}^{x=f} PU_x \cdot DWAD_x \qquad (1)$$

Upgradeability: Briefly explained, backbone networks can be implemented following organized interconnection schemes. Networks can be planned to be implemented in stages and at the conclusion of each stage, an organized topology can be used for transmissions. In this way, every time a network is upgraded by the addition of new links, the performance consequences can be more predictable. For more information it is recommended to read [12].

CO_2 emissions: Even though the final idea in the far future is to be able to produce energy with no emission, *"Zero Carbon"* concept, the reality is that the trends are going more in the way of the so called *"Carbon Neutrality"*, focused on feasible CO_2 reductions [17]. This idea is followed in this document.

Euclidean vs. Real distance: The physical length of the links is calculated as the Euclidean distance between end points. Specialized studies provide ratios Euclidean-Real distance of roads [13] and [14]. Thus, their use combined with the Euclidean distances gives an acceptable approximation avoiding the road layout design task.

Notation:
Emissions: E_{NT} are the total emissions of the network, ED_{xy}, ET_y, and EM_{xyz} are the emissions of deployment, transmission and maintenance where x can be n, a and l for Nodes, Amplifiers and Lines. y corresponds to the topology and it can be R, H and G for Ring, Honeycomb and Grid. In the maintenance case, z can be M for monitoring and F for failure.

Time values: TD_{xy}, TT_y and TM_y are the periods for deployment, transmission and maintenance. tD_{xyz}, tT_{yz} and tM_{xyz} are the instant times of each action where x is the element, y is the topology (just as the emissions notation) and z is 0 for the beginning of the period and 1 for the end. α_x, β_x and γ_x are the emission factors for each of the tasks. ρ_x, τ_x and δ_x are their respective decrement rates.

Other variables: TRF traffic, A_A average amplifiers per link, A_D average distance and PU_f time percentage of a state of f failures. Power consumptions, P_n and P_a are the power required to treat one bit at a node or amplifier respectively. P_{1bit} is the average power required to transmit 1 bit from a source to a destination.

3 The Model

The goal is to define a model to relate the GHG emissions of a network along its lifetime to the commented parameters in network planning. In this way, it is possible to evaluate the network design options from a new environmental perspective. The model includes some other parameters not strictly related to network planning, i.e emissions per watt generated and not controllable at the design stage. However, the model might help to provide guidelines of how their evolution should be in order to reasonably build environmental backbones. The model can be defined as two simple statements:

- The simplicity of the model allows flexibility of usage.
- The possibility of increasing progressively the complexity of each parameter allows a systematic approach of an efficient match *"model-real life"*.

Three main stages are considered to contribute to the emissions: Deployment, Transmission and Maintenance. There is the possibility that the power consumption and consequently the potential GHG emissions of one of these actions are not significant. For the definition of the model, everything that might contribute should be included. At the time of obtaining empirical results, maybe some factors will not significantly contribute to the global overview of the network and can be discarded.

Let ED, ET and EM be the emissions caused by the deployment, transmission and maintenance; then the emissions of a network along its lifetime (E_{NT}) is given by Eq. (2). X can be some other contribution not considered yet, but it leaves the model open for improvement.

$$E_{NT} = ED + ET + EM + X \ . \tag{2}$$

3.1 Deployment Emissions, ED

They cover the emissions related to the construction of the network and its elements. They can be directly related to the number of elements and length of the links. Similar concept can be found for FTTH (Fiber To The Home) implementation in [15].

There are three types of main affecting elements, number of nodes N, number of amplifiers A and network length (including ditches) L.

These elements are related to the emissions by defining the α emission factors. Let α_n, α_a and α_l be the emission factors corresponding to the production, transport and installation of the nodes, amplifiers and links equipment given as [CO_2(Kg)/node], [CO_2(Kg)/amp] and [CO_2(Kg)/km]. Thus, the format of E_D can be defined as Eq. (3).

$$ED = ED_n + ED_a + ED_l = \alpha_n \cdot N + \alpha_a \cdot A + \alpha_l \cdot L \ . \tag{3}$$

In reality, networks are not instantaneously built, it is a time process. The α parameters, will vary in time, i.e the process of producing fibre might involve lower emissions in 10 year. Hence, the variables should be continuous and time dependent. The elements rate of deployment might also be time dependent. Eq. (4) presents ED for a generic deployment time TD when considering time dependent parameters.

$$ED(TD) = \int_0^{TD} \alpha_n(t) \cdot N(t) + \alpha_a(t) \cdot A(t) + \alpha_l(t) \cdot L(t) dt \ . \tag{4}$$

The parameters calculations can be as complex as desired; however this work is not focused on getting into their specific details. In fact, some of them will require intense research work before they can be used in reality.

3.2 Transmission Emissions, ET

These emissions are related to the transmission of information. Every bit transmitted, routed or amplified at each of the active devices will consume energy [10]. To transmit one bit from any source to a destination is energy consuming and this energy is assumed to involve emissions. Let P_n and P_a be the power consumption to receive, treat and retransmit 1 bit at a node and amplifier respectively, both given as [W/bit]. Let A_D and A_A be the path average distance, given as [hops/bit] and average number of amplifiers per link. The calculation of A_D is introduced at Section 2 (*DWAD*) and it can be time dependent due to topology link upgrades for example. A_A is presented in Eq. (5). D_A is the distance between amplifiers or amplifier-node, currently around 70 km, and it can be time dependent $D_A(t)$ implying $A_A(t)$. *# Links* is the number of links.

P_n can depend on the type of signal processing at the nodes, *OxExO* or all optical, type of routing, hardware design or even cooling systems. Many concepts might be included on one variable. Its format or complexity is not relevant to generically present the model. But it is important to keep in mind that the accuracy of the model comes from the specific definition of all the parameters for each of the technologies.

Eq. (6) presents the format P_{1bit}, total average power consumption to transmit one bit from source to destination, including the time dependent format[1].

$$A_A = \frac{L}{\# Links \cdot D_A}. \tag{5}$$

$$\begin{aligned} P_{1bit} &= P_n \cdot (A_D + 1) + P_a \cdot A_A \cdot A_D \\ P_{1bit}(t) &= P_n(t) \cdot (A_D(t) + 1) + P_a(t) \cdot A_A(t) \cdot A_D(t) \end{aligned}. \tag{6}$$

Eq. (7) presents the format of *ET*, including the time dependent form, where *TRF* is the traffic aggregated to the network per year, β is emissions to generate 1 Watt given as [$CO_2(kg)/W$]. $TT = tT_1 - tT_0$ is a generic transmission period.

$$ET = \beta \cdot TRF \cdot TT \cdot P_{1bit} \; ET(TT) = \int_{tT_0}^{tT_1} \beta(t) \cdot TRF(t) \cdot P_{1bit}(t) \, dt. \tag{7}$$

3.3 Maintenance Emissions, EM

These emissions cover all the aspects related to the maintenance of the network. Two types of energy consuming actions are considered: Monitoring and Failure reparation and their corresponding emission variables are EM_M and EM_F, Eq. (8). They can also be presented as time functions similarly to Eq. (4). Like the deployment emissions, three elements are considered: nodes, amplifiers and links. The EM_F will be clearly conditioned to the size of the network since the failure rate is proportional to the physical length of the links [11].

The emission factors for monitoring actions are defined as γ_{Mx}, given as [$CO_2(kg)$/element*year] or [$CO_2(kg)$/km*year}] for the links. The emissions due to failure reparations, γ_{Fx} given as [$CO_2(kg)$/element*failure] and F_x is the failure rate in [failures/year]. x in the variables notation corresponds to the element, being n for nodes, a for amplifiers and l for links. The rest of the variables are: number of nodes N, number of amplifiers A and network length L. Both formulas can be expressed, but not presented in the document to avoid repetition, as time functions as previously presented for *ED* and *ET*.

$$EM = EM_M + EM_F = (\gamma_{Mn} \cdot N + \gamma_{Ma} \cdot A + \gamma_{Ml} \cdot L) \cdot TT + (\gamma_{Fn} \cdot Fn + \gamma_{Fa} \cdot Fa + \gamma_{Fl} \cdot Fl) \cdot TT \tag{8}$$

---

[1] The number of nodes in a path is considered to be $A_D + 1$ since the source and destination nodes also need energy to process the information.

4 Case Study

The following case study intends to illustrate one of the potential uses of the model. It is important to remark that, at this stage, it is not possible to provide final numerical solutions, but it is possible to analytically illustrate the idea. For the presentation of more clear equations several assumptions has been taken. The values of some are symbolic but they do not interfere with the presentation of the use of the model.

4.1 The Scenario and Cases

The scenario consists of a set of nodes to be interconnected. Three cases are compared for the same area: to implement a physical Ring, Honeycomb (4X5) or Grid (4x5).

For this purpose, the deployment technique commented in Section 2 is followed. The deployment is planned in stages so at the end of each stage there is an organized topology ready to be used for transmissions. As a result, emission equations are presented for three Cases over the same region to illustrate the influence of the network infrastructure parameters. The three cases are:

- *Case A*: A Ring topology is deployed and remains as final structure (Stage 1).
- *Case B*: A Ring topology is deployed and when it is installed the network is ready to be used (Stage 1). In that instant, the Honeycomb upgrade begins and this structure remains for the rest of the network's lifetime (Stage 2).
- *Case C*: As Case B but when the honeycomb is finished (Stage 2), an upgrade begins to form a Grid that will be the final topology (Stage 3).

The chosen scenario is to connect the 20 most populated metropolitan areas in continental Australia [2] . The shortest physical way to interconnect them is determined for each of the topologies and cases using genetic algorithms [3] [5]. The complexity of the topology problem is *NP* since theoretically there are *N!* possible solutions. Any search method can be used to solve this type of problems.

4.2 Assumptions

Deployment: Starts at $tD_{R0}=0$.

- The deployment is continuous until the definitive topology is deployed. Thus, for example for Case C: $tD_{R0}=0$, $tD_{R1}=tD_{H0}$ and $tD_{H1}=tD_{G0}$.
- All the nodes are deployed as soon as possible and at a constant rate. For *Case A* all nodes will be deployed at the Ring stage, $tD_{NT}=tD_{R1}$. For *B* and *C*, at the Ring stage 18 nodes are installed and the rest at the Honeycomb stage. If a 20 nodes Ring is implemented, some of its links cannot be used to form a Honeycomb. Therefore, it is not an efficient planning procedure. Links are deployed at a constant rate and amplifiers are installed at the same time.

---

[2] Sydney, Melbourne, Brisbane, Perth, Adelaide, Newcastle, Gold coast, Canberra, Wollongong, Sunshine coast, Bendigo, Geelong, Townsville, Cairns, Orange, Alburya, Darwin, Toowoomba, Ballarat, Shoalhaven. Coordinates and Population taken from [18].

[3] The same topology might have different length depending on the case since the optimized topology is the definitive. More information in [12].

- The α factors have a constant decreasing rate of τ per year. $\alpha_x(t)=\alpha_{x0}\cdot(1-\tau)^t$, α_{x0} is the initial value at $t=0=tD_{R0}$. There is a need to define a reference value, $\alpha_{xref.}$ corresponding to the emissions of implementing one node (amplifier or km of link) in one year. In this way $\alpha_{x0}=\alpha_{xref}/TD$. x corresponds to the element (n, a or l).
- $D_A=70$ km and it is kept constant (distance between amplifiers).

Transmission: Starts at $tT_{R0}=tD_{R1}$.

-The topology is not operable until the installation/upgrade is completed.
-The β factor have a constant decreasing rate ρ per year. $\beta_x(t)=\beta_{x0}\cdot(1-\rho)^t$, β_{x0} is the initial value at $t=0=tD_{R0}$.
-The average distance is calculated as $DWAD$, Eq. (1) and up to one failure at the same time. It is assumed shortest path routing and all the links have a constant equal weight when calculating the Spanning Tree in both cases, of 0 and 1 failures.
-Traffic transactions increase rate is kept constant, $TRF_0\cdot(1+\rho_{TRF})^t$.
- P_n and P_a are assumed to be always constant.

Maintenance: Starts at $tM_{R0}=tD_{R1}$.

-The γ factors have a constant decreasing rate δ per year. $\gamma_x(t)=\gamma_{x0}\cdot(1-\delta)^t$, γ_{x0} is the initial value at $t=0=tD_{R0}$.
-It is assumed that only link failures are significant to be included in the formulas to illustrate the example. Equipment at the nodes and amplifiers are highly reliable and very unlikely to fail [5]. However, human errors might be included in future.
-The values to calculate the failure rates and element *down-time* are taken from [4] and [11] and correspond to $MTTF=500$ FIT and $MTF=14,4$ h.

4.3   Analysis

For the rest of the case study, to indicate the case, a superscript (A, B or C) is added to each of the terms, and for example $tD_{R0}{}^A$ is the beginning of deployment of the Ring at case A. Table 1 presents the equations to be solved to determine the total emissions of Case A. These formulas act as a guideline and, to avoid repetition, for Cases B and C they are not presented. The concept is similar but considering the proper time periods, stages and parameters for the different tasks.

Table 1. Case A equations

Emissions	Case A
$ED_R(TD_R^A)$	$\int_0^{tD_{R1}^A} \alpha_{n_0}\cdot N\cdot(1-\tau_{\alpha_n})^t + \alpha_{a_0}\cdot A\cdot(1-\tau_{\alpha_a})^t +$ $\alpha_{l_0}\cdot L\cdot(1-\tau_{\alpha_l})^t\,dt$
$ET_R(TT_R^A)$	$\beta_0\cdot TRF_0\cdot(P_n\cdot(A_D+1)+P_a\cdot A_D\cdot A_A)\cdot$ $\int_{tT_{R0}^A}^{tT_{R1}^A}(1-\rho_\beta)^t\cdot(1+\rho_{TRF})^t\,dt$
$EM_R(TM_R^A)$	$\int_{tM_{R0}^A}^{tM_{R1}^A}(\gamma_{Mn_0}\cdot N\cdot(1-\delta_{\gamma_{Mn}})^t + \gamma_{Ma_0}\cdot A\cdot(1-\delta_{\gamma_{Ma}})^t +$ $\gamma_{Ml_0}\cdot L\cdot(1-\delta_{\gamma_{Ml}})^t)\,dt$

Fig. 1 presents the planning solutions for the considered cases including time lines illustrating the emissions periods. Some of the time parameters are indicated as

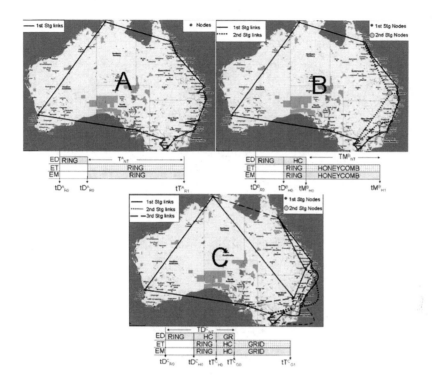

Fig. 1. Case A, B and C

examples for a better understanding. Table 2 presents the numerical values of the planning parameters. The information is divided by Case and Stage displaying for each the corresponding topology and all its parameters (nodes, length, amps ...). The variables NDp, ADp and LDp correspond to the nodes, amplifiers and km of link to be deployed at each stage. All the values are calculated, there are no assumptions. The information is displayed by case and stage. The information required in order to make these calculations is the following: City coordinates and population, $MTTF$ and MFT , a graph analysis script to calculate the average distance as $DWAD$, as mentioned in Section 2 and a ratio of *Euclidean-Real distance* of $\sqrt{2}$.

Finally, Table 3 presents the resulting equations. In order to provide reasonably short terms, all the τ, ρ and δ parameters are given a value of 0,05 (except for ρ_{TRF}). This implies a decrement of 5% per year. ρ_{TRF}=0,41, in the way that traffic volume is doubled every two years as predicted for a near future [16].

The equations are displayed by case, type and period, the total emissions of each case being the sum of all their emissions. The effect of each of the planning factors can clearly be identified in Table 2. In Table 3, these factors are indicated only in the first equation of each type for clearness of display, but for the rest it is similar.

One of the basic illustrated ideas is that the Grid network contributes more to ED and EM but less to ET than the Honeycomb or Ring. Depending on the values assigned to the stages periods, the emission factors or traffic trends, different options can be evaluated to find the most environmental.

Table 2. Planning results for cases A, B and C

Case	A	B		C		
Stage	st1	st1	st2	st1	st2	st3
Top.	R	R	H	R	H	G
Nodes (NDp)	20(20)	18(18)	20(2)	18(18)	20(2)	20(0)
Links	20	18	24	18	24	31
Length [km]	14870	14344	19800	20009	21684	28750
(LDp)	(14870)	(14344)	(5456)	(20009)	(1675)	(7066)
Amplifiers (ADp)	213(213)	205(205)	283(78)	286(286)	310(24)	411(101)
A_A	10,55	11,40	11,79	15,89	12,92	13,26
F_L(failures year)	65,13	62,83	86,72	87,64	94,98	125,92
PU_0	89,3	89,7	85,7	85,6	84,4	79,3
$DWAD_0$	5,28	4,73	3,81	4,8	3,69	3,27
$DWAD_1$	6,58	7,35	3,92	6,1	3,75	3,32
$DWAD_T$	5,42	4,99	3,83	4,98	3,70	3,28

The model and its solutions combined with some parameters analysis might contribute to some of the following ideas:

-Simply, which, among a set of options, implies the least emissions according to the expected trends of the emission factors or traffic growth.

- How the parameters evolution has to be so Case X is better than Case Y.

- How and when to upgrade a network to make it more environmentally efficient.

- Network planning has always been a matter of considering global optimization between different network properties to find a balance. The addition of the environmental aspect will not change this concept. In fact, the combination of different backbone models (i.e. performance, economical and environmental) can provide a better systematic planning procedure in future.

The three different cases show how the network planning parameters affect each type of emissions. However, it is possible to go a little further in the solution in order to illustrate more clear results; numerical values are given to the time periods. This way it is possible to compare the three solutions just as a function of the emissions factors. Obviously this value depends on the investment for the deployment, high investment more man power and machinery available, so the value is an example. Let the deployment speed be 3000 Km per year[4] and the corresponding nodes and amplifiers are implemented within the links deployment time. The network has an estimated lifetime of 40 years. Table 4 presents the resulting time periods (T) and instants (t) for these assumptions.

Finally, substituting all the numerical values, Table 5 gives the final results to be compared as a function of the emissions factors, these factors are constant and equal in the three cases. Briefly, the conclusion of this example verifies the affirmations previously stated and in [7].

In terms of deployment and maintenance, the physical length of the links significantly affects the emissions. To deploy and maintain a Ring causes considerably less emissions than a Grid. On the other hand, the reduction of the physical hops of the paths implies a reduction on the ET related to both amplifiers and

---

[4] In this way any of the cases, the deployment can be finalized in 10 years maximum.

Table 3. Cases' practical planning results

Case	ED
A,TD_R	$(\underbrace{20}_{NDp}\,\alpha_{nref} + \underbrace{213}_{ADp}\,\alpha_{aref} + \underbrace{14870}_{LDp}\,\alpha_{lref})(1 - 0,95^{tD^A_{R1}})/(0,05 \cdot TD^A_R)$
B,TD_R	$(18\alpha_{nref} + 205\alpha_{aref} + 14344\alpha_{lref})(1 - 0,95^{tD^B_{R1}})/(0,05 \cdot TD^B_R)$
B,TD_H	$(2\alpha_{nref} + 78\alpha_{aref} + 5456\alpha_{lref})(0,95^{tD^H_{H0}} - 0,95^{tD^H_{H1}})/(0,05 \cdot TD^B_H)$
C,TD_R	$(18\alpha_{nref} + 286\alpha_{aref} + 20009\alpha_{lref})(1 - 0,95^{tD^C_{R1}})/(0,05 \cdot TD^C_R)$
C,TD_H	$(2\alpha_{nref} + 24\alpha_{aref} + 1675\alpha_{lref})(0,95^{tD^C_{H0}} - 0,95^{tD^C_{H1}})/(0,05 \cdot TD^C_H)$
C,TD_G,	$(101\alpha_{aref} + 7066\alpha_{lref})(0,95^{tD^C_{G0}} - 0,95^{tD^C_{H1}})/(0,05 \cdot TD^C_G)$
	ET
A,TD_R	$\beta_0 \cdot TRF_0 \cdot (\underbrace{6,42}_{DWAD_T+1}\,P_n + \underbrace{57,18}_{A_A \cdot DWAD_T}\,P_a)((1,33)^{tT^A_{R1}} - (1,33)^{tT^A_{R0}})/0,28$
B,TT_R	$\beta_0 \cdot TRF_0 \cdot (5,99P_n + 56,89P_a)((1,33)^{tT^B_{R1}} - (1,33)^{tT^B_{R0}})/0,28$
B,TT_H	$\beta_0 \cdot TRF_0 \cdot (4,83P_n + 45,16P_a)((1,33)^{tT^H_{H1}} - (1,33)^{tT^B_{H0}})/0,28$
C,TT_R	$\beta_0 \cdot TRF_0 \cdot (5,98P_n + 79,13P_a)((1,33)^{tT^C_{R1}} - (1,33)^{tT^C_{R0}})/0,28$
C,TT_H	$\beta_0 \cdot TRF_0 \cdot (4,70P_n + 47,80P_a)((1,33)^{tT^H_{H1}} - (1,33)^{tT^C_{H0}})/0,28$
C,TT_G	$\beta_0 \cdot TRF_0 \cdot (4,28P_n + 43,49P_a)((1,33)^{tT^C_{G1}} - (1,33)^{tT^C_{G0}})/0,28$
	EM
A,TM_R	$(\underbrace{20}_{N}\,\gamma_{Mn0} + \underbrace{213}_{A}\,\gamma_{Ma0} + \underbrace{14870}_{L}\,\gamma_{Ml0} + \underbrace{65,15}_{F_L}\,\gamma_{Fl0})(0,95^{tM^A_{R0}} - 0,95^{tM^A_{R1}})/0,05$
B,TM_R	$(18\gamma_{Mn0} + 205\gamma_{Ma0} + 14344\gamma_{Ml0} + 62,83\gamma_{Fl0})(0,95^{tM^B_{R0}} - 0,95^{tM^B_{R1}})/0,05$
B,TM_H	$(20\gamma_{Mn0} + 283\gamma_{Ma0} + 19800\gamma_{Ml0} + 86,72\gamma_{Fl0})(0,95^{tM^H_{H0}} - 0,95^{tM^H_{H1}})/0,05$
C,TM_R	$(18\gamma_{Mn0} + 286\gamma_{Ma0} + 20009\gamma_{Ml0} + 87,64\gamma_{Fl0})(0,95^{tM^C_{R0}} - 0,95^{tM^C_{R1}})/0,05$
C,TM_H	$(20\gamma_{Mn0} + 310\gamma_{Ma0} + 21684\gamma_{Ml0} + 94,98\gamma_{Fl0})(0,95^{tM^C_{H0}} - 0,95^{tM^C_{H1}})/0,05$
C,TM_G	$(20\gamma_{Mn0} + 411\gamma_{Ma0} + 28750\gamma_{Ml0} + 125,92\gamma_{Fl0})(0,95^{tM^C_{G0}} - 0,95^{tM^C_{G1}})/0,05$

Table 4. Planning results for cases A, B and C

T variables	Years	t variables	Instant (years)
TD^A_R	5	$tD^A_{R0} = tD^B_{R0} = tD^C_{R0}$	0
TD^B_R	4,8	$tD^A_{R1} = tT^A_{R0} = tM^A_{R0}$	5
TD^B_H	1,8	$tD^B_{R1} = tT^B_{R0} = tM^B_{R0}$	4,8
TD^C_R	6,7	$tD^B_{H1} = tT^B_{H0} = tM^B_{H0}$	6,6
TD^C_H	0,5	$tD^C_{R1} = tT^C_{R1} = tM^C_{R0}$	6,7
TD^C_G	2,4	$tD^C_{H1} = tT^C_{H1} = tM^C_{H0}$	7,2
T_{NT}	40	$tD^C_{G1} = tT^C_{G1} = tM^C_{G0}$	9,6

Table 5. Emissions comparison

Emission(Case)	Values
$ED(A)$	$18,1\alpha_{nref} + 192,7\alpha_{aref} + 13455\alpha_{lref}$
$ED(B)$	$17,9\alpha_{nref} + 246,2\alpha_{aref} + 17223\alpha_{lref}$
$ED(C)$	$17,1\alpha_{nref} + 332,9\alpha_{aref} + 23288\alpha_{lref}$
$ET(A)$	$\beta_0 \cdot TRF_0 \cdot (2,06 \cdot 10^6 P_n + 1,86 \cdot 10^7 P_a)$
$ET(B)$	$\beta_0 \cdot TRF_0 \cdot (1,55 \cdot 10^6 P_n + 1,45 \cdot 10^7 P_a)$
$ET(C)$	$\beta_0 \cdot TRF_0 \cdot (1,37 \cdot 10^6 P_n + 1,40 \cdot 10^7 P_a)$
$EM(A)$	$258,1\gamma_{Mn0} + 2749\gamma_{Ma0} + 1,85 \cdot 10^5\gamma_{Ml0} + 840,5\gamma_{MFl0}$
$EM(B)$	$258,5\gamma_{Mn0} + 3590\gamma_{Ma0} + 2,51 \cdot 10^5\gamma_{Ml0} + 1100\gamma_{MFl0}$
$EM(C)$	$231,5\gamma_{Mn0} + 4566\gamma_{Ma0} + 3,19 \cdot 10^5\gamma_{Ml0} + 1399\gamma_{MFl0}$

nodes. The optimal design decision depends on the numerical values of these emission factors, which with the cooperation of other science disciplines, would be possible in future. In any case, this example can clearly illustrate the basics of the model and how to use and interpret it. The model can be implemented as an evaluation application and sweeps of several of the present variables in the model can be performed to observe the potential contributions depending on the planning decisions, future technological evolutions or even environmental legislation.

5 Conclusion

The main contribution is the presentation of a network planning model focused on the emissions generated along the lifetime of an optical backbone. This model relates the classical network planning parameters such as number of nodes, distances between pairs of nodes or physical network length to the emissions generated by the different elements. Three main types of emissions are defined based on Deployment, Transmission and Maintenance actions. The model can be defined as simple as desired but it provides the possibility of extending each of its elements to significant complexity levels. Several parameters present on the model are not strictly related to networks, i.e. emissions per watt generated, thus for the evaluation of environmental planning aspects of backbones, there are many different science fields involved and interrelated. Furthermore, a case study illustrates the potential use and analysis of the model in real networks. Several assumptions had to be made in order to provide solutions equations. It is possible to identify how each of the mentioned network planning parameters (Table 2) affects the emission levels.

The model is defined and presented, and even though it is not possible yet to provide final numerical solutions, the first step has been taken towards the inclusion of environmental aspects in optical network planning and design.

Further research on each of the parameters present in the equations is required to estimate their behavior in time. Each of the emissions factors can be extended or modified to be used for other environmental measurements such as toxicity. Maybe other factors can be included as well such as equipment replacement or recycling for *EM*. In general, there is potential new research on this model.

References

1. Chabarek, J., Sommers, J., Barford, P., Estan, C., Tsiang, D., Wright, S.: Power Awareness in Network Design and Routing Export. In: INFOCOM 2008 (2008)
2. Chiaraviglio, L., Mellia, M., Neri, F.: Reducing Power Consumption in Backbone Networks. In: ICC 2009, Dresden, Germany (June 2009)
3. Chiaraviglio, L., Mellia, M., Neri, F.: Energy-aware Backbone Networks: a Case Study. In: Workshop on Green Communications, ICC 2009 (2009)
4. To, M., Neusy, P.: Unavailability Analysis of Long-Haul Networks. IEEE Journal on Selected Areas in Communications 12(1) (January 1994)
5. Gutierrez, J., Imine, M., Madsen, O.: Network Planning Using GA For Regular Topologies. In: ICC 2008, Beijing, China (May 2008)

6. Nielsen, R.H., Mihovska, A., Madsen, O.B.: Energy-efficient deployment through optimizations in the planning of ICT networks. In: WPMC 2009, Japan (2009)
7. Gutierrez, J., Riaz, T., Pedersen, J.M., Madsen, O.B.: A Survey On Environmental Backbone Design and Implementation. In: ISABEL'09, Bratislava, Slovakia (2009)
8. Owens, W.: Life-cycle assessment: Constraints on moving from inventory to impact assessment. Journal of Industrial Ecology 1(1), 37–49 (1997)
9. Landman, P.: High-level power estimation. In: International Symposium on Low Power Electronics and Design, Monterey, CA, USA, August 12-14 (1996)
10. Idzikowski, F.: Power consumption of network elements in IP over WDM networks. TKN Technical Report TKN-09-006, Berlin (July 2009)
11. Challita, A., Tzanakaki, A., Tomkos, I.: Reliability Based Routing in WDM Optical Networks. In: ICTON 2005 (Mo.B1.5). IEEE, Los Alamitos (2005)
12. Gutierrez, J., Riaz, T., Pedersen, J., Madsen, O.: Upgradeability and Predictability Analysis for Mesh Topologies in Optical Distribution Networks. In: WOCN 2009, Egypt (2009)
13. Fernandez, J., Fernandez, P., Pelegrin, B.: Estimating actual distances by norm functions: a comparison between the $1_{k,p,\theta-}$ norm and the $1_{b1,b2,\theta}$ -norm and a study about the selection of the data set. Comput. Oper. Res. 29(6), 609–623 (2002)
14. Love, R.F., Morris, J.G.: Mathematical models of road travel distances. Management Science 25, 130–139 (1979)
15. Ecobilan for FTTH Council Europe, FTTH Solutions for a Sustainable Development (February 2008), http://www.ftthcouncil.eu/
16. Coffman, K.G., Coffman, K.G.: Internet growth: Is there a "Moore's Law" for data traffic. Handbook of Massive Data Sets, 47–93 (2001)
17. Vandenbergh, M.P.: The Carbon-Neutral Individual, vol. 82. University Law Review, New York (2007); Vanderbilt Law and Economics Research Paper No. 07-29
18. http://www.tageo.com/index-e-as-cities-AU.htm

Internet Sensor Grid: Experiences with Passive and Active Instruments

Peter Komisarczuk[1,2] and Ian Welch[2]

[1] School of Computing and Technology, Thames Valley University, Ealing, London, UK
peter.komisarczuk@tvu.ac.uk
[2] School of Engineering and Computer Science, Victoria University of Wellington,
P.O. Box 600, Wellington 6140 New Zealand
{ian.welch,peter.komisarczuk}@ecs.vuw.ac.nz

Abstract. The Internet is constantly evolving with new emergent behaviours arising; some of them malicious. This paper discusses opportunities and research direction in an Internet sensor grid for malicious behaviour detection, analysis and countermeasures. We use two example sensors as a basis; firstly the honeyclient for malicious server and content identification (i.e. drive-by-downloads, the most prevalent attack vector for client systems) and secondly the network telescope for Internet Background Radiation detection (IBR - which is classified as unsolicited, non-productive traffic that traverses the Internet, often malicious in nature or origin). Large amounts of security data can be collected from such sensors for analysis and federating honeyclient and telescope data provides a worldwide picture of attacks that could enable the provision of countermeasures. In this paper we outline some experiences with these sensors and analyzing network telescope data through Grid computing as part of an "intelligence layer" within the Internet.

Keywords: Internet Background Radiation, Drive-by-downloads, honeyclient, Network Telescope, Grid computing.

1 Introduction and Background

The Internet is constantly evolving with new emergent behaviours arising [1, 2], some of these new behaviours are benign but unfortunately many are malicious. For example complex distributed entities such as software robot armies (botnets) that make it hazardous to use or be connected to the Internet [3, 4]. The US NSF project GENI (Global Environment for Network Innovation) identifies security and robustness as the most compelling reasons to redesign the Internet [5]. Understanding how to design the network of the future to be more resilient to attack requires an understanding of the current malicious activity in the Internet. In this paper we provide an experience report and review around several tools developed to detect, study and analyse drive-by-downloads for client side attacks and a network telescope for Internet Background Radiation (IBR) detection.

Web-based exploits are currently the fastest growing attack on the Internet with around 1 in 150 web servers said to be compromised in early 2010 [from Kaspersky

A. Pont, G. Pujolle, and S.V. Raghavan (Eds.): WCITD/NF 2010, IFIP AICT 327, pp. 132–145, 2010.

2010]. Compromised or malicious web servers deliver "drive by downloads" [6,7] which are exploits that occur when your web browser visits a compromised server; your browser receives the requested web page but also receives targeted and usually obfuscated malicious content often causing a system to be compromised. For example, a keylogger program installed without the users permission in order to gather user name and password data. To discover these exploits instruments called honeyclients [8, 9, 10, 11, 12] have been developed of which there are two main classifications. A high-interaction honeyclient [8] is an instrument consisting of a complete operating system running a web browser where we classify a web server as either malicious or benign based on changes observed to the state of the operating system after visiting the web site. This is a relatively slow process but is highly accurate. On the other hand, low-interaction honeyclients [9] are faster but less accurate because they classify a web page for example by matching structures in the document against previously generated signatures of malicious content. They are prone to give false positive results and would miss new attacks for which there are no signatures.

Internet Background Radiation (IBR) is defined as unsolicited, non-productive traffic that traverses the Internet and is often malicious in nature or origin. An IBR sensor consists of a darknet (or network telescope) [13], which is an IP address range that is advertised but contains no real responders/systems. Instead a darknet passively records all packets. Additionally active responder systems can be deployed which respond to IBR to gain further information on the attacks.

Blocking IBR traffic may be possible if an Internet user, business or ISP can use control data derived from such Internet sensors to identify IBR traffic destined for their network and enable countermeasures. Unfortunately one technique used by attackers to avoid detection is to forge the IP source address of their attack packets. The effect of this is that a victim detects packets from a number of different innocent source addresses. The responses the victims make to these packets are sent back to the forged IP addresses and this traffic is commonly known as "backscatter". There are also benign sources of unsolicited traffic to an address space; such sources include the effects of network mis-configuration and network mapping studies [14]. Pang, el al. [15] showed that TCP traffic accounts for the majority of IBR traffic, ranging from 56.5% to 95.0% of traffic across individual monitors, with TCP ports 135 and 445 (loc-srv and Microsoft-ds respectively) being popular exploits. Likewise Yegneswaran, Barford, and Ullrich [16] showed that worm activity contributed between 20% to 60% of any one day's IBR traffic arriving at a network sensor.

Drive-by Downloads and IBR are just two parts of the overall malicious behaviour seen on the Internet. IBR forms part of the early phase of attacks where the Internet is probed for vulnerable hosts, or it shows the spread of malware through the Internet. IBR detection is based on passive measurement techniques, whereas Drive-by-Download detection is an active measurement that provides: maps of compromised web servers, redirection and exploit servers, detects malware delivery mechanisms, malware packers, malicious payloads and can lead onto detection of botnet command & control infrastructure and attack commands based on honeypot techniques. These, and other instruments can form part of a barometer – a weather map for the Internet.

In this paper we discuss the Internet Sensor Grid. Review some of the developments in active and passive sensors and measurements and discuss some of the Grid based analysis that can be undertaken on network telescope data.

2   The Internet Sensor Grid

We identify an Internet sensor grid [17] comprising active and passive measurement systems that encompasses a wide range of malicious activity measurements, allowing potential correlation between different attack components to be determined. Political, business, social, economic and technical difficulties, make a wide scale federated Internet sensor grid a difficult system to build and run. It requires careful dissemination of information; based on trust and reputation, with guarantees around the provenance of the data, the analysis undertaken and the control data or feedback disseminated.

Some service providers in this space have evolved in recent years, often as not for profit organisations, such as the Honeynet Project [10], ShadowServer [18] and Team Cymru [19] that have capability for large-scale data collection and analysis. Trust is provided through recommendation and vetting of individuals or organizations. These service providers are creating large-scale cooperative sensor and notification services. For example Team Cymru launched the Dragon Research Group in 2009 to deploy a large set of network telescopes to gather data and a community to develop tools [19]. Team Cymru disseminate a bogon routing reference, IP-ASN mapping, malware hash registry as well as Darknet monitoring data. The Honeynet Project are deploying the second phase of their Global Distributed Honeynet (GDH-II) which will incorporate thousands of active honeypot sensors across the world [10] allowing research and dissemination into host attack trends, techniques, malware and botnet command and control.

Networks of the future could develop more sophisticated systems, allowing federated security sensor data to be used to reduce malicious activity. Such systems may use Complex Adaptive Systems (CAS) concepts [1, 2, 20, 21] because of the combination of large numbers of software, hardware and human agents involved. The Internet Sensor Grid would be a CAS in itself as they would be collaborative systems of many components that detect, share, initiate protection or launch countermeasures [22]. Such a system may be based on biologically inspired immune system concepts [23], virally spreading the key information to enable reaction and countermeasures [24] like an immune system using antibodies [25]. Existing work on collective intelligence [26] may also be incorporated but needs to be evaluated to fit with this problem space. Key areas to be developed cover the creation of collaborative sensors and actuators [25, 17, 28, 29], detection and classification of emergent behaviour [3,4], inventing and testing system response and counter-measures. Current basic systems are proving successful, e.g. filtering and warning services currently allow ISPs or Telcos to effectively filter bogon space. Data from darknets, honeypots and honeyclients can be used to provide countermeasures, e.g. by CERTs, to warn typically innocent Internet users that their system is being compromised and used for illegal activities, such as spamming and distributed denial of service attacks.

3 Review of Developments in Active and Passive Sensors

There are a wide variety of sensors that can be employed in the detection of malicious behaviour, including active and passive measurements techniques – integrating network telescopes and active devices such as honeypots, honeyclients, DNS tools for fast flux detection etc. Data is gathered and analysed ranging from low-level protocol interactions through to geopolitical, network topology and network/service provider level. This paper specifically looks at the evolution and applications of the data and intelligence that can be extracted from network telescopes and honeyclients, and describes our experience and development of tools based on Grid computing used to scale systems or analyse the data collected. Below, we briefly review honeypot/honeynet, network telescopes and honeyclient developments.

A honeypot/honeynet is a computer system deployed as a "sacrificial lamb": "A security resource whose value lies in being probed, attacked or compromised" [30]. It has no production value; so anything going to/from the honeypot is likely to be a probe, attack or a compromise. It is used for monitoring, detecting and analyzing attacks and consists of the sacrificial system and a firewall to capture the packets sent and received. A honeypot is labour/skill intensive and has a limited field of view (scalability) and does not directly protect vulnerable end systems. Detection mechanisms tend to fall into one of two broad categories: Active Responders and Passive Monitors [16]. An Active Responder replies to incoming IBR traffic to solicit further traffic so as to more precisely detect its nature and intent. Examples include Honeypots [30] which are characterized as high interaction or low interaction host systems e.g. HoneyTrap [31], HoneyD [32], and simpler higher capacity "Stateless Active Responders" such as iSink [33] and the Internet Motion Sensor [34]. These systems are attached to the Internet in order to be probed and compromised and their value is in the intelligence gathered. A honeyclient on the other hand scans the Internet and is looking to be compromised by malicious servers in order to detect compromised or malicious servers and their exploit mechanisms.

A high interaction honeypot [30] is secured with a reasonable password on the common system userid's and is monitored by software and network hardware. The system is typically accessed through a Honeywall – a firewall that allows attackers in but limits the connectivity from the honeypot so that it cannot effectively be used to launch attacks, but does allow the attacker to incorporate the honeypot into a botnet for example. The return on investment or value obtained from such honeypots includes knowledge of botnet command and control infrastructure, attack plans, malicious actions etc.

Low interaction honeypot systems provide an emulated computer system, services and applications. These systems have limited capabilities, which make them more scalable and can emulate a large network address space and provide services that to some extent looks like the real thing. Such devices are relatively easy to deploy, with lower risk because they are not complete computer systems, however they capture more limited information. A number of low interaction systems exist, for example the HoneyTrap [31], often run in a virtual machine, accepts TCP connections to gathers information including at least the first data packet. It is designed to keep TCP connections open long enough to receive useful information on the exploit and it also provides a 'mirror mode' option where the attack can be reflected to the originator.

HoneyD [32] is a dynamic tool that fakes a number of IP addresses and emulates the fingerprints of various operating systems, making it harder for an attacker to detect it is talking to a honeypot. It can be deployed within an Enterprise using any un-used address space, so an attacker scanning for devices to compromise could pick an address used by HoneyD rather than a real system. HoneyD runs services on specific ports using scripts, which can show known security flaws in order to coax the attacker to launch an attack. Default operations can be applied, such as sending TCP reset, or accept commands for a given port. Data from honeypots is being aggregated and shared through the mwcollect alliance, see http://alliance.mwcollect.org.

The honeyclient has several forms like the honeypot. The high interaction honeyclient is a complete system driven to browse the web and uses system state changes to detect malicious behaviour e.g. that captures API calls, shown in Figure 1. The honeyclient system developed incorporates a server component (Capture-HPC) [8] and a Microsoft Windows behavioural analysis tool (Capture-BAT), running in a Virtual Machine environment controlled from the coordinating server. The latest developments have been to provide network API monitoring and extensions to the capture server to incorporate a database and checkpoints to optimize operations [35] and has been used in a variety of studies, including a long term scan of the .nz domain.

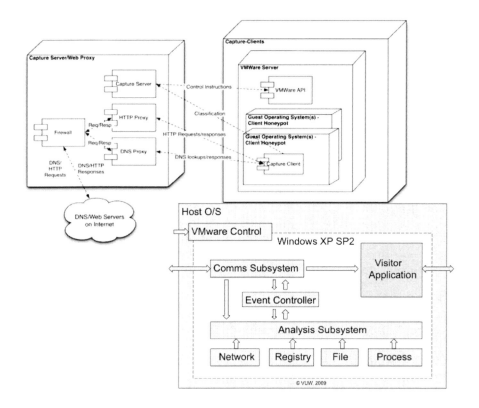

Fig. 1. Capture-HPC honeyclient architecture [8, 22]

Developments to scale the honeyclient system have been trialed using Grid computing which encapsulated the system for the Grid using the gRAVI toolkit [36] and using workflow engines to control Grid execution [28]. The use of workflow engines proved less effective than hoped at scaling honeyclient infrastructure. Alternatively low interaction honeyclients [9] can be employed, typically using fewer compute resources to classify a web page as potentially malicious. Static analysis of web page features can be used to provide a classification, e.g. the use of obfuscated JavaScript or small iframes [37] and it can use DNS data to form server maps [27] and detect fast-flux attacks to classify interactions that are likely to be malicious. Other low interaction systems, such as PhoneyC [38], provide a virtual HTTP honeyclient combining a web crawler and analysis engine. The input is provided through a call to Curl, which mimics a legitimate browser's behavior. The page is then evaluated, all content is downloaded, scripts are evaluated and a classification of the webpage made. The malicious web pages from the low interaction system are then checked using a high interaction honeyclient. Combining low and high interaction honeyclients into hybrid systems can optimise system performance and thus costs and helps develop the honeyclient business case [39]. These systems employ feedback loops for learning and automated signature generation [40].

Unlike low interaction honeypots or honeyclients, a darknet or network telescope is a passive monitoring system that records IBR traffic destined for a range of addresses. The darknet does not respond to any incoming packets, thus there are no scalability issues with respect to responding to incoming packets, nor is there a need to provide real or emulated services. The bottleneck is the speed at which we can record packets for analysis. Network telescopes require significantly less computing and bandwidth resources than active responder systems as no reply packets are generated [13, 15, 19, 41, 42, 43]. The network telescope does detect a wide range of malicious activity, but the data gathered is limited to the first packet in an exchange, so it may not be possible to determine the exact nature of the attack.

The size of the IP address range being monitored by a Network Telescope has a major impact on its ability to detect large-scale network events [13]. As it is purely passive the time to detect an event is based on the probability of an attacker selecting the darknet address range, so the larger a darknet the more likely it is to detect malicious activity, or be picked for scanning, or by a propagating worm. Detection time ranges from an average 1.82 hours for a /16 network address pool down to 19.4 days for a sensor using a /24 network [13]. Harder, Johnson, Bradley, and Knottenbelt [43] outline the difficulty of accurately detecting worm infection rates using a /24 network telescope. Unfortunately, increasing the size of a Network Telescope increases the packet rate that the sensor is expected to deal with. In circumstances where not all traffic can be captured, traffic sampling can be employed, or sensors can be segmented. Studies from Yegneswaran, Barford, and Ullrich [16]; and Pang, Yegneswaran, Barford, Paxson, and Peterson [15] have pioneered the use of various sampling methods for network telescope data. Nonetheless, there is a loss in accuracy because the entire population of IBR is not being captured.

The data captured by these sensors ranges from probes to attacks and to the exploitation of the attacked systems. The data captured includes protocols (packets), addresses of exploited systems, malware samples, command & control interactions, misuse and attacks. The data is stored in a number of formats, from PCAP and binary files through to logs of keystrokes, system and API calls, including temporal data. This data can be employed for example to identify the attackers and classify attacks [44, 37]. The IEEE Computer Security Group (ICSG) is beginning standardization of data exchange for the security industry using an XML schema for meta-data exchange [45], covering malware sample exchange, URLs, and events such as Conficker.

4 Network Telescope and Analysis Engine

The network telescope setup used at Victoria University is shown in Figure 2 consisting of the advertising router, providing routing advertisements of the address space used, a VLAN trunk to the capture server for data collection, which can be split up using multiple VLANs. This host captures any packets that are destined for this address space, packs them into PCAP files and these packets are sent for analysis periodically, reducing the real time processing overhead of the system. The trade off for the telescopes lower resource overhead is that no packets are ever sent back to the IBR source, which limits the ability to ascertain the source's true intent. With a darknet, for example, all that can be determined is that there is an incoming TCP connection to a specific port e.g. 135, a Blaster worm attack, but without a response to the source we are unable to see the confirming connection on port 4444 [34].

The capture server integrity is maintained by hardening the system, we use tcpdump to capture all packets to disk (in standard PCAP format) and use netfilter rules to identify if any traffic originates from the telescope indicating a breach of the system. The tcpdump process is monitored by the init process to ensure that the tcpdump process is kept alive. All data was captured and stored in 100MB files, which were compressed along with identifying metadata. Data processing was accomplished using a tool developed called pcapstat written in C using the libtrace library [46]. Pcapstat was deployed on a GT2 Grid and the resulting output analysed with the open source statistical package R [47]. Details can be found in the thesis from [48].

The network telescope deployed used a /16 address range located in New Zealand and was unused at that time; it has since been re-used by an organization for their IP needs. It was deployed continuously from 16th December 2004 to the 12th March 2006. The dataset collected by the network telescope consists of approximately 225.6 GBytes and the anonymised dataset is available at DATCAT (http://www.datcat.org, the Internet measurement data catalog), where the destination network address has been replaced with the loopback address, but all other data, including all the data contained within UDP or TCP packets has been preserved except for any destination address information. Anonymisation of the data was completed using a modified version of the libtrace anonymisation tool from the WAND group at Waikato University (http://research.wand.net.nz/software/libtrace.php). The PCAP data was anonymised by changing the first two octets of the destination address to 127.0 respectively, but preserving the lower 16 bits of the address. The libtrace library has a tool to anonymise packet headers and adjust the header checksum accordingly, the modified version of the tool also anonymised occurrences of the source address in binary or text form, or in reverse order as used for example in a reverse DNS lookups in the data field of packets.

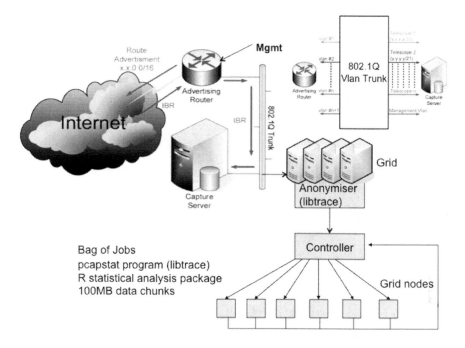

Fig. 2. Network Telescope Setup and Grid Analysis Engine

On average approximately 499Mbytes of data was collected per day over the 452 days of the experiment. Aggregating data from even a reasonably small number of /16 network telescopes, such as envisaged in medium to large scale experiments, would require processing of many 10's of GBytes of data per day in order to produce attack data, trend analysis, IP geo-location, black listing etc. Some data sources are required to anonymise data before sharing it and all data needs to be processed to provide base statistics and trend analysis, e.g. using the statistical package R. Our experiment developed some Grid based solutions that distribute data amongst a set of nodes using the "bag of jobs" paradigm, shown in Figure 2. Data is stored in the pcap format and our base analysis software (pacpstat), extracts core data [48]. Data is concatenated into 100MByte files to be processed and pcapstat was statically compiled to overcome issues with deployment on the Grid (availability of libtrace library).

The Grid setup for the analysis used a distributed computing architecture based on the Sun Grid Engine (Sun Microsystems). This Grid cluster has 232 execution nodes made up from desktop computers used by staff and students connected through a fast Ethernet network. Jobs can be submitted to this cluster and are assigned a node on which to run. A single Grid user is limited to submitting up to 90 concurrent jobs. All of the data file archives on which analysis was performed were stored on a shared file system. This network file system is made available to each of the computing nodes via NFS. This setup allowed up to 90 nodes to process data from the archive files, which initially caused a bottleneck at the file server. To overcome this bottleneck the scripts used to run these jobs copied compressed data files from the file server to local hard disc and to minimize the impact of file server congestion and network latency the extracted data was written to local disc and then the files were archived and transmitted in compressed form back to the NFS share once all analysis was complete. The distribution of Pentium IV processor speeds used were: 42% - 2600MHz, 37% - 2800MHz, 21% - 3200MHz. These computing nodes were required to analyse 2256 individual data files of 100Mbytes each. The distribution of node execution times for pcapstat on the data files is shown in Figure 3. The sum of the execution times is 504,264 seconds (almost 6 days) so parallel processing is essential for rapid analysis. Because the actual analysis runs were performed in a number of chunks to allow other users to make use of the computing grid, it is difficult to obtain a precise overall execution time. For an Internet control loop we may need more responsiveness – 10's of seconds rather than 100's. This raises a number of engineering questions: What is a good sample size from network telescopes? How do we aggregate large data sets? How do we detect changes in probe patterns, and categorise anomalous behaviour (anything captured by a network telescope is potentially malicious except for a few cases)?

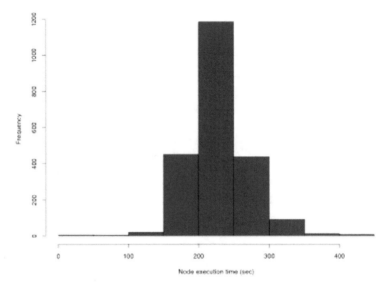

Fig. 3. Grid node processing time (seconds) for 100MB PCAP traces

Previously we identified the non uniformity of data hitting the network telescope from an address range perspective and identified the data sampling strategy that would be best employed to estimate the IBR hitting a larger address space [48, 49]. Here we outline other aspects of the dataset such as typical attack trends detected. The network telescope captured a set of TCP (60.7%), UDP (36.6%) and other traffic (2.7%), mainly ICMP, ARP and IGMP. In terms of IBR arrival rate the network telescope saw a wide range of arrival rates, the majority of activity seen related to port scans. Figures 4 and 5 show typical features, including the repetitive nature of scans on a weekly basis (UDP port 1434), the decay in attacks (e.g. TCP port 1023), step changes (e.g. TCP port 139) and ad hoc attacks (e.g. UDP port 135).

Geo-IP location and ASN determination are a useful component of IBR analysis. Typical results for each attack address are shown in Figure 6, using Google maps and the free Geolite database [50], which provides latitude and longitude of an IP address. Some country data is sparse, however it gives an indication of attack location.

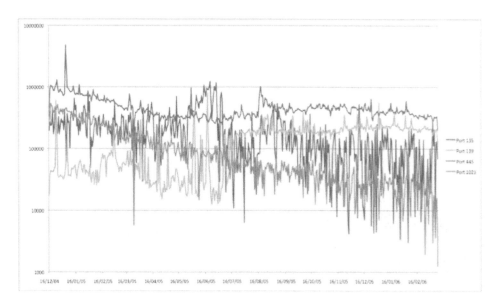

Fig. 4. Top 4 TCP port activity (packets/day)

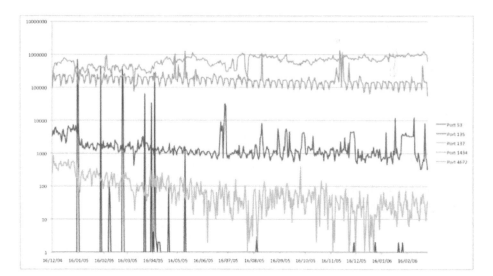

Fig. 5. Top UDP port activity (packets/day) and occasional port 135 attacks

The intensity of each attack location is shown using a colour scale. Red indicates a 50% attack intensity (China), green areas indicate a 1% attack intensity, blue areas indicates a low attack intensity (< 0.1%). For geo-IP analysis the dataset task was split into 1800 jobs, which were sent to Grid nodes sequentially using Ruby and the DRMAA framework (http://drmaa4ruby.sunsource.net/). Jobs downloaded a file containing 10,000 IP addresses and output a file for a second job summarising and collating information for mapping. Each Grid job finished within an hour.

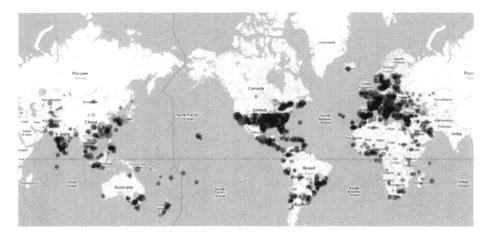

Fig. 6. Geo-heatmap, locating attacks using Google Maps and Geolite data

Using IBR data for traffic filtering was tested on a simplistic testbed. An analysis of a single 100MB sample from near the start of the telescope data indicated two prevalent attack types, the SQL slammer worm and Microsoft-ds from a total of 7,287 attacking hosts. Applying exclusion lists matching these source addresses and TCP characteristics over a sampled set of logged data files showed between 94.3% to 21.4% of all IBR traffic hitting the network telescope would be stopped through the filtering specifically for these addresses and exploits. This indicated the long-term activity of the exploited hosts and attackers prevalent throughout the experiment.

5 Summary

This paper has provided a review of work related to malicious activity detection on the Internet using active and passive measurement devices. We highlight work that is extending these measurement devices and discuss some of the key areas of investigation in developing honeyclients and network telescopes, including a discussion of some experiences with grid computing for scaling instruments and analysis. Internet Sensor Grids and network control infrastructure are becoming feasible, potentially using techniques from complex adaptive system theory, AI and biologically inspired system behaviour for deploying countermeasures. Even simple countermeasures could provide benefits through the application of filtering based on analysed IBR data.

Acknowledgments. The authors would like to acknowledge the work of research assistants Ben Palmer and , Tim Best, internee Jerome Selles, MSc students and David Stirling, PhD students Christian Seifert and Van Lam Le in the development of tools, techniques and analysis for this paper.

References

[1] Park, K.: The Internet as a Complex System, Purdue University, Technical Report (2002)

[2] Park, K., Willinger, W.: The Internet as a Large-scale Complex System. Journal of the Royal Statistical Society: Series A (Statistics in Society) 170(1), 260–260 (2007)

[3] Navarez, J., Seifert, C., Endicott-Popovsky, B., Welch, I., Komisarczuk, P.: Drive-By-Downloads, Victoria University of Wellington, New Zealand, Technical Report (2008)

[4] CERT, CERT/CC statistics (1998–2008),
http://www.cert.org/stats/cert_stats.html

[5] Clark, D., Shenker, S., Falk, A.: GENI Research Plan. GDD-06-28, Version 4.5 (2007)

[6] Seifert, C.: Know Your Enemy: Behind The Scenes Of Malicious Web Servers. The Honeynet Project (2008),
http://www.honeynet.org/papers/wek/
KYE-Behind_the_Scenes_of_Malicious_Web_Servers.pdf

[7] Seifert, C., Steenson, R., Holz, T., Yuan, B., Davis, M.A.: Know Your Enemy: Malicious Web Servers. The Honeynet Project (2008),
http://www.honeynet.org/papers/mws/
KYE-Malicious_Web_Servers.pdf

[8] Seifert, C., Steenson, R., Welch, I., Komisarczuk, P.: Capture - A Tool for Behavioural Analysis of Applications and Documents. In: The Digital Forensic Research Workshop, Pittsburgh, PA (2007)

[9] Seifert, C., Welch, I., Komisarczuk, P.: HoneyC - The Low-Interaction Client Honeypot. In: The Proceedings of the 2007 NZCSRCS, Waikato University, Hamilton, New Zealand (2007)

[10] The Honeynet Project, http://www.honeynet.org/misc/project.html

[11] Seifert, C.: Improving Detection Accuracy and Speed with Hybrid Client Honeypots. PhD Proposal, Victoria University of Wellington, New Zealand (2007)

[12] Komisarczuk, P., Seifert, C., Aval, C., Abbasi, F.: New Zealand Chapter Status Report For 2008. The Honeynet Project, Technical Report (2009)

[13] Moore, M., Shannon, C., Voelker, G.M., Savage, S.: Network telescopes. Technical report, CAIDA (2003)

[14] Plonka, D.: Flawed routers flood university of wisconsin internet time server,
http://pages.cs.wisc.edu/~plonka/netgear-sntp/

[15] Pang, R., Yegneswaran, V., Barford, P., Paxson, V., Peterson, L.: Characteristics of Internet Background Radiation. In: Proceedings of the 4th ACM SIGCOMM Conference on Internet Measurement, pp. 27–40. ACM Press, New York (2004) ISBN 1-58113-821-0

[16] Yegneswaran, V., Barford, P., Ullrich, J.: Internet intrusions: global characteristics and prevalence. In: Proceedings of the 2003 ACM SIGMETRICS International Conference on Measurement and Modeling of Computer Systems, pp. 138–147. ACM Press, New York (2003) ISBN 1-58113-664-1

[17] Komisarczuk, P., Welch, I., Pemberton, D., Seifert, C.: Grid Enabled Internet Instruments In: Proceedings of IEEE Globecom (2007)

[18] Shadowserver, http://www.shadowserver.org/wiki/

[19] Team Cymru. The Team Cymru Darknet Project,
`http://www.cymru.com/Darknet/index.html`, Dragon Research Group,
`http://drg.team-cymru.org/`

[20] Dooley, K.: Complex adaptive systems: a nominal definition, Arizona State University, Technical Report (1996)

[21] Foukia, N., Hassas, S.: Managing computer networks security through self-organisation: a complex system perspective. In: Engineering Self-Organising Systems, pp. 124–138. Springer, Berlin (2004)

[22] Green, I., Raz, T., Zviran, M.: Analysis of Active Intrusion Prevention Data for Predicting Hostile Activity in Computer Networks. Communications of the ACM 50(4), 63–68 (2007)

[23] Glickman, M., Balthrop, J., Forrest, S.: A machine learning evaluation of an artificial immune system. Evolutionary Computation 13(2), 179–212 (2005)

[24] Farrow, R., Geer, D.: Workshop Summary. In: HotBots '07, The First Workshop on Hot Topics in Understanding Botnets. USENIX, Cambridge (2007),
`http://www.usenix.org/publications/`
`login/2007-08/openpdfs/hotbots07sums.pdf`

[25] Shafi, K., Abbass, H.A.: Biologically-inspired Complex Adaptive Systems approaches to Network Intrusion Detection. Inf. Secur. Tech. Rep. 12(4), 209–217 (2007)

[26] Wolpert, D.H., Tumer, K., Frank, J.: Using collective intelligence to route internet traffic. In: Advances in Neural Information Processing Systems (1999)

[27] Seifert, C., Komisarczuk, P., Welch, I., Aval, C.U., Endicott-Popovsky, B.: Identification of Malicious Web Pages Through Analysis of Underlying DNS and Web Server Relationships. In: 4th IEEE LCN Workshop on Network Security (WNS 2008), Montreal (2008)

[28] Stirling, D., Welch, I., Komisarczuk, P.: Designing Workflows for Grid Enabled Internet Instruments. In: the 8th IEEE ccGrid 2008 Conference, Lyon, France (2008)

[29] Bagnasco, A., Poggi, A., Scapolla, A.M.: A Grid-Based Architecture for the Composition and the Execution of Remote Interactive Measurements. In: The Second IEEE International Conference on e-Science and Grid Computing (e-Science'06), Amsterdam, Netherlands (2006)

[30] Honeynet Project. Know your Enemy: Honeynets,
`http://prokect.honeynet.org/papers/honeynet/`

[31] HoneyTrap, `http://sourceforge.net/projects/honeytrap/`

[32] Honey, D.:, `http://www.honeyd.org/`

[33] Yegneswaran, Y., Barford, P., Plonka, D.: On the design and use of internet sinks for network abuse monitoring. In: Jonsson, E., Valdes, A., Almgren, M. (eds.) RAID 2004. LNCS, vol. 3224, pp. 146–165. Springer, Heidelberg (2004)

[34] Cooke, E., Bailey, M., Watson, D., Jahanian, F., Nazario, J.: The Internet Motion Sensor: A distributed global scoped Internet threat monitoring system. Technical report, Univerisity of Michigan, Electrical Engieering and Computer Science (2004)

[35] Capture-HPC, `https://projects.honeynet.org/capture-hpc`

[36] Chard, K., Tan, J., Boverhof, R., Madduri, R., Foster, I.: Wrap Scientific Applications as WSRF Grid Services using gRAVI. In: The IEEE 7th International Conference on Web Services (ICWS), Los Angeles, USA (2009)

[37] Seifert, C., Komisarczuk, P., Welch, I.: Identification of Malicious Web Pages with Static Heuristics. In: The Australasian Telecommunication Networks and Applications Conference (ATNAC), Adelaide, Australia (2008)

[38] Nazario, J., Phoney, C.: A Virtual Client Honeypot. In: USENIX, LEET Workshop (2010),
http://usenix.org/events/leet09/tech/full_papers/nazario/nazario.pdf

[39] Seifert, C., Komisarczuk, P., Welch, I.: True Positive Cost Curve: A Cost-Based Evaluation Method for High-Interaction Client Honeypots. In: The SECUREWARE Conference, Athens (2009)

[40] Le, V.L., Komisarczuk, P., Gao, X.: Applying AI to Improve the Performance of Client Honeypots. In: The Passive and Active Measurements Conference 2009, Seoul Korea (2009)

[41] Moore, D., Shannon, C., Brown, D.J., Voelker, G.M., Savage, S.: Inferring Internet denial-of-service activity. ACM Trans. Comput. Syst. 24(2), 115–139 (2006) ISSN 0734-2071

[42] Cooke, E., Bailey, M., Mao, M.Z., Watson, D., Jahanian, F., McPherson, D.: Toward understanding distributed blackhole placement. In: Proceedings of the 2004 ACM workshop on Rapid Malcode Analysis, pp. 54–64. ACM Press, New York (2004) ISBN 1-58113-970-5

[43] Harder, U., Johnson, M.W., Bradley, J.T., Knottenbelt, W.J.: Observing Internet Worm and Virus Attacks with a Small Network Telescope. In: Proceedings of the 2nd Workshop on Practical Applications of Stochastic Modelling, pp. 113–126 (2005)

[44] Man, V.K.: Clustering Malicious Networking Attacks. MSc Thesis, Victoria of Wellington, Wellington, New Zealand (2008)

[45] IEEE, Computer Security Group (ICSG), Industry Connections Activity Initiation Document Version: 1.0 (Approved),
http://standards.ieee.org/prod-serv/indconn/icsg/ICSG_ICAID.pdf

[46] WAND Network Research Group. The libtrace packet library,
http://research.wand.net.nz/software/libtrace.php

[47] R Development Core Team. R: A Language and Environment for Statistical Computing. R Foundation for Statistical Computing, Vienna, Austria,
http://www.R-project.org

[48] Pemberton, D.: An Empirical Study of Internet Background Radiation Arrival Density and Network Telescope Sampling Strategies. MSc Thesis, School of Mathematics, Statistics and Computer Science, Victoria University of Wellington, New Zealand (2007)

[49] Pemberton, D., Komisarczuk, P., Welch, I.: Internet Background Radiation Arrival Density and Network Telescope Sampling Strategies. In: The Proceedings of the Australasian Telecommunication Network Application Conference, Christchurch, New Zealand (2007)

[50] MINDMAX. Maxmind - geolite city free geolocation database,
http://www.maxmind.com/app/geolitecity

Data-Driven MAC for Efficient Transmission of Spatially Correlated Data in WSNs

Nahdia Tabassum and Guojun Lu

Faculty of Information Technology, Monash University, Australia
{Nahdia.Tabassum,Guojun.Lu}@monash.edu

Abstract. In Wireless Sensor Networks (WSNs), nodes closer to an event are able to detect the event earlier and more accurately, thus contain more important information. Also, tiny nodes are usually scarce of energy and a major portion of their energy is used through communication. Therefore saving the energy by allowing only a limited number of communications is desirable in designing protocols for WSNs. We propose a data-driven Medium Access Control (MAC) protocol which allows only the more useful information to enter into the medium by using a modified contention mechanism and also suppressing other spatially-correlated data that are of less importance. Simulation results show that the proposed MAC outperforms the existing ones in terms of event reporting delay and packet delivery ratio for urgent data.

Keywords: medium access control, data-driven, energy-efficiency, delay, sensor networks.

1 Introduction

Wireless Sensor Networks (WSNs) is a fascinating area with endless possibilities. It is envisioned as one of the most dominating futuristic technologies and promised to bring remote monitoring into the reality. In future almost every aspects of our life is going to be touched by this technology including home safety, wildlife habitat, industrial, medical, child care, aged care, bushfire, and military battle field monitoring [2,8].

In a typical WSN, nodes are deployed in a target field to monitor an event and can measure the usual physical phenomena like temperature, humidity, light, sound, gaseous concentration, radiation, nitrate level in the water etc. [6]. Collected information from the field is then transmitted back to the Base Station (BS) for further processing. But these battery-operated tiny sensor nodes are severely energy constraint because once they are deployed in a target field, it is impractical or often impossible to replace batteries in hundreds or thousands of nodes. Since communication is the most costly part in sensor network operation, the number of data transmission should be reduced to a possible minimum. Hence careful design of MAC protocol is required to allow only limited and meaningful information to enter into the medium.

A. Pont, G. Pujolle, and S.V. Raghavan (Eds.): WCITD/NF 2010, IFIP AICT 327, pp. 146–157, 2010.

Now the problem is to determine which data are to give priority in transmission and which one to suppress. In the case of an event monitoring system, occurrence of the particular physical event produce spatially correlated data around the event. In nature, many physical phenomena follow the diffusion laws. As a result, nodes have better information in the proximity of the phenomenon. For example, the values of the temperature are higher in the vicinity of a heat source and decrease with the distance to the source. Moreover, authors in [11] proved that if a sensor node is located far from the source, it is likely to observe more distorted version of the event. Therefore, the closer a node to the event source the more reliable and useful the information it holds. Now if we limit the number of data transmissions, we should allow only the most urgent/useful information to enter into the medium. Hence we emphasize the fact that in event monitoring application of WSNs, MAC protocol should allow the transmission based on the data characteristics and not by any random choice.

In this paper, we design a data-urgency based medium access technique. In this context our MAC protocol is data-driven, as we utilize node's data urgency levels and initiate data transmission accordingly. Neighboring nodes with less urgent data have to wait longer and if they overhear any transmission of more urgent data, they ultimately suppress their own data. Due to fewer transmission attempts, probability of collision is decreased to a significant amount which leads to a fewer retransmissions resulting in overall less energy consumption and lower delay in data delivery.

The rest of the paper is organized as follows: We discuss the related work in Section 2. The proposed data-driven MAC is discussed in details in Section 3. An environment model is presented in Section 4. The performances of our protocol are compared in Section 5. Finally, we present a brief conclusion in Section 6.

2 Related Work

Energy-efficient MAC protocols for WSNs have made contributions in mainly two parts. Firstly, the channel access mechanism is explored (i.e. the contention problem). Correlation-based Collaborative Medium Access Control (CC-MAC) [11], SIFT [7] etc. fall into this category where they demonstrated how restriction can be put on the number of data entering the medium in order to save energy in transmission. By limiting the number of data transmission within the network, they achieve higher energy efficiency and lower delay in data delivery. Secondly, researchers adopt the classic CSMA/CA based contention mechanism to access the media and made contribution in how nodes periodically follow sleep-wake cycles to save energy. Well known protocols like S-MAC [12], T-MAC [5] etc. fall into this category where they demonstrated how node-to-node data transfer can be made while following a periodic sleep-wake cycles. In this paper we focus on the contention part of the MAC protocol and propose a data-driven MAC utilizing the node's information level.

IEEE 802.11 DCF standard [1]: Though IEEE 802.11 DCF is not a protocol for WSNs; its contention mechanism is also the basic contention mechanism for many WSN MACs (e.g. S-MAC, T-MAC etc.). Therefore we discuss details about the IEEE 802.11 DCF contention mechanism. IEEE 802.11 DCF is a random access mechanism that combines the good features of Carrier Sense Multiple Access with Collision Avoidance (CSMA/CA) with Medium Access with Collision Avoidance Wireless (MACAW) [4] to lower the probability of packet collision. In CSMA, whenever a node intends to send data, it checks the status of the medium to find whether the medium is being currently used by any other neighboring nodes and this checking is called carrier sensing. After detecting the channel as being idle for a minimum duration called DCF Inter Frame Space (DIFS), sender performs a random backoff procedure. The duration of this random backoff time is determined as a multiple of a slot time. If the channel remains idle, the backoff time counter is decremented by one for each idle time slot. If the channel becomes busy, backoff counter is frozen until the medium becomes idle again. Once the backoff counter reaches 'zero', the device is allowed to access the medium and transmits. Each device maintains a so-called Contention Window (CW), from which sender chooses a random backoff time before transmission. Backoff Time (BT) in IEEE DCF is calculated as below:

$$BT = Random\,(0, CW_i) \times aSlotTime \tag{1}$$

Here, CW is the contention window. After each successful transmission, the contention window is reset to CW_{min}, otherwise CW_i is calculated as $CW_i = 2^{k+i-1}$, where i is the number of attempts (including the current one) that have been made to transmit the current packet, and k is a constant defining the minimum contention window CW_{min}. And $aSlotTime$ is the slot time determined by physical layer characteristics.

We can see from (1) that backoff time is a random integer value that corresponds to a slot-number. This slot-number is taken randomly from a uniform distribution. In shared wireless medium, access to the channel depends on the picked slot-number. For example, if two nodes want to access the medium at the same time, and both sense the medium is idle for DIFS amount of time, then both of them take a random backoff time (measured in slot-numbers) before actually transmit into the medium. The node which chooses lower slot-number gets access into the medium first. The node with higher slot-number waits for the other node to finish before transmits itself. But choice of the slot-number does not depend on the node itself and is completely random in nature.

CC-MAC: M.C. Vuran, and I. F. Akyldiz proposed CC-MAC for event-driven WSN applications. They were first to explore spatial correlation in designing MAC protocol for WSNs. To avoid spatial redundancy in transmitted information, CC-MAC proposes to choose only a few representative nodes to transmit data from the target field. One representative node is selected from a correlation region of the area determined by the correlation radius (r_{corr}). Authors claim that only one node is sufficient to transmit from a correlation region in order to achieve desired performance at the sink. To find the representative nodes, all sensor nodes with event information contend for the medium using random access mechanism similar to that of the IEEE 802.11 standard where some sensor nodes can access the channel while others have to backoff. After the initial contention phase, node that captures the medium first becomes the representative node of the area determined by the r_{corr}. Other nodes within the correlation region suppress their data upon overhearing the transmission of the representative node. Neighbors of the correlation region can sleep and only participate in forwarding the packets thus saving energy.

In CC-MAC, though spatial redundancy in data transmission is eliminated, but there is no control on representative node selection. Representative nodes are selected as a result of the random contention protocol, and due to the random characteristics of CSMA-based MAC protocol, there is no means to ensure that nodes with the more urgent data get prior chance in transmission.

SIFT: Jamieson et al. described SIFT as a non-persistent CSMA wireless MAC protocol. But instead of taking a random number from uniform distribution (as used in [12,5,1]), they propose to take a random number from geometric distribution to determine the transmission-slot. The non-uniform, truncated increasing geometric distribution is given in (2).

$$p_r = \frac{(1 - \alpha) \, \alpha^{CW}}{1 - \alpha^{CW}} \times \alpha^{-r} \quad \text{for } r = 1, 2, \cdots CW \tag{2}$$

Here $0 < \alpha < 1$ is a parameter and is defined by $\alpha = N_{max}^{-\frac{1}{CW-1}}$, where N_{max} is the maximum number of nodes that can be supported by the protocol.

By using this geometric distribution, nodes have higher probability to pick up the later transmission-slots. Only a few nodes choose lower transmission-slots and get access to the medium first. Sift also allows only R number of event reports to transmit toward the BS through message suppression. Applying the geometrically increasing distribution, SIFT can reduce the collision while there is a sudden increase in traffic load, but there is no control on which node can access the channel first. Nodes near the event with urgent data may not get opportunity to access the medium, because, with the geometrically increasing distribution, it is not possible to determine which node is finally winning the shared medium. In this paper, we propose a data-driven MAC to improve the above schemes. The details are discussed in Section 3.

3   Data-Driven MAC

In event detection applications of WSNs, users are interested in getting the event-source information quickly and reliably. MAC protocols designed for such event-driven applications should give higher priority to the critical data (e.g. high temperature/gaseous concentration reading) than normal data (i.e. low temperature readings) in accessing the medium. By critical data we mean that readings that are highly indicative to the occurrence of an event under observation. For example, temperature reading that indicates an ignition nearby for bushfire monitor application or higher gaseous concentration that indicates a leakage nearby for an industrial leakage monitor application. By allowing only meaningful and

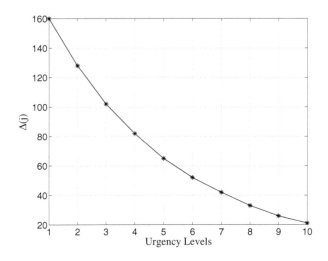

Fig. 1. Relationship between urgency levels and $\Delta(j)$

urgent information to enter into the media, MAC protocol can reduce redundant transmissions and energy consumption while reducing data delay.

While CC-MAC chooses a random number from uniform distribution and SIFT chooses a random number from geometric distribution in order to determine the index of the transmission-slot, we propose to directly calculate the slot-number within the CW based on the urgency of the data. The main disadvantage of CC-MAC and SIFT's contention mechanism is, due to the inherent randomness in choosing the index of transmission-slot, a node with some urgent information may not have any opportunity in accessing the medium.

Instead of using any probability distribution to choose the slot-number from we propose the following equation to choose the index of the transmission-slot.

$$
BT = \begin{cases} Random(0, \Delta(j)) \times aSlotTime & \text{when } j = j_{max} \\ Random((\Delta(j+1)+1), \Delta(j)) \times aSlotTime & \text{otherwise} \end{cases} \quad (3)
$$

Here, $\Delta(j)$ is given by the following equation:

$$
\Delta(j) = \left\lfloor \frac{(1-\alpha)^j}{\alpha \times [1-(1-\alpha)^{jmax}]} \times \beta \right\rfloor \quad \text{where } 0 < \alpha < 1 \quad (4)
$$

Here, j represents different urgency levels namely, $1, 2, \cdots, j_{max}$. The values of j are chosen based on the sensor's measurement about the event's effect. Mapping of j's to the data readings are discussed in details in subsection 4.2.

The α is a skewness parameter and β is a scale factor. The values of these two parameters are used to adjust the size of CW. The bigger the value of α, the smaller the $\Delta(j)$ s resulting in smaller CW size and vice versa. We have seen from experiments that if the CW is too small, it creates more collisions and at the same time if the CW is too big, it can introduce unnecessary delay. Based

Table 1. Urgency levels and corresponding CW boundaries

Urgency Levels	CW boundaries (Lower - Upper)	Urgency Levels	CW boundaries (Lower - Upper)
10 (highest)	0 - 21	5	53 - 65
9	22 - 26	4	66 - 82
8	27 - 33	3	83 - 102
7	34 - 42	2	103 - 128
6	43 - 52	1 (lowest)	129 - 160

on our observation we have taken $\alpha = 0.2$ and $\beta = 45$ and, Fig. 1 and Table 1 show the CW boundaries for different priority levels from (3) and (4), for these values of α and β.

Equation (4) ensures that node with urgent information have shortest waiting time as shown in Table 1. But considering the fact that more than one node may possess the same urgency level, we retain a small random part in our algorithm in order to alleviate the probability of nodes with same urgency levels colliding with each other.

Now, we further explain our algorithm by taking a particular scenario with different urgency levels, i.e. $j = 1, 2, \cdots, 10$ (highest-urgency-level). At first, nodes while sensing events determine their own urgency level on the basis of sensor's measurement about the event's effect (i.e. sensed-data). After deciding on the urgency level, nodes calculate the appropriate backoff time using (3). For example, if it has the highest urgency level (i.e. j_{max}), it takes a random number within the first CW (i.e. within 0 and 21) and gets chance to transmit first. Neighboring nodes suppress their own data if they overhear transmission of higher urgency data packet. If there is no data in the highest urgency level, then the nodes with second highest urgency level send their data and so on.

In order to reduce the number packets to enter into medium, we introduce a threshold in the urgency level as X_{th}. Nodes having data above X_{th} are allowed to transmit. Threshold is setup in a way that only the nodes with useful-data can access the medium. For example, no data should be transmitted when the temperature is in normal range. The urgency level is embedded in the data packets so that intermediate nodes can also access the medium appropriately based on the urgency levels of route-through packets.

4 Environment Model

In this section, we explain how urgency levels used in our proposed scheme are determined.

4.1 Modeling the Environment

Event's Effect. We used the similar environment model used in [6] to populate data in various sensor nodes around the event source. Authors in [6] argues that every physical event produces a fingerprint in the environment in terms of the event's effect; e.g., fire increases temperature, chemical spilling increases contamination, and gas leakage increases gaseous concentration. Moreover, most of the physical phenomena follow diffusion property [3] with distance, d and time t, and can be modeled as a function of distance and time, $f(d, t)$. Now, considering sensors reading at particular time instance, say t_1, diffusion can be expressed as a function of distance only, i.e., $f(d) \propto 1/d^a$, where d is the distance from the point having maximum effect of the event, $f(d)$ is the magnitude of the event's effect at d and a is the diffusion parameter depending on the type of effect; e.g., for light $a = 2$, heat $a = 1$.

Environmental Noise. A sensor readings may include noise due to surrounding condition, such a humidity, prolonged heat exposure, obstacles etc. The amount of noise included in sensor readings is less where the distance between the event source and sensor is less [11]. The noise level gradually increases with distance from the source. Including this noise, sensor's reading can be modeled as follows,

$$f(d_i) = f^*(d_i) \pm f_{env}(f^*(d_i)) \qquad (5)$$

Here, $f_{env}(f^*(d_i)) \propto (f_{max} - f^*(d_i))$, d_i = distance of the location from peak information point (i.e., the event), $f(d_i)$ = gradient information of the location with environmental noise, f_{max} = peak information, $f^*(d_i) = f_{(max)}/d^a$ = gradient information of the location without environmental noise. In the simulation, $a = 0.8$ is taken [6]. The proportional constant is considered 0.03 as in [6] to model the environmental for our protocol, i.e., 3% environmental noise is considered.

4.2   Mapping of Sensor Data to the Urgency Levels

Mapping of sensed data to the urgency levels depends entirely on the target application of WSN and the nature of the physical phenomena under observation. Based on the target application, sensor readings can be varied widely including but not limited to temperature, humidity, seismic vibration, motion, acceleration etc. For example, in bushfire detection application nodes sense the ambient temperature among other possible sensing parameters and hence the ambient temperature reading can be affected by various factors like distance, obstacles, wind direction etc. As shown in Table 2, higher urgency levels are given to the higher temperature readings while the lower end (e.g. urgency levels 1, 2, and 3) actually refers to non-threat situation because these temperatures fall within the normal range. Urgency level 4 can be assumed as the upper threshold and temperatures above the threshold need reporting. For real applications, these urgency levels and upper/lower threshold can be easily further fine-tuned to suit the desired accuracy level.

5   Performance Analysis

We use $ns - 2$ [9] simulator for analyzing the performance of the proposed data-driven MAC protocol. Comparisons will be made with (1) IEEE 802.11 standard and (2) SIFT which is one of the recent protocols to manage spatially correlated

Table 2. Mapping of temperatures with urgency levels

Ambient Temp. ($^\circ C$)	Urgency Level	Ambient Temp. ($^\circ C$)	Urgency Level
80 and above	10	50 - 59	5
75 - 79	9	40 - 49	4
70 - 74	8	30 - 39	3
65 - 69	7	20 - 29	2
60 - 64	6	0 - 19	1

data. Though IEEE 802.11 standard is not suitable for WSN but its contention mechanism is used as the basic access mechanism by many renowned WSN-MACs (i.e. S-MAC, T-MAC etc.) and in this paper we are focusing on the contention part to allow urgent data to reach the destination quickly. The performance of the data-driven MAC protocol has been studied in the following two scenarios: (1) a single node in the network has data of maximum-urgency and (2) multiple nodes have data of maximum-urgency. We are going to measure the following performance metrics for data-driven MAC, SIFT and IEEE 802.11 standard:

- Event reporting delay: The total delay experienced by data packets. The lower the reporting delays for the important data, the better.
- Packet delivery ratio: The ratio of the number of data packets actually delivered to the destinations versus the number of data packets supposed to be received. This number presents the effectiveness of a protocol.

These measurements indicate how quickly and reliably the urgent data are sent to the sink. They also indirectly indicate the energy consumption: lower delay means lower number of collision and lower number of retransmission resulting in lower energy consumption.

In the subsection 5.1, we discuss simulation topology and parameters. We compare the performance of the proposed MAC in subsection 5.2. In the subsection 5.3, the impact of parameter on the performances of our protocol is analysed.

5.1   Simulation Topology and Parameters

We arrange 100 nodes in a 10 by 10 grid as shown in Fig. 2. Nodes are separated by five meter from each other and the sink is located at the upper-right corner ($x = 50$ meter, $y = 50$ meter). As in [5], a radio range chosen for all nodes so that non-edge nodes all have 8 neighbors. As well, two-ray ground reflection model is used for signal propagation. The sensor nodes are modeled according to the $ns - 2$ wireless node module [9]. In routing layer, we have used Ad hoc On-Demand Distance Vector (AODV) routing protocol [10] for all MACs. Data traverse a multi-hop route from source to the sink.

Event-Based Traffic: Constant-bit-rate (CBR) or TCP flows do not suffice to evaluate protocols for sensor networks, because they capture neither the bursti-ness inherent in the network, nor some underlying physical process that the network should be sensing [7]. We therefore propose two event-based workloads to evaluate our design. In the first, a single node is having maximum-urgency: a fire event (E) is simulated with $f_{max} = 200^\circ C$ at $x = 3$, $y = 3$ as shown

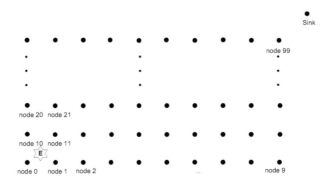

Fig. 2. 100-node network with sink situated at the right-top corner

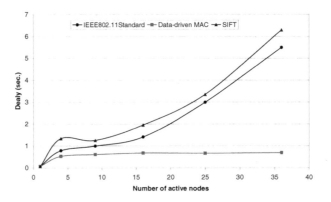

Fig. 3. Average reporting delay with respect to increasing number of active nodes

in Fig. 2. Any surrounding node calculates its urgency level based on the temperature data it has which is in turn dependent on the distance from the event source and the noise factor as discussed in Section 4. Nearby nodes have higher urgency levels than the far-away nodes. With this setup; we observed, only node 11 which is closest the event have maximum-urgency level. This can resemble to the early stage of forest fire which is just ignited. In the second, multiple nodes have maximum-urgency: we have simulated the fire with higher temperature (i.e. $f_{max} = 370°C$) and found that up to nine surrounding nodes may have maximum-urgency level. This situation can resemble to the situation when fire is reasonably spread over.

In the simulation, every node sensing the event calculates its urgency level, and then determines its backoff time using (3). After that, nodes start trying sending data (if their data is above the threshold). Neighboring nodes, upon overhearing any ongoing transmission, compare the data with their own. If the over-hearer has less important data, it suppress its data, otherwise it compete for the medium. Whenever, a node has data to send and takes transmission attempt, we call it in active mode and otherwise it is in the flat mode. In the

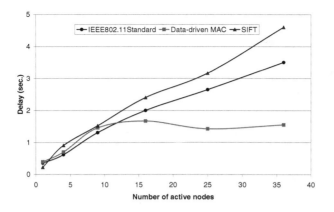

Fig. 4. First reporting delay for multiple source having maximum urgency

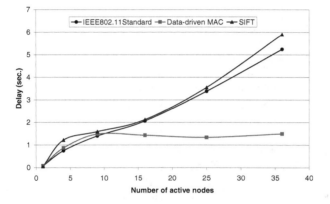

Fig. 5. Average reporting delay for multiple source having maximum urgency

flat mode, nodes do not have their own data but they take parts in forwarding other's data towards the sink. To create the worst case scenario to test protocol performance, data generation is engineered in such a way that all active nodes start to send data at the same time. For the observation purpose, at first node 11 is put into active mode and all others are taking part in forwarding. Then, the four surrounding nodes (i.e. nodes 0, 1, 10, and 11) are put into active mode. In this way 9, 16, 25 and 36 surrounding nodes are put into active modes to observe the performance under heavy traffic.

5.2   Simulation Results

Event reporting delay. This delay is calculated by subtracting (simulation) time when the maximum-urgency data are generated at a node from the time when that is received at the sink. We ran the simulation for 100 times with random seeds and calculated average delay.

a) Average reporting delay is given in Fig. 3 for single node having maximum-urgency scenario. The reporting delay increases with increasing number of active

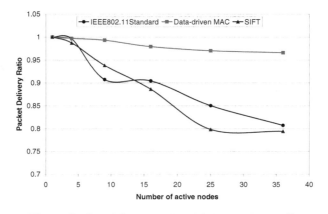

Fig. 6. Packet delivery ratio with increasing traffic

nodes in SIFT and IEEE 802.11. This is expected because with increasing number of contenders, probability of collision would also increase and results in higher network delay. In data-driven MAC, however the delay remains almost constant despite the increasing number of active nodes. This is because, in the single node having maximum-urgency scenario, other surrounding nodes have bigger backoff time and even far-off nodes have such low priority they eventually suppress their data allowing the maximum-urgency data to traverse quickly.

b) Average reporting delay (single report is required at the sink) for multiple nodes having maximum-urgency scenario is shown in Fig. 4. From Fig. 4, we see that all three protocols are performing closely until nine actives nodes. This is because, up to this point all the active nodes have maximum-urgency level and they are competing with each other. So the delays increase almost linearly with the number of active nodes. But after that when more nodes are active (i.e. in the case of 16, 25, and 36), they all compete with each other on both cases of SIFT and IEEE802.11, causing increased delay. For the data-driven MAC, the number of real competition remains almost same beyond nine active nodes (i.e. for the scenario of 16, 25 and 36 active nodes). So the reported delay remains low and almost constant.

c) Average reporting delay (multiple reports are required at the sink) for multiple nodes having maximum-urgency scenario is shown in Fig. 5. We have calculated the average delay for the three protocols when more than one reports are required at the sink to ensure the event reliability. In this case 10 reports are sent from each source. In this scenario, we also find that data-driven MAC outperforms the others.

The above discussion proved the proposed data-driven MAC protocol can deliver the urgent data more quickly.

Packet delivery ratio. This is a measure of reliability in data delivery. For the measurement of packet delivery ratio of maximum-urgency packets, ten packets are sent from each source in every run. Temperature is set up in such a way that up to four nodes may have maximum-urgency levels at any time. Simulation is repeated 100 times with different random seeds. So the ratio is calculated from the total number of packets received at the sink out of the total number packets sent from the nodes with maximum-urgency level. We see from the Fig. 6, the delivery ratio is higher in the proposed MAC than the IEEE802.11 and SIFT, and proposed protocol performs better with increasing number of contenders.

This shows that the proposed protocol is more reliable to send urgent data.

6   Conclusion

In this paper, we propose the data-driven MAC which exploits information level exists in sensor's reading in taking transmission decision. Medium access is favored to the higher-urgency level nodes which have more accurate and reliable event information. Energy efficiency is preserved by suppressing the redundant transmission from any neighboring node that has less urgent and noisier version of event information. Simulation results show that the event reporting delay is lower in our protocol than SIFT and the traditional IEEE 802.11 standard. Also the reliability factor (e.g. higher packet delivery ratio) is much higher in our proposed contention scheme than the IEEE802.11 standard and SIFT. Therefore, we can conclude that, our proposed data-driven MAC is more suitable for the event detection application of WSNs.

References

1. Wireless LAN Medium Access Control (MAC) and Physical Layer (PHY) Specification. IEEE Std. 802.11 (2007)
2. Akyildiz, I.F., Su, W., Sankarasubramaniam, Y., Cayirci, E.: Wireless sensor networks: a survey. Computer Networks 38(4), 393–422 (2002)
3. Askeland, D.R.: The Science and Engineering of Materials. Wadsworth Publishing Company (1994)
4. Bharghavan, V., Demers, A., Shenker, S., Zhang, L.: MACAW: a media access protocol for wireless LAN_s. In: Proceedings of the conference on Communications architectures, protocols and applications, SIGCOMM, pp. 212–225 (1994)
5. Dam, T.V., Langendoen, K.: An adaptive energy-efficient mac protocol for wireless sensor networks. In: SenSys, pp. 171–180 (2003)
6. Faruque, J., Helmy, A.: RUGGED: Routing on fingerprint gradients in sensor networks. In: ICPS, pp. 179–188 (2004)
7. Jamieson, K., Balakrishnan, H., Tay, Y.C.: Sift: A mac protocol for event-driven wireless sensor networks. In: Römer, K., Karl, H., Mattern, F. (eds.) EWSN 2006. LNCS, vol. 3868, pp. 260–275. Springer, Heidelberg (2006)
8. Kredo II, K., Mohapatra, P.: Medium access control in wireless sensor networks. Computer Networks 51(4), 961–994 (2007)
9. Network Simulator - ns (Version 2): ns, http://www.isi.edu/nsnam/ns/
10. Perkins, E.C., Royer, E.M.: Ad-hoc On-Demand distance vector routing. In: WMCSA, pp. 90–100 (1999)
11. Vuran, M.C., Akyildiz, I.F.: Spatial correlation-based collaborative medium access control in wireless sensor networks. IEEE/ACM Trans. Netw. 14(2), 316–329 (2006)
12. Ye, W., Heidemann, J., Estrin, D.: An energy-efficient mac protocol for wireless sensor networks. In: Proc. IEEE INFOCOM, pp. 1567–1576 (2002)

Leveraging Trusted Network Connect for Secure Connection of Mobile Devices to Corporate Networks

Kai-Oliver Detken[1], Hervais Simo Fhom[2],
Richard Sethmann[3], and Günther Diederich[3]

[1] DECOIT GmbH, Fahrenheitstraße 9, 28359 Bremen, Germany
detken@decoit.de
[2] Fraunhofer Institute for Secure Information Technology, Rheinstrasse 75, 64295
Darmstadt, Germany
hervais.simo@sit.fraunhofer.de
[3] University of Applied Science of Bremen, Flughafenallee 10, 28199 Bremen, Germany
{sethmann,guenther.diederich}@hs-bremen.de

Abstract. The approach described in this paper is part of the German national research project VOGUE. VOGUE leverages trusted network connect concepts as a key to implement/design a holistic and vendor neutral network access system while addressing shortcomings of traditional network access control mechanisms. The rest of the paper is organized as follows: Section 2 provides the motivation that outlines the importance of validating mobile devices state of health before allowing access to the enterprise network and gives a brief overview of the background on Trusted Network Connect (TNC). Furthermore, the section describes the security risks, challenges and requirements that are relevant to interoperable network access control and authorization. Next, we discuss in section 4 existing solutions and other industry standards and specifications that have had an influence on our work. The paper concludes with section 5.

Keywords: Network Access Protection (NAP), Network Access Control (NAC), Trusted Computing Group (TCG), Trusted Network Connect (TNC), Trusted Platform Module (TPM), SIMOIT, TNC@FHH, VOGUE.

1 Introduction

Wired and wireless communication networks grow together and service access is becoming more and more ubiquitous, multimodal and standardized solutions are necessary. However, mobile devices and systems pose specific requirements and because of the diversity of network access technologies, the increasing numbers of services, mobile devices are more vulnerable with respect to IT-security. Reliable identification of both the user and the device itself is mandatory for authorization and authentication when requesting access to networks or services. In general, IT-based business processes demand administration and control of access privileges with automated and role-based allocation/withdrawal of user privileges – the so called "user-provisioning" und "de-provisioning".

A. Pont, G. Pujolle, and S.V. Raghavan (Eds.): WCITD/NF 2010, IFIP AICT 327, pp. 158–169, 2010.

The Trusted Network Connect (TNC) approach addresses this issue, specified by the Trusted Computing Group (TCG) with the aim to define a common standard. Besides the more significant authentication (user and device identification), a quarantine-zone for unsecured equipment has been introduced. TNC avoids any modifications of devices and thus excludes security lacks caused by weak device configuration, security breaches in software applications and operating systems. With this framework the configuration state of devices are communicated to a dedicated server, which decides upon its trustworthiness.

The core specification has been completed and some products such as switches, routers, and VPN-gateways are already available in the market. However, a seamless integration of mobile users into an enterprise user-centric identity management system is still far from being a reality. Platform-independent solutions do not exist in the market. Authentication mechanisms and synchronization of user identities and rights are not compatible.

Especially for SMEs identity management and access is a complex issue and challenge. This target group cannot afford dedicated departments for IT-security and has to face restricted budgets and personnel resources. As mobile networking and communications becomes more complex, administration is tedious and error-prone, demanding mechanisms for central administration and configuration. The German R&D project VOGUE (http://www.vogue-project.de) has identified this problem and implemented the TNC approach partly in the form of a vendor-neutral prototype. [1]

2 Motivation and Background

Let us consider an enterprise that provides its employee, named Bob, with a mobile communication device (e.g. smartphone) running several critical business applications that he require for carrying out his job responsibilities. As mobile employee, Bob uses the firm-owned mobile device to remotely access critical components of his enterprise's network and retrieve sensitive business information remotely. In order to limit access for non-authorized users and devices, Bob's enterprise relies on a traditional network access control approach deployed as a combination of 802.1X, EAP/EAoP, IPsec and RADIUS. That scenario will lead us to the motivation of the project VOGUE, the security risks/challenges, and requirements, described in the next sub-chapters.

2.1 Motivation Scenario

In order to enter his employer network, Bob first connect his mobile device to a wireless access point (AP). The latter can be either a public hotspot or one located at a foreign[1] enterprise network perimeter. By applying the foreign enterprise's and public hotspot's operator routing policy respectively, the AP relays Bob and his device through a potentially unsecured network, i.e. Internet, to his home security gateway.

The AP's network control policy as well as related processes is for simplicity reasons not further discussed. The security gateway, which is designed to enforce

---

[1] Any network other than Bob's employer network to which Bob's mobile device may be connected.

Bob's employer network access policy blocks, by default, all traffics form devices that have not yet been authenticated. It basically blocks all traffic towards back-end components like for instance critical database servers and other services provisioning servers, except those traffics towards entities needed to establish trust, e.g. AAA server. The mobile device then authenticates to the security gateway by sending it all necessary security parameters including Bob's identity attribute (user name and correct password) as well as his smartphone credentials. These security parameters are then relayed to relevant back-end validator entities (e.g. AAA server), which proceed to determine whether Bob and his smartphone are compliant with the enterprise's policy requirements. If the compliance check is successful, i.e. if user and device along with their respective attributes (e.g. identity and role in the company) are authentic and allowed to access company critical servers, then the back-end validators instruct the security gateway about access rules and conditions to be enforced. Finally, the gateway provides the smartphone with the enforced access decision. An example of such a decision might be the establishment of a secure VPN-connection between Bob's mobile device and one of his company critical services provisioning servers.

However, since the employer, being the owner of the smartphone, might also allows Bob to use the device in foreign networks (e.g. while working from a partner's premise) and perhaps install applications that he need for his daily use, it wants to be able to validate access to its network based on the smartphone's state of health and security. It thereby wants to mitigate potential threats posed to his network infrastructure by getting assurance about the mobile device integrity and the fact that there is no malware-infected application running on it.

2.2 Security Risks and Challenges

Regarding the described scenario we have the following security risks and challenges:

a. **Endpoints misconfiguration:** Traditionally, enterprises deployed NAC solutions relying on strong isolation of network segments by means of firewalls and routers. Dedicated routers are configured to perform simple network packet filtering while the firewalls deployed as proxies performed more fine-grained filtering or allow the setting of a "demilitarized zone" (DMZ). However, firewalls configuration might contain errors and even well configured firewalls can be circumvented. On the other hand, vulnerable networked devices (incl. smartphones) posing huge security threats to the overall enterprise information and communication technology are typically secured by means of patching of their OS, update or by installation of latest versions of security software. The challenge here is related to the difficulty and cost of patching, updating and managing security patches manually, especially when non-security aware employees (re-)introduce infected mobile devices into the enterprise network. Moreover, the ubiquitous nature of smartphones makes it hard the kind of automatic, continuous and centralized management required for a broader and secure adoption of smartphones as endpoints in enterprise network infrastructures.

b. **Open and ubiquitous nature of mobile endpoints:** the growing popularity of smartphones is attracting more and more enterprises to deploy them as integrated components of their enterprise network. Designed as open and programmable-networked embedded devices, smartphones are used by mobile and external employees to access and manage critical business data in a ubiquitous way (see section 2.1). This fact has introduced new technologies and new security challenges to the urgent need for machine-to-machine identification and authentication, and cross-layer network access authorization. Machine level platform-authentication is crucial for the security and authorization of network-access requests at both layer-2 and layer-3. Furthermore, due to recent attacks at the higher layers (e.g. attributable to the increasing number of smartphones malwares) a major problem that needs to be addressed is that of achieving integrity of mobile endpoints. The problem of endpoint integrity concerns in our case the trustworthiness of the smartphones and that of enterprise servers with regard to their respective integrity states, including their identities. By the term integrity, we understand relative purity of the smartphone platform from software (and hardware) that are considered harmful to the phone itself and others with whom it interacts. The growing number of smartphone malwares best exemplifies this problem for corporate networks. As illustrated in the motivation scenario, today employees connect their mobile devices to unsecured networks, at home or when they are away on business, often resulting in malware being inadvertently downloaded onto the smartphone. When (re-) connected to the corporate network, the device becomes a distributor of the malware to other devices on the enterprise network. [2]

2.3 Security Requirements

For the aforementioned scenario and with regard to the security risks and challenges described above, we define the following requirements:

a. **Backward compatibility and scalability:** it is not reasonable to build an entirely new NAC solution that does not interwork with already existing solutions, industry standards and open specifications. Therefore, proposals for a new NAC system have to be interoperable systems leveraging a number of existing and emerging standards, products, or techniques such as IEEE 802.1X and/or others. Moreover, a new NAC system should provides features required to guarantee good scalability and performance especially for large-scale enterprise environments, e.g. centralized configuration and policy management. The complexity of maintaining such a deployed NAC system should be reasonable.
b. **Enterprise's network security policy should be reliably enforced:** additionally to user and device credentials, the mobile endpoint's state of health and security should be considered for validation during the access control and authorization process. Validation rules and conditions specified as technical security/ integrity policy have to be reliably enforced. Such a policy might require the presence, status, and software version of mandated

applications, and the OS patch level of the mobile device. Reassessment methods are required to enforce post-admission control, i.e. revalidation, at regular time interval, of mobile device platforms that are already admitted to the enterprise network.

c. **Isolation and automatic remediation:** in order to provide flexibility with regard to the isolation of critical enterprise networked resources from less critical ones, mobile devices should be reliably isolated and quarantined from the rest of the network if they fail to meet the security policy requirements for endpoint compliance. If allowed, smartphones and employees redirected to a quarantine zone should be provided with necessary security updates, helping them becoming compliant. In order to reduce the effort for performing such a strategy, especially in large-scale enterprise, the remediation process has to be automatic.

d. **Endpoints platform authentication:** NAC mechanisms should enable mobile devices and employees to reliably detect rogue access requestors and rogue security gateways respectively. Furthermore, the proof of identity of communication endpoint (smartphones, access point or back-end servers) and the assessment of platform integrity of those devices have to be reliably verified.

e. **Support of federation of trust:** since corporations defined different network access control and authorization policies, methods are required for exchanging security attributes and integrity information about a mobile device and about the employee associated with it across enterprises' security domains. This is an important requirement considering corporation boundaries becoming more elastic and mobile devices roaming between different corporations' networks.

f. **Usability:** NAC solutions should be designed while keeping both network administrators and end users' (employees) conveniences in mind.

2.4 Trusted Network Connect (TNC)

With the TNC specification, the TCG developed an open and vendor-neutral specification for the integrity check of communication endpoints, which requests access to a resource. The architecture supports existing and well-established security technologies such as VPN, 802.1X, Extensible Authentication Protocol (EAP) and RADIUS. The TCG's TNC offers hardware support by means of the Trusted Platform Module (TPM), so that e.g. the accuracy of the platform integrity information used in the network access control process is guaranteed. Built in desktop PCs and notebooks this integrated chip protects data on a hardware level. Together with 802.1X, it guarantees the TNC architecture, so that solely certified (digitally signed) application software may be used. Furthermore, this technology uses an authorization token (e.g. a X.509 certificate), which is communicated together with the client status information. These are being validated at the target system against policy conformity. Access management relies on client identity and system status.

The architecture of TNC should be divided into three main areas:

a. **Access Requestor (AR):** contains a Network Access Requestor, the software that is used by the client to connect to the network – an 802.1X supplicant, a VPN client, or similar. The Access Requestor also contains a TNC Client (software that manages the overall NAC process) and Integrity Measurement Collectors (IMCs, plug-in software modules specialized for reporting the status of anti-virus software, patches, or other things).

b. **Policy Decision Point (PDP):** contains a Network Access Authority, software that makes the final decision on whether network access should be granted. The Policy Decision Point also contains a TNC Server (software that manages the NAC process on the server) and Integrity Measurement Verifiers (IMVs, plug-in software modules that compare reports from IMCs against policy, supply access recommendations to the TNC Server, and send remediation instructions to the IMCs).

c. **Policy Enforcement Point (PEP):** PEP is responsible for the assessment of the Integrity Measurement Collectors (IMC) and the TNC client measurement data. PEP doesn't have any internal components. The TNC server will do this work.

The following diagram illustrates the TNC architecture, as specified in [2]:

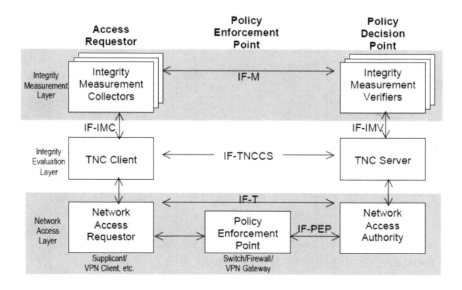

Fig. 1. TNC architecture overview

The interfaces of TNC are really vendor-independence. Every component in the TNC architecture has been implemented by multiple vendors and these products have been tested to ensure they actually work together. Customers retain full choice and are not tied down to any one vendor. Similar but proprietary approaches are NAP from Microsoft and NAC from Cisco Systems. [2]

3 Related Work

Endpoint security solutions are being implemented in routers, switches, WLAN access points, software and security appliances. Authentication and authorization information of mobile devices are being communicated to a policy server, which decides if the device may have access or not. Furthermore, an access protection enables a state check ("health check") of the client. Such a check typically consists of requests for specific information about the client platform. Some of the gathered data is e.g.: version of the anti-virus software, configuration of the personal firewall, and of other software, and the patch level of the device (also of the operating system). In case that the client does not fulfil the security policy, it can be isolated into a dedicated VLAN with a consecutive "decontamination". [3]

Beside the licensed software products, "Cisco Network Admission Control (NAC)" and "Microsoft Network Access Protection (NAP)", an open source solution exists: "Trusted Network Connect (TNC)". For this solution, some projects implemented their own approach, like SIMOIT (http://www.simoit.de) and TNC@FHH (http://trust.inform.fh-hannover.de).

3.1 Network Access Protection (NAP)

Microsoft's Network Access Protection is similar to the TNC functionality. However, the nomenclature of the components varies (NAP client = TNC client, TNC server = Network Policy Server (NPS), Integrity Measurement Collector is comparable to SHA (System Health Agent), and the task of the Integrity Measurement Verifier can be dispatched by the System Health Validator). [6]

Similar to the TNC technology, NAP addresses the following aspects:

a. **Validity check of network policies:** The validation of the mobile devices against policy conformity such as the current patch level of the operating system.
b. **Fulfillment of network policies:** Updating mobile devices, so that they meet the security policies (in an isolated quarantine network segment).
c. **Network access:** After a positive authentication validation and policy validation, access to the network is granted.

Through the so called "Statement of Health"-protocol interoperability between TNC and NAP is given. Furthermore, a licence agreement between Cisco and Microsoft allows NAP clients to communicate with both the "Statement of Health" protocol and the Cisco Trust Agent protocol. [5]

3.2 Network Admission Control (NAC)

Cisco's Network Admission Control is a further architecture, which can be compared with TNC. It is an "Enforcement and quarantine technology on API level", which is integrated in the Cisco network infrastructure. Here, the trusted module "Cisco Trusted Agent" is used for user authentication and authorization. It is implemented in the mobile devices and in Cisco routers and switches. [7]

A prerequisite for using the NAC framework architecture are the following Cisco components: [5]

a. **Trusted Network Agent:** Collects information from the clients, which NAC applications are installed. These information are sent to the Network Access Device (NAD) on request.

b. **Cisco Secure ACS:** Acting as policy server, it checks the information coming from the Trust Agent and determines the access privileges of the clients, and sends this information to the Network Access Devices (NAD).

c. **Network Access Devices (NAD):** This is a Cisco device (switch, router, VPN concentrator or access point) supporting Network Admission Control and defining the client access privileges based on the information received from the Cisco Secure ACS.

3.3 SIMOIT

According to the requirement specifications to mobile devices and the application scenarios of the pilot-user the project SIMOIT (http://www.simoit.de) specified the architecture and implemented a prototype, which evaluated the TNC approach. The core element of the prototype platform is represented by the Mobile Security Gateway (MSG), consisting of different modules (VPN, firewall, TNC, RADIUS, and LDAP). Here, for the sake of an openness and flexibility, mainly open source solutions have been selected. [1]

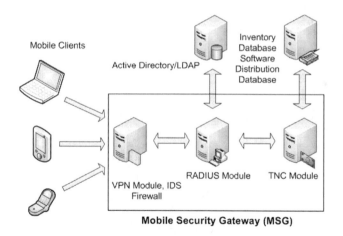

Fig. 2. Overview of the modules of the SIMOIT system

SIMOIT is able to interact with unmodified clients having a standard configuration, whereas complete TNC-architectures require software-agents and integrity measurement collectors on the client-side. SIMOIT aimed at the development of a mobile IT security platform for heterogeneous environments using standards. The method and solutions developed in this project can be deployed for IT infrastructures in small and medium sized enterprises. The essential aim was to develop a modular and vendor-neutral system.

According to the requirements and the application scenarios of the pilot user SIMOIT realized a development and test platform, which evaluated the TNC methodology. The main platform is represented by the Mobile Security Gateway (MSG) as mentioned before. The project specifically evaluated open source software projects and methods with the aim to realize a standard solution. At the same time, SIMOIT paid high attention to flexibility, so that typical security components such as firewalls can be integrated as well. In this case, instead of using the SIMOIT module an interface was provided. Also, it was stipulated that existing inventory databases can be interconnected in order to retrieve software versions and patch levels. The pilot user required the interconnection of an Active Directory Server (ADS), which made it necessary to develop an interface via LDAP. Through this, all user profiles crucial for authentication can be retrieved, and routed to the Mobile Security Gateway (MSG).

For the sake of high flexibility, SIMOIT mainly focused on a server-side solution. The reason for this is the fact, that in the future mobile device vendors will provide their own access software. Hence, on the server side any TNC implementation can be customized.

3.4 TNC@FHH

The TNC@FHH approach (http://trust.inform.fh-hannover.de) is also an open source implementation of the TNC architecture for integrity check of mobile devices. In order to enable an open and standardized implementation, open source software has been analyzed. As in the SIMOIT project the TNC@FHH approach allows integration of conventional security components such as firewall systems. A further precondition was to develop a framework based on the IEEE 802.1X standard in order to be used in Ethernet-based network environments.

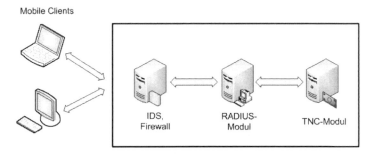

Fig. 3. TNC@FHH implementation

The realization of the project bases on two essential and separated software packages. On the client-side specific IMCs have been developed, which analyze and communicate the current security status of the systems. This critical information is communicated to the IMV residing on the RADIUS/TNC server and validated against the security policy. After the evaluation has been accomplished and the mobile device meets the requirements, the RADIUS server sends an access-accept notification to the Network Access Server (IEEE 802.1X compatible switch or router), which then grants the client the respective network access.

4 The VOGUE Approach

Until now transferring the TNC approach to mobile phones has not been the subject of R&D projects. It is a favourable point in time to realise such a project, because modern mobile platforms such as Android and iPhone OS, now permits application development on mobile devices, thus enabling the security components for TNC and the integration of a root-of-trust on smartphones. Such a root-of-trust is capable of vouching for the integrity of the platform, collecting and reporting the device platform configuration to a challenger in a trustworthy manner. This aspect is one of the core themes of VOGUE project. Such a root-of-trust for mobile systems, named Mobile Trusted Module (MTM) 0, which is a modified version of the TPM, has been specified by the The TCG Mobile Phone Work Group and will soon be introduced into the market. A software emulator 0 also used in VOGUE has being developed to allow the development of products for this emerging security technology.

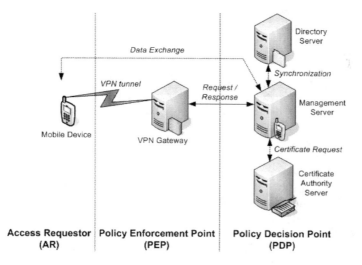

Fig. 4. VOGUE platform overview

According to the scenario and requirements discussed above, the project VOGUE specified the following platform assumption for the first prototype. The core element of the platform is represented by the VPN gateway. Additionally, a management server (e.g. RADIUS), a directory server (e.g. LDAP), and a certification authority server is necessary. In the first step, the user has to be identified for the correct access with the VPN gateway. All criteria are available on the directory server and assign the user to different profiles and user groups.

Each user group has different security policies for different access rights. The management system synchronizes continuously in intervals the user information with the directory server. That includes that user from the directory server with VPN access rights, if they are not yet available on the management server, will synchronize with all user group membership automatically after one interval. As an option a public certification authority (CA) can be adapted. If a new user is created on the management server, a certificate will apply. The management server platform is then a registration authority. The VPN gateway has to be configured that all requested clients will be authenticate via the management server. Therefore, the gateway site does not need adaptations for new user. That will be done automatically by the communication with the management server.

Next to the authentication of the user, the smartphone platform (hardware and software configuration) is checked according to the enterprise TNC's requirements. After the establishment of a VPN connection, the network access of the mobile device is limited to the quarantine zone. Within this area, it is only possible to update software components of the mobile device like anti-virus-software or operating system patches. The access to other network areas of an enterprise network is forbidden. Information about the status of the mobile device is available by the access requestor (AR) on the client-site. The AR includes the network requestor (as a component of the VPN client), the TNC client (as an interface between the network access requestor and plug-in software), and the integrity measurement collector (describes the plug-ins which allows different software products like antivirus software to communicate with TNC).

In detail, the following points will initiate for a mobile device communication (also depicted in figure 5):

1) A VPN connection is established.
2) The management server (TNC server) initializes an integrity check.
3) The mobile device (TNC client) collects integrity measurements (IM) information using the local Integrity Measurement Clients (IMC) on the mobile device.
4) The management server (TNC server) forwards the IM information for a check to the integrity measurement verifier (IMV).
5) The Integrity Measurement Verifier (IMV) checks the IMs and sends the results with a recommendation to the management server (TNC server).
6) The management server (TNC server) takes access decision und forward this information to the VPN gateway (PEP) and the mobile device (AR).
7) The VPN gateway (PEP) allows or does not allow the access to the network for the mobile device (AR).

Summarized, the integration of the MTM allows a further check of the software components on the mobile device. This simplifies the detection of rootkits. Furthermore it is possible to sign and encrypt messages with key material of the MTM. That means a strong security check of the origin of the information.

5 Conclusions

The TNC approach within VOGUE presented in this paper is a viable solution to raise the security level in mobile networks. Though the core specifications are already accomplished and various network components are available on the market, there are still shortcomings and manufacturers differ in their approaches. With Microsoft's "Statement-of-Health Protocol" future interoperability can be reached, but Cisco Systems will go its own way and will not be interoperable with the standard.

The projects SIMOIT and TNC@FHH are based on TNC too, but include only the server-side implementation of the standards. The TNC approaches of both projects presented in this paper are different, but are similar trusted computing implementations for mobile scenarios. They allow a relatively high security level for mobile and scalable identity and access management. Both platforms are modular, extensible, and can be combined with conventional security components such as VPN and firewalls.

The VOGUE project will improve existing TNC approaches with own developed TNC clients for mobile operating systems (e.g. Android) in order to extend the applicability beyond laptops or notebooks, since smartphones are widely used in corporate networks. With this work, it is hoped, that the integration of smartphones for "Trusted Computing" will bring the TCG initiative one step further in the development and standardization process.

Acknowledgements

The project VOGUE (http://www.vogue-project.de) is fund by the Federal Ministry of Education and Research (BMBF) of Germany. The project started in October 2009 and will end at September 2011. The authors would like to thank the BMBF for their support. We also wish to express our gratitude and appreciation to all VOGUE partners for their strong support and valuable contribution during the various activities presented in this paper.

References

1. Detken, G., Bartsch, S.: Trusted Network Connect - sicherer Zugang ins Unternehmensnetz; D.A.CH Security 2008: Bestandsaufnahme, Konzepte, Anwendungen und Perspektiven; Herausgeber: Patrick Horster; syssec Verlag; Berlin (2008) ISBN 978-3-00-024632-6
2. TCG, Trusted Network Connect Architecture for Interoperability, Specification 1.3, Revision 6 (April 2008)
3. Nispel, M.: Enterasys Secure Networks: Was Sie über NAC wissen sollten, http://www.computerwoche.de/knowledge_center/security/1871427/index.html
4. Eren, E., Detken, K.-O.: Mobile Security - Risiken mobiler Kommunikation und Lösungen zur mobilen Sicherheit. Carl Hanser Verlag, München Wien (2006) ISBN 3-446-40458-9
5. Eren, E., Detken, K.-O.: Identity and Access Management according to the implementation of the SIMOIT project and TNC@FHH. International Journal of Computing, Ukraine (2010) ISSN 1727-6209
6. http://www.infowan.de/index.html?windows_2008_profvogl2.html
7. Cisco NAC Appliance - Clean Access Manager Installation and Configuration Guide, Release 4.1(2)
8. TCG, TCG Specication Architecture Overview v1.2. Technical report, Trusted Computing Group, pp. 11–12 (April 2004)
9. TCG Mobile Phone Work Group, Mobile Trusted Module Overview Document (2006)
10. Strasser, M., Stamer, H., Molina, J.: Software-based TPM Emulator, http://tpm-emulator.berlios.de

OpenFlow and Xen-Based
Virtual Network Migration*

Pedro S. Pisa, Natalia C. Fernandes, Hugo E.T. Carvalho,
Marcelo D.D. Moreira, Miguel Elias M. Campista,
Luís Henrique M.K. Costa, and Otto Carlos M.B. Duarte

Universidade Federal do Rio de Janeiro - GTA/COPPE/UFRJ
Rio de Janeiro, Brazil

Abstract. Migration is an important feature for network virtualization
because it allows the reallocation of virtual resources over the physical
resources. In this paper, we investigate the characteristics of different
migration models, according to their virtualization platforms. We show
the main advantages and limitations of using the migration mechanisms
provided by Xen and OpenFlow platforms. We also propose a migration
model for Xen, using data and control plane separation, which outperforms the Xen standard migration. We developed two prototypes, using
Xen and OpenFlow, and we performed evaluation experiments to measure the impact of the network migration on traffic forwarding.

1 Introduction

To experiment new alternatives in the Internet core using production traffic is
considered unpractical. Internet providers do not feel comfortable to perform
modifications that could damage their service. This problem causes a dead lock,
on the one hand Internet must evolve to handle new demands, but on the other
hand, new mechanisms that change the Internet cannot be applied in the underlying infrastructure. Many works tackle this problem by using virtualization
techniques [4, 9] because, in a virtualized environment, the physical substrate is
shared among many virtual networks. Virtual networks are isolated and, consequently, new proposals could be run together with the current Internet without
disturbing the production traffic. Network virtualization requires new control
and management primitives for redistributing physical resources among the virtual nodes. One of these primitives is the live virtual network migration. The
idea is to move virtual networks among the available physical resources without
disrupting the packet forwarding and network control services [11].

Virtual network migration allows dynamic planning of physical resources and
traffic management on demand. Network migration can also be applied to create
green networks [1], because virtual networks could be placed on different physical routers according to the traffic demand to reduce energy consumption. This

---

* This work was supported by FINEP, FUNTTEL, CNPq, CAPES, and FAPERJ.

A. Pont, G. Pujolle, and S.V. Raghavan (Eds.): WCITD/NF 2010, IFIP AICT 327, pp. 170–181, 2010.

concept is also compatible with the idea of cloud computing, which is an attempt to efficiently share power, storage devices, user applications, and network infrastructure over the Internet as if they were services [7]. Virtual network migration could also be used to solve security problems. For instance, a link shared by different virtual networks could be jammed because of a denial of service attack to one of the virtual networks. In this case, the non-attacked networks could be migrated to different physical routers until the attack is solved. In the current Internet, none of the above mentioned applications is possible because live migration services are not available.

In this paper, we compare and evaluate different migration models, according to the type of virtualization in use. First, we evaluate the use of Xen[1] standard migration to verify the impact of this migration model over a virtual network. We also analyze virtual network migration models based on plane separation. The plane separation is a technique for dividing each network node in two parts: a control plane, responsible for running all the control algorithms and for constructing the routing table; and the data plane, which is responsible for forwarding the traffic. We propose a model for applying the plane separation on Xen migration and we evaluate the advantages and the disadvantages of this new migration model. Also, we analyze the use of OpenFlow migration techniques, which is a platform natively based on plane separation for virtualizing switched networks. We present an algorithm for migrating virtual flows without impacting the traffic forwarding service. We also compare the OpenFlow link migration technique with the link migration in Xen.

Traditional management and control activities are also benefited by the use of network migration. The planned maintenance, in which a server or a router is rebooted or even turned off for a period of time for upgrading hardware and software, is a typical operation in any network. When a router service is restarted, the time for re-synchronizing the routing protocol states with the neighbor routers can lead to high delays. If we use virtual routers with live migration, the service downtime during planned management can be reduced to zero. Another service that takes advantage of the virtual network migration is the deployment of new network services. While a service is still under tests or is still an initiative with a low number of users, it can be placed on a smaller AS or in low capacity physical node. As the service develops, it can be moved to a more adequate infrastructure. With the current network model, the network administrator must invest in equipments for the new services without knowing the real significance of each service. Therefore, network virtualization with migration brings not only a service innovation incentive, but also an economic incentive in equipments, management, and power consumption.

We developed two prototypes for migrating virtual networks without losses in the data plane using Xen and OpenFlow. We evaluate these two prototypes according to the packet losses during migration and we compare them to Xen standard migration. Besides, we measured the delays for the data plane in Xen and OpenFlow prototypes. Hence, we can estimate the impact of the migration

---

[1] Xen is a virtual machine monitor used for machine virtualization.

over the network and also the delay for migrating a virtual network. This delay is important in situations where the virtual network migration is being executed because of high link usage. If migration takes too long, the link congestion will also persist for a long period causing messages losses.

The remainder of the paper is structured as follows. Section 2 presents an analysis of virtual network migration models according to the virtualization platform. It also presents the proposal for migration in Xen with plane separation and an efficient algorithm for migration in OpenFlow. In Section 3, we describe the developed prototypes and the experimental results. Finally, Section 4 concludes the paper.

2   Virtual Network Migration

Virtual network migration is a function to rearrange the virtual network topology over the physical topology. Such rearrangement can even promote changes in the virtual network topology. The primary objective is to move virtual nodes and links minimizing the impacts on the virtual networks, such as requiring virtual routers to be reconfigured, disturbing virtual IP-level topology, or increasing the convergence time of the virtual network routing algorithms due to message losses caused by the migration process [12].

There are two basic approaches for virtualizing a network element [5]. Next, we show how the migration process works, according to the virtualization approach in use. We assume the existence of an entity that decide when and how to migrate nodes or paths in the network [2]. This entity can be implemented in a centralized way, for simplicity, or in a distributed way, for guaranteeing scalability, for instance. This entity is aware of the physical network topology and all the virtual network topologies and loads. As a consequence, this entity is able to define the new physical topology of a virtual network that will be migrated. Also, the existence of an arbiter raises an issue about security. Since we have an entity that has power over the whole network, the communication among this entity and the virtual/physical nodes must be completely safe. Moreover, the arbiter cannot be influenced by malicious network nodes that want to divert resources from one network to other.

2.1   1st Approach: Data and Control Planes on the Same VM

In this virtualization approach, a virtual network is composed of virtual nodes, each one containing both data and control planes, and virtual links, as shown in Fig. 1(a). To maintain the virtual network topology, when migrating a node, we must find a new physical node that has the same virtual neighbors of the source node. Then, the whole virtual environment is migrated to the new physical node. For instance, in Fig. 1(b), the virtual node B is migrated from the physical node 2 to 5, because this modification does not change the virtual network topology.

One way of implementing this first virtualization approach is by using Xen, a virtualization platform created for commodity hardware [3]. In Xen architecture,

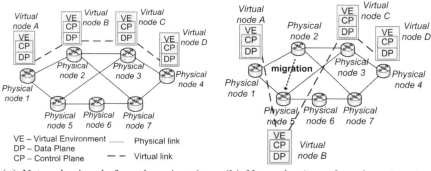

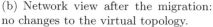

(a) Network view before the migration of virtual node B.

(b) Network view after the migration: no changes to the virtual topology.

Fig. 1. Virtual network migration assuming no data and control plane separation

a virtual machine monitor (VMM), also known as hypervisor, is placed over the hardware and provides a virtual x86 hardware interface to virtual machines (VMs). Thus, each VM has its own virtual resources, such as CPU, memory, disk, and also its own operating system and application software. Xen also presents a privileged virtual machine, called Domain 0, which has full access to the physical devices and is responsible for providing reliable I/O-hardware support for the other virtual machines.

When we use Xen to create virtual networks, we assume that each VM works as a virtual router. Hence, to migrate a VM means to migrate a router. Because the VM is running a live service, we need to reduce the migration downtime, which is the time that the virtual machine is unavailable during the migration. It is also important to minimize the total migration time to guarantee that we can quickly free the resources of the initial physical machine. Xen has a built-in mechanism to migrate virtual networks [2]. This mechanism is based on some assumptions: the migration occurs inside a local network and the machine disk is shared over the network[2]. The main idea of this procedure is that migrating a virtual machine is the same of copying the memory of the virtual machine to the new physical location and reconfiguring the network links without breaking connections.

The simplest way to migrate the VM memory is to suspend the VM, transfer all the memory pages to the new physical location, and then resume the VM. To reduce the downtime, this procedure is evolved to a pre-copy migration, in which the memory copy is accomplished through two phases. The first phase, called iterative pre-copy, transfers all memory pages to new physical machine,

---

[2] This shared disk assumption can be relaxed in our scenario, because routers from the same vendor usually implement the same small set of applications [11]. Then, we assume that the new physical router also has this set of programs and is able to load them onto the file system of the new VM. Hence, only virtual router memory and configuration files must be migrated.

except for the 'hot pages', which are frequently modified pages. Consequently, the downtime is reduced, because only a few pages, instead of the whole memory, are transmitted while the VM is down. The next phase is called stop-and-copy. In this phase the VM is suspended and the hot-pages are transferred with the maximum transfer rate. Then, the new physical node confirms the reception of the whole memory to the old physical node.

The Xen built-in migration is inadequate for virtual networks due to the high packet loss rate during the VM downtime. Other problem of Xen built-in migration for virtual routers is that it assumes a migration within a local area network, which does not fulfill our objectives of migrating routers. Indeed, we cannot assume that physical nodes, such as nodes 1, 2, and 5 of Fig. 1, always belong to the same local network.

2.2   2nd Approach: Data and Control Plane Separation

In the second virtualization approach, we separate data and control plane to migrate the control plane without message losses in data plane, which is an important characteristic for router virtualization. There are two different ways of implementing control and data plane separation. One way, which applies for virtualization platforms such as Xen, is run the control plane in the virtual environment, while the data plane runs in a shared area of the physical node. Another way is based on the OpenFlow platform [8], in which the network control is centralized in a special node, while each network node has a share data plane that is shared by different virtual networks.

Migration in Xen with plane separation. To reduce the packet loss in data plane during live migration, we propose to separate data plane and control plane in Xen. A similar approach was proposed for OpenVZ, a virtualization platform that provides multiple virtual user spaces over the same operating system [11]. Xen, however, presents a more programmable virtualization platform, because each virtual router can have its own software set, including operating system and protocol stack.

We developed a prototype that maintains in the VM the control plane, while the data plane is implemented in Domain 0. Each virtual router has its own forwarding table in Domain 0 and each table is a copy of the original forwarding table created by routing software running in the VM. When Domain 0 receives a control message, it checks which network the message belongs to and forwards the message to the corresponding VM. When Domain receives a data message, it is forwarded by Domain 0 using the forwarding table that corresponds to that virtual network.

The proposed migration mechanism works as follows. First, the Xen standard migration is started to migrate the VM. After the iterative pre-copy phase, the VM is paused and the remaining dirty memory pages are transferred. During this time, the data path is still working at Domain 0, with no interruptions or packet losses. Also, a daemon is started in Domain 0 to buffer the control packets for the VM that is being migrated. When the whole memory is copied, the VM is resumed on the new physical machine (PM) and the network connections are created in the new Domain 0 using a dynamic interface binding module, which is responsible for mapping the virtual network interfaces to the physical network interfaces of the new PM. After that, a tunnel from the old PM to the new PM is created in order to transfer the control packets that were buffered in the old Domain 0 and also the new control packets. Finally, the ARP reply is broadcast to update the links and the data path in the old PM is removed.

Our migration mechanism guarantees no packet loss in the data plane during the VM migration, which is an important characteristic for a virtual router. Moreover, there is also no control packet loss. Our mechanism inserts only a delay in the control packet delivery. The proposed mechanism, however, is based on Xen default migration, which means that it still needs that routers are within the same local area network. In addition, the mapping of a virtual link over multiple physical links is still an open issue that depends on solutions such as IP tunnels or instantiating new virtual routers on the network. For instance, in Fig. 2, we migrate virtual node B from physical node 2 to physical node 6. Physical node 6, however, is not a one-hop neighbor of physical node 1. Consequently, to complete the link migration, we need to create a tunnel from physical node 6 to physical node 1 to simulate a one-hop neighborhood. The other solution is to instantiate a new virtual router to substitute the tunnel. This solution, however, modifies the virtual topology and influences the routing protocol functioning.

Migration with OpenFlow. OpenFlow is a platform to provide network virtualization which is natively based on plane separation [8]. In OpenFlow, all network elements, such as routers, switches, and access points, work as "OpenFlow switches" and compose the data plane. Hence, OpenFlow networks are switched networks with support to virtualization. The control plane is centralized in a special element called "controller" [6], which runs in a separated machine. The controller knows the whole network topology and executes applications to configure flows according to the virtual network policies.

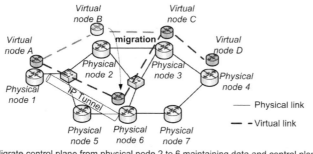

1) Migrate control plane from physical node 2 to 6 maintaining data and control planes.
2) Do interface dynamic binding and create tunnel between physical nodes 1 and 6.
3) Create a new forwarding table in Domain 0 of physical node 6
4) Reconfigure links with ARP reply
5) Delete data plane on physical node 2.

Fig. 2. Example of router migration in Xen when a virtual link is mapped to a multiple-hop path in the physical network

Network virtualization in OpenFlow is done in two different modes. In the first mode, there is one controller and each set of applications executing in the controller corresponds to each virtual network control plane. In the second mode, which provides more isolation between virtual networks, there is another machine besides the controller in the network, called FlowVisor [10]. In this mode, the control plane of each virtual network runs in a different controller and FlowVisor is responsible for giving/restricting the access of each controller to OpenFlow switches. In both modes, OpenFlow switches run a shared data plane, which is the concatenation of the forwarding tables of each virtual network. Indeed, the OpenFlow switches have no knowledge about the virtual networks or about which network each message being forwarded belongs to. OpenFlow switches are just hardware with a configurable forwarding table.

Since a controller is able to configure all OpenFlow switches, to migrate flows is the same of reconfiguring forwarding tables. The algorithm for migrating flows in OpenFlow is described in Fig. 3. First, when the controller decides to migrate the flows from a physical node to another, it creates new flow entries in each switch of the new path, except for the first common switch between the new and the old path, which is node 1 in the figure. After, the controller modifies the entries in this switch, redirecting the flows from the initial output port to the new output port. Finally, the controller deletes the old flow entries in the switches of the original path, which are node 2 and 3 in the figure.

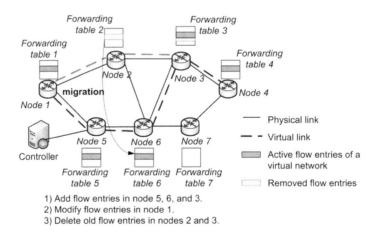

1) Add flow entries in node 5, 6, and 3.
2) Modify flow entries in node 1.
3) Delete old flow entries in nodes 2 and 3.

Fig. 3. Example of flow migration in OpenFlow

The advantages of OpenFlow migration are that it avoids the need for a local network, such as in Xen, because OpenFlow assumes a wide area switched network with configurable forwarding tables. Moreover, since we have a switched network and a centralized controller, there is no need to create tunnels after a migration. Since the control plane is now centralized and has a whole view of the physical network, there is no need to maintain the virtual topology. In Xen, it is necessary to guarantee that the communication between the shares of the

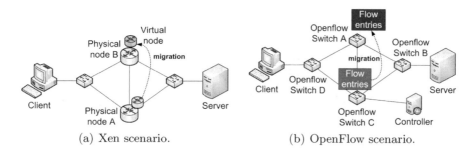

(a) Xen scenario.   (b) OpenFlow scenario.

Fig. 4. Experimental scenarios for virtual network migration

control plane in each physical node is not impacted by the migration. Indeed, when we have a distributed control plane, a modification in the network topology will cause an update in the routing data and, consequently, a convergence delay until all nodes agree on the same routes again. OpenFlow provides an easier infrastructure for reallocating network resources. It is, however, based on a centralized controller, which may not scale for large area networks.

3 Developed Prototypes and Experiments

We implemented a prototype built on Xen with plane separation and a prototype built on OpenFlow. In Xen prototype, we modified the Xen standard packet forwarding scheme, because Xen architecture confines both data and control planes inside a virtual machine. Our prototype implements the plane separation with a mechanism that synchronizes the data plane, placed at Domain 0, with the routing information base (RIB) created by the control plane inside the virtual machine. The implemented migration mechanism uses the Xen standard migration mechanism to migrate the control plane as its first step. After that, the destination Domain 0 creates a forwarding table to the migrating virtual router and synchronizes the forwarding table with the RIB on the virtual machine. Finally, the link migration is done through ARP replies and then the source Domain 0 removes the old data plane. In OpenFlow prototype, we migrate the virtual data planes by moving flows from the old to the new physical switches. We developed a NOX application that creates a flow from "Client" to "Server" and vice-versa when the network is started, as shown in Fig. 4(b). When the migration is started, the controller constructs new flow table entries on the new path and, after that, delete the old flows entries, as described in Section 2.2. Accordingly, there is no packetloss during OpenFlow migration.

We developed a testbed, described in Fig. 4, to evaluate the presented migration prototypes, comparing with the Xen standard migration, which has no plane separation. In the Xen scenario, we have two physical machines, Physical Node A and Physical Node B running Xen 4.0. The experiment consist of generating an UDP data traffic and migrating a virtual router from Physical Node A to Physical Node B while the virtual router forwards the data traffic from the client to the server. To not disturb the data traffic, we use a separated link to transmit the migration traffic during the migration process. In the Xen standard migration, the data traffic is forwarded by the virtual machine. In the Xen with plane separation, the data traffic is forwarded by the shared data plane in Domain 0 and the control traffic is forwarded by the virtual machine. In the Openflow scenario, the two physical machines with Xen are replaced by OpenFlow switches, running OpenFlow v 0.8.9. There is also a centralized NOX controller that accesses and controls all OpenFlow switches.

Results

In our experiments, we measured the delays and losses due to the migration with different data packet rates. We present experiments with 64-byte and 1500-byte packets, which respectively represent the minimum Ethernet payload and the most common Ethernet MTU, but there were no significant differences in the results when the packet size varies.

Fig. 5 presents the time elapsed during the downtime stage. The results show that the downtime is roughly constant with the growth of the data packet rate for all migration schemes. Compared with the Xen standard migration, the Xen with plane separation has a downtime that is 200 milliseconds lower on the average. This difference exists because in Xen standard migration, the virtual machine must forward all data and control packets, which increases the number of 'hot pages' in virtual machine memory and, consequently, raises the downtime. In the Xen with plane separation, the data traffic is forwarded by Domain 0 and the memory pages dirtied in the virtual machine come only from the routing software running in the virtual machine, which reduces the downtime.

Fig. 6 shows the number of data packets that were lost during downtime in the experiments. As expected, in the Xen standard migration, the number of lost packets increases linearly with the packet rate, because the downtime is constant and the data packet rate grows linearly. OpenFlow and Xen with plane separation tackle this issue. Xen with plane separation has a downtime only during the

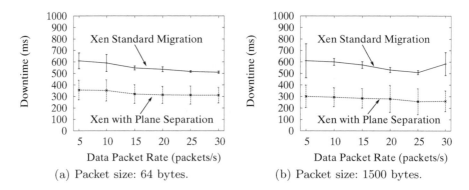

(a) Packet size: 64 bytes.   (b) Packet size: 1500 bytes.

Fig. 5. Migration downtime as a function of the data packet rate

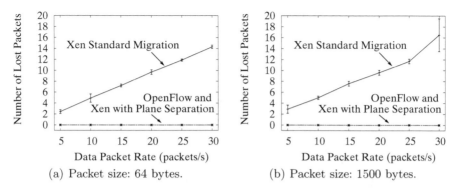

Fig. 6. Number of lost packets during downtime as a function of the data packet rate

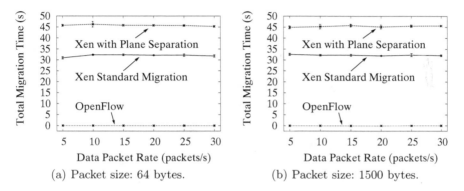

Fig. 7. Total migration time as a function of the data packet rate

control plane migration and the data plane is not frozen during migration.. In OpenFlow, the migration mechanism moves the data traffic to a new path without migrating the control plane. Indeed, OpenFlow has no downtime, since neither the data plane nor the control plane are stopped due to the migration.

Fig. 7 shows the total migration time, which consists of the time between the migration triggering and the moment when the data packets start to pass through the destination machine. The difference between Xen standard mechanism and Xen with plane separation is about 15 seconds. This variation occurs in our prototype due to data plane synchronization after control plane migration and the remapping of the virtual interfaces to the appropriate physical interfaces, which does not exist in the Xen standard migration. OpenFlow total migration time is about 5 milliseconds, because OpenFlow only migrates the data plane. This time comprises the interval between the beginning and the ending of sending flow change messages from the controller to all switches. In our scenario, the controller reaches all the switches with two hops at the most, as we can see in Fig. 4(b). Nevertheless, if the distance between the controller and the Open-Flow switches rises, the total migration time increases. Besides, if the number of migrated flows grows, the total migration time also increases. This happens due to the increased number of messages sent to the switches.

4   Conclusions and Future Directions

We evaluated the impact of different virtual network migration models with Xen and OpenFlow virtualization platforms. We observed that data and control plane separation is a key feature for reducing packet losses during the migration. Moreover, in the proposed migration mechanism for Xen, the packet forwarding through Domain 0 also reduced the number of dirtied pages in the virtual machine. Therefore, the downtime of the control plane during migration is reduced by 200 milliseconds. We obtained a significant difference in the packet loss rate and control plane downtime during migration when comparing the Xen standard migration and the proposed migration mechanism with plane separation for Xen. Besides, the analysis of the proposed migration algorithm for OpenFlow showed that it is an efficient approach for migrating virtual networks, because it provides a downtime of less than 5 milliseconds and no packet losses during the migration process.

The control plane downtime and the mapping of a virtual link over multiple physical links are the main observed drawbacks in the Xen migration. OpenFlow has none of these disadvantages, but it is based on a centralized controller, which can restrict the size of the network. Other approaches for migrating the data plane in Xen should also be analyzed, such as the instantiation of new virtual routers instead of mapping virtual links on multiple physical links. In addition, we intend to analyze the real impact on the traffic forwarding of buffering the control plane messages during downtime in the Xen migration model assuming data and control plane separation.

References

[1] Bolla, R., Bruschi, R., Davoli, F., Ranieri, A.: Energy-aware performance optimization for next-generation green network equipment. In: PRESTO'09: Proceedings of the 2nd ACM SIGCOMM Workshop on Programmable Routers for Extensible Services of Tomorrow, pp. 49–54 (2009)
[2] Clark, C., Fraser, K., Hand, S., Hansen, J.G., Jul, E., Limpach, C., Pratt, I., Warfield, A.: Live migration of virtual machines. In: NSDI'05: Proceedings of the 2nd Conference on Symposium on Networked Systems Design & Implementation, pp. 273–286. USENIX Association, Berkeley (2005)
[3] Egi, N., Greenhalgh, A., Handley, M., Hoerdt, M., Mathy, L., Schooley, T.: Evaluating Xen for router virtualization. In: ICCCN'07: International Conference on Computer Communications and Networks, August 2007, pp. 1256–1261 (2007)
[4] Feamster, N., Gao, L., Rexford, J.: How to lease the Internet in your spare time. ACM SIGCOMM Computer Communication Review 37(1), 61–64 (2007)
[5] Fernandes, N.C., Moreira, M.D.D., Moraes, I.M., Ferraz, L.H.G., Couto, R.S., Carvalho, H.E.T., Campista, M.E.M., Costa, L.H.M.K., Duarte, O.C.M.B.: Virtual networks: Isolation, performance, and trends. Tech. rep., Grupo de Teleinformática e Automação - GTA/COPPE/UFRJ, Rio de Janeiro, Brazil (March 2010)

[6] Gude, N., Koponen, T., Pettit, J., Pfaff, B., Casado, M., McKeown, N., Shenker, S.: NOX: Towards an operating system for networks. ACM SIGCOMM Computer Communication Review 38(3), 105–110 (2008)

[7] Han, S.M., Hassan, M.M., Yoon, C.W., Huh, E.N.: Efficient service recommendation system for cloud computing market. In: ICIS'09: Proceedings of the 2nd International Conference on Interaction Sciences, Seoul, Korea, pp. 839–845 (2009)

[8] McKeown, N., Anderson, T., Balakrishnan, H., Parulkar, G., Peterson, L., Rexford, J.S., Turner, J.: OpenFlow: Enabling innovation in campus networks. ACM SIGCOMM Computer Communication Review 38(2), 69–74 (2008)

[9] Ratnasamy, S., Shenker, S., McCanne, S.: Towards an evolvable Internet architecture. ACM SIGCOMM Computer Communication Review 35(4), 313–324 (2005)

[10] Sherwood, R., Chan, M., Covington, A., Gibb, G., Flajslik, M., Handigol, N., Huang, T.Y., Kazemian, P., Kobayashi, M., Naous, J., Seetharaman, S., Underhill, D., Yabe, T., Yap, K.K., Yiakoumis, Y., Zeng, H., Appenzeller, G., Johari, R., McKeown, N., Parulkar, G.: Carving research slices out of your production networks with OpenFlow. ACM SIGCOMM Computer Communication Review 40(1), 129–130 (2010)

[11] Wang, Y., Keller, E., Biskeborn, B., der Merwe, J.V., Rexford, J.: Virtual routers on the move: Live router migration as a network-management primitive. In: ACM SIGCOMM, August 2008, pp. 231–242 (2008)

[12] Wang, Y., der Merwe, J.V., Rexford, J.: VROOM: Virtual routers on the move. In: Proceedings of the ACM SIGCOMM Workshop on Hot Topics in Networking, November 2007, pp. 1–7 (2007)

Virtual Network Urbanization

Othmen Braham, Ahmed Amamou, and Guy Pujolle

Pierre and Marie Curie University,
Place Jussieu. 4, 75005 Paris, France
{othmen.braham,ahmed.amamou}@virtuor.fr,
guy.pujolle@lip6.fr
http://www.lip6.fr/phare

Abstract. Adapting virtualization concepts to satisfy network telecommunication challenges receives more and more attention. The virtual network environment is formed by the amount of bounded virtual resources provided by physical network equipments. Deploying virtual network infrastructure has recently caught more research interests due to its flexibility and manageability. However, virtual network deployment is not evident as it should be. Therefore, it is now necessary to provide virtual environment design to coexist virtual networks and their respective operators. In this article, we describe our virtual network environment architecture. We explain the proposed organization strategies to improve virtual network urbanization. The initial results and quantitative analysis of the architecture deployment are exposed.

Keywords: Virtualization, Network, Management, Urbanisation.

1   Introduction

It is widely accepted that virtualization is taken more and more importance for IT platform. The virtualization is a way for sharing physical resources into separate and isolated virtual resources. It permits simultaneous multiple machines to run within one physical computer. The virtual network is based on physical network equipment virtualization. The connected virtual machines composing the virtual network share currently the amount of provided virtual resources.

Advances in virtualization technologies have created new opportunity for network operators to take advantage of network resources more efficiently. There is growing need for an architecture that allows network managers to instantiate virtual networks in an organized and easy-way. Related works, which describe virtual network [1], are more interested on network communication mechanism behaviour due to virtualization overhead. This research explores the design and strategy to be considered to fulfil virtual network operator needs. And in this context is where we want to implement the proposed architecture and test the performance and availability of virtual network.

In our approach, each virtual network could propose a different network service with isolation guarantees. The virtual machine could be any kind of network

A. Pont, G. Pujolle, and S.V. Raghavan (Eds.): WCITD/NF 2010, IFIP AICT 327, pp. 182–193, 2010.
© IFIP International Federation for Information Processing 2010

equipment used within real network: Routers, Label Switch router, firewall, access point, SIP router, IP PBX... Virtual machine could implement any protocol stack such as: IPv4, IPv6, MPLS... A virtual network is created by the instantiation of each virtual machine that compose its topology. These virtual machines are linked through virtual link. A virtual network router could use any routing protocol such as: OSPFv2, OSPFv3, Rip, RIPng, BGP...

This paper describes an architecture that facilitates the management of high-evolutive virtual network environment. Although many virtual management applications have been developed to offer their special features and tools, few works has been reported on providing support for developing virtual network urbanization application. It permits the instantiations of virtual networks within a virtualized environment and the ability to configure each part.

Aiming to provide an environment for building virtual networks, we have developed our architecture which combines the following features:

- Virtual network isolation;
- Defining a gap between physical and virtual resources management;
- The virtual machines that compose virtual networks could be any network equipment;
- Easy configurable and easy manageable.

To present an overview of our virtual network management application, this paper focuses on our architecture and its key elements. The rest of this paper is structured as follows. Section 2 describes the virtual network environment platform. Section 3, describes the overall virtual network application architecture. Section 4 presents the design and mechanisms underlying the virtual network platform. Section 5 presents the experimental evaluations. Finally, Section 6 concludes the paper with the description of our future work.

2   Virtual Network Environment Platform

The physical nodes are connected through physical network link. Each physical node offers its virtualized resources via a hypervisor. The hypervisor guarantees concurrent virtual machine running isolation conforming to their allocated resources. The Physical Node is the component upon which all virtual machines reside. It corresponds to the physical machine with a real location and hardware specification. Its resources are characterized in term of CPU, memory and network I/O as we are focusing on network equipments. We have used in our platform physical equipment with 4Go RAM, C2D-2.4 Ghz CPU and six 1 Gbyte network interface.

We have adopted XEN [2] as hypervisor because it is open source and increasingly popular among virtual network infrastructure researches. Xen is also a high performance resource-managed virtual machine monitor (VMM) comparing to other technologies as mentioned in literature [3,4]. The VMM provides isolation and safety for running virtual machines. Despite the advances in virtualization technology and technique, the overhead of network I/O through Xen virtualization still have a negative impact on the performance of virtual network applications. Though, the performances are close to those of non virtualized software routers if the need for processing overhead is satisfied and allocated resources are oversized to support unfairness in resources share.

The virtual machines share physical host resources. An instantiation of a virtual machine needs: kernel, files system, network application and configuration description of resources that will be allocated. We have used small size virtual machines that can support different network application. We have integrated some available open source project inside virtual machines such as: Xorp [5], Quagga [6], Asterisk [7], MPLS-Linux [8], Opensip [9]. We have elaborated a virtual machine list that covers different kind of network equipment. We have adapted virtual machine operating system to support several type of protocol stack. We have deleted unused operating system modules to eliminate their effect on network traffic. Using light weight virtual machine increases routing performance and managing action such as instantiation, migration and backup.

The virtual network environment as shown in Fig. 1 consists of several virtual networks. Each virtual network can guarantee different kind of service to satisfy the requested Service Level Agreement (SLA). The virtual network creation is achieved by the instantiation of each virtual machine that compose it. The virtual machines must correspond to the offered service in term of protocol stack and network application.

As exposed in Fig. 1, we have different protocol stack IPv4, IPv6 and MPLS network running on the same physical nodes and isolated down to hypervisor isolation. The IPv4 network is extended by IP PBX functionalities to support video conference service. MPLS network is used for video streaming service due to its minimal delay grantee. The IPv6 network guarantees data exchange service between its users. The clients must have the same protocol stack as their virtual network and configure them self to be connected to it. They can be connected to several virtual networks at the same time to take advantages of the different proposed services.

This platform could be used by several operators. They can share the deployed physical infrastructure by allocating available virtual resources. The amount of allocated resources could be used to create different instantiation of virtual networks. Depending on resources needed by each machine that composes the network, virtual machines have to be placed appropriately to an available resources location that satisfies the virtual network topology.

The network is distributed by nature. Due to virtualization level capability, it becomes also dynamic. A new operator can allocate available virtual resources and instantiate a new virtual network with a new kind of service. Another operator could delete a virtual network that is not any more in use to free the allocated resources. The virtual machine migration could be used for different purpose in this kind of platform to ensure high availability and load-balancing. In the next section, we describe our architecture to manage virtual resources and establish heterogeneous virtual networks that guarantee different qualities of service.

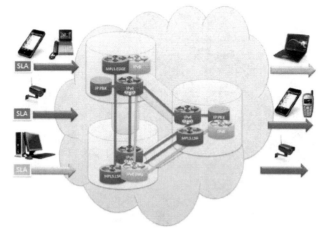

Fig. 1. Virtual network environment platform

3   Application Architecture Overview

The architecture, as shown in Fig. 2, consists of three principal abstraction layers. The lowest layer is the Infrastructure Provider Domain (IPD). It is the management domain of the infrastructure provider. The IPD includes all physical network resources. Each Physical Node has its own unique identity within the Infrastructure Provider Domain.

The second layer is the Network Provider Domain (NPD). The amount of virtual resources in terms of processor, memory and network interfaces represent the NPD. The IPD administrator defines the namespace boundary for these virtual resources as a NPD. The Network Provider Domain is an aggregation of all the different types of virtual objects. The NPD administrator could be represented as a virtual operator.

Each physical node offers an amount of virtual resources in term of CPU, Memory and network I/O. This amount is shared between virtual operators. To separate between concurrent NPDs in the same physical node, we propose in our architecture a logical border assimilated to a container of virtual resources. The container corresponds to a logical resources amount in term of CPU, memory and network I/O. It defines the limit of allocated resources for a virtual operator. A virtual operator can allocate on each physical node the estimated container capacity depending on its client proportion and location. The request of resources by the NPD could not exceed container capacity. The container will enclose as many virtual machines as its capacity allows that. It guarantees the availability of resources amount allocated by operators. The service level agreement of virtual operators must be satisfied in any case unlike the operator subscribers SLA which are more flexible.

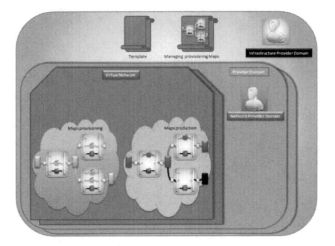

Fig. 2. Application Architecture

The third layer is composed by virtual networks (VN). The Virtual Network provides the ability to monitor and manage logical groups of resources within the Network Provider Domain. A Virtual Network could be represented by physical location, a subnet range, or a logical grouping of virtual machines. The NPD Administrator creates Virtual Networks for its clients to satisfy their service level agreement request. Each VN has two maps view to bring management simplicity for virtual network resources. The map production shows the virtual resources allocated and already in use within virtual network. It provides a representation of the network topologies. It corresponds to unavailable amount of resources within the map of containers. The Map Production shows the actual running virtual machine and current used virtual resources inside each virtual network in the Network Provider Domain. The monitored objects includes virtual machines, network interfaces, and templates. The NPD Administrator can manage running virtual machine through the map production. The Map Provisioning represents allocated virtual resources not yet in use. It corresponds to the available amount of resource in the map container. The Map Provisioning provides views and capabilities to understand the relationships between the available amount of virtual resources and their physical location within the infrastructure provider domain. It indicates the available virtual resources that could be used by VN to be extended. The NPD Administrator has a view on the available virtualized resources that it could request from IPD through map provisioning.

We have defined a template for each virtual machine that describes its configuration. A template is a picture of a virtual machine that can be used as a master copy to create and provision new virtual machines. This image typically includes a specified operating system and configuration that provides virtual counterparts to real hardware equipments. The template is a combination of three level abstractions: physical template, operating system template and virtual domain template. Physical template describes hardware resources that will be allocated to the virtual machine. This description includes hardware specification that will be seen by the virtual machine such as: CPU, memory, virtual network interfaces. Operating system template includes the operating system specification and system files that will be used on the boot and during the execution of the virtual machine. Virtual domain template indicates the type and functionality that would offer the virtual machine. The NPD Administrator requests an instance of virtual machines according to the defined templates.

The roles are separated into two groups that correspond to domain action. The infrastructure provider domain administrator manages the physical resource level and allocates them to network provider domain. The IPD could accept several NPD depending on its resources offers. The IPD Administrator has the ability to manage and organize Physical Nodes. He can also create new Network Provider Domain and manages role memberships throughout the entire Infrastructure Provider Domain for NPD Administrators.

Unlike an Infrastructure Provider Domain, which is used to organize physical object type, a Network Provider Domain is an aggregation of all virtual resources level which is composed by virtual machines. The network provider domain administrator interacts with its IPD to allocate available virtual resources on each physical node. The NPD clients ask for specific network in term of protocol routing, protocol stack, and network equipment type. VN are then created and configured by their NPD. The NPD Administrator can manage running virtual machine through the map production. The NPD aims to optimize the use of its containers on each physical node to satisfy maximum virtual heterogeneous network. An NPD Administrator has read-only access to the available resources within Infrastructure Provider Domain level shown by provisioning map and no access to other Network Provider Domains. Access or visibility to Maps provisioning depends on the NPD Administrators administrative privileges. He cant manage any physical node because he has permissions on virtual resources only. The NPD Administrator has full management on the owned resources shown by the maps production.

4   Deployment Architecture Platform

We have implemented a management tool as described in the proposed architecture to control virtual resources and establish heterogeneous virtual networks that guarantee different qualities of service. After authentication step, the tool offers multiple functionalities that help to manage physical network resources for IPD administrators and virtual network resources for NPD administrators. It gives them an amalgam of options to control different instantiations of virtual networks and the ability to configure every virtual object within the virtualized environment.

As shown in Fig. 3, we opted for a central decision server with distributed agents on each physical node. The management server is based on web server

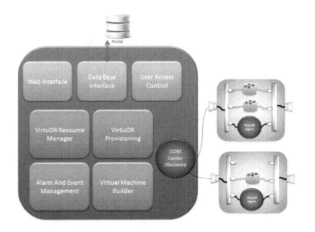

Fig. 3. Platform architecture deployment

application and uses a data base for virtual network environment information persistence. Each actor must be identified by the server before it could act on its resources and interact with agents. Each agent runs continuously in the background, performing monitoring and executing managing activities even when no actor is logged on the physical node where it resides. It is installed on the privilege domain to permit the execution of privilege instructions on virtual resources and to have a local view of them. The agent has access to the entire physical node resources and can manage from outside the running virtual machine.

All the running virtual machines on managed physical nodes are automatically discovered and shown into correspondent Map Production within their Network Provider Domain. The migrating process describes the action of moving a virtual machine from one physical node to another. The virtual machine migration is a life transferring of a virtual machine snapshot image to another physical node without service interruption. In our case, we can easily migrate from one container to another if resources of destination container permit that.

To manage virtual network, we have created a management network. The management network is formed by the different agents that control each physical machine. In response to NPD needs, IPD administrator creates a container which is a logical resources border on the selected physical node. The NPD administrator instantiates virtual machines of its virtual network through map provisioning. When virtual network instantiation is completed, the NPD can access and configure each virtual machine. He could reach virtual machines using the network that he has created or through the management network.

A virtual operator would not share routing information tables inside virtual machines with any other actor. This information could give indications about its clients activities and location. To guarantee virtual network isolation, our deployment allow only for NPD administrator to configure the inside of its virtual machine instantiations such as routing table, network application and other configuration. The NPD must be recognized by the identification system of the virtual machine to configure it. The IPD administrator can manage the instantiation of virtual machine but cannot access inside or interfere with the execution behaviour of the running network application.

To guarantee feather extensions to our tool, we have used REST [10] as web service architecture because there is no need to keep session. We have used XML data exchange format between server, agents and actors. Each virtual network environment entity has its own Uniform Resource Identifiers (URI) [11] that permit to execute on it all REST standard action like: GET, POST, DELETE, PUT and the other related resource type actions.

5   Experimental Setup

Our experimental testbed consists of 5 physical machines. The witness virtual network connects two client laptops. Each one has C2D 1.6 GHz CPU, 2Go RAM, 100Mb network interface. The same configuration is deployed for the charged virtual network. The Physical node that will host all virtual Network has 4Go RAM, C2D-2.4 GHz CPU, six 1 GByte network interface and XEN 3.4 installed ont it. All instantiated Virtual Routers have this configuration: one x86 virtual CPU, two 100 MB virtual interfaces, 20 Mb image disk size, 80Mb RAM and Quagga router as network application.

As shown in Fig. 4, the physical node will host 2 virtual networks: the witness virtual network and the charged one. The witness network will support all performance tests. The charged virtual network aims to charge the physical node in term of CPU and memory use. It is composed from several virtual routers that are connected to each other in cascade. The network traffic generated by clients keeps the virtual resources in use. The two networks are not connected to the same physical interfaces to avoid influence between the two virtual networks packets. For our experiments, we try to only charge the virtual resources. Connecting the two networks with the same interfaces would produce false results.

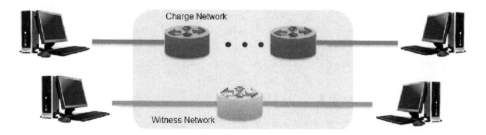

Fig. 4. Testbed description

The test consists of measuring witness network performance while incrementing routers number in the other one. Test purpose is to prove that a virtual router can work with acceptable performance when competed by several other routers. On charged network all routers are placed in cascade to be sure that all of them work in the same time. We will use Iperf with default parameters to charge the second virtual network. In these tests will not present the performance of charged Network. We remarked that it has equivalent performance to witness network.

First, we will present throughput measurement result. We will use Mgen to generate series of 100000 TCP packets with Poisson distribution of 1Kb each to evaluate throughput and to more generic. We have chosen this number because on client we have 100Mb network interfaces and to reach the max routing number of packet. Each scenario test was repeated 30 times for standard point and 100 for interesting point (where throughput have a big variation).The duration of each test was fixed to 5 minutes.

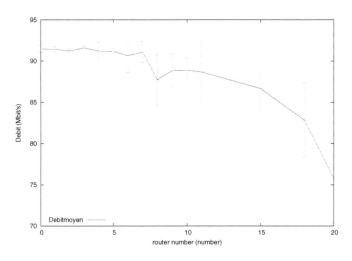

Fig. 5. Throughput measurement results

We noticed after measurements that until eight machines on charged network we have a relative constant throughput. Starting from the 9th router throughput began to decrease gradually to reach 75 Mb per second with 20 routers as shown in Fig. 5. Throughput's decrease is due to the router scheduling. We estimate that system overload with context switching between routers is the causes of this throughput decrease. Despite the decrease these results demonstrate that even with extreme charge on physical node the throughput remain almost acceptable to satisfy local networking application.

Second, we will present the Round Time Trip (RTT) delay measurement. For delay measurement, we used the Ping RTT result. Ping is generally the most used way to evaluate delay as in [12]. It can be inexact if routers give low priority to ping packets. For our testes as we haven't changed ICMP packet priority inside

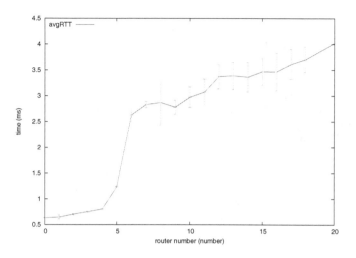

Fig. 6. RTT delay measurement results

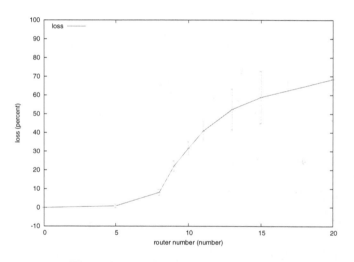

Fig. 7. Paquet loss measurement results

virtual router. Ping packet has the same priority as all other packets. Also for this test, duration is 5 min and each test is repeated 30 times for irrelevant point and 100 times for critical one. As shown in Fig. 6, the RTT in witness network remains under 1ms for a charged network composed from less than 5 routers which is a relatively good value for RTT. For the case of 8 Router we have values under 3ms. Then the RTT begins to increment until reaching 4ms in the worst case with 20 routers. The virtual environment context switching delays the router response and affects RTT variation. However, this delay is acceptable for VoIP communication.

Finally, we will present paquet loss measurement. We have changed the flow nature compared to throughput measurement. Iperf measures the loss rate only for UDP Flow. It was also an occasion to view UDP flow variation in virtual network context. We have also changed the charge network flow to UDP. The Test duration is 5 min and each test is repeated as precedent tests. As we have seen with TCP throughput, we have noticed that with the 8th machine we began to have significant problem with a relatively high loss percentage. As shown in Fig. 7, the loss percentage continues to grow gradually to finally reach 70% in a configuration with 20 routers in the charged network. Over this number of machines the performance is decreasing gradually to reach critical level with 21 routing working in the same time. As we have explained before the decrease in performance is due to the increasing number of virtual machine context switching in the Hypervisor. We have also observed during these tests that the most part of resource is used by the privileged domain dom0 which consumes the most significant part of CPU and memory resources.

6   Conclusion

Advances in virtualization technologies have created new opportunities for network operators to take advantage of network resources more efficiently. We try to adapt virtualization concepts to satisfy many of today's network telecommunication challenges.

We have proposed virtual network environment architecture. We have presented the design and mechanisms underlying the virtual network platform. We have started the implementation of this approach with a real prototype. Using experiments with realistic virtual router network applications and benchmarks, we demonstrated the performance/cost benefits and the effortless applicability of our architecture to manage virtual network environment. We have measured the performance of this architecture with a real Testbed. The experimentations show that we have obtained significant result until 10 Virtual routers in the same physical Node.

Our future work will focus on distributed management algorithm of virtual network resources. We will also investigate different means to increment network efficiency by reducing system resources waste in privileged domain, virtual machine size and their resources consumption.

Acknowledgments. We would like to acknowledge VirtuOR start-up to have supported our researches. It helps us to develop our architecture and validate it on a real platform.

References

1. Anhalt, F., Primet, P.: Analysis and evaluation of a XEN based virtual router. In: HAL-CCSD (2008)
2. Barham, P., Dragovic, B., Fraser, K., Hand, S., Harris, T., Ho, A., Neugebauer, R., Pratt, I., Warfield, A.: Xen and the art of virtualization. In: ACM Symposium on Operating Systems Principles, SOSP (2003)

3. Deshane, T., Shepherd, Z., Matthews, J.N., Ben-Yehuda, M., Shah, A., Rao, B.: Quantitative Comparison of Xen and KVM. In: Xen Summit, Boston (2008)
4. Santos, J.R., Janakiraman, G., Turner, Y.: Xen Network I/O Performance Analysis and Opportunities for Improvement. HP Labs (2007)
5. Xorp, http://www.xorp.org
6. Quagga, http://www.quagga.net
7. Asterisk, http://www.asterisk.org
8. MPLS-Linux, http://sourceforge.net/apps/mediawiki/mpls-linux
9. Opensips, http://www.opensips.org
10. Fielding, R.T.: Architectural Styles and the Design of Network-based Software Architectures. Doctoral Thesis, University of Califormia, Irvine (2000)
11. Berners-Lee, T., Fielding, R., Masinter, L.: Uniform Resource Identifiers (URI): Generic Syntax. RFC Editor (1998)
12. Wang, G., Ng, T.S.E.: The Impact of Virtualization on Network Performance of Amazon EC2 Data Center. In: IEEE INFOCOM'10, San Diego (2010)

New Routing Paradigms for the Next Internet

Djamel H. Sadok, Luciana Pereira Oliveira, and Judith Kelner

Federal University of Pernambuco (UFPE), Brazil
{jamel,lpo,jk}@gprt.ufpe.br

Abstract. This work suggests that current and future could be seen as flexible architecture structured by societies. Information sharing and routing are then studied in this context. A proposal, namely evidence-based knowledge sharing routing is described and evaluated. Information sharing in social networks looks to be a promising venue for next Internet routing.

Keywords: Social Networks, Information Sharing, Architecture, Internet and Networks.

1 Introduction

One may expect the next Internet to offer a new living space for working, entertaining, a sort of second life, rather than a simple transport or information distribution channel. Simply put, where there is information, there should be an Internet access to it. Despite the large debate on whether one should consider a clean slate approach for a "new" Internet, the authors chose to define a socially inspired flexible structure that may embrace many possible new networking contexts. For years we have been intrigued by the way bio-inspired models from ants, bees, humans and other animal species organize on a large scale their societies. The question is: how much would one gain by extending some of these models to the Internet.

A critical look shows that the current Internet already mimics human behavior to an extent, continuously spawning more and more virtual communities. Hence, elements of the next architecture(s) may take on roles characterizing them within their societies while using rules and policies to achieve their goals and make predictable decisions. Recent research from content centric networks [1] emphasized this. Here, routers should be seen as objects acting on content according to their context. Hence it is the context that defines the role and not otherwise.

In this paper, we propose and discuss the Internet as a structure based, among other things, on the concepts: 1) usage of a society-based structure with rules or policies governing their existence; 2) roles and relationships and finally; 3) knowledge sharing between society members for information routing. It is this last item, namely knowledge sharing, which is examined in this paper.

2 Embracing the Societies for the Internet Architecture

A simplified one size fits all approach is no longer practical. The authors see the next Internet as one that consists of different societies, governed by different policies,

A. Pont, G. Pujolle, and S.V. Raghavan (Eds.): WCITD/NF 2010, IFIP AICT 327, pp. 194–205, 2010.

having different goals and technological characteristics. Somehow, these societies get together in an attempt to offer some common good or services.

Within a single society one expects to see relatively more homogeneity, stability, common rules and vocabulary (ontology) being applied. Some cultures become more dominant at some time of history, others remain peripheral to the global picture. Among societies, different views may be adopted to achieve similar objectives and to enforce internal autonomy. Despite diversity, societies need to talk to each other and harmonize with their environments. Hence one expects some order in such disorder, common, through probably weakly coupled, roles that ensure end to end cooperation.

The overlay networks are interesting model to exemplify societies. They constituted virtual communities like Peer-to-Peer (P2P) networks (such as Skype and BitTorent), Newgroups, mailing lists, video and music file sharing over physical network. They are exemplified by the context of global interworking in Fig. 1.

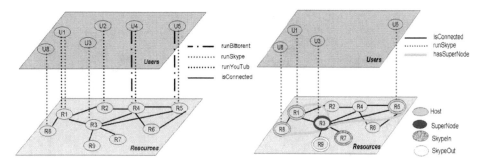

Fig. 1. View of a Society Based Internet   **Fig. 2.** Skype society

Fig. 2 depicts a Skype society extracted from the example in Fig. 1 [2]. For this scenario, connectivity resources include user desktops, routers and the public phone service (PSTN) gateways. The roles responsible for stability within this society include the following special servers: Supernodes, Skype-in and Skype-out gateways. A host can be a Skype client used to place voice calls and send text chat messages. A Supernode is a special one with a public address (or external role in society terminology) possibly having sufficient CPU, memory, and network bandwidth. Skype-in and Skype-out gateways reach users and applications from other communities or societies such as the public phone service and other VoIP application users. Hosts and Supernodes organize the P2P overlay, while the Skype-in and Skype-out elements provide PC-to-PSTN and PSTN-to-PC bridging.

We envisage a next Internet where, for example, Skype and Orkut users may talk to each other through special gateways. Similarly, YouTube users may get to know MSN and POTS users and interact with them. Future societies or groups would be plug-and-play connectible as long as they follow some simple proposed social structure and stability requirements.

Therefore, our societies must have some basic knowledge on how to forward such requests among themselves. A request could visit many societies in between, asking them about given knowledge or services, if they could have suggestions on forwarding a request. Such requests may die out slowly in the meta-societies hyper-space unless they locate their target society. Our approach implicitly adopts the late binding mechanism as users are not required to know the exact path or even have the full information on their communication partners. Time to live flags should be associated with forwarded queries or information for them to be removed when unsuccessful.

3   Relevant Advances the Social Approach in Routing

Many protocols have been based on social phenomena such as regional gossiping [3] and rumor routing [4]. The following are some new routing related concepts:

- *Proximity*: represents how nearby and further away a node is using a predefined distance concept;
- *Knowledge*: represents if someone knows, heard of, has never seen before or knows someone (make a referral to) who may help;
- *Volatility*: reflects the presence of highly dynamic societies with limited scope in time and space. A new emergency network setup to deal with an earthquake or one covering a sport event are such examples.
- *Connectivity level*: shows how high (important) a society is. It is therefore, likely, that we have different connectivity levels, including: global societies that are present all over the world and connect to many others; big, regular and small societies. A power Law or mass amount disparity phenomenon may be expected as many societies will have little connectivity and the global ones may be limited in numbers.

Data fusion strategies, such as the Dempster-Schaffer [5], [6] technique, may then be used to combine the evidence gathered by a node to make a routing decision. Such decisions may be cached for possible future reference. Although routing has been used to refer to mechanisms responsible for forwarding information, a more suitable name reflecting a new Internet scenario where societies are cooperating with each others could be knowledge sharing. Our scenario is that of a community of societies constantly conducting knowledge diffusion activities, by far, a wider scope.

Cultural diffusion models have not been effectively adopted for large scale systems such as the Internet. They have been developed to illustrate the processes of knowledge diffusion between knowledge workers, and factor the coefficients of distance, willingness, motivation, and ability of comprehension and expression [6].

Gossip-based models have, for instance, extensively been used in knowledge diffusion work [7]. This is however an oversimplified model, as we need to use asynchronous models where there is call for more interaction rather than relying on old acquaintances to lead with the future. In [8], a barter process is assumed between the members that can trade different types of knowledge.

Considerable work has also gone into partially connected networks [9], [10]and Epidemic Routing (ER) [11]. Such work introduces ER, where random pair-wise exchanges of messages among mobile hosts ensure eventual message delivery. Similarly, Chen and Murphy propose a protocol called Disconnected Transitive Communication which involves the application in locating the node among a cluster of currently connected nodes that it is best to forward the message to [12]. Given that messages are delivered probabilistically in ER, the application may require the use of acknowledgments. Some optimizations may be further made using techniques such as bloom filters [13].

Relevant ideas may also come from recent work on disruptive networks (DTN). Here a number of routing strategies have been evaluated including flooding, random walk, replica forwarding with staggered attempts [9], even enhanced link state protocols and hybrid approaches. Similarly, Zhang in [13] and Small and Haas in [14] studied analytically algorithms derived from ER. Spyropoulos proposed a multi-copy scheme for DTN routing in [15]. In [16], a DTN routing strategy that minimizes packet loss is developed.

4 Knowledge Sharing and Routing

The social routing algorithms are based on the observation that information reaches more people and destinations when going through popular nodes [17]. For such context, we suggest the knowledge network could be measured to classify the society's evolution and such classification could be coordinating the routing of messages.

4.1 Evolution of Societies and Routing Information

We expect that the first step in evolution of a society corresponds the processing where a society gets to know itself, who are its members, their reachability towards other societies and their capacity and willingness to work as gateways. We expect every society to implement some basic internal discovery mechanisms allowing it to reach one or more representative nodes, that know about its connections to other societies and has at least a partial description of what others do. The interaction among the societies will continue its evolution and consequently the classification changes.

Global societies will give priority to learning about each others. They would accept even weak evidence within passing routing information (or recent overheard gossip). The lower we go into the connectivity index, the less persuasive their evidence is considered. There could be an exception however, for example that of volatile (highly dynamic) societies. This class could be given special treatment as a slow spread of gossip may work against it due to the time it takes for other societies to know about it. Hence a society may inflate its connectivity or knowledge metrics just to ensure that the knowledge sharing converges rapidly allowing others to discover it. Alternatively, a society may chose to restrict its connectivity information and operate in an almost "silent mode". Note that this may also be subject to policy guidelines. We do not consider the effect of wrong or malicious information as part of this work at present. Apart from the global societies, each society seeks to know about similar and higher level ones. Although we already used the term "know about" yet we did not define this. So what are the implications of knowing about a given society? These are three: first its identification is no longer strange to your "gateways" or similar entities, its purpose (services) in life is known and third, we know some information on the societies it is capable of reaching i.e. its external topology.

Unlike the existing Internet, duplicate knowledge is not removed but kept and some accumulative levels of evidence are associated to each of the entries. All evidence is sorted according to its levels and eventually the lower ones are removed. Even evidence may get old and consequently weaker to reflect the fact that old knowledge may no longer be valid. Special, per society policies should be defined to enforce such decisions. A lifetime may explicitly be associated with an evidence message by the issuing society.

Changes within the connectivity level of a society should be communicated to its siblings. When trying to find out about a path to a society, a query with a maximum society hop count may be made. Upon failure, this threshold may be increased. A lesson to be learned from this, is that knowledge of distant societies is more precious and should be maintained and spread to nearby siblings. A society that knows many distant societies could have its connectivity level increased (improving its status in a world of societies – where you are who you know!).

Unlike deterministic routing, societies may live with uncertainty and incomplete knowledge. We may simply need to locate a node that is close enough and avoid loops. By close we mean some society that knows about the destination. This is in line with current new Internet architecture proposals that use late binding. Nonetheless, we need to maintain delivery rates high while minimizing resource utilization. We also need to derive upper and lower bounds on the delay.

One or more metrics, both quantitative and even qualitative, need to be established to measure its effectiveness. As an example, we select a probabilistic metric called delivery predictability, $P(a \Rightarrow b) \in [0,1]$, at every node a for each known destination b.

The routing could be seen as a multiple copy scheme that operates according to probability or predictability with support for both on-demands versus table driven modes. Routing needs to learn, which members lack some knowledge, and which member owns it. When knowledge is shared between two societies on a given destination or services, then a society's knowledge on that first one increases. Knowledge aging is also taken into account. Hence with time, it is expected that the delivery predictability to a given destination will decrease. This is similar to ant based routing that adopts the idea of dissipating pheromone trails.

Further, societies may be characterized by different coefficients of knowledge sharing willingness and knowledge learning motivation. It is also expected that a society detaining a high level knowledge may not be willing to share knowledge with one with a lower knowledge level. We need to characterize societies with wide ranging possible knowledge sharing willingness and knowledge learning motivation.

However, if there is a small gap between the knowledge of societies they probably reside within the same "class" of societies. A threshold representing the knowledge gap may be used to determine when societies should exchange knowledge. Distance between the members may also influence knowledge sharing. Such distance may be regarded as one of the following categories or some combination: 1) geographical distance; 2) cultural distance: such as languages, values, and 3) technology distance, etc;

4.2   Elements of Proposal Routing Algorithm

The proposed routing may be viewed as one that consists of the following algorithms or blocks:

1. Knowledge sharing mechanisms: algorithms may be based on gossip, scoped broadcast, etc. These take into consideration knowledge sharing willingness of a given society, status of a society, local policies, etc.

2. Knowledge adoption algorithms: such class of algorithms determines when a society may accept some incoming information and how to associate a validity level to it. A receiving society maintains total autonomy in deciding whether it will accept new information. For example, it may determine that it is unwilling to carry messages larger than a given size or destined for certain societies. Hence we see room for policies in our proposal to govern the knowledge sharing and evidence acceptance in the future Internet. One may also assume an implicit trust model, where societies with the same degrees of connectivity (number of neighboring societies) trust the announcements made from others. We will not examine any further this point however in this work.

3. Society lookup: represents strategies that may be adopted in finding out the whereabouts of a given society and its reachability information. Such strategies may be based on intelligent algorithms, brute force, semantic queries, dedicated known overlay servers such as society Oracles, etc.

4. Strategies for the update and retrieval of society information: determine when and how to seek some information it owns and tell those interested of possible changes in its status. Examples of mechanisms that may be used to offer such functionalities range between publish and subscribe, push models, broadcast, etc.

5. Society clustering algorithms: may be seen as a future attractive mechanism for optimizing knowledge sharing. It may be modeled by averaging the proportion of neighbors of a society who are also connected together. Societies may also use third party knowledge to deal with forwarding issues. Such optimization steps are left for future studies.

5 Knowledge Sharing Model

In this work, we evaluate the first element of proposed routing algorithm (knowledge sharing) analyzing the society evolution. We modeled the algorithm such that its knowledge flow will be inversely proportion to the distance among societies, and directly proportion to knowledge gap. Existing Internet based social networks have been described as power-law or scale-free degree distribution networks with distinct epidemiologic properties from those of random networks [6]. We need to investigate how future Internet society will evolve and whether they would maintain a linear expansion of the existing power Law model or change into multiple different topologies. The network topology impact on knowledge diffusion models has been shown in [7].

Techniques such as adaptive percolation [18], [19] may be used to show that by propagating knowledge from a small number of specially chosen societies we can drastically increase the probability of the network becoming almost fully connected (aware of its societies and their whereabouts).

Attending such characteristics, our algorithm model was defined as $S = \left\{ S_i : i \in N^* \right\}$ been a set of societies and $\|S\|$ their cardinal. Let d_i be the degree of the ith society S_i. We divide societies into K classes $\{C_1, ..., C_k\}$ according to their connectivity level or degree (of knowledge). This division is done in a way that it should take a long time for a society before being able to leapfrog to a next level in order to maintain a stable network connectivity state. Hence there should be a small number of classes that are distant enough. The simulated world (or the next Internet) starts up with a small number of classes and will grow to create new levels by continuously upgrading those with a larger degree of connectivity.

At the top level there are more stable societies with a high connectivity degree. A society gets first to know about its physically sibling neighbors through more than one interface or gateway. This will have a weight factor equal to one and reflects direct contact in this case. If a society learns about another one through a given path, it also knows about those along such path. Hence such knowledge is accumulative and may be represented by independent (separate) logical links within a graph for instance.

Let $l_{i,j}$ be a path to society j from i (information on society j from i) and $\|l_{i,j}\|$ be the total number of such knowledge elements. Hence we have (1). Without loss of generality we may assume that a society S_i with degree d_i belongs to class C_k with $k \in \left\{1...K\right\}$ given we have (2) and (3). Hence if we choose for example B as 100 and K as 4 then we have the four classes: C_1, C_2, C_3 and C_4 should have as members societies with degrees immediately bellow the thresholds $10^2, 10^4, 10^6$ and 10^8. The larger the base B is, the more distant are the classes. Hence we may view B as a tunable factor that separates the big from the riffraff. Let N_i be the number of elements within a given class C_i for $1 \le i \le K$.

$$d_i = \sum_{j=1;\, j \neq i}^{\|S\|} \left\| l_{i,j} \right\| \tag{1}$$

$$k = \text{Min}\{K, \text{Max}\{1, \text{Ceiling}\,(log_B\, d_i)\,\}\} \tag{2}$$

$$C_j = \left\{ S_i : B^{j-1} \le d_i < B^j \right\}. \tag{3}$$

In contrast to the static probability percolation strategy our approach uses a dynamic probability for responding a knowledge request from society i about j to its known colleagues given by (4) where α_k is a per class tunable constant. For our evaluations we assume that death may occur at any C_i level according $p_i = b_k/d_i$, where b_k is also a per class tunable constant. In other words, we can introduce different levels of death at the classes or define a limitation such as setting up societies at the bottom level of the stability graph (C_1 class) to it only cease to exist. Knowledge sharing works by associating a weight for each new information. Knowledge related to a small society (limited connectivity degree) will have a smaller probability for being spread to the rest of the world. Hence it is very likely that only nearby societies know about a low degree one as this knowledge dies out the further we get from this society.

$$p_{i,j} \sim \alpha_k * d_i * d_j \tag{4}$$

Knowledge is exchanged under different conditions:

1. When two societies need to exchange knowledge. For example, when a new society is born, it is then eager to tell the world about itself;
2. A request is made to locate or search for a given society using some information known about it.
3. Currently, knowledge accumulates. However, we some knowledge may become unavailable when a society dies out. Others may be alerted about this;

6 Evaluation of Knowledge Sharing Model

The simulation studies the mechanisms to build paths that corresponds the evolution of the societies in terms of learning, accumulating and disseminating information (paths).

6.1 Simulation Metrics and Parameters

We evaluate the membership of each class. The presence of a large number of nodes in some class shows that its nodes learn more each round and more frequently. The dissemination of knowledge is a second potential metric to evaluate the knowledge flow. Societies propagate more response messages when the nodes are "young" as need to know more about their neighbors. The forwarding of lookup requests adds latency and increases the lookup traffic load. Hence, the analysis investigates both the accumulated knowledge as well as the frequency of learning and dissemination of knowledge. We assume that the network starts with a small number of nodes (set to 10 nodes here) and we simplify the simulation by using fixed numbers of classes and set the constant B to, respectively 4 and 10. To reduce memory allocation requirements, each node may obtain up to a maximum of a hundred direct connections.

The following tunable α_k constants were used: 9, 60, 300 and 1000. Moreover, we suppose that the nodes are not homogenous, so these are randomly born with knowledge between 0 and 3 (little amount of information). Based on these assumptions, the analysis of the Knowledge Sharing based routing protocol attempts to quantify the knowledge properties of the Societies architecture. The analysis computes the dissemination of information, knowledge accumulated and learning frequencies.

6.2 The Results

Fig.3 presents the number of nodes classified in each class. Class 1 contains the largest total number of nodes created. This is the class where nodes are initially born. Class 2 has fewer nodes classified than both classes 1 and even 3. This is due to the fact that the threshold between class 1 and class 2 is relatively small (10 points of knowledge). Consequently, many nodes from class 2 do not spend too much time in this class and move rapidly to class 3, sometimes not even going through it. On the other hand, the threshold between class 3 (α_k =100) and class 4 (α_k =1000) is larger, hence leading to a slower flow of societies between the two categories. Note that the choice of these disparate threshold values was made on purpose in order to highlight the evolution under such peculiar circumstances and highlights the importance of choosing α_k .

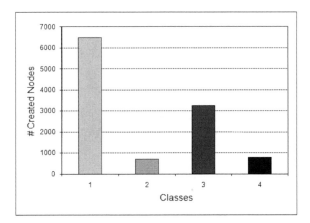

Fig. 3. Skype society

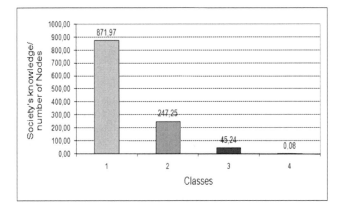

Fig. 4. Skype society

Fig 4. presents the total count of acquired knowledge per node of each class, so it also shows the evolution of nodes learning. Class 1 received more information, because a node from this class has a high probability to accept knowledge sharing. It follows, or mimics, the young behavior, because the learning allows the survival of nodes, and giving the necessary knowledge to cross over to a next class. This figure also presents the dissemination flow. We can see the knowledge flow; it decreases more when the node goes to a high class, as this has less information received.

Fig. 5 depicts the learning curve with the graphical relation between the average learning of nodes and the time taken to learn. Classes 2, 3 and 4 use the blue, red and green colors respectively. Due to limitations in the OMNET simulator, class 1 learning curve is not displayed due to the large number of values it has, more than the OMNET graphical tool may handle. It seems that knowledge stabilizes at some moment. The authors plan to conduct more simulations.

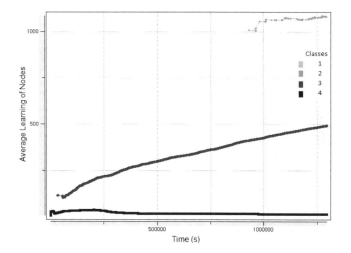

Fig. 5. Learning curve

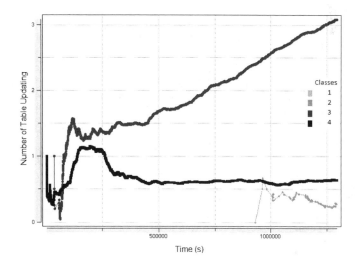

Fig. 6. Learning curve

The knowledge sharing and routing algorithm was implemented using knowledge tables. Each node has a table that is updated when it receives information. Therefore, Fig. 6 shows the average number of table updating.

7 Conclusions and Future Directions

Routing is an important part of any future Internet architecture. Societies and their communication styles are expected to be at the core the architectural mechanisms. The author introduces an approach for quantifying the information sharing/routing among societies in Internet, based on the society classification and information adoption model, but we intend to analyze such model in-depth studies to understand inter-society information routing using real traces.

The initial experiment studied the evolution of societies and the information sharing among such simulated societies. Knowledge believe and probable forwarding based on trust, evidence have shown that despite leading to apparent unexpected non deterministic routing results, they could nonetheless be used as a basis for next Internet to reach all possible groups.

Problems such as email spam and unwanted traffic may be dealt with using such inter-society policy based routing. We plan to expand the simulations in order to gain more understanding of the results.

References

1. Smith, T.F., Waterman, M.S.: Identification of Common Molecular Subsequences. J. Mol. Biol. 147, 195–197 (1981)
2. Jacobson, V., Mosko, M., Smetters, D., Garcia-Luna-Aceves, J.J.: Content-Centric Networking. Whitepaper Describing Future Assurable Global Networks. Palo Alto Research Center, Inc. (January 30, 2007)
3. Baset, S.A., Schulzrinne, H.G.: An Analysis of the Skype Peer-to-Peer Internet Telephony Protocol. In: INFOCOM. 25th IEEE International Conference on Computer Communications, pp. 1–11 (2006)
4. Li, X.Y., Moaveninejad, K., Frieder, O.: Regional gossip routing for wireless ad hoc networks. Mobile Networks and Applications 10(1-2), 61–77 (2005)
5. Braginsky, D., Estrin, D.: Rumor Routing Algorithm For Sensor Networks. In: WSNA'02, USA (2002)
6. Dempster, A.P.: A generalization of Bayesian inference. Journal of the Royal Statistical Society, Series B 30, 205–247 (1968)
7. Shafer, G.: A Mathematical Theory of Evidence. Princeton University Press, Princeton (1976)
8. Cointet, J.-P., Roth, C.: How Realistic Should Knowledge Diffusion Models Be? Jour. of Artificial Societies and Social Simulation 10(3, 5) (2007)
9. Cowan, R.: Network structure and the diffusion of knowledge. Journal of Economic Dynamics and Control 28(8), 1557–1575 (2004)
10. Vahdat, A., Becker, D.: Epidemic routing for partially connected ad hoc networks, Duke University, Tech. Rep. CS-200006 (April 2000)

11. Lindgren, A., Doria, A., Schelen, O.: Probabilistic Routing in Intermittently Connected Networks. In: 1st. International Workshop on Assurance with Partial and Intermittent Resources

12. Kenah, E., Robins, J.: Network-based analysis of stochastic SIR epidemic models with random and proportionate mixing. J. Theor. Biol. 249(4), 706 (2007)

13. Chen, X., Murphy, A.L.: Enabling disconnected transitive communication in mobile ad hoc networks. In: Proc. of Workshop on Principles of Mobile Computing, pp. 21–27 (2001)

14. Zhang, X., Neglia, G., Kurose, J., Towsley, D.: Performance Modeling of Epidemic Routing. MIT Rep. 05-44 (2005)

15. Hass, Z.J., Small, T.: A New Networking Model for Biological Applications of Ad Hoc Sensor Networks. IEEE/ACM Transactions on Networking (February 2006)

16. Spyropoulos, T., Psounis, K., Raghavendra, C.: Efficient Routing in Intermittently Connected Mobile Networks: The Multi-copy Case. ACM/IEEE Journal of Transactions on Networking (2007)

17. Lipsa, G.: Routing Strategy for Minimizing the Packet Loss in Disruptive Tolerant Networks. Information Sciences and Systems, 1167–1172 (2008)

18. Sadok, D.H., França, J., Abreu, R., Oliveira, L.: Knowledge Sharing to Improve Routing and Future 4G Networks. In: Adibi, S., Mobasher, A., Tofighbakhsh, M. (eds.) Fourth-Generation Wireless Networks: Applications and Innovations IGI-Global, ch. 10 (2009) ISBN: 9781615206742

19. Han, S., et al.: Collaborative Blog Spam Filtering Using Adaptive Percolation Search. In: WWW 2006, Edinburgh, UK, May 22-26 (2006)

20. Moore, C., Newman, M.: Epidemics and Percolation in Small-world Networks. Physical Review 61(5), 5678–5682 (2001)

End-to-End Performance Evaluation of Interconnected Optical Multi-ring Metropolitan Networks*

Tülin Atmaca and Tuan Dung Nguyen

Institut Telecom/Telecom SudParis, 9 rue Charles Fourier, 91011 Evry-France
{tulin.atmaca,dung.nguyen}@it-sudparis.eu

Abstract. Metropolitan ring networks are usually used to connect the high speed backbone networks with the high speed access networks. In this paper, we focus on the end-to-end performance of a multi-ring architecture in which metropolitan access networks (MANs) are interconnected by a metropolitan core network. These rings are synchronized and can be interconnected transparently through single access nodes (Hub node) or multiple access nodes. A multi ring architecture consisting of two slotted MAN rings connected by a ring-based slotted metro core will be simulated. The major problem in this architecture is how to resolve the synchronization shift between rings while assuring the traffic routed efficiently from the metro access to the metro core networks. To ensure this efficiency, we use some optical packet filling mechanisms such as Aggregation Mechanism, CUM (CoS-Upgrade Mechanism), DCUM (Dynamic CoS-Upgrade Mechanism). Through various simulations, we present some performance results in terms of jitter and mean end-to-end delay which show that the use of the pair of Aggregation/DCUM improves the transmission capability at Hub nodes as compared with others pairs and provide a cost-effective solution.

Keywords: Metropolitan Area Network (MAN), Optical Multi-Ring metro architecture, performance, synchronization, simulation, jitter, end-to-end delay.

1 End-to-End Network Architecture

Transport and switching network elements responsible for the data transmission between network users is referred to as the transport (or data) plane. It is important to note that the architecture required to construct an efficient transport plane has evolved differently in the backbone, metro, and access levels. Backbone networks (also called long haul networks) carry huge loads of information between countries, through mountains to keep the signal clear and the loss minimal. Backbone networks provide connectivity between points of presence (PoPs), consist of multiple edge and core routers. Each serves one or multiple MAN. The number of nodes and links in a backbone network can vary significantly among the different service providers (typically 30–100 nodes and 40–120 links) [1]. The distances between node pairs are in the order of several hundreds or even thousands of kilometres, and the traffic

* This work was partially supported by the ECOFRAME ANR French national research project and NoE/Euro-NF project.

A. Pont, G. Pujolle, and S.V. Raghavan (Eds.): WCITD/NF 2010, IFIP AICT 327, pp. 206–216, 2010.

demand between them is usually meshed and specified in multiples of the wavelength granularity (i.e., 2.5 or 10 Gbits/s). The average bandwidth on a backbone link can be up to several hundreds of Gbits/s.

Metro networks (MAN) interconnect a number of central offices (CO) within a given metropolitan area. These networks have been traditionally deployed using synchronous optical network/synchronous digital hierarchy (SONET/SDH) rings, as the traffic grooming technique was needed to guarantee efficient use of the network bandwidth (the capacity required between pairs of CO has been smaller than the wavelength granularity of SONET/SDH systems). Unlike long-haul networks, which transport point-to-point traffic, metro networks are ring-based in multiples of the wavelength granularity.

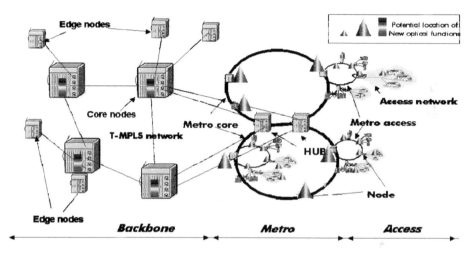

Fig. 1. Access, Core and Backbone Metro Networks [2]

As showed in Fig. 1, metro rings (core/region networks) interconnect the high-speed backbone networks and the high-speed access networks. The metro rings can be interconnected transparently through single access node (Hub node) or multiple access nodes. Current metro networks are typically SONET/SDH-over-WDM rings which carry the huge amount of bursty data traffic. The metro core and regional networks are normally both 2-fiber rings. A fiber failure in a metro access ring does not affect the traffic in the core and other access rings. The network thus becomes more reliable.

The technology evolution for an end-to-end architecture can be: ADSL towards Passive Optical Network (PON) in the access network [3] and SONET/SDH/WDM towards all-optical packet switching/Dense WDM in the metro network. Besides, upstream traffic flux from Optical Line Terminal (OLTs) to the access metro is statistically multiplexed through a DSCU (Distant Subscriber Connection Unit). A DSCU can be connected with several OLTs while an access node of the access metro can be connected with several DSCUs. As a result, an access metro (about 10 ring nodes) can support some thousands of PONs. A simplified end-to-end architecture in the metropolitan network is shown in Fig 2.

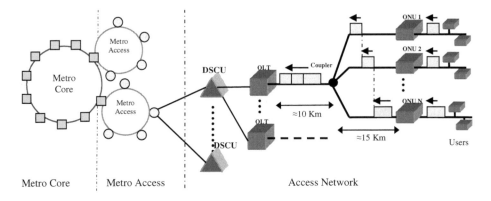

Fig. 2. End-to-End Metro Network Architecture

In this architecture, there are about 2 million subscribers which are connected to the metro core (primary ring with 10 core stations) through access networks and metro networks. Each core station is connected with a secondary ring (access metro) composing of 4 access stations (access nodes). So we have a total of 40 stations which are accessible. Each access station connects with 25 DSCUs which manages approximately 2000 subscribers across 60 PONs. We suppose that the amount of traffic from each network PON is approximately equal to 32Mbits/s, which requires an access metro with a capacity exceeding 200Gbit/s (40 wavelengths of 10Gbit/s responsible for 50%). Note that optical frames are transmitted from ONUs to OLT and from OLTs to DSCU under point-to-point connections.

2   Multi-ring Network Simulation

Now, we focus on the proposed simulation. For the sake of simplify, we use 3 metro rings in which 2 access metro rings connected to 1 core network through Hub nodes as shown in Fig. 3. All access nodes of a metro access (the left one) sends its local traffic to a destination node residing on another metro access network (the right one) by passing through a metro core network. These traffics are then transported to the left Hub node (Hub 1 - the node interconnecting the metro access network in the left side with the core network) before being routed to the core metro network into optical fixed-size packets. Inside the Hub 1, the traffic can be aggregated with other traffic coming from other access nodes (because they have the same destination) or with the Hub node's local traffic. Since the network architecture is configured with active components as Packet Optical Add/Drop Multiplexer (POADM [4]), hence both metro types support the synchronous transmission which allows transporting optical fixed-size packets in the slotted mode. In the following, we use the bus-based network referring to the left metro access's upstream path in the figure.

In our simulation, the uniform traffic pattern is considered in the bus-based network. From an access node residing in the bus-based network, electronic packets are encapsulated into optical packets and then transported to the Hub 1. Depending on

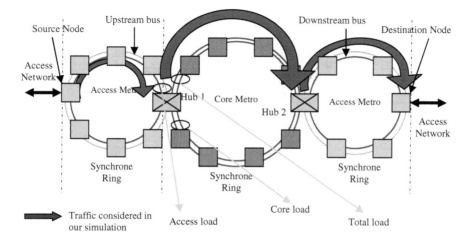

Fig. 3. Multi-Ring Network Simulation

the mechanism used in the Hub node, the optical packets might be directly put on optical buffers (to be ready for being routed to the core network) or be separated again into electronic packets which will be then contained in electronic buffers. The second one leads to the situation that incoming electronic packets (from different access nodes) might be together combined (mutual combination) or be combined with local electronic packets (local combination) of Hub node (Hub node can be a point of presence) or both in order to create a new optical packets with a higher filling ratio. This behaviour is very similar to GPFO mechanism [5] (that we have developed in order to increase the filling ratio of the optical packets by entering electronic packets in intermediary nodes), so-called GPFO behaviour. In order to limit the complexity of the simulation, we consider only GPFO behaviour formed by mutual combination in resuming that Hub node does not function as a POP.

There are two key challenges to simulate a Hub node. The first one is the synchronization between interconnected rings. Transmitting transparently optical packets through Hub node needs to consider this synchronization shift. The other challenge to simulating Hub node is the optical packets size supported by different rings. This is referred as "granularity" problem. In the second one, optical packets must be disassembled and re-aggregated, but in different sizes before being switched to the core network. The problem of synchronization shift is shown in the Fig. 5.

For simplicity, we suppose that three simulated rings support the same optical packets size and hence the same slot duration. So the synchronization shift has a 'minor' impact on the Hub node performance. In general, a control packet will be dropped when corresponding data packets which come from access nodes, are received in Hub node. At Hub node, a new control packet needs to be created when a data packet sent to the core network. Certainly, this created control packet must be according to characteristics of the core network. The insertion of data packets must satisfy the discipline of the traffic priority at Hub node (Fig. 4) which is described as follows: the traffic in the core network has the priority higher than that in Hub node.

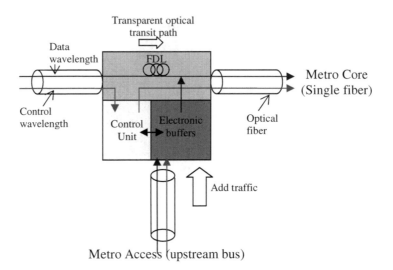

Fig. 4. Hub node's traffic

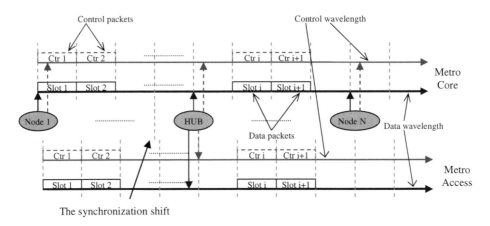

Fig. 5. The synchronization shift between interconnected rings

3 Simulation Parameters

Generally, many performance requirements must be met in order to transport specified data from the access network to the backbone network across a pair of metro core/region (access) networks. Based on parameter requirements for the metropolitan Ethernet network defined in MEF of IETF we use performance parameters in an end-to-end metropolitan network (metro access/core/access networks) as follows: the end-to-end Packet Loss Ratio (EPLR), the end-to-end Accumulated Packet Delay (EAPD) and the Electronic Packet Jitter (EPJ). EPJ is one of the most important parameters which support for real-time data transfer in quality-of-service (QoS).

We suppose that networks support the fixed-size optical packets of 12500 bytes corresponding to the duration of 10μs @10Gbps. We use the multi-class approach for both network types [4]. We assume 8 CoS for client packets in the electronic domain. The premium traffic is generated from CBR sources, with the packet size of 810 bytes. The non premium traffic is modelled by an aggregation of IPP sources with different burstiness levels. Generated packets are of variable lengths according to the Internet packet length statistic ([6]) for each non premium CoS (classes ID from 3 to 8). The optical buffer size is equal to 200 Kbytes for the premium traffic class, 500 Kbytes for silver and bronze traffic classes, 1000 Kbytes for the BE traffic class.

Since Hub node has not a function as a point of present, we propose three scenario cases to study as table 1. Our previous works [4, 7, 10] has shown that PEM (Packet Erasing and Extraction) mechanism does not improve the network performance under medium load, so it is disabled in this work. DCUM and Aggregation Mechanism offer the best performance (in terms of access delay and PLR) [7], so we choose them for metro core network to compare. The GPFO-behaviour can be activated or deactivated, depending on each scenario.

Table 1. End-to-End cases

	Metro Access (10Gbps)	Metro Core (10Gbps)	Metro Access (10Gbps)
Case 1	Aggregation	DCUM	Aggregation
Case 2	T = 150μs	DCUM	T = 150μs
Case 3	Aggregation	Aggregation	Aggregation

4 Numerical Results

Before analyzing simulation results, we note that all mean values in our simulation results are computed with an accuracy of no more than a few percents at 95% confidence level using Batch Means method [8].

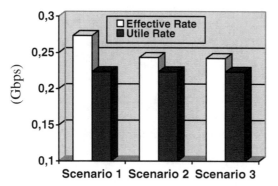

Fig. 6. The total utile and effective rates (from node 1 to 7) in the left-side access metro network

Let's call "effective rate" be the rate of optical containers being transported on the optical ring, and let "utile rate" be the rate of electronic client packets which are travelling inside the optical container (being encapsulated in the optical container). Fig. 6 shows the total utile and effective rates from node 1 to node 7 in the left-side access network for three scenarios without GPFO. We observe that the utile rate has the same value from node 1 to node 9 while the effective rate becomes smaller as long as the timer value increases. This is due to the fact that when the Timer duration is small, the number of created optical containers is higher than it is obtained with bigger Timer values and increases the probability of having not full-filled optical containers. The effective rate with small timer values thus becomes more important, leading to the waste of bandwidth. This shows advantage of simple aggregation mechanism compared to limited-timer mechanism [10].

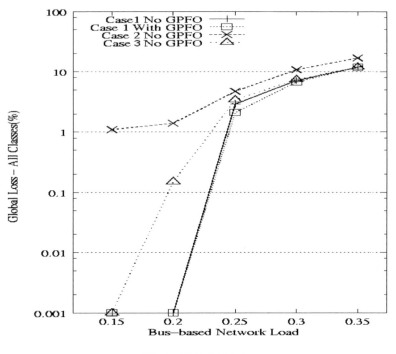

Fig. 7. PLR at Hub 1

Now, we focus on the Hub 1 which interconnects the bus-based network with the metro core network. Fig. 7 presents the total PLR (all classes of service) obtained at Hub node with three cases in function of the access load. Since the core load in observation (shown in Fig. 3) is set up to 70% (that we have supposed), so the total load can be up to a very high proportion over the core network capacity (e.g. it occupies about 95% core network capacity when the access load equal to 25%). As expected, all four curves show a very high loss as considered load increases. This is due to the fact that as the access load increases, the total load of the core network increases also. When the access load reaches 0.3, the Hub node's output capacity hence becomes saturated (100% core network capacity filled). As a result, a very high packet loss is observed when the access load surpasses this threshold.

For this reason, we focus on access loads which are smaller than 0.3. Regarding case 1, with or without GPFO, the difference of the packet loss is not significant. Since the simple aggregation always provides a maximum filling ratio, thus the remaining space inside an optical packets filled by the simple aggregation is not enough to be continuously filled in intermediate nodes. Hence GPFO-behaviour is not necessary when the simple aggregation is enabled.

Among three studied cases without GPFO-behaviour, Hub node in case 2 performs the worst performance, followed by case 3 while case 1 offers the best performance. Case 2 begins show the packet loss earlier than that in case 1 and 3 (15% in comparison to 20% of the access load). Moreover, in case 2, although DCUM is used in the core network, the timer size of 150µs set up at metro access network cannot improve the PLR, even under lightly loaded network (PLR observed with the access load of 0.15 has shown more than 1% loss). So, we think that the simple aggregation used in the metro access network, connecting to a metro core network implementing DCUM is the best choice, based on obtained performance results. Theoretically, DCUM can be implemented in metro access side, but it is more expensive in terms of consumed resource since the algorithm used in DCUM is more complex than that in the simple aggregation.

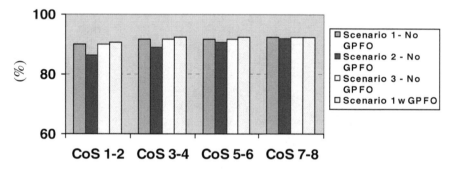

Fig. 8. Filling Ratio observed at Hub 1

Fig. 8 shows the filling ratio obtained for 3 scenarios with and without GPFO. Having a lower filling ratio, the optical container in the scenario 2 without GPFO wastes more bandwidth than other cases, notably for the Premium class. We observe that the filling ratio obtained in scenarios 1 and 3 without GPFO is the same for 4 CoS and always smaller than that obtained in scenarios 1 with GPFO. The difference of the filling ratio obtained from different scenarios is clearer for the premium traffic but it becomes vaguer as the priority of traffic decreases. An explanation for this phenomenon is that we use the factor 1 for the premium traffic's timer (T1 = T) while we use respectively the factor 2, 10 and 20 for other classes of service (T2 = 2*T, T3 = 10*T and T4 = 20*T) [10].

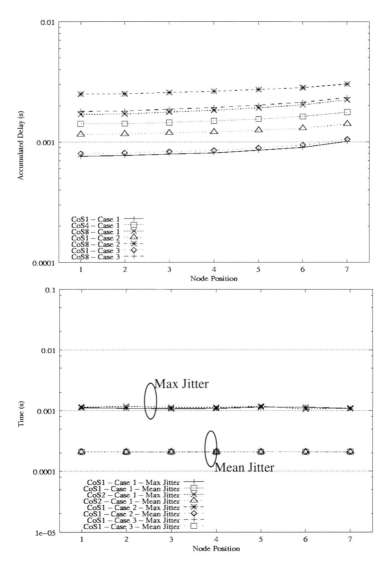

Fig. 9. Average accumulated delays and standard of electronic packet jitter at each node for different cases with the access load equal to 5%

Fig. 9a plots the accumulated access delay in function of access nodes with bus-based network load fixed to 15%. We observe that classes of lower priority provide slightly higher accumulated access delay for all cases as compared to that obtained with classes of high priority. For instance, Premium traffic with the simple aggregation provides a low average accumulated delay (less than 1 ms) at all nodes as compared to accumulated delays obtained by classes of lower priority (e.g. CoS 4 and CoS 8). Regarding the maximum and the average of the electronic packet jitter shown in Fig. 9b, we observe that three cases provide nearly identical average electronic packet jitter at all nodes. Additionally, electronic packet jitter obtained from CoS 1 and 2 seems to be the same. This is due to the fact that electronic packets which are encapsulated in an optical packet will be received in the same time when the optical packets finish its travel at the destination node. In general, there are about from ten to hundred electronic packets encapsulated inside an optical container, leading to small inter-arrival time measured at the destination node. Packet jitters obtained by CoS 1 and 2 are smaller than values specified by MEF. This could be considered as satisfaction in terms of QoS, even for strictly delay-sensitive voice traffic, regardless of used access mechanisms.

5   Concluding Remarks and Future Works

In this article, we have presented an interconnection architecture of optical multi-rings metropolitan networks. We studied the end-to-end performance and the functionality of the interconnection interface of synchronous metropolitan rings. Comparing three cases scenario of optical packet filling mechanisms: CUM/DCUM, Aggregation/Aggregation and Aggregation/DCUM, respectively used for metro access and metro core networks, we have observed that the pair of Aggregation/DCUM mechanisms was the best choice thanks to the algorithmic simplicity of the aggregation mechanism in access and to efficiency of DCUM in metro core to obtain quite good results in terms of jitter and end-to-end delay.

Aggregation/DCUM mechanisms implemented in a pair of metro networks have well achieved its objective: its configuration can strongly improve the network performance, providing an end-to-end metro network with the capability of being stable while guaranteeing good performance in terms of low packet loss, low accumulated delay and high resource utilization under various workloads.

In the future, we will take into account the "granularity" problem in which each network supports different size of the optical packets. This work also will include the performance evaluation of a network where an asynchronous ring (i.e DBORN [9]) connected to a synchronous ring, while the capacity of the metro core should be several times larger than that of the metro access network.

References

[1] Alanqar, E., Jukan, A.: Extending End-to-End Optical Service Provisioning and Restoration in Carrier Networks: Opportunities, Issues and Challenges. IEEE Communications Magazine (January 2004)

[2] Atmaca, T., Nguyen, V.H., Eido, T., Nguyen, T.D.: Report 2 on Comparative Study between Fix Packet Format & Variable Packet Format in an Optical Ring Network. Collaboration 2006 Alcatel-Lucent / GET-INT; Performance Analysis of DATA Oriented Metro Area Networks, PERFOMAN (2007)

[3] Kramer, G., Pesavento, G.: Ethernet passive optical network (EPON): building a next-generation optical access network. IEEE Commun. Mag. 40(2), 66–73 (2002)

[4] Delivrable D2.1: Définition du Plan de Transport (MAC, Protocoles), French ANR Project / ECOFRAME (Eléments de convergence pour les futurs réseaux d'accès et métropolitains à haut débit), Conventions 2006 TCOM 002 -01 à -08, Alcatel-Lucent, Orange-Labs, Télécom-SudParis, Télécom Bretagne, UVSQ (January 2008)

[5] Eido, T., Nguyen, D.T., Atmaca, T.: Packet Filling Optimization in Multiservice Slotted Optical Packet Switching MAN Networks. Paper Accepted for the Advanced International Conference on Telecommunications, AICT'08, Athens (June 2008)

[6] http://www.caida.org/analysis/AIX (still accessible)

[7] Nguyen, T.-D., Eido, T., Atmaca, T.: DCUM: Dynamic Creation of Fixed-Size Containers in Multiservice Synchronous OPS Ring Networks'. In: International Workshop on the Evaluation of Quality of Service through Simulation in the Future Internet, IEEE QoSim'09, Roma, Italy (March 6, 2009)

[8] McDougall, M.H.: Simulating Computer Systems: Techniques and Tools. The MIT Press, Cambridge (1987)

[9] Le Sauze, N., Dotaro, E., Dupas, A., et al.: DBORN: A Shared WDM Ethernet Bus Architecture for Optical Packet Metropolitan Network. Photonic in Switching (July 2002)

[10] Nguyen, T.D., Eido, T., Nguyen, V.H., Atmaca, T.: Impact of Fixed-Size Packet Creation Timer and Packet Format on the Performance of Slotted and Unslotted Bus-Based Optical Man. In: International Conference on Digital Telecommunications IEEE ICDT'08, Bucharest, Romania, June 29-July 5 (2008)

[11] Popa, D., Atmaca, T.: On Optical Packet Format and Traffic Characteristics. In: Proceedings of IEEE/EuroNGI SAINT'05 Workshop on Modelling and Performance Evaluation for Quality of Service in Next Generation Internet, Trento, Italy, January 31-February 4 (2005)

[12] Haciomeroglu, F., Atmaca, T.: Impacts of packet filling in an optical packet switching architecture. In: Advanced Industrial Conference on Telecommunications, AICT'05, Lisbon, Portugal (July 2005)

[13] Fall, K., Varadhan, K.: The ns Manual , UC Berkeley, LBL, USC/ISI, and Xerox PARC (December 13, 2003)

[14] Atmaca, T., Nguyen, H.: Optical MAN Ring Network: Performance Modelling and Evaluation, Springer ©, Performance Handbook – Next Generation Internet: Performance Evaluation and Applications- SPIN 12440030, LNCS 5233, ISBN 978-3-540-99500-5, Edited by Prof. Demetres Kouvatsos, University of Bradford, United Kingdom (2009)

A Relative Bandwidth Allocation Method Enabling Fast Convergence in XCP

Hanh Le Hieu[1], Kenji Masui[2], and Katsuyoshi Iida[2]

[1] Graduate School of Science and Engineering, Tokyo Institute of Technology
[2] Global Scientific Information and Computing Center, Tokyo Institute of Technology
hanhlh@netsys.ss.titech.ac.jp, {kmasui,iida}@gsic.titech.ac.jp

Abstract. The eXplicit Control Protocol (XCP), which explicitly sends feedback information on the current network resource condition to end-hosts to control congestion, is a promising protocol for the network supported congestion control that will be needed in the future Internet. Because of its flexibility, XCP can provide relative bandwidth allocation service that is impossible with other protocols. However, with the existing version of this XCP service, the convergence time to network stability is long due to the gradual resource allocation. We have analyzed the existing allocation method and propose a new allocation method for use at XCP routers. The effectiveness of the proposed method has been evaluated through simulation and the results are discussed here.

Keywords: convergence, relative allocation, QoS, congestion control, XCP, NGN.

1 Introduction

Technology trends indicate that the use of high-bandwidth and high-latency links (e.g., satellite links) with throughput of up to tens of Gb/s will be widespread in the future Internet [2]. However, theory and experimental confirmation show that in such a high bandwidth-delay product network environment end-host congestion control in Transmission Control Protocol (TCP), in which packet drop is used as a signal to implicitly control congestion to end-hosts, will become inefficient and prone to instability [7]. To deal with this issue, starting with [4], recently a number of network supported congestion controls have been performed. Among of them, the eXplicit Control Protocol (XCP) [5], which controls network congestion by returning feedback information in packet headers to end-hosts, is a promising means of congestion control.

Furthermore, as the Internet has grown, relative bandwidth allocation has received much attention. Relative bandwidth allocation is a service to differentially allocate network bandwidths to flows transversing the network according to predefined weights. This service is offered because users differ in the value they assign to network reliability. A number of users or application/content service providers are willing to pay more than others to obtain better bandwidth at times of congestion. For instance, in the future Internet, the demands of high-definition movie viewing, high-quality live streaming, huge bulk-data exchange,

A. Pont, G. Pujolle, and S.V. Raghavan (Eds.): WCITD/NF 2010, IFIP AICT 327, pp. 217–228, 2010.

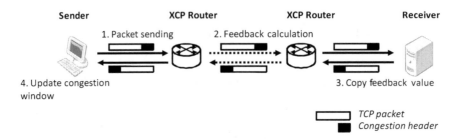

Fig. 1. XCP Illustration

etc., will be considerable. In such cases, users from a higher class who pay more will obtain better quality of service than ones from a lower class. This will make the relative bandwidth allocation service more and more important and requisite.

In the current Internet, where TCP dominates, several relative bandwidth allocation solutions have been reported, such as RIO[3], CSFQ [9] and WPFRA [6]. XCP compares favorably to these solutions in that its unique flexible resource allocation schemes make it possible to provide relative bandwidth allocation service to targeted flows transversing a network with higher performance and it is easier to implement [5]. However, the relative bandwidth allocation method in XCP treats such targeted flows equally with the remaining ones in a network when converging to stability. In XCP, it takes multiple round-trip times (RTTs) for most flows to reach their fair rates, so when a new flow starts arriving in a network with a low transmission rate, the convergence time of this flow to stability, as well as that of the total network, becomes quite long.

This paper describes two relative bandwidth allocation methods implemented at XCP routers to enable fast convergence to stability. First, a Basic Method of utilizing the correct feedback value provided by a normal XCP router is tried. After that, an Improved Method that overcomes a problem in the Basic Method is proposed. The remainder of this paper is organized as follows. First, we provide an overview of XCP and the existing relative bandwidth allocation method proposed in [5] in Section 2. We describe our proposed methods for use at XCP router in Section 3, and summarize the simulation experiment and discuss the results in Section 4. Concluding remarks and possibilities for future work are given in Section 5.

2   XCP and Relative Bandwidth Allocation Method in XCP

2.1   XCP

While TCP concurrently allows the two congestion-control goals of high utilization and fairness to be achieved, XCP [5] is a protocol for Internet congestion control that is based on decoupling congestion control from the resource allocation policy. The XCP protocol is illustrated in Fig. 1. Each XCP packet carries a three-field congestion header. The **H_throughput** and **H_RTT** fields show the current throughput and RTT estimates of senders. They are filled in by the senders and never modified in transit. The remaining field **H_feedback**, takes positive or negative values and is initialized by senders. Routers along the communication path modify this field to directly and explicitly control the throughput of the sources in a way that causes the system to converge to optimal efficiency and max-min fairness. When the feedback reaches the receiver, it is returned to the sender in an acknowledgment packet and the sender accordingly updates its rate.

2.2   Relative Bandwidth Allocation Method in XCP (XCP Method)

The relative bandwidth allocation method provided in [5] works as follows. XCP uses the current throughput of each flow to converge each flow's rate to a fair rate, so the sender replaces the **H_throughput** field with the current throughput divided by the weight of the flow. As a result, at times of congestion, the throughput of each flow becomes $\frac{throughput_i}{weight_i} = \frac{throughput_j}{weight_j}$, hence $\frac{throughput_i}{throughput_j} = \frac{weight_i}{weight_j}$, which shows the relative bandwidth allocation between flows in the network.

This paper focuses on the relative bandwidth allocation at routers, where each flow's throughput replacing process is shifted to XCP routers. Specifically, we suppose that whenever a packet arrives, XCP routers identify the source of the packet and change the throughput value using a corresponding predefined weight. The method that enables this is called XCP Method.

Note: A provision algorithm to determine weights in relative bandwidth allocation has been proposed in [8].

3   Proposals

In this section, two methods to enable fast convergence for relative allocation of network bandwidth to targeted flows at XCP routers are proposed.

These two methods have a common first step of estimating the specific bandwidth of a target flow. Next, the Basic Method converges the targeted flow's congestion window by using a corrected feedback value for both the increasing and decreasing process of the targeted flow's congestion window, while the Improved Method only uses this value in the decreasing process.

3.1   Basic Method

Targeted Flow Throughput Estimation. First, whenever a packet arrives, XCP routers identify its source (e.g., from the flow ID, flow source, etc.).

Then, if the packet belongs to a targeted flow, the optimized congestion window corresponding to the desired bandwidth of the flow is calculated at the router through Eq. (1):

$$cwnd_{opt} = \frac{Bandwidth \cdot RTT}{PacketSize} \cdot \frac{weight}{\sum_{all\ flow} weight}, \tag{1}$$

where $cwnd_{opt}$ is the optimized congestion window, *Bandwidth* is the possible bandwidth of a network link, *RTT* is round-trip time, *PacketSize* is the size of

Table 1. Definitions

weight	$0 < weight < 1$	$weight = 1$	$weight > 1$
Type of flow	Targeted flow	Background flow	Targeted flow
Type of service	Deprioritizing		Prioritizing

each packet, and *weight* is a parameter to adjust the desired bandwidth for the targeted flow. In this paper, based on the value of *weight*, the type of flows and service in a relative bandwidth allocation service are defined as shown in Table 1.

Targeted Flow Throughput Convergence. In this step, the current congestion window of the flow is converged to the optimized congestion window calculated from Eq. (1) at the routers. This is achieved by simply using the feedback value that was earlier correctly calculated at the XCP routers. In detail, the congestion window of a target flow is increased when smaller than the optimized congestion window and decreased when larger. Furthermore, to ensure smoothness when converging the adjusting flow's congestion window, the current congestion window status of this flow and the feedback value that is correctly calculated at the routers are also taken into consideration. Equation (2) expresses this process:

$$feedback_{adj}(\alpha_{inc}, \alpha_{dec}, \varepsilon) = \begin{cases} d^{\alpha_{inc}} \cdot |feedback| & cwnd < (1 - \varepsilon) \cdot cwnd_{opt}, \\ -d^{\alpha_{dec}} \cdot |feedback| & cwnd > (1 + \varepsilon) \cdot cwnd_{opt}, \\ 0 & \text{otherwise.} \end{cases} \quad (2)$$

where $cwnd$ is the current congestion window, $d = \left| \frac{cwnd - cwnd_{opt}}{cwnd_{max}} \right|$, and $cwnd_{max} = \frac{Bandwidth \cdot RTT}{PacketSize}$. Here, α_{inc} and α_{dec} are used to decide whether or not the converging process considers the difference between the current adjusting congestion window and the optimized one. In addition, ε is a parameter to adjust the precision of the method. The smaller this parameter is, the more accurate the method becomes. The sender uses this $feedback_{adj}$ to adjust its own congestion window.

3.2   Improved Method

Targeted Flow Throughput Estimation. The first step in this method is the same as that of the Basic Method.

Targeted Flow Throughput Convergence. When the *weight* parameter in Eq. (1) for a targeted flow is higher than one, the Basic Method will take a longer time to converge to the desired value (a detailed analysis is provided in the next section). To solve this problem, in this step, instead of using the correct feedback value, right from first RTTs, the method aggressively allocates the desired bandwidth to a specific flow as shown by Eq. (3):

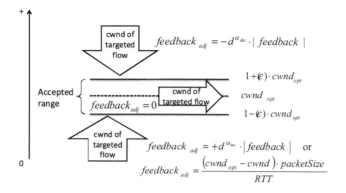

$$feedback_{adj} = -d^{\alpha_{dec}} \cdot |\, feedback \,|$$

$$feedback_{adj} = 0$$

$$feedback_{adj} = +d^{\alpha_{inc}} \cdot |\, feedback \,| \quad \text{or}$$

$$feedback_{adj} = \frac{(cwnd_{opt} - cwnd) \cdot packetSize}{RTT}$$

Fig. 2. Illustration of calculation in the convergence process of proposals

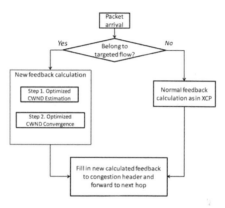

Fig. 3. Proposal overview

$$feedback_{adj}(\alpha_{dec}, \varepsilon) = \begin{cases} \frac{(cwnd_{opt} - cwnd) \cdot packetSize}{RTT} & cwnd < (1 - \varepsilon) \cdot cwnd_{opt}, \\ -d^{\alpha_{dec}} \times |feedback| & cwnd > (1 + \varepsilon) \cdot cwnd_{opt}, \\ 0 & \text{otherwise.} \end{cases} \quad (3)$$

The image of convergence calculation in this step of the two proposed methods is shown in Fig. 2.

An overview of our proposals is given in Fig. 3.

4   Experiments and Analysis

The goal of this work has been to develop relative bandwidth allocation methods for use at XCP routers to enable fast convergence. In this section, the performance of the proposed methods is verified in terms of the convergence time compared with that of the XCP Method, how precisely they allocate bandwidth to target flows as expected, and the stability of the whole network.

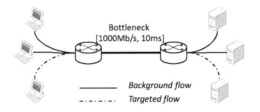

Fig. 4. Dumbbell topology

4.1   Basic Method

Experiment Setup. For the experiments, the classes relating to XCP in ns-2.33 [1] were modified to enable control of feedback value at routers.

In these experiments, the typical dumbbell topology was used, as shown in Fig. 4. To evaluate the effect that applying this method to a specific flow had on the remaining background flows, a scenario of starting *Normal* background flows at 0.1-s intervals and then initiating a targeted flow after a 3-s interval was set. The bandwidth at the bottleneck link, delay, and packet size were respectively fixed to 1,000 Mb/s, 10 ms, and 1,000 Byte. The buffer size at each router (i.e., the product of the link's bandwidth and delay) was kept as in normal XCP [5]. The experiments were performed with 10 background flows and one targeted flow. Furthermore, to evaluate the proposed method for both prioritized and deprioritized targeted flows, the *weight* parameter in Eq. (1) was fixed to 0.5 or 3. Also, based on preliminary experiment results, α_{inc}, α_{dec}, and ε were set to 0, 1, and 0.1, respectively. We did not consider the difference between the current congestion window and the optimized one in the increasing case because *distance* is always smaller than one (and greater than 0), which diminishes the value of $feedback_{adj}$. This is contrary to the purpose of increasing congestion windows for a targeted flow.

Experiment Results and Analysis. The experiment results for comparing the convergence time between the Basic Method and the XCP Method are shown in Fig. 5. These results were averaged over a 0.1-s period. As the number of background flows was 10, the starting time of the targeted flow was at 4 s.

In Fig. 5, the x-axis shows the time and the y-axis indicates the normalized proportion of the target flow's throughput to the desired one. Figures 5(a) and 5(b) show the results when the *weight* was 0.5 and 3, respectively. In Fig. 5(a), the Basic Method outperformed the XCP Method by nearly 2 s, but when the *weight* was 3, the Basic Method converged target flows to the optimized value much more slowly than the XCP Method. The reason for this can be understood as follows by referring to Fig. 6.

Although the XCP Method relatively allocates bandwidth to flows, it actually converges to the weighted allocation status as it does in normal allocation. Figure 6 describes the convergence to fair status process for a simple case of two flows with throughput (X_1, X_2) in a network. In this figure, $X_{goal-deprior}$ is the estimation rate in deprioritizing, X_{fair} represents the fair rate, and $X_{goal-prior}$ corresponds

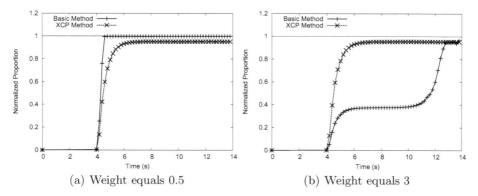

(a) Weight equals 0.5   (b) Weight equals 3

Fig. 5. Convergence time comparison between the Basic Method and the XCP Method

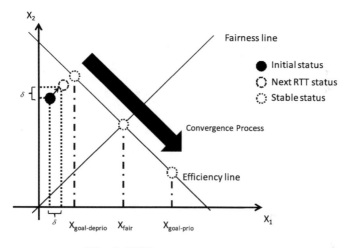

Fig. 6. XCP convergence process

to the estimation rate in prioritizing. The targeted flow's throughput is X_1 and the XCP Method needs time to converge X_1 from the initial status, normally near 0, to X_{fair}. The feedback value at XCP routers is calculated in a way that allocates bandwidth from flows whose throughput is greater to flows whose throughput is smaller than fair one. As the Basic Method simply uses this feedback value, the throughput of X_1 can consequently reach $X_{goal-deprio}$, then X_{fair}, and finally $X_{goal-prio}$. Given the situation that the convergence time in the XCP Method is the same for all cases (fair, deprioritizing, prioritizing), it is easy to understand why the convergence time with the Basic Method was faster/slower than that with the XCP Method in the deprioritizing/prioritizing cases.

4.2 Improved Method

The goal of this experiment was to evaluate the performance of the Improved Method described in Sec. 3.2. First, a simple simulation experiment with the

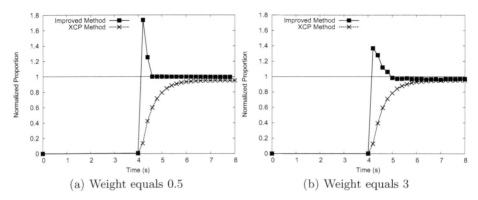

(a) Weight equals 0.5   (b) Weight equals 3

Fig. 7. Convergence time comparison between the Improved Method and the XCP Method

same scenario used to evaluate the Basic Method's performance is discussed. Next, the effect of parameter ε from Eq. (3) on the precision of this method is evaluated. The influence of the number of background flows on the performance of the proposed method is then considered. Finally, the impact of the number of targeted flows is discussed.

Experiment Setup. In this experiment, the network topology and other parameters (such as the link bandwidth, delay, packet size, buffer size at router, and α_{dec}) were kept as in the experiment described above.

Experiment Results and Analysis. In this part, in the coming figures showing the experiment results, the x-axis and y-axis represent the simulation time and the normalized proportion to the desired throughput of a targeted flow, consequently.

Simulation Result in Simple Scenario. Figure 7 shows the simulation results with the same scenario as in Sec. 4.1, where 10 background flows were started at 0.1-s intervals and one targeted flow was entered at 4 s. Figures 7(a) and 7(b) show the results when the *weight* was set to 0.5 and 3, respectively.

The Improved Method significantly affected performance in the prioritizing case, i.e., when the *weight* was fixed to 3. Specifically, it shortened the convergence process time by nearly 1.5 s compared with that of the XCP Method. This result confirmed that it is possible to aggressively allocate network bandwidth to a certain flow right from the beginning of connection.

Effect of Precision Parameter. The effect of precision parameter ε was evaluated by changing ε in Eq. (3) from 0.05 to 0.1, 0.15, and 0.2. As ε becomes smaller, the method becomes more precise.

Figures 8(a) and 8(b) show the results when weight parameters were fixed to 0.5 and 3, respectively. For ease of evaluation, the normalized throughputs of the targeted flows were averaged over a 0.2-s period. Figure 8(a) shows that the

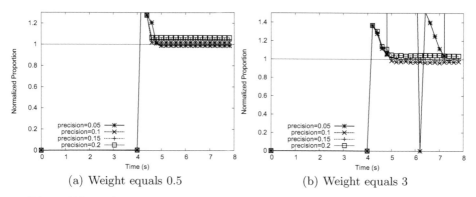

(a) Weight equals 0.5   (b) Weight equals 3

Fig. 8. Effect of precision parameter ε to the Improved Method's performance

proposed method worked well enough in precisely allocating bandwidth to the targeted flow for all cases. However, if the convergence time is also taken into consideration, 0.1 was the best option.

Figure 8(b) shows that the method had trouble ensuring convergence to the goal value when ε was 0.05, which was not the case when the *weight* was 0.5. The reason for this is that the desired value in prioritizing is larger than that in deprioritizing, and this made it harder for the method to converge to the targeted congestion window within that precise range. The best performance was when ε equaled 0.15, but the difference from when ε was 0.1 was not large. Therefore, an optimized range of ε from 0.1 to 0.2 seems reasonable.

For convenience, for the later experiments the precision parameter was consequently fixed to 0.1 or 0.2.

Effect of the Number of Background Flows. This experiment was to evaluate the effect of the number of background flows on the performance of the Improved Method. The number of background flows was fixed to 5 or 20, and both the convergence time and the stability of the whole network were taken into consideration. Because of the difference in the number of background flows, the entering time for the targeted flow was approximately 3.5 s or 5 s.

These results are shown in Figs. 9 and 10. Figures 9(a) and 9(b) show the results when *weight* was set to 0.5 and the number of background flows was 5 and 20, respectively. Figures 10(a) and 10(b) describe the results when *weight* was fixed to 3 and the number of background flows was 5 or 20. Figure 9 shows that the method was quite robust in the case of deprioritizing, i.e., when the *weight* was 0.5. The method shortened the convergence time to about 2 s for both cases. This is because the method takes advantage of the convergence process to fair status from normal XCP. However, as shown in Fig. 10(a), the method failed in its attempt to converge the targeted flow's congestion window to the optimized value. To investigate the reason for this result, we further examined the raw data from the simulation result and discovered packet loss at the targeted flow. The cause of the packet loss was the method suddenly allocating a huge amount of bandwidth to the targeted flow within a short time while the buffer size of routers

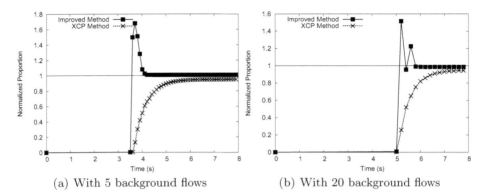

Fig. 9. Effect of the number of background flows to the Improved Method's performance when the weight parameter equals 0.5

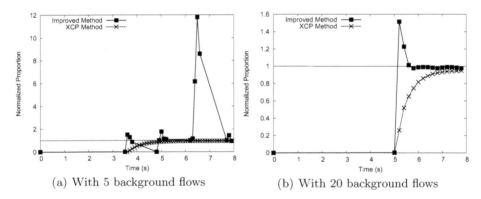

Fig. 10. Effect of the number of background flows to the Improved Method's performance when the weight parameter equals 3

were fixed as in XCP (i.e., the product of the link's bandwidth and delay). The successful result shown in Fig. 10(b) is consistent with this explanation. In this case, as the number of background flows increased, the optimized value of the targeted flow's congestion window became smaller. Accordingly, packet loss did not occur and the proposed method enabled a convergence time approximately 1 s shorter than that of the XCP Method.

Effect of the Number of Targeted Flows. In contrast to the above experiment, in this part we verified the performance of the Improved Method by changing the number of targeted flows to three while keeping the number of background flows the same (i.e., 10 flows).

The results when the *weight* was fixed to 0.5 or 3 are shown in Figs. 11(a) and 11(b), respectively. As in the above experiment, in the prioritizing case the proposed method did not work as well as the XCP Method. As packet loss occurred, it took the last arriving targeted flow about 1 s to re-setup its congestion window and be converged to the optimized value. Hence, the convergence time with the Improved Method was 1 s longer than that with the XCP Method.

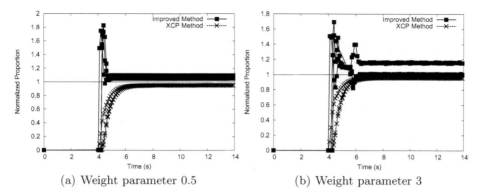

(a) Weight parameter 0.5   (b) Weight parameter 3

Fig. 11. Convergence time comparison between the Improved Method and the XCP Method with three targeted flows

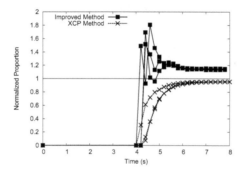

Fig. 12. Convergence time comparison between the Improved Method and the XCP Method with three targeted flows when the buffer size at routers was enlarged

As a result, it seems that to get good performance, the Improved Method needs the buffer size at routers to be enlarged to ensure packet loss does not occur. Figure 12 compares results for the Improved Method and the XCP Method when the router buffer size was enlarged by the packet loss quantity, i.e., about 1500 packets. It can be seen that the convergence time with the Improved Method was slightly shorter, by about 0.5 s, than that with the XCP Method.

5   Conclusion and Future Directions

In this paper, we proposed two relative bandwidth allocation methods for use at XCP routers to achieve faster convergence compared to that with the XCP Method. This is implemented by adjusting the targeted flow's congestion windows. We evaluated the two proposed methods through experiments using network simulation. The results for the Basic Method show that it outperformed the XCP Method for deprioritized targeted flows, but it took noticeably longer to converge a targeted flow's throughput to the desired one. The results also indicated that the Improved Method succeeded in allocating bandwidth to a targeted flow within a shorter convergence time at precision from 10% to 20% with a small ratio of targeted flows. It also was found in the Improved Method that the network's stability could be effected due to allocating large amount of packets at the beginning to targeted flows in prioritizing.

In the future, we would like to work on the following issues. Firstly, the problem of packet loss with the Improved Method needs to be solved by considering the queue status at routers. We would then like to evaluate the proposed method under more realistic conditions than could be obtained in the research reported in this paper. Specifically, the network topology should be extended to more complex scenarios that include a larger number of flows as well as cross flows. In addition, to deal with the scalability of dynamic network, the possibility of implementing the proposals as in DiffServ model should be considered. The bandwidth estimation is brought to edge routers while the converging process is performed mainly in core routers. Lastly, the applicability of the proposed method to hierarchical link-sharing mechanisms should be investigated. Such mechanisms are widely used by ISPs to provide bandwidth management inside their domains.

Acknowledgment

This work was supported in part by Grant-in-Aid for Young Scientists (A) (1) (21680006) of the Ministry of Education, Culture, Sports, Science and Technology, Japan.

References

1. The Network Simulator ns-2.33., http://www.isi.edu/nsnam/ns
2. 10 Gigabit Ethernet Technology Overview (2003), http://www.intel.com/network/connectivity/resources/doc_library/white_papers/pro10gbe_lr_sa_wp.pdf
3. Clark, D., Wenjia, F.: Explicit Allocation of Best-effort Packet Delivery Service. IEEE/ACM Trans. Netw. 6(4), 362–373 (1998)
4. Floyd, S.: TCP and Explicit Congestion Notification. ACM SIGCOMM Comput. Commun. Rev. 24(5), 8–23 (1994)
5. Katabi, D., Handley, M., Rohrs, C.: Congestion Control for High Bandwidth-Delay Product Network. In: Proc. ACM SIGCOMM 2002 (2002)
6. Lee, C., Chen, C., Chen, W.: Weighted Proportional Fair Rate Allocations in a Differentiated Services Network. IEICE Trans. Comm. 85(1), 116–128 (2002)
7. Low, S., Paganini, F., Wang, J., Adlakha, S., Doyle, J.: Dynamics of TCP/AQM and a Scalable Control. In: Proc. IEEE INFOCOM 2002., vol. 1, pp. 239–248 (2002)
8. Shimamura, M., Iida, K., Koga, H., Kadobayashi, Y., Yamaguchi, S.: Provisioning Algorithm for Minimum Throughput Assurance Service in VPNs Using Nonlinear Programming. In: IEEE Australasian Telecommunication Networks and Applications Conference (ATNAC), pp. 311–316 (2007)
9. Stoica, I., Shenker, S., Zhang, H.: Core-Stateless Fair Queueing: Achieving Approximately Fair Bandwidth Allocations in High Speed Networks. ACM SIGCOMM Comput. Commun. Rev. 28(4), 118–130 (1998)

On the Interest of Introducing Randomness in Ad-Word Auctions

Patrick Maillé[1] and Bruno Tuffin[2]

[1] Institut Telecom; Telecom Bretagne
2 rue de la Châtaigneraie CS 17607
35576 Cesson Sévigné Cedex, France
patrick.maille@telecom-bretagne.eu
[2] INRIA Rennes - Bretagne Atlantique
Campus universitaire de Beaulieu
35042 Rennes Cedex, France
btuffin@irisa.fr

Abstract. Search engines play and will still play a major role in the use of networks. Sponsored search auctions is the basic tool for a return on investment in this industry, accounting for an increasing part of the business. We introduce here a model for consumer behavior in the context of ad-word auctions. Considering that unsatisfying answers of the ad-word engine will lead some consumers to perform again the same request later on, we show that displaying only the highest bidding or highest revenue-producing advertisers in a deterministic way is not always the best strategy for the ad-word engine. Instead, some randomization among advertisers can provide higher revenues. We also design a Vickrey-Clarke-Groves auction rule for a display probability and compare it with the current generalized-second-price scheme.

Keywords: Auctions, Random processes.

1 Introduction

Search engines play a crucial role in the Internet, allowing, just by giving keywords, to reach the most relevant web pages. This role is expected to be at least as important in next generation networks. Search engines make money by proposing advertising slots to potential advertisers, usually displayed at the top and/or at the right of the page of results corresponding to the keyword(s). Actually search engine advertising has become an important business, the combined revenue of the two main actors in the area, Yahoo! and Google, being more than $11 billion in 2005 for instance [1], and this business is expected to count for about 40% of total advertising revenue [2].

Keyword ads work as follows: an Internet user seeking for a web site types keywords on a search engine. Based on those words, the search engine proposes a list of links ranked by relevance, but also some commercial links chosen according to criteria which depend on the engine. Our goal is to investigate the

A. Pont, G. Pujolle, and S.V. Raghavan (Eds.): WCITD/NF 2010, IFIP AICT 327, pp. 229–240, 2010.
© IFIP International Federation for Information Processing 2010

allocation of commercial slots to advertisers. For a nice overview of the general and recent modeling issues, an interested reader can for instance look at [3]. We focus in this paper on a single keyword, the best strategy of advertisers in terms of keyword selection being not addressed here as in most of the literature. Slot allocation is based on auctions, and most of existing works deal with a game of complete information [1,4,5,6,7] where advertisers make a bid for the keyword corresponding to the maximum price they would accept to pay if the link is clicked through. Advertisers are ranked according to a prespecified criterion, for instance the bid value (initially for Yahoo!), or the revenue they will generate (more or less corresponding to Google's situation), taking into account the click-through rate (CTR) for each advertiser. The K available slots are then allocated according to the above ranking to the K first advertisers. Advertisers pay the search engine each time their link is clicked through, the amount they are then charged being, in the literature, either exactly the bid (corresponding to the so-called first price auction), the opportunity cost that the considered advertiser's presence introduces to all the other advertisers (the so-called Vickrey-Clarke-Groves (VCG) auction), or the generalized second price (GSP) where each advertiser pays the bid of the advertiser just below itself in the ranking (that latter scheme is applied by Google and Yahoo!, and yields the same incentives to bid truthfully than VCG auction if the game is not one-shot and advertisers anticipate the effects of the strategies of their competitors [8]). Most models differ on the assumptions about the CTR modeling, the budget limit of the advertisers, the game being static or played several times, or the pricing rule applied.

But all the above works, and to our knowledge all the literature, assume that an Internet user will make a search only once and will never come again. We propose here to investigate the consequences of users potentially composing several times the same keyword, the interval between two searches being random. This is typical of users looking for new or additional information, or who do not remember the previous results. In that situation, *always* presenting the same advertisers on the sponsored slots may be a bad option since if a user has not clicked through the links once, he is likely to proceed the same way again. A random strategy for the allocation, still dependent on the bid of the advertisers but allowing advertisers with small bids to be displayed with a positive even if small probability, may produce a higher expected revenue than the current deterministic strategy. This paper aims at illustrating the relevance of that approach. We therefore introduce here a model describing users searching the same keyword a random number of times, and compare according to the parameter values the revenues generated by the random or deterministic allocation of slots. Only $K = 1$ slot and two advertisers are considered to simplify the analysis and for comparison purposes. We show that *for fixed bids and prices*, applying a random allocation can increase revenue. We then build a VCG auction scheme based on this allocation rule, and compare the revenues and social welfare at equilibrium of the bidding game among advertisers with those obtained using a deterministic GSP rule.

Remark that randomness has already been considered in ad-word auctions. In [6,9], a Markovian model is used to represent the user behavior when looking at the ranked ads: she looks at the first ad then clicks and quits or goes to the second with a given probability, which she clicks or not, then goes to the following, up to the number K. In [10], randomness is introduced on the size of the population and the type of advertisers but the allocation rule is kept deterministic. The closest work to ours is maybe [11]. In that paper the authors discuss the ad-slot placement and pricing strategies maximizing the expected revenue of search engine over a given interval of time. They find the optimal allocation rule and show that the $c\mu$-scheduling rule (i.e., maximizing selling probability times (virtual) valuation) is a good suboptimal policy, but the randomness is rather on the types of advertisers. To the best of our knowledge, no paper is actually considering randomness in the behavior of users, coming several times, and the consequence on slot allocations as we do.

The paper is organized as follows. Section 2 introduces the model and describes users' behavior. Section 3 computes the average revenue generated using a random allocation strategy with fixed price per click for users and shows that this rule can increase revenue. Then Section 4 suggest to use Vickrey-Clarke-Groves auctions to allocate the ad display probabilities among the advertisers, when implementing a randomized instead of deterministic ad display policy. Section 5 illustrates the fact that such an auction scheme can perform better than a deterministic GSP display mechanism in terms of advertiser revenue and overall wealth generated by the ad slot. Our conclusions and some directions for future work are given in Section 6.

2   Model

In this section, we introduce a mathematical model aimed at representing the behavior of a customer when faced with a search engine implementing an ad-word auction. The particularity of that model is to explicitly express the retry rate of customers, when previous answers have not resulted into a sale.

Since the paper is mainly focused on illustrating a phenomenon (i.e., the fact that introducing randomness in the selection of the advertisers to display may be profitable to the search engine), we consider an extreme case to simplify the analysis, both for the auction engine and the customer population. The model can be complicated in order to better fit reality.

2.1   Search Engine Basic Model

We consider a search engine providing only one commercial slot, and two advertisers, say, 1 and 2, competing for that slot on a given ad-word. In an auction, players (here, advertisers) submit bids, from which allocation and pricing rules are applied. Each advertiser $i = 1, 2$, is therefore characterized in the auction by

– b_i the bid of advertiser i for that keyword,

– π_i the probability that advertiser i's ad is displayed (which should depend on the bid profile (b_1, b_2)),
– p_i the price-per-click that advertiser i is charged, also dependent on (b_1, b_2).

2.2   User Behavior Model

The population of users likely to search for that ad-word is assumed to be heterogeneous, made of two types: some users, called type-A users, can only be interested in purchasing the good sold by advertiser 1, but can potentially click on the ad of advertiser 2 without purchasing it eventually. On the other hand, type-B users are potential buyers of advertiser 2 only (likewise, they will never purchase advertiser 1's product even if they click on its ad when displayed).

Formally, customer (new) requests occur randomly over time: we denote by λ_A (resp. λ_B) the average number of *first* requests per time unit of type-A (resp. type-B) customers.

For a type-A user who performs a search with the considered keyword:

– if the search engine displays the ad of advertiser 2, then the probability of the user clicking the ad is denoted by $c_{A,2}$, but recall that even if the user clicks on the ad, he does not purchase the good;
– if the search engine displays the ad of advertiser 1, we denote by $c_{A,1} > 0$ the probability of the user clicking on that ad, and by $h_{A,1} > 0$ the probability that the user purchases the good after clicking on the ad.

As a result, for one search, the probability that a type-A user buys its wanted product is $\pi_1 c_{A,1} h_{A,1}$: indeed, that probability is $c_{A,1} h_{A,1}$ if advertiser 1 is displayed in the ad-word slot, and 0 otherwise.

Inevitably, some users do not end up buying their wanted good, because of the bad ad displayed or for other reasons (e.g., lack of time to finish the purchase, or hesitation). In this paper, we assume that some of those users will try again later and perform a search with the same keyword, after some time, independently of the number of previous search attempts. For those retries, we assume that the user has the same behavior, i.e., the same probabilities of clicking on the ad, of purchasing the good, and of trying again later in the case of no purchase.

As a result, the average number of retries per time unit only depends on the total average number of searches λ_A^{tot} (including new attempts and retries from previous attempts): Let us denote by R_A the probability of a not-buying type-A user to retry the keyword later. Define by θ_A^{retry} the overall probability of retry, given by

$$\theta_A^{\text{retry}} := R_A(1 - \pi_1 c_{A,1} h_{A,1}).$$

The overall behavior of type-A users is illustrated in Figure 1, representing new searches, retries and users definitely leaving the search.

In steady-state -which can be easily shown to exist, the system behaving like an infinite server queue with instantaneous service time-, the mean number of retries per time unit should equal the total mean number of search tries λ_A^{tot} multiplied by the overall probability of retry θ_A^{retry}.

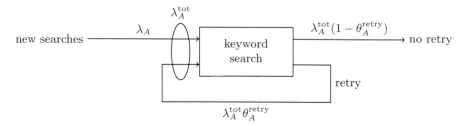

Fig. 1. Type-A users search behavior. Arcs are labeled with the average number of occurrences per time unit.

We clearly see in Figure 1 that the total mean number of requests by type-A users per time unit verifies

$$\lambda_A^{\text{tot}} = \lambda_A + \theta_A^{\text{retry}}\lambda_A^{\text{tot}},$$

which gives, since $\theta_A^{\text{retry}} < 1$,

$$\lambda_A^{\text{tot}} = \frac{\lambda_A}{1 - \theta_A^{\text{retry}}} = \frac{\lambda_A}{1 - R_A(1 - \pi_1 c_{A,1} h_{A,1})}. \tag{1}$$

For type-B users, we define the probabilities $c_{B,1}, c_{B,2}, h_{B,2} > 0$, and R_B in the same way as for type-A users. With the same reasoning, the mean number of requests by type-B users per time unit is $\lambda_B^{\text{tot}} = \frac{\lambda_B}{1 - R_B(1 - \pi_2 c_{B,2} h_{B,2})}$.

3   Search Engine Revenue

Let us consider fixed values of the advertiser bids b_1 and b_2, and assume that the corresponding display probabilities are π_1 and $\pi_2 = 1 - \pi_1$, with prices per click p_1 and p_2, respectively.

The mean revenue (utility) per time unit for the search engine (for the considered keyword auction) is

$$U = p_1\,\underbrace{\pi_1(\lambda_A^{\text{tot}}c_{A,1} + \lambda_B^{\text{tot}}c_{B,1})}_{\text{nb of clicks on ad 1}} + p_2\,\underbrace{\pi_2(\lambda_B^{\text{tot}}c_{B,2} + \lambda_A^{\text{tot}}c_{A,2})}_{\text{nb of clicks on ad 2}}$$

$$= \lambda_A\frac{\pi_1(p_1 c_{A,1} - p_2 c_{A,2}) + p_2 c_{A,2}}{1 - R_A(1 - \pi_1 c_{A,1} h_{A,1})} + \lambda_B\frac{\pi_1(p_1 c_{B,1} - p_2 c_{B,2}) + p_2 c_{B,2}}{1 - R_B(1 - c_{B,2} h_{B,2} + \pi_1 c_{B,2} h_{B,2})} \tag{2}$$

where we used the fact that $\pi_1 + \pi_2 = 1$.

To simplify the analysis, we will first assume that users types are symmetric, and that users never click on an ad that does not correspond to their type.

Assumption A. *Users of both types have a similar behavior with respect to their preferred/less preferred advertisers, in terms of click probability, conversion rate, and retry probability. Formally,*

$$c_{A,1} = c_{B,2} := c$$
$$h_{A,1} = h_{A,2} := h$$
$$R_A = R_B := R.$$

Moreover, users are only likely to click on the ad of their preferred advertiser, i.e., $c_{A,2} = c_{B,1} = 0$.

Under that simplifying assumption, the auctioneer revenue is

$$U = \lambda_A p_1 c \frac{\pi_1}{1 - R(1 - \pi_1 ch)} + \lambda_B p_2 c \frac{1 - \pi_1}{1 - R(1 - ch + \pi_1 ch)}. \tag{3}$$

For a real ad-word auction mechanism implementing randomization, the price per click p_i charged to each advertiser $i = 1, 2$ should increase with the probability π_i of displaying each ad. However, if for a moment we fix those prices as given and look at (3) as a function of π_1, we remark that the revenue-maximizing strategy does not necessarily consist in always displaying the ad with the highest price, or the ad with the highest product $\lambda_{X_i} \times p_i$, with X_i the type of users potentially interested in buying advertiser i's product. Indeed, if the retry rate R is sufficiently close to 1, the revenue in (3) attains its maximum for a π_1^* in the interior of $(0, 1)$. The rationale is that potential consumers of the not-displayed advertiser will perform again the search, giving a large overall request rate for that type of consumers, which makes it beneficial for the auctioneer to display the ad.

That result is formalized by the following proposition.

Proposition 1. *The value π_1^* of π_1 maximizing the search engine revenue is*

- $\pi_1^* = 0$ *if* $\sqrt{\frac{\lambda_A p_1}{\lambda_B p_2}} \leq \frac{1-R}{1-R(1-ch)}$,
- $\pi_1^* = 1$ *if* $\sqrt{\frac{\lambda_B p_2}{\lambda_A p_1}} \leq \frac{1-R}{1-R(1-ch)}$,
- $\pi_1^* = \frac{1}{R \cdot ch} \frac{1 - R + R \cdot ch - (1-R)\sqrt{\frac{\lambda_B p_2}{\lambda_A p_1}}}{\sqrt{\frac{\lambda_B p_2}{\lambda_1 p_1}} + 1}$ *if* $\frac{1-R}{1-R(1-ch)} < \sqrt{\frac{\lambda_A p_1}{\lambda_B p_2}} < \frac{1-R(1-ch)}{1-R}$.

In other words, when R is sufficiently close to 1, we are in the third case, and the search engine gets a higher revenue than when always showing one of the advertisers.

Proof. It can be easily seen that for $R < 1$ the revenue (3) is a continuous, derivable and strictly concave function of π_1 on $[0, 1]$, with derivative

$$U'(\pi_1) = (1 - R)c \left(\frac{\lambda_A p_1}{[1 - R(1 - \pi_1 ch)]^2} - \frac{\lambda_B p_2}{[1 - R(1 - (1 - \pi_1)ch)]^2} \right).$$

Due to the strict concavity of U, we have three possibilities:

- either $U'(0) \leq 0$, i.e., $\sqrt{\frac{\lambda_A p_1}{\lambda_B p_2}} \leq \frac{1-R}{1-R(1-ch)}$, then $\pi_1^* = 0$;
- or $U'(1) \geq 0$, i.e., $\sqrt{\frac{\lambda_B p_2}{\lambda_A p_1}} \leq \frac{1-R}{1-R(1-ch)}$, then $\pi_1^* = 1$;
- or $\frac{1-R}{1-R(1-ch)} < \sqrt{\frac{\lambda_A p_1}{\lambda_B p_2}} < \frac{1-R(1-ch)}{1-R}$, which is always the case when R is sufficiently close to 1, then $\pi_1^* \in (0, 1)$, i.e., it is in the interest of the auctioneer to randomize when choosing which ad to display.

Example 1. Consider a simple and arbitrarily chosen example illustrating the kind of gain that can be obtained through randomization. Use the probability values $c = 1/2$, $h = 1/2$, the rates $\lambda_A = 1$, $\lambda_B = 0.8$ and prices per click $p_1 = 1$, $p_2 = 0.8$. The retry probability is taken as $R = 0.8$ so that we are in the third situation presented in the proposition. The revenue (3) is maximized at $\pi_1^* = 2/3$ and given by 1.4. If we compare it with the optimal revenue when only one ad is displayed, $\max(\lambda_A p_1, \lambda_B p_2) = 1$, a gain of 40% is observed. This gain is even increased for a larger value of R.

A similar result applies in the general case, as illustrated by the following proposition.

Proposition 2. *In the non-symmetric case, there also exists a unique π_1^* maximizing the revenue $U(\pi_1)$ of the search engine given by (2). The solution is in the interior of the interval $[0,1]$ if $U'(0) > 0$ and $U'(1) < 0$.*

Proof. The proof is similar to the one of Proposition 1, given that the revenue defined by (2) is still a strictly concave function of π_1 with $R_A, R_B < 1$.

Remark 1. Notice that the randomization proposed here transfers some of the complexity from the advertiser to the auctioneer, since in most current auctions the advertisers develop quite complex bidding strategies to adapt over time to the opponents' bids and to the flow of requests, so that it appears effectively that not always the same ads are displayed when users perform the same request several times. With the randomization suggested here, we might imagine that advertisers fix their bid for a time period, and the auctioneer computes the ad displaying probabilities based on the bids and some knowledge of the demand (which it is more likely to be able to estimate than the advertiser is).

4   A VCG Auction Mechanism for Display Probability

In this section, we highlight a utility function for an advertiser i, that depends on the display probability π_i of its ad. Such a utility function being continuous and increasing in π_i, we propose to define an auction scheme among providers to allocate and price the "probability range", i.e., the interval $[0,1]$, as an infinitely divisible resource. We then study a game where advertisers submit their bid representing how much they are accepting to pay per click, and the display probability is allocated and charged according to VCG auction rules.

4.1   Advertiser Willingness-to-Pay in Terms of the Ad Display Probability

We first quantify the average revenue in terms of display probability for each advertiser. With the same notations as in the previous sections and under Assumption A (symmetry among both types of customers, customers only interested in clicking for one advertiser), the mean sales income per time unit due to the keyword searches for, say, provider 1, is

$$V_1(\pi_1) = \lambda_A^{\text{tot}} \pi_1 ch v_1$$
$$= \frac{\lambda_A \pi_1 ch}{1 - R(1 - \pi_1 ch)} v_1, \qquad (4)$$

where v_1 is the benefit that the advertiser makes on each sale (i.e., the selling cost of the product minus its production cost). We call that function V_1 the *valuation* function of provider 1, since it represent the monetary benefit due to the ad display probability. Remark that exactly the same form would be obtained when computing the valuation $V_2(\pi_2)$ of provider 2.

As a result, the overall utility (revenue) for an advertiser i who has to pay a price p_i to have its ad displayed with probability π_i is *quasi-linear*, that is,

$$U_i = V_i(\pi_i) - p_i. \qquad (5)$$

Interestingly, we remark that for each $i = 1, 2$, V_i is a continuously derivable, nondecreasing and concave function on $[0, 1]$, and that $V_i(0) = 0$. Such properties are often needed when designing some pricing and allocation mechanisms with nice properties -both from economic and computational perspectives-.

In the following subsection, we therefore propose an auction scheme to efficiently allocate the overall resource (display probabilities) among advertisers.

4.2   VCG Auctions for Allocating an Infinitely Divisible Good

In this subsection, we use the possibility of randomization to define an auction on ad display probabilities. The auction is interpreted as an auction for an infinitely divisible good, with total quantity 1. Indeed, from the formulation of the previous subsection, advertisers are only sensitive to their display probability and the price they pay, while the total sum of advertiser (probability) allocations cannot exceed 1.

The problem of the auctioneer is therefore to share that total amout 1 of resource among bidders. In this work, we look at the well-known Vickrey-Clarke-Groves (VCG) [12,13,14] mechanism, which is the only auction mechanism with the properties below for bidders with quasi-linear utility functions [15]:

- *Incentive compatibility*: truthfully declaring one's value for the good is a dominant strategy, i.e., there is no gain to expect from lying about one's willingness-to-pay.
- *Efficiency*: when bidders are truthful, allocations maximize social welfare, that is the sum of all bidders willingness-to-pay.
- *Individual rationality*: every bidder pays less than his declared willingness-to-pay, so there is always an interest in participating in the auction.
- *Non-negativeness of prices.*

The VCG mechanism works as follows: Each bidder i is asked to declare its entire valuation (willingness-to-pay) function $V_i(\cdot)$. Then,

- (**allocation rule**) the auctioneer computes an allocation vector $(\pi_i)_{i \in \mathcal{I}}$ that maximizes social welfare, i.e., the sum of bidders declared valuations;
- (**pricing rule**) the price that each bidder has to pay equals the loss of social welfare that it imposes the others through its presence.

4.3   Applying VCG

Based on (4), declaring one's willingness-to-pay function consists in revealing the four parameters of V_i, namely for provider 1: λ_A, R, v_1, and the product ch. However, as pointed out in Remark 1, some parameters like the retry rate R are more likely to be measured by the search engine itself: We can therefore consider that provider 1 only has to declare the parameters λ_A, v_1, and ch. Since being truthful is a dominant strategy for advertisers, we consider that they reveal their real valuation parameters.

Allocation rule. The auctioneer computes the display probabilities π_i solving the strictly convex optimization problem

$$\max_{\pi_1, \pi_2 \text{ s.t. } \pi_1 + \pi_2 \leq 1} \bar{V}_1(\pi_1) + \bar{V}_2(\pi_2), \tag{6}$$

where $\bar{V}_i$ is the declared willingness-to-pay function of advertiser i ($\bar{V}_i = V_i$ if i bids truthfully). Remark that since the functions $\bar{V}_i$ are strictly increasing, the solution of (6) lies in the set where $\pi_1 + \pi_2 = 1$. Therefore, the declared-welfare maximizing allocation $(\bar{\pi}_1, \bar{\pi}_2)$ is such that

$$\bar{\pi}_1 = \arg \max_{\pi_1 \in [0,1]} \frac{\pi_1 \lambda_A ch}{1 - R(1 - \pi_1 ch)} v_1 + \frac{(1 - \pi_1)\lambda_B ch}{1 - R(1 - (1 - \pi_1)ch)} v_2 \tag{7}$$
$$\bar{\pi}_2 = 1 - \bar{\pi}_1.$$

The optimization problem (7) is exactly the same as in (3), with v_i playing the role of p_i for each advertiser i. Therefore, from Proposition 1, $\bar{\pi}_1$ is given by

- $\bar{\pi}_1 = 0$ if $\sqrt{\frac{\lambda_A v_1}{\lambda_B v_2}} \leq \frac{1 - R}{1 - R(1 - ch)}$,
- $\bar{\pi}_1 = 1$ if $\sqrt{\frac{\lambda_B v_2}{\lambda_A v_1}} \leq \frac{1 - R}{1 - R(1 - ch)}$,
- $\bar{\pi}_1 = \frac{1}{R \cdot ch} \frac{1 - R + R \cdot ch - (1 - R)\sqrt{\frac{\lambda_B v_2}{\lambda_A v_1}}}{\sqrt{\frac{\lambda_B v_2}{\lambda_1 v_1}} + 1}$ if $\frac{1 - R}{1 - R(1 - ch)} < \sqrt{\frac{\lambda_A v_1}{\lambda_B v_2}} < \frac{1 - R(1 - ch)}{1 - R}$.

Pricing rule. Finally, to determine the charge to each advertiser, the auctioneer computes the loss of value (in terms of declared willingness-to-pay) that each advertiser imposes on the other through its presence. Since we consider only two advertisers, then, had one of them been absent from the auction, the whole resource (i.e., display probability 1) would have been given to the other. As a result, the total price t_i per time unit that each advertiser i is charged under the VCG rule is given by $\begin{cases} t_1 = \bar{V}_2(1) - \bar{V}_2(\bar{\pi}_2) \\ t_2 = \bar{V}_1(1) - \bar{V}_1(\bar{\pi}_1). \end{cases}$

Such an average charge per time unit can easily be converted to a price per click, to fit current auctions charging base. The mean number of clicks per time unit for advertiser 1 is $\lambda_A^{\text{tot}}\bar{\pi}_1 c$, where λ_A^{tot} is given in (1); as a result, under Assumption A the auctioneer may charge advertiser 1 a price per click

$$p_1 = \big(\bar{V}_2(1) - \bar{V}_2(\bar{\pi}_2)\big)\frac{1 - R(1 - \bar{\pi}_1 ch)}{\lambda_A \bar{\pi}_1 c}.$$

Likewise, the price per click for advertiser 2, whose ad is displayed with probability $\bar{\pi}_2$, should be

$$p_2 = \big(\bar{V}_1(1) - \bar{V}_1(\bar{\pi}_1)\big)\frac{1 - R(1 - \bar{\pi}_2 ch)}{\lambda_A \bar{\pi}_2 c}.$$

4.4   Asymmetric Case

The asymmetric case can easily be handled equivalently. The valuation functions $V_1(\pi_1)$ and $V_2(\pi_2)$ are then respectively the first and second terms of the revenue (2), with again p_1 and p_2 replaced by v_1 and v_2. The rest of the discussion follows as well, invoking Proposition 2 instead of Proposition 1.

5   VCG for Randomizing Displayed Ads versus Deterministic GSP

In this section, we consider a simple illustrative example comparing the consequences of a VCG auction on display probability to those obtained with a deterministic GSP pricing scheme. We consider a symmetric case, with $v_1 = 1$, $v_2 = 0.8$, $\lambda_A = \lambda_B = 1$, $c = h = 0.5$. Since the main phenomenon we want to model in this paper is the fact that consumers try out the same research several times, we make the retry probability R vary.

The currently used GSP auction consists in asking each advertiser the price it is willing to pay to be displayed (with probability 1). In the numerical computations we make here, we assume that advertisers bid truthfully, i.e. they declare their real value of a customer click if their ad were to be displayed with probability 1. Under Assumption A, $b_1 = v_1 h = 0.5$ and $b_2 = v_2 h = 0.4$. As a result, GSP will always result in advertiser 1's ad being displayed. At each click on its ad, advertiser 1 will be charged $b_2 = 0.4$. The corresponding revenue per time unit for the auctioneer is thus $\lambda_A^{\text{tot}} cb_2 = \frac{0.8}{4-3R}$, while the per-unit net benefit of provider 1 is $\lambda_A^{\text{tot}} c(v_1 h - b_2) = \frac{0.2}{4-3R}$. Provider 2 gets no benefit from the auction, since its ad is never displayed and it does not pay any charge to the search engine.

In Figure 2, we compare the advertiser as well as auctioneer net benefits under VCG and GSP auction schemes. Social welfare, i.e., the sum of those utilities (or in other words, the total wealth generated by the ad slot), is shown in Figure 3.

This example illustrates that when a VCG auction is applied on the display probability, the revenue of advertisers is larger than when applying a deterministic GSP pricing. and the difference increases with R, while it is the opposite

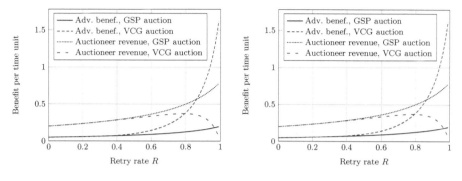

Fig. 2. Benefits of participants   **Fig. 3.** Social welfare

for the search engine revenue. In the case of a search engine in the situation of a monopoly, a deterministic GSP would be preferable than a random VCG in terms of revenue, but in the case of competitive engines with comparable quality (for instance Yahoo! against Google), advertisers would prefer the one applying VCG due to their larger revenue, and the advantage may change. Also, as seen on Figure 3, social welfare is larger with our new VCG scheme, which points out a better use of the resource (here, the ad slot).

6   Conclusion

This paper proposes a new randomized allocation rule for ad-word auctions, based on the idea that users often retry the same search. We have shown that *for fixed bids and prices*, applying a random allocation can increase revenue. We have also designed a VCG auction scheme based on that allocation rule, and compared the revenues and social welfare at equilibrium of the bidding game among advertisers with those obtained using a deterministic GSP rule. The search engine revenue is lower with our scheme, but not social welfare nor advertisers' revenue. Due to that last point, we claim that in a competition between engines, our new scheme will be preferred, and therefore could also generate more revenue.

Next works will go into several directions. First, we would like to study theoretically the competition game between two engines, to support our claim. Studying the case of multiple slots, as well as the game between advertisers under the randomized allocation rule but with a GSP pricing rule and a reserve price are also important issues we intend to address.

References

1. Varian, H.: Position auctions. International Journal of Industrial Organization 25, 1163–1178 (2005)
2. Liu, D., Chen, J., Whinston, A.: Competing keyword auctions. In: Proc. of 4th Workshop on Ad Auctions, Chicago, IL, USA (2008)

3. Jordan, P., Wellman, M.: Designing an ad auctions game for the trading agent competition. In: IJCAI-09 Workshop on Trading Agent Design and Analysis (TADA), Pasadena, California, USA (2009)
4. Edelman, B., Ostrovsky, M., Schwarz, M.: Internet advertising and the generalized second-price auction: Selling billions of dollars worth of keywords. American Economic Review 97(1), 242–259 (2007)
5. Lahaie, S., Pennock, D.: Revenue analysis of a family of ranking rules for keyword auctions. In: Proc. of the EC'07, San Diego, California, USA (2007)
6. Aggarwal, G., Feldman, J., Muthukrishnan, S., Pál, M.: Sponsored search auctions with markovian users. In: Proc. of 4th Workshop on Ad Auctions, Chicago, IL, USA (2008)
7. Chakrabarty, D., Zhou, Y., Lukose, R.: Budget constrained bidding in keyword auctions and online knapsack problems. In: Proc. of the 3rd Workshop on Ad Auctions, Banff, Canada (2007)
8. Bu, T., Deng, X., Qi, Q.: Dynamics of strategic manipulation in ad-words auction. In: Proc. of the 3rd Workshop on Ad Auctions, Banff, Canada (2007)
9. Kempe, D., Mahdian, M.: A cascade model for externalities in sponsored search. In: Proc. of 4th Workshop on Ad Auctions, Chicago, IL, USA (2008)
10. Dellarocas, C., Viswanathan, S.: The holy grail of advertising? Allocative efficiency and revenue implications of pay-per-action advertising in environments with quality uncertainty. In: Proc. of 4th Workshop on Ad Auctions, Chicago, IL, USA (2008)
11. Menache, I., Ozdaglar, A., Srikant, R., Acemoglu, D.: Dynamic online-advertising auctions as stochastic scheduling. In: Proc. of NetEcon (2009)
12. Vickrey, W.: Counterspeculation, auctions, and competitive sealed tenders. Journal of Finance 16(1), 8–37 (1961)
13. Clarke, E.H.: Multipart pricing of public goods. Public Choice 11, 17–33 (1971)
14. Groves, T.: Incentives in teams. Econometrica 41(3), 617–631 (1973)
15. Green, J., Laffont, J.J.: Characterization of satisfactory mechanisms for the revelation of preferences for public goods. Econometrica 45(2), 427–438 (1977)

The Role and Future Challenges of Wireless Communication Networks for Cooperative Autonomous City Vehicles

Andrei Furda, Laurent Bouraoui, Michel Parent, and Ljubo Vlacic

Intelligent Control Systems Laboratory (ICSL)
Griffith University, Brisbane, Australia
a.furda@griffith.edu.au, l.vlacic@griffith.edu.au
Intitut National de Recherche en Informatique et en Automatique (INRIA)
Team IMARA, 78153 Le Chesnay, France
laurent.bouraoui@inria.fr, michel.parent@inria.fr

Abstract. This paper elaborates on the use of future wireless communication networks for autonomous city vehicles. After addressing the state of technology, the paper explains the autonomous vehicle control system architecture and the Cybercars-2 communication framework; it presents experimental tests of communication-based real-time decision making; and discusses potential applications for communication in order to improve the localization and perception abilities of autonomous vehicles in urban environments.

Keywords: communication for autonomous city vehicles, Cybercars-2 communication framework, cooperation.

1 Introduction

Communication for autonomous city vehicles is crucial for enabling them to perform cooperative driving maneuvers, and important for improving their safety and efficiency. Vehicle-to-Vehicle (V2V) communication allows nearby vehicles to exchange relevant information about their traffic environment (e.g. potential hazards, accidents, etc.), and/or about their driving intentions, even when they are not in line-of-sight (e.g. around corners or at intersections). In addition, Vehicle-to-Infrastructure (V2I) communication can be used to improve the road network efficiency and reduce pollution by informing autonomous vehicles about traffic conditions (e.g. traffic congestions, alternative routes, etc.) and guiding them accordingly.

The remainder of this paper is structured as follows. Section 1.1 elaborates on the state of technology, Section 2 gives an overview of the autonomous vehicle control system and the Cybercars-2 communication framework, Section 3 explains experimental tests, Section 4 elaborates on potentials of future communication networks for autonomous city vehicles, Section 5 explains current limitations of communication networks, and Section 6 concludes this paper.

A. Pont, G. Pujolle, and S.V. Raghavan (Eds.): WCITD/NF 2010, IFIP AICT 327, pp. 241–251, 2010.
© IFIP International Federation for Information Processing 2010

Fig. 1. ICSL/INRIA demonstration of cooperative driving in 2002 [1]

1.1   State of Technology

Although the great potentials of using wireless communication for autonomous vehicles are obvious, so far, with the exception of a small number of experimental tests, the numerous ideas about how ad-hoc communication among autonomous vehicles can be used, have not been implemented yet. One of the few early demonstrations were made in 2002, when Griffith University's Intelligent Control Systems Laboratory (ICSL) and INRIA's IMARA Laboratory demonstrated a solution for on-road cooperative autonomous driving. The autonomous vehicles performed driving maneuvers which required inter-vehicle cooperation or synchronization through wireless communication [1]. For example, the vehicles were able to cooperatively overtake each other, and to establish an order of priority before traversing unsignalized intersections (Fig. 1).

Although most recent autonomous vehicle projects do integrate wireless communication functionalities, communication is mainly only used for monitoring the autonomous vehicles and for safety reasons (emergency stopping), and not for enabling cooperative tasks, or for extending the vehicles' input of information regarding the road environment or road infrastructure.

Nevertheless, worldwide standardization efforts addressing the requirements for V2I and V2V communication are currently in progress. One of the most significant efforts is ISO TC204 WG16 and its CALM (Continuous Air Interface for Long and Medium Range) concept. CALM is a set of standards which provides protocols and parameters, specifically addressing the requirements for ITS communication networks [2].

2   Autonomous Vehicle Control System Overview and the Cybercars-2 Communication Framework

2.1   Autonomous Vehicle Control System

The ICSL autonomous vehicle control system consists of the following four functional subsystems (Fig. 2):

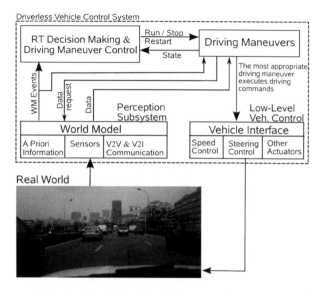

Fig. 2. Autonomous vehicle control system

- Perception Subsystem,
- Real-Time Decision Making & Driving Maneuver Control,
- Driving Maneuvers,
- Vehicle Interface.

The purpose of the Perception Subsystem is to collect available information about the vehicle's road traffic environment, to manage and process it, and to provide it in an adequate form to the Real-Time Decision Making & Driving Maneuver Control, and Driving Maneuvers. The Perception Subsystem's components are (Fig. 3):

- A Priori Information: software components providing information available before the vehicle begins its journey.
- Sensor Components: software and hardware components providing information obtained from on-board sensors.
- Communication: software and hardware components providing information obtained through communication with other vehicles (V2V) or infrastructure (V2I) (e.g. traffic management centre).
- World Model (Fig. 3): software component which collects information from subsystems, maintains an up-to-date view of the vehicle's environment, actively notifies other subsystems about relevant events in the traffic environment, and provides access to all its information to other software components through an API (Application Programming Interface).

Based on the information provided by the Perception Subsystem, the Real-Time Decision Making & Driving Maneuver Control subsystem makes driving decisions. This software subsystem decides about the activation and the execution of the most appropriate driving maneuver for any given traffic situation.

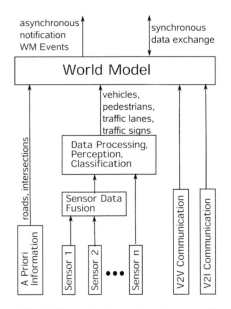

Fig. 3. World Model information input and output

The Driving Maneuvers subsystem contains a set of closed-loop control algorithms, each able to maneuver the vehicle in a specific traffic situation. The driving maneuvers direct their output to the Vehicle Interface subsystem.

The Low-Level Vehicle Control subsystem contains hardware and software components, which control the vehicle's speed, steering angle, and other actuators (e.g. transmission).

The data contained in the World Model is constantly updated in real -time. The main purpose of the World Model within the vehicle control software is to provide the Real -Time Decision Making & Driving Maneuver Control module, with accurate information about the vehicle's environment. This is accomplished in two ways:

- by actively notifying registered observer modules when the status of World Model Events changed, and
- by allowing other modules to access all information stored in the World Model structure.

The V2V/V2I component of the developed World Model is realized in compliance with the Cybercars-2 communication framework, which is presented in the following subsection.

2.2   The Cybercars-2 Communication Framework

The main objective of the Cybercars-2 Communication Framework [2,3] is to enable autonomous vehicles to safely perform cooperative driving maneuvers.

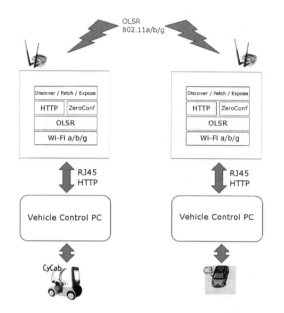

Fig. 4. The Cybercars-2 Communication Framework architecture

Cybercars are Intelligent Transportation Systems [4,5] based on road vehicles with fully automated driving capabilities. In the current stage, Cybercars are not intended to operate in public traffic, but in restricted environments, such as airports or theme parks.

The communication framework consists of five layers: Physical Layer, MAC Layer, Network Layer, System Service Layer, and Application Layer (Fig. 4).

Physical and MAC Layers: The Cybercars-2 Communication Framework accommodates the use of the following three communication standards / recommendations: IEEE 802.11p, IEEE 802.11a/b/g and WWAN technologies, such as GPRS, UMTS or WiMAX. The IEEE 802.11p recommendation is used for V2V/V2I communication, IEEE 802.11a/b/g for support information, and WWAN to monitor the traffic flow and to improve its efficiency.

At the current stage, communication equipment compliant to IEEE 802.11b/g is used for V2V and V2I communication. Therefore, the MAC Layer includes the functionalities which are available for the commercial IEEE 802.11 compliant equipment. The hardware and software enabling communication is integrated into the 4G-Cube (Fig. 5), which is a MIPS-based computer running Linux. It is equipped with one or two Mini-PCI Wi-Fi(b/g) cards and an Ethernet interface [2].

Network Layer: In order to fulfill the main objective, which is to enable cooperative maneuvers, the focus is mainly on close proximity communication between nearby vehicles. In this highly dynamic application environment, involving moving vehicles, dynamic routing is a major requirement. For this purpose, the

Fig. 5. The 4G-Cube is a small MIPS-based computer with integrated Wi-Fi(b/g) and Ethernet interfaces

Optimized Link State Routing protocol (OLSR) is used. The OLSR protocol provides the functionality required for vehicle communications. It was designed specifically for multihop networks with a strong and efficient mechanism for data flow delivery and it enables the quick creation and reconfiguration of vehicle mesh networks [6]. OLSR operates as a table driven, proactive protocol, allowing the exchange of topology information between network nodes. Each node selects a set of its neighbor nodes as multipoint relays (MPR). Only MPR nodes are responsible for forwarding control traffic, which is intended to be delivered over the entire network. MPRs provide an efficient mechanism to control traffic flooding by optimizing the number of transmissions required, and therefore it helps to avoid network overload.

System Service Layer: As part of the system service layer, the service discovery mechanism Zeroconfiguration from Apple has been adopted, as it helps to improve the network establishment procedure. Multicast DNS (mDNS) is used to provide a local namespace in order to abstract the vehicle's network addresses. On top of DNS (or mDNS), Service Discovery (DNS-SD) can be used by the 4G-Cube to publish or query information about the applications or services running in the neighborhood [6].

Application Layer: The communication protocol is based on the HTTP 1.1 protocol and uses the HTTP GET and POST requests. The following three functions are provided:

- Discover: to list available services,
- Expose: to send data (i.e. to make data available to all network nodes),
- Fetch: to receive data from a specific network node.

The discover function is used to list all available services. Its main use is for retrieving the list of all communicating vehicles (network nodes) along with the types of information they are able to send. The expose function is used to send communication data. The variety of information sent over the communication network is virtually unlimited. It can include for instance the vehicle's

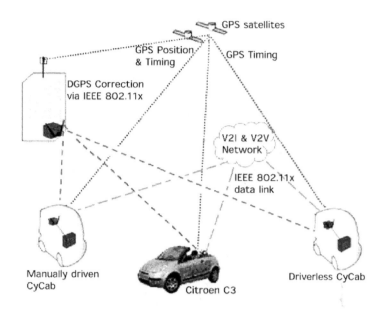

Fig. 6. Overview of the example communication setup (adapted from [2]). The autonomous CyCab communicated with a manually driven CyCab and a conventional car.

current GPS position, speed, heading, data from any on-board sensors, information about its future travel direction, etc. The fetch function is used to receive communication data from a specific network node.

3   Experimental Decision Making Tests with the Cybercars-2 Communication Framework

Experimental tests have been carried out in 2009, which show not only the communication performance, but also the potentials of communication for real-time decision making. For these experiments, we used an autonomous vehicle (Cycab, manufactured by Robosoft, France), a second, manually driven Cycab and a conventional car (Citroen C3). All vehicles, sensors, and test facilities haven been provided by the French research institute INRIA (team IMARA), while the decision making approach [7] has been developed at ICSL, Griffith University.

In our experiments, all vehicles, including the conventional car, were equipped with differential GPS (DGPS) and were able to communicate over the communication infrastructure (Fig. 6). In addition to its own GPS position, the autonomous vehicle was able to receive the GPS positions of the other two vehicles. Furthermore, the autonomous vehicle's world model included a priori information, such as the position of intersections and positions of imaginary stop signs. In order to test the decision making approach, three different traffic scenarios

(a) Experiment 2   (b) Experiment 3

Fig. 7. Real-time Decision Making experiments using communication

have been set up, all showing a common decision situation: passing a stopped
vehicle under different traffic conditions.

- Experiment 1: In the first traffic scenario, the autonomous vehicle approached
  a stopped vehicle. Safe passing was possible, and the oncoming traffic lane
  was free of any obstacles. In this first scenario, the autonomous vehicle immediately started the passing maneuver when it approached the stopped
  vehicle.
- Experiment 2: The second traffic scenario was similar to the first, however
  another manually driven vehicle was oncoming, making safe passing impossible (Fig. 7.a). In this second scenario, the autonomous vehicle waited behind
  the stopped vehicle, and started passing the stopped vehicle when the oncoming traffic lane was free.
- Experiment 3: In the third traffic scenario, a manually driven vehicle was
  stopped at an intersection (Fig. 7.b). The autonomous vehicle waited behind
  the stopped vehicle until it crossed the intersection. Then the autonomous
  vehicle continued driving, stopped at the imaginary stop sign before continuing across the intersection.

The main goal of the experiments related to real-time decision making was to
demonstrate that the ICSL autonomous vehicle control software, and most of all
the ICSL real-time decision making approach works with real vehicles and real
sensors, and meets the real-time decision making requirements. The integration
of the Cybercars-2 Communication Framework developed by INRIA into the
ICSL control software gave us the first opportunity to test the decision making
approach under real-world conditions, while at the same time proving the usability of the Cybercars-2 Communication Framework. During the experimentation
phase at INRIA, all experiments were repeated numerous times. Often, new
software or hardware related problems were detected and solved. Consequently,
these experimental results cannot be regarded as a rigorous test benchmark for
the quality of the entire system.

Although there were a number of remaining problems, such as the unreliable execution of driving maneuvers, and occasional problems related to unreliable DGPS and communication connections, the results show that in all repeated experiments, the decision making module was always able to avoid collisions with other vehicles and make appropriate driving decisions in real-time. Consequently, as real-time decision making was purely based on communication, the results also show that the used communication framework proved to be useful for improving the safe operation of autonomous vehicles.

4 Future Potentials of V2V and V2I Communication Networks

4.1 Vehicle Localization

One of the major remaining challenges for autonomous city vehicles is the accurate and reliable vehicle localization in urban environments. The currently used Differential GPS (DGPS) technology offers very accurate information, however only when the vehicle is able to receive GPS satellite signals, and, additionally, the position correction signals from a stationary beacon. In urban environments, for example between high buildings or under bridges, the direct reception of satellite signals is not reliable. Therefore, Inertial Navigation Systems (INS) are often used in combination with DGPS, which allow the estimation of position and heading based on inertial measurements and vehicle velocity. However, the accuracy of INS-based estimations decrease within a very short period of time, making such systems useful only for minutes after the GPS satellite reception is lost.

Future communication networks could provide a solution to the localization problem by enabling the vehicles to receive their position on the road from the road infrastructure. Road infrastructure sensors could be used, which detect autonomous vehicles, and inform them about their current position.

Additionally, autonomous vehicles could receive other close-by vehicles' position information which have GPS reception, and, knowing the distance to these vehicles from on-board sensors, calculate their own position.

4.2 Perception

Another major challenge is the autonomous vehicle's ability to reliably recognize relevant traffic features, such as traffic signs, intersections, other vehicles, and pedestrians. While currently used LIDAR and RADAR sensors are able to provide very accurate information regarding the distance and velocity of obstacles, they are not able to recognize the type of obstacle. On the other side, in their current state of development, computer vision systems do not seem to provide the required accuracy and reliability in bad weather and light conditions.

As demonstrated in the experimental tests, V2V communication can be used to improve the autonomous vehicles' perception capabilities of communication-enabled vehicles. In the same way, the road infrastructure network could provide relevant information, for example about traffic signs and intersections.

Since today the majority of people already carry communication devices, such as mobile phones, future networks could use communication with such devices to improve, in addition to vehicle's on-board sensors, the recognition of pedestrians.

5   Current Limitations and Future Challenges

5.1   Current Limitations

While the currently available wireless communication technology satisfies the needs for mobile non-safety-critical applications such as speech, email, web surfing, entertainment, etc., the currently available wireless networks are not sufficient for safety-critical applications, such as V2V and V2I communication for autonomous vehicles.

The most critical current limitations for wireless V2V and V2I communication networks are:

– Low communication reliability,
– Unsatisfactory network reachability,
– Unsatisfactory real-time performance,
– Inadequate network security.

5.2   Future Challenges

Autonomous city vehicles are safety-critical systems. Therefore, if communication is used for purposes which can affect their safe operation, such networks need to guarantee reliability, reachability, fulfillment of real-time requirements, as well as network security requirements.

While occasional communication dropouts are acceptable for non-safety-critical applications, V2V/V2I networks require a very high level of communication reliability. Furthermore, such networks need to guarantee reachability everywhere within the network area, even close to high-voltage power lines, or in tunnels. The worst-case communication times need to be guaranteed within specified real-time limits, regardless of the number of communicating vehicles, amount of transmitted data, or network load.

Network security is another major challenge for future autonomous vehicle communication networks. On such networks, security breaches could have a devastating impact, causing major traffic delays, or, in worst-case scenarios, enable network intruders to take over control over autonomous vehicles.

6   Conclusion

This paper has elaborated on the potentials of future wireless communication networks for autonomous city vehicles. After presenting an overview of the autonomous vehicle's control system, the Cybercars-2 communication framework, and experimental tests with wireless communication for real-time decision making, the paper has elaborated on the potentials of V2V and V2I communication to help overcome today's biggest challenges for autonomous city vehicles: the vehicle localization and perception. Furthermore, the paper has addressed current limitations and future challenges for future wireless networks for autonomous city vehicles.

References

1. Kolodko, J., Vlacic, L.: Cooperative Autonomous Driving at the Intelligent Control Systems Laboratory. IEEE Intelligent Systems 18(4), 8–11 (2003)
2. Molinete, B., Bouraui, L., Naranjo, E., Kostense, H., Hendriks, F., Alonso, J., Lobrino, R., Isasi, L.: CyberCars-2: Close Communications for Cooperation between CyberCars. Technical Report Project No IST-2004-0228062 (2009)
3. Bouraoui, L., Parent, M.: Cybercars-2 Close Communications for Cooperation between CyberCars. In: Field Testing Reports, INRIA Technical Report D.4.2 (2006)
4. Parent, M., Gallais, G.: Intelligent transportation in cities with CTS. In: ITS World Congress, Chicago, USA (2002)
5. Parent, M., Gallais, G.: Cybercars: Review of first projects. In: Ninth International Conference on Automated People Movers, Singapore (2003)
6. Clausen, T., Jacquet, P., Laouiti, A., Muhlethaler, P., Qayyum, A., Viennot, L.: Optimized link state routing protocol. In: IEEE INMIC (2001)
7. Furda, A., Vlacic, L.: Towards increased road safety: Real-time decision making for driverless city vehicles. In: 2009 IEEE International Conference on Systems, Man, and Cybernetics, San Antonio, TX, USA (2009)

Performance Analysis of User-Centric Network Selection and Network-Centric Resource Allocation Approaches in Wireless Networks

Sahin Albayrak, Manzoor A. Khan*, Fikret Sivrikaya,
Ahmet C. Toker, and Cuong Troung

DAI-Labor, Technische Universität Berlin, Germany
ManzoorAhmed.Khan@dai-labor.de

Abstract. The possible leveraging of high deployment costs, and the possibility to increase revenue have also introduced the concept of network sharing between different operators. On the other hand, the realization of a user-centric paradigm in future heterogeneous wireless networks, which implies free and automatic choice among different available wireless and mobile access networks, will revolutionize future wireless networks. For this innovative concept to materialize a paradigm shift is required from a long-term contractual based service delivery to a short-term contractual and dynamic service delivery. In this paper we formulate and compare the network-centric resource allocation and and user-centric network selection problems in a multi-operator scenario using two different flavors of game theory, namely bargaining games (for network-centric resource sharing) and multi-attribute auctions (for user-centric interface selection). We also compare the contributed solutions to one another to investigate their performance in terms of efficient resource allocation, call blocking probability, and user satisfaction.[1]

1 Introduction

We observe an increasingly heterogeneous landscape of wireless access technologies, including UMTS, GSM, WiFi, WiMAX, etc, which are specialized for different environments and user contexts. The development as well as the business cycles of these technologies can assure us that they will be available simultaneously for the years to come. Consequently, there has been significant research activity on the integration and inter-operability of these fundamentally different access technologies, which exhibit different service characteristics in terms of bandwidth, coverage, pricing, and Quality of Service (QoS) support. *Common Radio Resource Management* (CRRM) [1] is the concept that multiple such radio access technologies (RAT) can be combined in an operator network to diversify the service offer, as well as make use of trunking gains. The CRRM problem, which involves the allocation of call requests of different service types to the

---

* Corresponding author.

[1] This research activity is partially funded under the EU ICT project PERIMETER (FP7-224024).

A. Pont, G. Pujolle, and S.V. Raghavan (Eds.): WCITD/NF 2010, IFIP AICT 327, pp. 252–264, 2010.
© IFIP International Federation for Information Processing 2010

different Radio Access Networks (RANs), has been approached mostly from a single operator perspective, where different Radio Access Technologies (RATs) deployed as radio access networks belong to the same operator.

As in many areas of the networking field, application of game theory concepts to CRRM problem has been considered using both cooperative [2], and non-cooperative / competitive [3] game models to obtain efficient resource allocation schemes. All these studies that apply game theory to CRRM are confined to a single network operator scenario. A parallel development in the communications industry is the emergence of the concept of network sharing [4], [5], where operators share RANs to leverage investment, and to improve utilization of their investments. In this *network-centric* view, the decisions of resource allocation are solely coordinated and taken by the operators, with the aim of resource optimization. With the emergence of multi-interface terminals that run increasingly diversified applications with different QoS requirements, the simple resource allocation and connectivity issue has started to shift into a more rewarding resource allocation problem. The main concept of *user-centric* view in network selection is to place end users, and the applications running on their terminals, at the center of decision making with the aim of improving the user experience for all different service types, while ensuring efficient resource utilization.

Keeping the above mentioned multi-dimensional issues in view, we propose both network-centric resource allocation and user-centric interface selection solutions in this paper and evaluate their performance. In the network-centric domain, we formulate the interaction in terms of two games, the intra-operator and the inter-operator games. In the former, the RANs belonging to an operator play a bargaining game to share the bandwidth of an incoming application bandwidth request. If an operator needs extra bandwidth to support the service request, it does so by playing the second game with other operators who have excess bandwidth and and are willing to share.

In the user-centric interface selection domain, where the decision of network selection resides at the mobile terminal, we model the interaction between mobile terminal and network operators using auctioning theory. Earlier research in the direction of user-centric networking concentrates on defining users' utility without taking into account the operators' benefits, hence omitting the motivation to realize the user-centric ABC vision. In this work, we are trying to address this by modeling the negotiation between users and operators using auctions, and to define the utilities of both operators and users.

1.1 Model and Assumptions

We consider a region R covered by various RANs owned by different operators. An area may be covered by a single RAN, by multiple RANs belonging to a single operator, or by multiple RANs belonging to multiple operators. We assume there are m different operators and n different RATs which are combined into RANs by the network operators. A consequence of this hierarchy is the different definition of load and congestion for the RAN, cost incurred and area that is covered by different RANs.

Before presenting our network-centric and user-centric models for network selection and resource allocation, we introduce or clarify a set of terms that will be utilized in the rest of the paper:

RAN Congestion – A RAN is said to be in congestion region if its available bandwidth falls below some pre-defined threshold value.

Aggregated Congestion – An operator network is said to be in the aggregated congestion region in an area a if the aggregated available bandwidth of the RANs belonging to the operator in area a falls below some threshold value.

Operators' Incurred Costs on Network Technologies – Operators' cost on technology mainly depends on radio equipment, backhaul transmission equipment, license fees, site build-outs, and installation of equipments. Such deployment costs are constants and can be normalized to user pool. Whereas the service management, operation and maintenance (O&M) costs can be used to categorize users.

2   Network-Centric Cooperative Resource Allocation

In this section we consider the traditional telecom model where users have contractual agreements with a *home operator* and generate application bandwidth requests of different QoS classes. Upon initial access selection, which is not a part of this work, a user connects to the home network using some RAN belonging to its home operator first, and generates bandwidth requests for applications of different service classes. The home operator first allocates this bandwidth request to different *home* RANs in the coverage area. We assume there is a functional CRRM entity that coordinates RANs of an operator in the area. If the operator is experiencing aggregated congestion in the area where the user is located, it will not allocate the bandwidth right away, but will request additional bandwidth from *foreign operators* which have RANs in the area, and are willing to share bandwidth. We assume that operators are in contractual agreements with each other to share resources, in terms of *service level agreements* (SLA). The interaction between operators is monitored by an *SLA broker*, which is an independent neutral entity. After the interaction, the requested bandwidth is distributed among those operators who are willing to share bandwidth and their RANs are present in the area. Each operator treats its share of the bandwidth as a new bandwidth request.

We use cooperative games to formulate the resource allocation management problem in multi-operator heterogeneous wireless networks at two levels. The first step in which the requested bandwidth is shared between the RANs of the same operator is called the *intra-operator resource allocation*, and the second allocation step is called the *inter-operator resource distribution*. At the intra-operator level operator's RANs in an area bargain over the requests coming from users that belong to the operator. Intra-operator game is played in order to find an optimal distribution of divisible application bandwidth among RANS, and is based on our previous work [6]. The request is *allocated* to different RANs, and the utility function of different RANs is set to be the amount of allocated bandwidth above a certain disagreement point.

Utility Function of Network Technologies – Let $U_{w,o}$ represent the utility function of technology $w \in W$ owned by operator o, $B_o^a(q)$ the vector of bandwidth offer $b_{o,w}^a$, and $c_{w,o}$ the incurring cost (specifically O & M). Then the utility function of w is given by: $U_{w,o}(Q_o^a(q)) = x_{w,o}^a(q)\pi_{w,o} - c_{w,o} \quad \forall b_o^a(q) \in B_o^a(q)$, where $x_{w,o}^a(q)$ represents the allocated bandwidth and $\pi_{w,o}$ the price per unit bandwidth over the technology w in area a. Since we concentrate on fixed rate pricing, the operator charges the same amount over all technologies owned by itself, irrespective of the cost incurred on technology. However this utility function strengthens the concept of priorities over network technologies set by the operator for different services, which is reflected in the offered bandwidth. The upper bound on the allocation bandwidth is defined by the feasible set [6].

Utility Function of Network Operators – Intuitively, the aggregated utility of all network technologies constitutes the operator utility:

$$U_{o \in O}(Q_o^a(q)) = \sum_{w \in W} U_{w,o}(Q_o^a(q)) \quad \forall b_{o,w}^a(q) \in B_o^a(q). \tag{1}$$

If a bandwidth request cannot be fulfilled by the RANs of a home operator, then the inter-operator game is played. The inter-operator resource distribution problem is formulated such that each operator present in a coverage area bargains over the additional (excessive) bandwidth requests.

We model the allocation and distribution problems as bankruptcy problems and obtain the utility distribution rules. These rules dictate the allocation of requested bandwidth to RANs and the distribution of excess bandwidth to operators. We employ game theoretic approach of *bargaining* and the KSBS to obtain the allocation and distribution rules. The distribution rule is enforced by the SLA-broker, whereas the allocation rule is enforced by the CRRM manager. For computing the bandwidth offers in intra-operator games, we use the solution of *proportional allocation rule* to *zero*-associated bargaining problem presented in our previous paper [6].

For the inter-operator game, let $\bar{r}_o^a(q)$ represent the excess bandwidth request for a service class q that an operator o cannot fulfill, and would like to offer in the inter-operator game to other operators. Moreover, let the vector $\bar{Q}^a(q)$ represent all these requests from different operators in the region that are in aggregated congested regions. The operators play the game by making a bandwidth offer b_o^a, which can be grouped into the vector $B_o^a(q)$. The bargaining comes up with allocation of requested bandwidth to different operators, x_o^a, which should be a member of the compact and convex feasibility set:

$$S(\bar{Q}^a(q), B_o^a(q)) = \left\{ x_o^a : x_o^a \leq b_o^a, \sum_{i \in O} x_i^a \leq \sum_{i \in O} \bar{Q}^a(q) \right\}$$

Let C_o represent the aggregated capacity of operator o, which is calculated from the capacities of the RANs belonging to operator o in that area. Similarly the condition for the bankruptcy formulation is: $\sum_{i \in O} \bar{r}_i^a(q) \leq \sum_{i \in O} b_i^a \leq \sum_{i \in O} C_i$. Contrary to the intra-operator game the disagreement point $D(q) = (d_1(q), \ldots, d_n(q)) \in \mathbb{R}^n$ is calculated from the bandwidth requests and offers of the operators. To depict a realistic scenario we select the disagreement point as the characteristic function in our bankruptcy problem at inter-operator level. The characteristic function of a bargaining problem is defined as the amount of utility conceded to a player by all other players. operators. That is, for an operator i and foreign operators $\forall j \neq i$ the disagreement bandwidth is given by $d_i(q) = max\{0; \sum_{k \in O} \bar{r}_k^a(q) - \sum_{i \neq j} b_j^a(q)\}$.

Let $X^a = (x_1^a, ..., x_m^a)$ denote the solution obtained by applying KSBS to our inter-operator bargaining problem. Then $X^a = F^{KS}(S(\bar{Q}^a(q), B^a(q)), D(q))$, which represents a D associated bargaining problem. Recommendations made by *KSBS* when applied to D associated bargaining problem coincides by adjusted proportional distribution rule [7]. This distribution rule is applied by the SLA broker.

$$x_o^a = d_o(q) + \frac{(b_o^a(q) - d_o(q))}{\sum_{i \in O} (b_i^a(q) - d_i(q))} \cdot (\sum_{i \in O} \bar{r}_i^a(q) - \sum_{i \in O} d_i(q)). \tag{2}$$

The operator sums the most up-to-date bandwidth offers from the RANs in the area for the service class. Then this aggregated offer is scaled with the motivation factor of the operator $0 \leq \mu_o \leq 1$. By setting this factor, the operator is able to adjust the cooperative nature of its strategy. There is an incentive for cooperative behavior as operators can allocate unused bandwidth to increase utilization and therefore revenues. Then we have $b_o^a(q) = \mu_o \cdot \sum_{i \in W_o^a} b_{o,i}^a(q)$, where $b_{o,i}^a(q)$ represents bandwidth offer by network technology $w \in W_o^a$.

3   User-Centric Multi-attribute Auction Based Interface Selection

For a study of user-centric interface selection problem that is comparable to our network-centric resource allocation model, we consider user terminals that are equipped with at least as many interfaces as the network technologies available in any given coverage area. Upon receiving a request for an application class, network operators available within the coverage area present service offers that satisfy the minimum application requirements, which are evaluated by the users' expected values of different parameters. Parameters include technology-specific, application-specific and user-specific preferences. Users select the network technology / operator for any application whose offer matches closest to the user expectation.

In this section we formally define our user-centric network selection model as a multi-attribute auction game using the *sealed bid second price Vickery* auction format. For game-theory basics specific to this paper, our previous work [6], [8] can be referred. Let $U = \{u_1^a, ..., u_n^a\}$ be the set of users, $O_w^a = \{o_1^a, o_2^a, ..., o_m^a\}$ be the set of network operators, where w is the network technology in area a and $\{(r^a(q), \theta_k) \mid r^a(q) \in Q', \theta_k \in \theta\}$ be the user request within coverage area a, where Q' represent the set of application classes, which in turn is characterized by different amount of required bandwidth resource. θ defines the vector of various QoS attributes and expected ranges of these attributes for user request and $r^a(q)$ is the required bandwidth by application of QoS class q. In our model of user-centric interface selection, *buyers* are analogous to *application users*, *sellers* to *network operators* of available network technologies within coverage area a and the *requested bandwidth* with associated attributes is considered as *auctioned item*. For any application request the user announces intention to acquire the item $(r^a(q), \theta_k)$ through the auctioneer residing on user terminal. Auctioneer broadcasts this request in the coverage area a, which is received by the operators owning network technologies in that area. Upon receiving this request the operator(s) submit their bids that identify the offer against the requested bandwidth.

The candidate operators create bids after they receive the *broadcasted* application bandwidth request by auctioneer in that area. Let the bid b by operator technology w be $bi^a_{w,o}$, which is given by the tuple:

$$bi^a_{w,o}(r^a(q), \theta_k) = ((r^a(q), \theta_k), \pi^a_{w,o}) \tag{3}$$

where $bi^a_{w,o}(r^a(q), \theta_k)$ is bid offer from operator o through network technology w in an area a against the application required bandwidth $r^a(q)$, associated attribute vector θ_k and $\pi^a_{w,o}$ is per unit bandwidth payment. Both users and network operators are characterized by their utility functions. The bid formation is dictated by the operator *utility function*. Framing this simply, we can say that the *bidding mechanism* is influenced by candidate operators' strategies that increase their payoffs, before we define the *utility function* of a network operator. let us assume that $D = max_{\{\bar{w}, \bar{o} \neq o\}} bi_{\bar{w}, \bar{o}}((r^a(q), \theta_k), \pi_{\bar{w}, \bar{o}})$ be the maximum suitable bid if operator $o \in O$ does not participate in the game. We also assume that the value of every QoS attribute is the simple linear function of cost incurred by network operator, meaning thereby cost increases linearly with increasing value of any QoS attribute in the direction of improving QoS. We also know that the operator receives amount against its extended service(bandwidth in our case) on per unit basis. Thus the utility function of operator in user-centric interface selection will be:

$$U_{w,o}(r^a(q), \theta_k) = \begin{cases} (\gamma_q, \theta_k)\pi^a_{w,o} - \sum_{k \in \theta} c_{w,o}(\theta_k) \text{ if } D \leq bi_w(\theta_k) \\ 0 \text{ if } D \geq bi_w(\theta_k) \\ \lambda((r^a(q), \theta_k)\pi^a_{w,o} - \sum_{k \in \theta} c_{w,o}(\theta_k)) \text{if} D = bi_w(\theta_k) \end{cases} \tag{4}$$

where $c_{w,o}(\theta_k)$ is the cost incurred on a single attribute value and we assume it to be the linear function of attribute values, meaning thereby increasing / decreasing the values of attribute that result in better user perceived QoS increases the network cost linearly. $\sum_{k \in \theta} c_{w,o}(\theta_k)$ is the operators' reservation price for service. λ is tie breaking co-efficient that can take any value $\{0, 1\}$ randomly.

It is straightforward to prove that the formulated auction is strategy proof, where each operator (bidder) maximizes its utility by bidding truthfully. The following lemmas follow from similar proof constructs given in [9,10], which we omit here due to space restriction.

Lemma-1 – *For every bid $bi^a_{w,o} \neq \widehat{bi^a_{w,o}}$ of an operator $o \in O$ there is a bidding profile $bi_{\{-w,-o\}}$ of other operators such that $u_{w,o}(bi^a_{\{-w,-o\}}, bi^a_{w,o}) < u_{w,o}(bi^a_{\{-w,-o\}}, \widehat{bi^a_{w,o}})$, where $bi^a_{w,o}$ is operator $o's$ bid with false valuation of request and $\widehat{b^a_{w,o}}$ represents the bid with true valuation.*

Lemma-2 – *In the strategy proof auction and for any value of offered bandwidth and associated QoS attributes $(r^a(q), \theta) = argmax_{(r^a(q),\theta)}((r^a(q), \theta)\pi^a_{w,o} - \sum_{k \in \theta} c_{w,o}(\theta_k))$ holds, where $(r^a(q), \theta)\pi^a_{w,o} \in \bigcup_{\theta, r^a(q) \in Q}$ which maximizes bidder's utility based on payment $\pi_{w,o}$.*

Winning bid is the consequence of user satisfaction. The degree of users satisfaction is translated using user utility function, which captures users' preference relationship over various QoS attributes and their behavior towards the amount of offered bandwidth. Since QoS attribute vector is n-dimensional, therefore user preference to every single attribute is represented by assigning weights to attributes. User evaluate amount of offered bandwidth and each relevant attribute quoted in the offer from network provider using its utility function(scoring function) and compute the utility of overall bid by using *weighted sum* over each utilities attained for each individual attribute and the utility obtained from the offered bandwidth as:

$$U_i(bi^a_{w,o}(r^a(q), \theta_k)) = \frac{u_i(r(q)^o)}{\sum_{k \in \theta} \psi_k \zeta_{w,o}(\theta_k)} - C_i(r^a(q), \theta_k) \tag{5}$$

where $\zeta_{w,o}(\theta_k)$ represents the normalized value of each associated attribute θ_k, ζ can be normalized in various expectancies i) the smaller the better, ii) the nominal the better, and iii) the greater the better. π_w represents the payment per unit bandwidth over network w, ψ_k is the user assigned weight to attribute k, and $u_i(r(q)^o)$ is the utility obtained by the offered bandwidth. The application utility is given by [11][12]

$$u_i(\gamma^o_q) = \begin{cases} 0 & \text{if } \gamma_f \leq \gamma_{min} \\ u_0 + \alpha \frac{1 - e^{-\beta(\gamma^o_q - \gamma_{min})}}{1 - e^{-\beta(\gamma_q - \gamma_{min})}} & \text{if } \gamma_{min} \leq \gamma_f \leq \gamma_{max} \\ u_0 + \alpha & \text{if } \gamma_f \geq \gamma_{max} \end{cases} \tag{6}$$

where $\gamma_{min}, \gamma_{max}$ are minimum and maximum required application bandwidths respectively. u_0 is the private valuation of user, which in our case is the minimum application required bandwidth.i.e, for any value of offered bandwidth that is less than minimum application required bandwidth, users' utility is equal to *zero*. A careful look at the utility curves in [8] reveals that utility is concave for different services like video, audio and data. The assessment of different weights to various associated QoS attributes are of prime importance for decision of optimal interface selection. Various proposed techniques that compute these

Table 1. QoS parameters and ranges

Parameters	Range		Score	Category
	70ms ~ 100ms		10	Excellent
Delay	100ms ~ 150ms		8	Good
	150ms ~ 200ms		6	Fair
	30ms ~ 50ms		10	Excellent
Jitter	50ms ~ 60ms		5	Good
	60ms ~ 70ms		3	Fair
	~ 10^{-6}		10	Excellent
Packet Loss	10^{-6} ~ 10^{-5}		7	Good
Rate	10^{-5} ~ 10^{-4}		4	Fair

Table 2. Predefined offer bandwidth

Class	GSM	WiMAX	UMTS
Voice	500	240	400
Data	900	1000	800
Video	500	1600	500

weights include Analytical Hierarchy Process (AHP), Fuzzy sets, Multi-attribute Utility Theory (MAUT), Smart Multi-attribute Rating Technique (SMART), etc. $C_i(r^a(q), \theta_k)$ in (5) represents the cost of service paid by user in terms of price. Auctioneer evaluates the offered service price as $C_i(\gamma_q, \theta_k) = \frac{\pi_{w,o}^a}{\pi_i^{max}}$, where the user specifies her maximum valuation of the service through π_i^{max}.

For a typical user it is difficult to describe technically the preferences over communication parameters for any application. This can be addressed by providing a Graphical User Interface (GUI) to the users, as in [13], which takes the following inputs: i) service request class – *Data, Video, Voice*; ii) service preferred quality – *Excellent, Good, Fair*; iii) Service price preferences – *Always Cheapest, Indifferent*. Once these inputs are specified, they need to be translated into technical communication requirements. In this context, Table 1 [14] is used in order to map user defined *service preferred quality* to the technical communication parameters:

An auctioneer computes the wining bid from the matrix such that the wining bid maximizes the users' utility, i.e. by (5). Auctioneer also determines the price that user pays to the winning network operator for the service. However the costs posed by user-centric network selection solution in terms of frequent handover is addressed by using fuzzy logic approach, explained in our earlier work [8].

4 Results and Analysis

In order to evaluate our approach for both network-centric resource allocation and user-centric interface selection, we have developed our own Java-based discrete event simulator, which generates user defined network operators, access technologies, users, different application quality classes and coverage areas with user defined RANs belonging to different operators [6]. We investigate the performance of our approach in randomly generated coverage areas for multi-operator heterogeneous wireless networks, consisting of GSM, UMTS, and WiMAX technologies.

We assume that a GSM RAN has a capacity of 4.500 kbps, UMTS 12.000 kbps, and WiMAX 20.000 kbps. The RAN overload thresholds are set to 10% for

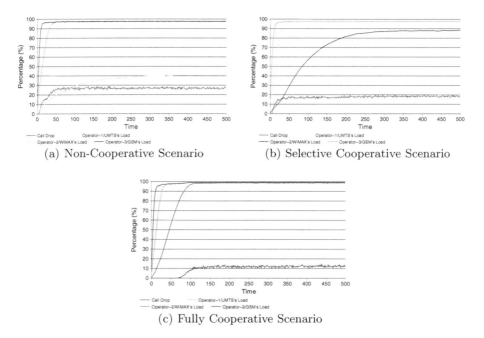

(a) Non-Cooperative Scenario   (b) Selective Cooperative Scenario

(c) Fully Cooperative Scenario

Fig. 1. Resource utilization and call blocking rate for different cooperation levels

UMTS and GSM, and to 3% for WiMAX. Users request generation is modeled by a poisson process, call holding time is exponentially distributed, and the service class is chosen randomly among voice, data, and video uniformly. The sizes of the requests are assumed to be static, and are 60 kbps, 150 kbps, and 500 kbps for voice, data, and video respectively. After the allocation and distribution algorithms, the allocated bandwidths are subtracted from the bandwidth pools of the RANs. The operators share the same predefined offered bandwidth values in kbps, which are given in Table 2. We assume a coverage area a covered by three technologies owned by three different operators, such that operator-1 has UMTS, operator-2 has WiMAX and operator-3 has GSM in the area.

To investigate the game-theoretic *network-centric resource allocation*, we assume that there are different number of users who have contractual agreements with different available operators. Users of each operator are assumed to generate service requests according to different poisson distributions with means $\tilde{\mu}_{op-1}$, $\tilde{\mu}_{op-2}$ and $\tilde{\mu}_{op-3}$. For the network-centric allocation case, we simulate operators' strategies when they cooperate under under-utilized and in-congestion conditions, or when they are non-cooperative. We assume that the requests are generated using $\tilde{\mu}_{op-1} = 2$, $\tilde{\mu}_{op-2} = 1$, and $\tilde{\mu}_{op-1} = 2$. Here we discern three cases based on different motivation factors of the involved operators. In the cooperative case all operators have a motivation factor of 1. In the selective cooperative case operators 1 and 2 have a motivation factor of 1, and operator-3 has a motivation factor of 0. In the non-cooperative case all operators have a motivation factor of 0.

Fig. 1(a) represents the non-cooperative case, which depicts that operator-2 is under-utilized and the aggregated call blocking is around 30% owing to the fact that all the operators are non-cooperative. In Fig. 1(b), the selective coopera- tive case, call blocking is reduced by 30% and resource utilization of operator-2 is increased by almost 100% when compared with the non-cooperative case. In the fully cooperative case, as shown in Fig. 1(c), the aggregated call blocking percentage is reduced to almost 10% whereas the resources of all operators in the area are fully utilized. This demonstrates the performance of proposed co- operative approach in terms of resource utilization, call blocking and ultimately the revenue of operators (which is a function of utilization).

In order to investigate the performance of *user-centric interface selection* gain of users in terms of their utility, we consider users randomly generate requests of different quality of service class audio, video and data specifying service pre- ferred QoS i.e., excellent, good and fair. These requests are generated using poisson distribution with the mean $\tilde{\mu}_{uc}$. To make this scenario comparable to network-centric scenario, the mean $\tilde{\mu}_{uc}$ is kept as $\tilde{\mu}_{uc} = \sum_{i=1}^{3} \tilde{\mu}_{op-i}$, meaning thereby the same number of users' requests are generated in the coverage area as in network-centric case, but now users have no long-term contractual agree- ments with operator, and they are free to get associated with any operator. Op- erators' offer vary over time specially in terms of offered prices and offered QoS attribute values owing to the network condition, congestion and operator prefer- ences. This results in triggering the interface selection decision. Performance of our auction-based interface selection approach is evaluated against the network- centric approach in terms of average values over user's throughput, delay, jitter, packet-loss and payed price over 500 simulation instances are depicted in Fig. 2(a). As can be seen that auction-based approach performs better by about 10% in user throughput and about 9% in the price.

The improvement is achieved at the cost of frequent handovers, which is re- vealed in the CDF curve in Fig. 2(c). To address the tradeoff between handover frequency and ABC goal, we also simulate the *auction-based with fuzzy* approach [8]. The results reveal that in terms of both throughput and price, auction-based with fuzzy approach performs almost the same as auction-based approach, but with almost half time the handovers as shown in Fig. 2(c). In parallel a compar- ison over the price is shown in the CDF graph in Fig. 2(b).

We also compare auction based interface selection in terms of call blocking rate and resource utilization with our game-theoretic network-centric resource allocation. Fig. 2(d) reveals that user-centric approach performs better in terms of resource utilization, owing to the fact that users are always able to connect to any operator if blocked by one operator. Comparing the results in Fig. 2(d) with our game-theoretic approach in Fig. 1(c) it can be concluded that user-centric approach behaves somewhat similar to the cooperative game theoretic approach in terms of resource utilization and call blocking, and performs better than other network-centric approaches (please refer to [6] for the related comparison). This result dictates that auction-based user-centric and cooperative network-centric

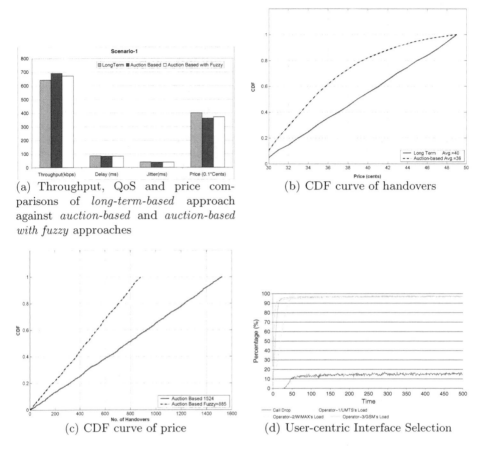

(a) Throughput, QoS and price comparisons of *long-term-based* approach against *auction-based* and *auction-based with fuzzy* approaches

(b) CDF curve of handovers

(c) CDF curve of price

(d) User-centric Interface Selection

Fig. 2. Results of User-Centric Interface Selection

approaches provide similar incentives in terms of better resource utilization, less call blocking, and more satisfied users. Moreover, assuming that efficient resource utilization ultimately means higher revenues for the operators, these two approaches also increase operator satisfaction.

5   Conclusion

In this paper we have presented game theoretic formulations of network-centric multi-operator CRRM and user-centric network selection problems. On the one hand, at the network level CRRM manager employs an allocation rule to distribute bandwidth requests from user applications among operator RANs based on the offers they make. On the other hand, we present the network selection decision mechanism in a user-centric network scenario where users dynamically select the best available network. We have provided comparisons for both approaches with one another in terms of the gain of both stake-holders, i.e. satisfaction and reduced costs for users and resource utilization and call blocking probability for operators. The results signal that user-centric (auction-based) network selection has a significant potential for satisfying both user and operators, thereby improving user experience and operators' resource utilization. Interestingly, the results for auction-based network selection in the user-centric scenario resembles to those of the cooperative game-theoretic approach in network-centric scenario. One can intuitively infer that these two approaches also result in higher revenues for operators compared to other approaches, although the actual revenue is dependent on the pricing scheme adopted by the operators. As a future work, we plan to incorporate the operators' pricing schemes into our model and investigate the dependencies between pricing, resource utilization, operator revenue, and user satisfaction.

References

1. Perez-Romero, J., Sallent, O., Agusti, R., Karlsson, P., Barbaresi, A., Wang, L., Casadevall, F., Dohler, M., Gonzalez, H., Cabral-Pinto, F.: Common radio resource management: functional models and implementation requirements. In: IEEE 16th International Symposium on Personal, Indoor and Mobile Radio Communications, PIMRC 2005, vol. 3, pp. 2067–2071 (2005)
2. Niyato, D., Hossain, E.: A cooperative game framework for bandwidth allocation in 4g heterogeneous wireless networks. In: Proc. IEEE International Conf. on Communications ICC '06, vol. 9, pp. 4357–4362 (2006)
3. Das, S., Lin, H., Chatterjee, M.: An econometric model for resource management in competitive wireless data networks. IEEE Network 18(6), 20–26 (2004)
4. Beckman, C., Smith, G.: Shared networks: making wireless communication affordable. IEEE Wireless Communications, [see also IEEE Personal Communications] 12(2), 78–85 (2005)
5. Hultell, J., Johansson, K., Markendahl, J.: Business models and resource management for shared wireless networks. In: 2004 IEEE 60th Vehicular Technology Conference, VTC 2004-Fall, vol. 5, pp. 3393–3397 (2004)
6. Khan, M.A., Trong, C., Geithner, T., Sivrikaya, F., Albayrak, S.: Network level cooperation for resource allocation in future wireless networks. In: Proceedings of the IFIP Wireless Days Conference '08 (2008)
7. Dagan, N., Volij, O.: The bankruptcy problem: a cooperative bargaining approach. Nir Dagan, Economic theory and game theory (1993)
8. Khan, M.A., Sivrikaya, F., Mengal, K., Albayrak, S.: Auction based resource allocation in heterogeneous wireless networks. In: Proceedings of the IFIP Wireless Days Conference '09 (2009)
9. Nisan, N., Roughgarden, T., Tardos, E., Vazirani, V.V. (eds.): Algorithmic Game Theory, September 2007. Cambridge University Press, Cambridge (2007)
10. Suyama, T., Yokoo, M.: Strategy/false-name proof protocols for combinatorial multi-attribute procurement auction. In: AAMAS '04: Proceedings of the Third International Joint Conference on Autonomous Agents and Multiagent Systems, pp. 160–167. IEEE Computer Society, Washington (2004)
11. Wu, Z., Yin, Q.: A heuristic for bandwidth allocation and management to maximize user satisfaction degree on multiple mpls paths. In: 3rd IEEE Consumer Communications and Networking Conference, CCNC 2006, January 2006, vol. 1, pp. 35–39 (2006)

12. Chan, H., Fan, P., Cao, Z.: A utility-based network selection scheme for multiple services in heterogeneous networks. In: 2005 International Conference on Wireless Networks, Communications and Mobile Computing, June 2005, vol. 2, pp. 1175–1180 (2005)

13. Toker, A.C., Cleary, F., Fiedler, M., Ridel, L., Yavuz, B.: Perimeter: Privacy-preserving contract-less, user centric, seamless roaming for always best connected future internet. In: 22th World Wireless Research Forum (2009)

14. Kim, H.J., Lee, D.H., Lee, J.M., Lee, K.H., Lyu, W., Choi, S.G.: The qoe evaluation method through the qos-qoe correlation model. In: Fourth International Conference on Networked Computing and Advanced Information Management, NCM '08, September 2008, vol. 2, pp. 719–725 (2008)

Author Index